D0212715

HANDBOOK OF CONTEMPORARY GROUP PSYCHOTHERAPY

Handbook of Contemporary Group Psychotherapy

Contributions from Object Relations, Self Psychology, and
Social Systems Theories

Edited by

ROBERT H. KLEIN, Ph.D.
HAROLD S. BERNARD, Ph.D.
DAVID L. SINGER, Ph.D.

INTERNATIONAL UNIVERSITIES PRESS, INC.
Madison   Connecticut

Library of Congress Cataloging-in-Publication Data

Handbook of contemporary group psychotherapy : contributions from
   object relations, self psychology, and social systems theories /
   edited by Robert H. Klein, Harold S. Bernard, David L. Singer.
      p. cm.
   Includes bibliographical references and index.
   ISBN 0-8236-2285-1
   1. Group psychotherapy. 2. Object relations (Psychoanalysis)
3. Self psychology. 4. Social systems. I. Klein, Robert H.
II. Bernard, Harold S. III. Singer, David L.
   [DNLM: 1. Psychotherapy, Group—methods. WM 430 H2355]
RC488.H35 1992
616.89′152—dc20
DNLM/DLC
for Library of Congress   92-1472
                                                                        CIP

Manufactured in the United States of America

To our wives and children

Contents

Contents

Foreword

Psychodynamic psychotherapy is at a point of creative crisis in its development. Besieged by a cultural move toward symptom-relieving treatments and time-limited modalities, psychodynamic theory is nonetheless flourishing. Contributions to and modifications of classical theory have come from object relations theory, self psychology and social systems theory. These contributions, each in its own way, emphasize the importance of others in the formation of personality, the etiology of psychopathology, and the healing of psychopathology.

It is natural, therefore, that group psychotherapy has benefited enormously from these theoretical advances. Group therapy by its very nature emphasizes the interpersonal approach. In its early days, group therapy rested uneasily upon classical instinct/drive theories of personality. With the advent of the newer schools of psychodynamic theory, group therapists found voice for the healing factors they had long witnessed in their groups. The projective identifications of the object relations school, the mirroring of self psychology, the impact of individual roles on systems of social systems theory—these and other healing factors have long been observed at work in therapy groups.

Drs. Klein, Bernard, and Singer have gathered a stellar group of authors to finally bring order to these disparate contributions to the field of group therapy. In an organized and comprehensive manner, the theoretical contributions from each of these schools is presented. Then the clinical relevance of these contributions is examined. Finally, the implications for the behavior and focus of the therapist are explored. The result is a masterful volume that brings together the most important contributions from various fields in one readable book. The reader's understanding of the various schools is enhanced by the comparison and contrast afforded by presenting different approaches chapter by chapter. The editors' well-planned organizational efforts help the book read more like an authored book than an edited book.

All who were involved in this project are to be congratulated. Your hard work will be rewarded by readers' enjoyment of this fine book.

J. Scott Rutan, Ph.D.
Director, Center for Group Therapy
Massachusetts General Hospital
Boston, Massachusetts

Contributors

THE EDITORS

Robert H. Klein, Ph.D. is Associate Clinical Professor of Psychiatry and Senior Group Therapy Supervisor, Albert Einstein College of Medicine; and Clinical Associate Professor of Psychiatry, Yale University School of Medicine. Formerly Director of Education and Training and Director of Psychology, Yale Psychiatric Institute, and Director, Adult Individual and Group Psychotherapy, West Haven Mental Health Clinic, he is a Fellow of the American Group Psychotherapy Association, and is a long-term member of the Editorial Committee of the *International Journal of Group Psychotherapy*. In addition to supervising multidisciplinary staff and trainees, he is in private practice in Milford and Wilton, Connecticut.

Harold S. Bernard, Ph.D. is Clinical Associate Professor of Psychiatry and Chief, Group Psychotherapy Program, Psychology Service, New York University Medical Center. He is serving as President of the Eastern Group Psychotherapy Society from 1991–1993, and he is a member of the Board of Directors of the American Group Psychotherapy Association for the 1991–1994 term. He is the Book Review Editor for the *International Journal of Group Psychotherapy*. He was formerly a member of the national Board of Directors of the A. K. Rice Institute. He is in private practice in Manhattan and in Westport, Connecticut.

David L. Singer, Ph.D. is Dean for Institutional Advancement and Core Faculty, Department of Clinical Psychology, Antioch New England Graduate School in Keene, New Hampshire, where he was previously founding director of its doctoral program in clinical psychology. President of the National Council of Schools of Professional Psychology for 1990–1991, he is a former President of the New Hampshire Psychological Association and a former member of the national Board of Directors of the A. K. Rice Institute, of which he is a Fellow. He also conducts a private practice in individual, group, and family therapy in Keene, New Hampshire.

THE AUTHORS

Charles J. Ashbach, Ph.D. is on the faculty of the Institute for Psychoanalytic Psychotherapies, and is director of research for the National Family Foundation. He is coauthor of *Object Relations, the Self and the Group,* and is in private practice in Philadelphia, Pennsylvania.

Howard A. Bacal, M.D., F.R.C.P.(C) is Associate Professor, Department of Psychiatry, University of Toronto. He is a training and supervising analyst and former director of the Toronto Institute of Psychoanalysis. He is a faculty member of the Canadian Group Psychotherapy Association Group Therapy Training Programme, Toronto Section. He is coauthor of *Theories of Object Relations: Bridges to Self Psychology.* He is in private practice in Toronto, Ontario.

John F. Borriello, Ph.D. is Chief, Group, Family and Organizational Consultation Branch, and Chief, Clinical Psychology Training, D.C. Commission on Mental Health Services, and Clinical Professor of Psychology, George Washington University. He is a Diplomate in Clinical Psychology of the American Board of Professional Psychology and a Diplomate and Fellow of the American Board of Medical Psychotherapists. He serves on the Editorial Committee of the *International Journal of Group Psychotherapy.* He has been President of the Mid-Atlantic Group Psychotherapy Society and the District of Columbia Psychological Association. He has held consultant positions at the Sheppard and Enoch-Pratt Hospital, the NIH Clinical Center and the National Science Foundation. He was formerly a Distinguished Professor of Psychology for the US Air Force.

Howard D. Kibel, M.D. is Associate Professor of Clinical Psychiatry at Cornell University Medical College and Coordinator of Group Psychotherapy at the New York Hospital–Cornell Medical Center, Westchester Division, in White Plains, New York. He served as President of the American Group Psychotherapy Association from 1986–1988. He is a Contributing Editor to *GROUP,* and is a reviewer for other publications. At the Westchester Division of Cornell, he trains psychiatric residents, psychology interns, and others, conducts research, and has a private practice.

Edward B. Klein, Ph.D. is Professor, Department of Psychology, University of Cincinnati; faculty member, Cincinnati Psychoanalytic Institute; member, national Board of Directors, A. K. Rice Institute; and a coauthor of *Seasons of a Man's Life.* His interests in group, systems, and adult development are reflected in teaching, research, organizational consultation, and clinical work.

Cecil A. Rice, Ph.D. is Director of the Postgraduate Center, Boston Institute for Psychotherapy, in Boston, Massachusetts. He is serving as Director of the American Group Psychotherapy Association Training Board, is a Fellow of the American Group Psychotherapy Association, and is a past President of the Northeastern Society for Group Psychotherapy. He practices group, individual, and marital psychotherapy in Needham, Massachusetts.

Victor L. Schermer, M.A. is a psychologist in private practice in Philadelphia, Pennsylvania. He is Outpatient Director of Mirmont Treatment Center/Riddle Memorial Hospital, in Lima, Pennsylvania. He is Executive Director of the Study Group for Contemporary Psychoanalytic Process, and faculty member of the Institute for Psychoanalytic Psychotherapies. He is coauthor of *Object Relations, the Self, and the Group,* and coeditor of the forthcoming volume *Ring of Fire,* about primitive affects and object relations in group psychotherapy.

Marvin Skolnick, M.D. is Clinical Professor of Psychiatry, George Washington University Medical School; Senior Faculty, Washington School of Psychiatry; former Dean of the Washington School Group Psychotherapy Program; and Associate of the A. K. Rice Institute. He is currently serving as Clinical Director of an Intensive Day Treatment Therapeutic Community, and is in private practice in Alexandria, Virginia.

Walter N. Stone, M.D. is Professor of Psychiatry at the University of Cincinnati College of Medicine. He is currently President of the American Group Psychotherapy Association.

Saul Tuttman, M.D., Ph.D. is Clinical Professor of Psychiatry, Albert Einstein College of Medicine; Training and Supervising Psychoanalyst, New York Medical College Psychoanalytic Institute; Treasurer, American Group Psychotherapy Association; and Fellow and Chairman of the Committee on Programs, American Academy of Psychoanalysis. He is the editor of the recently published volume, *Psychoanalytic Group Theory and Therapy.*

1

Introduction

ROBERT H. KLEIN, Ph.D., HAROLD S. BERNARD, Ph.D., and DAVID L. SINGER, Ph.D.

New developments within psychodynamic theory and practice have generated more heat than light. Recently, a colleague of ours—a highly competent, gifted senior clinician and recognized leader in the field of group psychotherapy—leaned over and apprehensively whispered to one of us in the context of a departmental Grand Rounds presentation on the role of object relations in the treatment process, "I hope they don't ask me to discuss this stuff in relation to group therapy." We believe that her level of discomfort and subjectively experienced lack of clarity regarding the contributions of object relations to the theory and practice of group therapy accurately mirrors what many of us feel. In fact, much the same might be said about recent developments in the areas of self psychology and social systems thinking and their implications for the group therapist. That this situation exists is all the more remarkable given that, over the past several years, psychoanalysis has maintained an intense focus on object relations and the notion of the self. The traditional psychodynamic framework for understanding and treating persons suffering from emotional difficulties is undergoing renewed and vigorous scrutiny. In view of the fact that most group therapists are trained in such a traditional psychodynamic model, the lack of such conceptual integration is particularly disquieting.

DEVELOPMENTS IN TRADITIONAL PSYCHODYNAMIC THEORY

The recent controversies stirred in psychoanalytic circles by theoretical contributions in the areas of object relations and self psychology

1

have stemmed from the increasing experience of clinicians in treating patients with narcissistic and borderline personality disorders. It is these patients, as well as those with schizophrenic disturbances, whose primary difficulties appear to be preoedipal in nature, rather than the consequence of unresolved oedipal-level conflicts.

On a more fundamental level, however, certain basic tenets of traditional Freudian theory have been called into question. Specifically, these new theoretical developments challenge the very essence of traditional theory, namely, instinct theory. They raise profound questions as to whether traditional theory, by maintaining that all human behavior occurs in the service of expressing and gratifying instinctual drives, can adequately account for object relations and the development of a coherent self. Does the significance of objects lie solely in their being the things in relation to which or through which (i.e., the means by which) drive reduction takes place (Freud, 1915)? Or are human beings object-seeking, that is, inherently searching for relationships and attachments with significant others, independent of or in addition to seeking gratification of sexual and aggressive drives? Put another way, is the formation of interpersonal attachments secondarily derived from the gratification of "primary" biological drives, or is it a fundamental, inborn propensity? Furthermore, is it drive gratification or early object relational experiences that play the determining role in the development of personality and self structure (Eagle, 1984)? Where one stands on these issues has a direct and critical bearing on understanding human development and psychopathology and has major implications for how one conceptualizes and implements the treatment process.

Greenberg and Mitchell (1983), in their review of the current state of psychoanalytic theory, suggest that "a less reductionistic, more synthetic approach is needed" to deal with the enormous complexity and heterogeneity evident in the field, and the lack of communication among the various schools. They note that in the fifty years following Freud, the most important movement within the field has been centrifugal, spinning out from Freud's theory of instinctual drive. Here they include the theoretical departures of Jung and Adler, the revisions of classical technique advocated by Rank and Ferenczi, the development of the neo-Freudian schools of Fromm, Sullivan, and Horney, and the three-way theoretical split among the Freudians into those who supported Freud's drive-structure model, those endorsing the contributions of Melanie Klein, and those who became proponents of American ego psychology.

In contrast, the past twenty-five years have been marked by a gradual convergence of basic concerns, particularly with regard to the role and importance of individuals' interactions with others, according to Greenberg and Mitchell (1983). This issue they label "the problem of object relations," since there is a lack of consensus as to the origins and meanings of object relations and the means by which they undergo transformations. Two different strategies have been developed for dealing with this problem, one which preserves, stretches, and adapts the original drive model, and the other, more radical strategy, which replaces drive discharge with a fundamentally different model that maintains that relations with others are the cornerstone of mental life. The central conceptual problem for current psychoanalytic thinking has been how to account for the enormous clinical significance of object relations; the solution to this problem "sets the foundation for subsequent theorizing" (Greenberg and Mitchell, 1983, p. 4).

In their discussion of modern-day psychopathology, Rutan and Stone (1984) call attention to the central role of "the ability to effect, experience and enjoy intimate and sustaining relationships" (p. 6). They suggest that whereas during the Victorian era the individual struggled with internal conflicts about wishes and impulses, a contemporary person has much more permission to experience and sometimes to enact those wishes but has fewer stabilizing family, church, and neighborhood structures that constitute sources of identity. Modern patients often come to treatment because their relationships are disabled or inadequate, not, as in Freud's time, because a body part is disabled. Hence, Rutan and Stone (1984) maintain that the refinements of psychoanalytic theory represented by object relations and self psychology have been mandated by differences in culture. To the extent that there is an active interplay between theory building and clinical practice, these theoretical developments need to be understood in a broader cultural context.

Clearly, the recent theoretical contributions from object relations and self psychology are in the process of moving psychoanalytic developmental psychology from a closed-system libido theory that focuses on the intrapsychic to a more open-system conceptual model that is increasingly concerned with relating the intrapsychic to the interpersonal (Ashbach and Schermer, 1987). The contributions from social systems theory similarly move current psychodynamic thinking beyond an exclusive focus upon a single level of analysis toward a richer, more complicated, holistic perspective that considers the intrapsychic, interpersonal, and group levels of analysis, and the reciprocal interactions among them.

The term "social systems theory" is being used here to refer primarily to the contributions of Wilfred Bion and Melanie Klein, whose works lie within the psychoanalytic tradition, and to those of Eric

Miller and Kenneth Rice, who focused attention upon the structural as well as the sentient (emotional) aspects of open systems. Social systems theory, as we are defining it for our purposes, conceives of psychotherapy as a throughput process with input, conversion, and output phases. In the realm of group psychotherapy, the treatment group is seen as a special case of the work group, in which task, structure, process, and culture all reciprocally affect each other.

A prominent feature of social systems theory is its focus on identifying, maintaining, and regulating various boundaries that define the treatment process. This involves a consideration of the group as a whole as an evolving social system and the relationships among its component parts. The theory assumes that when a part within a system changes there are implications for all other components of that system. An important concern is understanding how the authority needed for increasing personal responsibility, exercising executive decision-making, and enhancing individual autonomy and growth is gradually shifted from the therapist to the patient. Although social systems theory does not necessarily make assumptions about the nature of the intrapsychic and interpersonal motivations of the individuals within a given system, it does examine the social roles individuals assume in groups and the functions they fulfill on behalf of themselves and others. With the introduction of a social systems perspective that is itself rooted in both psychoanalytic and general systems considerations, this transactional model moves even further in the direction of an open-systems framework that permits simultaneous examination of intrapsychic, interpersonal, and group-as-a-whole levels of analysis.

DEVELOPMENTS IN GROUP PSYCHOTHERAPY THEORY AND PRACTICE

The notion of examining the ongoing process of psychotherapy at multiple conceptual levels—intrapsychic, interpersonal, and group-as-a-whole—has long fascinated psychodynamic group therapists. Indeed, anyone who has worked for any period of time leading a psychotherapy group quickly comes to appreciate the enormous and, at times, bewildering complexity of group therapy as an enterprise. The problem for most of us is that so much is happening so quickly. The inherent tension between individual- and group-dynamic issues invariably occupies our attention, as does the rapid-fire sequence of who is doing what to whom, for what reasons, and with what consequences. Grotjahn (1971) has suggested that in the group one must "shoot from the hip" without the luxury of time to theorize.

One of the most frequently asked questions by trainees is some variant of "How and when should I intervene, and at what level in the group process?" For example, in a recent group therapy seminar devoted to working with borderline and narcissistic patients, one trainee asked, "When should we confront these patients and when should we use more empathic responses?" Behind this question, the answer to which was eagerly awaited by all the seminar participants, was the wish to be given a simple solution to a complex problem and to be told precisely what to do in the face of an ambiguous situation.

We might all agree that it is not possible to answer this type of question in the abstract without first carefully assessing the levels of individual patient functioning, the developmental phase of the group, the therapist's level of technical expertise, the nature of the therapist's personality structure and countertransference responses, his or her theoretical orientation, plus a host of other potentially relevant variables. In addition, there is the larger art-versus-science issue with regard to the practice of group psychotherapy: whether our current levels of theoretical specificity permit us to logically deduce particular therapist responses. Finally, there is the highly questionable assumption, often maintained by our least experienced trainees, that there may be one right answer about when to confront or to empathically support patients.

Nonetheless, there is something compelling about the challenge to carefully articulate our theories, critically assess their efficacy, and provide clinically useful and readily teachable models for how to lead psychotherapy groups effectively. Perhaps the underlying question is whether we can make some sense out of what we are doing and why we are doing it. Only in this fashion can we hope to eventually arrive at a comprehensive theoretical model that will furnish practical guidelines for governing clinical decision-making and therapist behavior.

Of course, the history of group psychotherapy is replete with valiant attempts to develop such a comprehensive model. Yet it is clear that this process remains incomplete. To a large extent, previous efforts have tended to be partial and fragmented, rather than additive and integrative. Our purpose here, however, is not to provide an exhaustive review of the history of group psychotherapy, nor do we wish to examine in detail the historical development of the psychological theories that underlie approaches to group therapy. Several such excellent reviews have been provided by others (e.g., Anthony, 1972; Yalom, 1975; Rosenbaum, 1978; Shaskan, 1978; Scheidlinger, 1980,

1982; R. H. Klein, 1983; Sadock and Kaplan, 1983; Rutan and Stone, 1984; Ettin, 1988, 1989). But inasmuch as this volume is devoted to efforts to apply recent developments in psychodynamic and social systems thinking to the practice of group psychotherapy, it may be useful to selectively highlight the major trends in the field so that the reader may place these newer perspectives into some historical context. Our focus here will be primarily upon developments within one branch of group psychotherapy, namely, psychoanalytic/psychodynamic treatment; we will not attempt to address developments in other branches of the field that have gone a more structured and directive route, looking less at group process and more at the individual member (e.g., Transactional Analysis, Gestalt, Bioenergetics).

EARLY HISTORICAL DEVELOPMENTS

While Tuttman (1986) traces the roots of group therapy to ancient Greek drama, the medieval morality play, and eighteenth-century mesmerism, most historians identify Pratt (1906) as the father of modern group therapy. His pioneer efforts with tubercular patients, as well as the contributions of Lazell (1921), who treated hospitalized schizophrenic and manic–depressive patients, and Marsh (1931), who also worked primarily with a hospitalized psychotic population, were based upon a "repressive–inspirational," psychoeducational approach. Through the use of small and large group formats that incorporated techniques such as lectures, patient testimonials, homework assignments, diary keeping, role-playing and dramatic procedures, bibliotherapy, and class discussions, patients were taught effective medical and mental hygiene (Ettin, 1988).

These early group therapy practices took shape against the background of critical theoretical contributions by Wilfred Trotter, Gustav LeBon, William McDougall, and Sigmund Freud. As noted by Anthony (1972), World War I proved to be a great impetus for the development of group psychology, while World War II spurred the development of group therapy. Trotter, a neurosurgeon, developed the notion of a "herd instinct" that accounted for the tendency of human beings, consistent with evolutionary trends, to form multifunctional, multiskill groups in order to ensure survival. LeBon popularized the idea of the "group mind" in which he hypothesized that individuals in the context of the large group lose their sense of personal responsibility and individuality. Because individuals in groups experience a sense of increased strength, a hypnotic state called "contagion," and increased suggestibility, he maintained that crowds become regressive, primitive, and uncivilized. McDougall, like LeBon, recognized that the unorganized group could indeed behave in an emotional, suggestible, irresponsible, and violent fashion. However, he also introduced the contrasting idea that if the group were properly organized it could enhance individual member functioning and be used as a means of changing behavior. The problem that he highlighted, and with which subsequent generations of group therapists would continue to struggle, was how to harness the emotional energy of the group so as to make therapeutic use of the "primitive sympathetic response" that might bring with it mutative affective experience (Anthony, 1972). In assessing the contributions of these early writers, Rutan and Stone (1984) point out that they recognized "the power of groups to affect the behavior of individuals; the presence of 'contagion' or the capacity of groups to fill each of the members with affects; and the importance of organization, contracts, and goals" (p. 13).

Building upon the work of LeBon and McDougall, Freud reasoned that a collection of individuals is not a group unless clear leadership and a sense of purpose were to develop. He viewed the role of the leader as critical and placed identificatory processes at the heart of group formation. Specifically, he reasoned that groups form when members develop libidinal ties to the leader, as those ties serve to bond one member to another. The group as a collective is then endowed with ego-ideal value as the individual relinquishes his ego ideal in favor of the group leader's goals and ideals in a fashion analogous to what happens when a loved object is overvalued and idealized. Nevertheless, since the relation to the leader is rooted in ambivalence, rebellion is inevitable. Freud likened this to the "symbolic representation of the primal horde's killing and eating of its leader to secure instinctual aims" (Ettin, 1988, p. 158). While Freud himself never conducted a therapy group, some have suggested that his theories about group development were vividly and ironically borne out by the dissolution of the (nontherapy) Vienna Circle group in the wake of rebellion and acrimonious debate between Freud and Alfred Adler (Ettin, 1988).

In addition, Freud highlighted the role of empathy as a means of resolving the regressive effects of becoming a group member. The process of empathy permits a redifferentiation of each individual to occur by means of imitation and then temporary emotional identification with others. Individuals in groups thereby can reverse the dedifferentiation resulting from initial membership and, in the process, learn more about their own emotional life and that of others (Rutan and Stone, 1984).

As the efforts of the pioneer practitioners and theorists began to become more widely known, others, including psychoanalysts, soon began to successfully experiment with treating emotional and mental problems in a group setting. Trigant Burrow (1927), who saw neurotic patients in groups, developed what he called "group analysis," which he later spoke of as "phyloanalysis." His key contributions included an emphasis on the here-and-now and a "refusal to polarize the therapeutic situation into a sick patient needing help on the one side and a well physician giving him help on the other hand" (Anthony, 1972). Alfred Adler, who was concerned with the social context of human behavior, was instrumental in the establishment of guidance clinics fostering family and group techniques (Dreikurs, 1956). Dreikurs, who brought Adler's counseling methods to America and reportedly conducted the first private therapy groups (Rutan and Stone, 1984), emphasized the importance of group dynamics, interactions among patients, and establishment of cohesion as fundamental to the treatment process (Ettin, 1988). Wender, in his treatment of hospitalized "psychoneurotics," viewed the hospital as a substitute family, with transference to the therapist as symbolic parent and to the other patients as siblings (Wender, 1936). Ettin (1989) reports that although Wender's early efforts to apply group therapy were in the psychoeducational tradition, his later work more closely resembled modern therapy groups. Schilder (1939), who had a background in psychiatry, neurology, and psychoanalysis, began practicing psychotherapy in groups in the 1930s and was quite influential in advocating more active therapy for psychosis. Following the development of his early group therapy, called "analysis of ideologies" (reminiscent of more modern "values clarification"), he went on to establish more psychoanalytic approaches to group therapy, focusing on the patients' relation to the group therapist, member rivalries and competition for the leader's attention, and stages in group development.

Moreno (1932, 1953), who claimed to have been the father of sociometry, psychodrama, and group therapy proper, apparently began experimenting with group methods prior to 1910 and reached increasing prominence with his development of the actional methods of psychotherapy during the late 1920s. He founded the first psychotherapy journal and the first society for group therapy, made many important contributions to the language of group psychotherapy (e.g., "encounter," "interpersonal communication," and "group psychotherapy"), provided numerous technical innovations and new methods (e.g., psychodrama, sociodrama, role-playing), and remained vitally concerned with group dynamics and the roles members assumed within groups. Although an admirer of Freud, Moreno emphasized spontaneity, creativity, and here-and-now interactions, claiming that Freud's resistance to "acting out" blocked the progress of psychotherapy.

Slavson (1940, 1964), another of the founding fathers of group psychotherapy, was a "prominent proselytizer, prolific writer, and vigilant watchdog for the field of group psychotherapy" (Ettin, 1989). A self-taught psychoanalyst with no formal training, Slavson relied upon traditional psychoanalytic concepts (e.g., transference, resistance, insight) and adapted a classical individual psychoanalytic model for his group psychotherapy, conducted primarily with disturbed children and adolescents. He devised the term "group dynamics" in 1939 but believed that such phenomena interfered with treatment, where the emphasis should remain on the individual patient, not on the group as a whole. He stressed the expression of fantasies and drives through play and action in the context of a stable and accepting group atmosphere, which permits constructive reliving of the earlier conflict as a result of the interaction of the children with each other and with the therapist (Tuttman, 1986).

LATER HISTORICAL DEVELOPMENTS

During the 1930s and early 1940s, practitioners continued to develop and popularize group therapy as a modality of treatment suitable for use with a diverse and widening patient population seen in a variety of settings. The utilization of group psychotherapy was greatly expanded during World War II due to the limited supply of psychiatric personnel, coupled with the increased need for psychiatric services.

A related and important development was the changing conceptualizations about the nature of mankind and the etiology of psychological ill-health. A social rather than an intrapsychic theory of illness became more prevalent. This interpersonal view of humanity, which suggested that psychological disturbance might be intrinsically linked to problems of relationships between people, paved the way for broader acceptance of multiperson treatment situations. It ushered in a phase of exuberant expansion of group psychotherapy, which was offered to persons of all ages, with every conceivable type of problem.

Paralleling these developments in the field of group psychotherapy, but in many respects completely separate and independent from them, were a series of developments emanating primarily from the fields of sociology, anthropology, education, and social psychology that collectively established a growing climate of concern about how groups work and how they could be utilized to implement social purposes. Prior to 1940, relatively little scientific effort had been devoted to understanding group processes. However, against the backdrop of World War II and the hopes of implementing democratic principles and methods, social scientists in the early 1940s, led by Kurt Lewin, began to study group climate, leadership styles, and intergroup conflict in order to understand how methods of leadership influenced the properties of groups and the behavior of their members.

Lewin's assumptions about the causes of behavior and his emphasis on forces and constraints in the social field led to a focus on the here-and-now dimension of group life. Under the auspices of the National Education Association, and in conjunction with the Research Center for Group Dynamics established by Lewin and his associates, the National Training Laboratory (NTL) was founded in 1947. Initially, this was an educational and research enterprise devoted to conducting research on behavior in groups and training leaders to function more democratically and effectively within their home organizations; there was no special interest in encouraging personal growth, mental health, sensitivity, and interpersonal relations (Lewin, 1951).

However, one aspect of this form of human relations training, the T-group ("T" for training in human relations) was quickly recognized as a vehicle that could be used to promote personal learning and change. The historical forerunner of the encounter group, the T-group emerged from the serendipitous discovery of a powerful technique of human relations education: experiential learning. It was noted that the learning of group members was significantly enhanced by studying the very interactional network they were involved in creating. What began as a member of the research team reporting to the group his or her process observations soon became an integral part of the group with members providing feedback to each other (R. H. Klein, 1983).

During this same time period, Carl Rogers and his colleagues in Chicago had initiated a group training project for mental health counselors which emphasized emotional education for human growth. Rogers's ideas on individual development, interpersonal communication, and the maintenance of relationships were quickly incorporated into the T-group format. Over the years the T-group came to focus on interpersonal behavior, with greater emphasis given to feedback, interpersonal honesty, self-disclosure, "unfreezing," and participant observation (Rogers, 1970).

Two distinctly different emphases soon emerged within the NTL: one, whose roots lay with Lewin and his associates, maintained an allegiance to learning about group dynamics, group development, group pressures, and leadership roles; the other, whose traditions derived from the work of Rogers, focused on human growth, authenticity, interpersonal style, and communication among members. The subsequent development of the human potential movement with its emphasis on high-risk, high-adrenaline, high-contact encounter group participation quickly mushroomed into a commercially viable enterprise that existed largely outside society's traditional help-giving institutions. Controversies raised within the field of group psychotherapy about theories and techniques that defined the field during the 1950s were dwarfed by the furor that surrounded the emergence of the new encounter groups during the 1960s and 1970s (R. H. Klein, 1983).

To a large extent, the primary concern of practicing professionals during this period was to establish psychoanalytically oriented group psychotherapy as a distinct, legitimate, and therapeutically valid enterprise. However, within this field there was continuing conflict about the acceptability of group dynamics and process-oriented approaches. Kauff (1979), in examining the diversity of analytic group psychotherapy, indicated that the technical differences among "analytic" practitioners were far greater than their common title might suggest.

Parloff (1968) proposed that the field of group psychotherapy could be classified into three different approaches: the intrapersonal or intrapsychic, the transactional or interpersonal, and the integral or group-as-a-whole. The intrapsychic approaches transposed the individual psychoanalytic model to the group setting, as, for example, in the work of Wolf and Schwartz (1962). In this model, emphasis is placed on the individual-within-the-group; this is psychoanalysis in the round, where the group is simply the setting. Group dynamics are not focused upon; indeed, noting their presence or encouraging their development is viewed as antitherapeutic. Rather, group dynamics are seen as impediments to and interferences with the primary task, which is the elucidation and interpretation of individual transference and resistance by uncovering and making conscious the historical antecedents of the patient's pathological conflicts and working them through. This approach has been subject to criticism for failing to adequately consider those factors that make group treatment unique, namely, group-dynamic issues.

Therapists who maintain an interpersonal or transactional approach focus on the subgroup or the dyad in the group; Irvin Yalom's (1975) orientation is an example. This view holds that the group provides a range of opportunities for interpersonal involvement that will enable members to demonstrate their idiosyncratic ways of relating to others as the group evolves into a social microcosm, representing each patient's social universe. Patients learn about their maladaptive interpersonal transactions and their parataxic (perceptual) distortions through feedback and consensual validation during group interaction as it takes place in the here-and-now. From this point of view, the "corrective emotional experience," arising from authentic human interactions in the group, rather than the analysis of individual transference and defense, lies at the heart of the change process. Group dynamics are examined only when they impede the work of the group. The approach developed by Yalom has been criticized as being a commonsense, practical, but largely atheoretical point of view that does not integrate or make sufficient use of more traditional psychodynamic concepts.

In contrast to these approaches, therapists advocating an integral or group-as-a-whole perspective emphasize the interpretation of (primarily preoedipal) group dynamics, as exemplified in the contributions of Bion (1959). In developing the "Tavistock method," Bion drew upon the object relations work of Melanie Klein, adapting formulations of primitive dynamics, the paranoid-schizoid position, and the role of psychotic anxieties to characterize the foundation of group culture. He began by focusing on the group attitude toward the leader as a basis for interpretation, formulated the existence of the work group and the basic assumption modes of group functioning, and then investigated the relationship of the basic assumption mentality to its mystical leadership, as that relationship impedes work group functioning (Kibel and Stein, 1981). According to this perspective, it is only through study of the group as an entity (group as a whole) that the functioning of the individual member can be understood in its full complexity. In its most extreme form this point of view holds that the therapist who intervenes at the level of individual problems presented by individual members is promoting resistance; only the shared anxiety and the defenses against it should be interpreted to the group as a whole (Kauff, 1979).

Over the past three decades, numerous contributors have attempted to extend, modify, and integrate these fundamental approaches. With regard to the group-as-a-whole approach, for example, Ezriel (1952, 1957, 1973) modified Bion's notions to include hypotheses derived from object relations theory and clinical work with individual patients. Ezriel (1952) viewed the total material produced by all the members of the group as if it had come from a single patient in an individual session. He emphasized the interpretation of what he termed the required, the avoided, and the calamitous relationships which arise in the here-and-now as the group develops a common group tension based upon unconscious transference wishes toward the therapist. No interpretation was complete unless these object relationships could be spelled out for the group as a whole, and the contribution of each of the members to the common theme specified.

The group focal-conflict model (Whitaker and Lieberman, 1964), another modification of a group-as-a-whole approach, hypothesizes that one can understand the behavior of patients in a session as attempts to solve an intragroup conflict that involves a disturbing impulse (a wish), opposed by a reactive motive (a fear), that results in a group solution (compromised expression). The therapist's job is to observe the group process, that is, the manner in which the group deals with its focal conflicts, so as to promote through interpretation the adoption of "enabling" as opposed to "restrictive" solutions.

Attempts to apply these group-as-a-whole models, however, led to the identification of some dilemmas. The Tavistock approaches have been criticized because they encourage the group to remain leader-centered as a result of the exclusive focus on group-as-a-whole interpretations of transference to the therapist. This keeps members from turning from their dependence on the leader toward each other; phases of group development are thereby inhibited and potential therapeutic benefit is lost since peer interaction is neglected (Kibel and Stein, 1981). In addition, members of the group often feel that their particular individual concerns are overlooked when interpretations are consistently addressed to the group as a whole. The focal-conflict model has been regarded as "an oversimplified adaptation of an individual psychological approach" that is not particularly well suited to the complexities of the clinical situation (Anthony, 1972).

Nevertheless, Tuttman (1986) has suggested that group therapists in the United States have been strongly influenced by the contributions of the British psychoanalytic schools (e.g., the group concepts of Ezriel, 1950; Bion, 1959; Foulkes, 1964; and Pines, 1981; and the psychoanalytic object relations theories of M. Klein, 1932, 1937, 1957; Fairbairn, 1954; Winnicott, 1957, 1965; Balint, 1968; Guntrip, 1969). He also notes that those group therapists who maintain a psychodynamic orientation have been substantially influenced by American practitioners of psychoanalytic developmental and ego psychology, object relations theory, and self psychology (e.g., Hartmann, Kris, and Lowenstein, 1946; Jacobson, 1964; Mahler, 1971; Kernberg, 1975; Kohut, 1977).

Rutan and Stone (1984), in their excellent contribution to psychodynamic group psychotherapy, have highlighted the more recent integrative advances provided in the work of Henrietta Glatzer (1960, 1962, 1975) and Helen Durkin (1964, 1975, 1982, 1983). Specifically, they sought to integrate individual psychoanalytic theory with group therapy and practice by focusing upon the use of group interactions as a means of clarifying individual as well as group transferences and resistances. Glatzer, in applying a psychoanalytic developmental approach to treatment, suggests that the presence of peer group members helps to create a supportive atmosphere that can yield significant advantages for the treatment of patients with developmental defects. Group interactions can not only reduce archaic preoedipal envy toward the omniscient therapist, but they can promote the development of a strong working alliance by providing support, reducing resistance, interpreting defenses, and encouraging reality testing (Tuttman, 1986). Durkin, whose early work resembles that of Glatzer, viewed group-dynamic concepts as complementary, not contradictory, to group-analytic therapy. She attempted to understand the reciprocal relationships between each person's unconscious motivations and group members' interactions, plus the relationship between individual and group-as-a-whole inputs (Durkin, 1975).

Horwitz (1971, 1977), working from an object relations perspective, proposed a hierarchy of group-as-a-whole to interpersonal to intrapsychic formulations (Rutan and Stone, 1984). Thus, he advocated the use of a holistic approach that capitalizes on the advantages and minimizes the disadvantages of the group-as-a-whole method (Tuttman, 1986). Emphasizing the need for collaboration and the importance of maintaining a solid working alliance between the therapist and each individual group member, he proposed that the leader should focus first on individual characterological features of each participant before a holistic interpretation is made.

Kernberg (1975) also has proposed a model for integrating group-as-a-whole with other levels of intervention. He maintains that the group-as-a-whole intervention is most suitable for addressing preoedipal issues of development, while higher levels of object relationships require a different level of intervention. The therapist must choose the intervention based upon an assessment of group and individual levels of functioning (Rutan and Stone, 1984).

Scheidlinger (1964, 1974, 1980, 1984), too, has remained vitally concerned with developing a broader understanding of the group therapy process that adequately encompasses both group and individual dynamics. He has written extensively about identification and regression in group therapy, has suggested that on archaic symbolic levels the group represents the nurturing mother with whom members wish to restore an unconflicted state of psychological unity, and has addressed the issue of how individuals' attitudes and perceptions develop at different psychological levels toward the group as a whole (Tuttman, 1986).

Developments within the group-as-a-whole approaches have served, to a large extent, as the conceptual forerunners to general systems theory (GST) (Ganzarain, 1959; von Bertalanffy, 1968; Durkin, 1975; Tuttman, 1986). GST, which is neither a conflict nor a deficit theory but a change/growth theory, also seeks to address the interrelationships among the intrapsychic, interpersonal, and group-as-a-whole levels. This model emphasizes common processes that occur simultaneously at each of these three levels. According to GST, all systems share certain structural features called isomorphies, as well as sharing laws of operations. Thus, whatever one learns about one system can be useful in clarifying another. The group therapist who examines the group, its members, and their individual personality structures as three levels of systems can draw upon new sources of information while avoiding becoming ensnared in whether individual psychodynamics or group factors are the crucial aspects of therapy. By examining these three systems as different levels of complexity in continuous interaction, locating their boundaries, and studying how transactions across these boundaries are conducted, the therapist can maintain a single uniform approach to all levels. Thus, the therapist assumes major responsibility for the opening–closing boundary maintenance function so as to regulate exchanges between members until they have developed their own "steady states" along with mechanisms to implement boundary control.

This GST approach focuses on the organizational structure, not the content of the various systems within the group. The structural bases of systems can be examined and the group can explore transferential modes of interacting and forms of resistance as a means of facilitating boundary change. Helen Durkin (1981), a major theoretical contributor to GST, has suggested that this model complements the psychodynamic orientation and may constitute a metatheory or conceptual umbrella that can accommodate the major current approaches.

Social systems theory, as elaborated by Eric Miller and Ken Rice at the Tavistock Institute, embraces many of these same tenets plus an emphasis on issues of task and authority relations that are especially germane for social organizations.

Within the past several years, paralleling developments in the area of individual psychotherapy, there have been increasing attempts to incorporate both object relations and self psychological notions into the theory and practice of group psychotherapy. Although these efforts, too, have aimed at further integration of intrapersonal, interpersonal, and group-as-a-whole levels, for the most part many recent contributions have tended to focus upon work with a particular patient population (e.g., Stone and Gustafson, 1982; Roth, Stone, and Kibel, 1990), applications to a specific setting (e.g., R. H. Klein, 1977, 1981; Kibel, 1981; R. H. Klein, Brown, and Hunter, 1986; Rice and Rutan, 1987), and the investigation of concepts that have special relevance for group treatment (e.g., projective identification [Horwitz,

1983]). With some notable exceptions (e.g., Ashbach and Schermer, 1987; Ganzarain, 1990), relatively fewer contributions have been devoted to articulating a broader, more comprehensive model that applies these newer theoretical developments to group therapy as an enterprise.

SUMMARY AND CONCLUSIONS

In summary, then, the early history of group psychotherapy was marked by the development of psychoeducational and "repressive–inspirational" approaches. This was followed by the gradual application of psychoanalytic principles to group treatment. Limited consideration was given to group dynamics and emphasis was placed upon psychoanalyzing individuals in the context of a group. As different patient populations in various settings began to be treated successfully in groups, there was a growth spurt in group psychotherapy that was greatly accelerated as a result of World War II. Psychodynamic approaches began to evolve that moved away from an exclusive focus on the individual toward a greater appreciation of the multiple levels (intrapersonal, interpersonal, and group-as-a-whole) that characterize the group. In recent years, increasing attention has been devoted to integrating psychodynamic and group-dynamic considerations and to incorporating new theoretical contributions regarding how individuals and systems grow, develop, and change.

Clearly, not only is classical Freudian metapsychology being reevaluated in light of recent theoretical contributions from object relations, self psychology, and social systems theories, but so too is the theory and practice of group psychotherapy. New insights are available for those seeking to understand the development of the ego and the self, the nature and origin of psychic conflict, and the drive for human connectedness. The individual patient is increasingly being viewed from a relational perspective, in terms of the early contacts with important others in his or her life and the emotional roles the patient has assumed within the family. From the perspective of self psychology, vicissitudes in the empathic connection between the individual and the selfobject are determinants of impairment, vulnerability to injury, and cohesiveness of the self. From the perspective of object relations theory, the relationships one establishes are centrally influenced by these early life experiences, which leave internalized residues (schemata) that not only shape one's sense of self but fundamentally affect the nature and quality of all subsequent interpersonal relationships.

From the perspective of social systems theory, the individual can be looked upon as an evolving open system that is continuously and reciprocally interacting with other interrelated systems at various levels of complexity: for example, with individuals, families, groups, and organizations. Thus, any individual cannot be fully understood or effectively treated without an adequate appreciation of the ways in which the self, relationships, and social systems form, function, and promote or hinder individual change, differentiation, autonomy, and psychological growth.

These notions about fundamental aspects of the human condition have profoundly influenced how we define and treat psychopathology. Increasingly, mental health professionals from all disciplines are attempting to incorporate these fascinating but often difficult to comprehend ideas into their own clinical, supervisory, and teaching practices. Yet these developments do not seem to have found their way into the mainstream of group therapy in a coherent and comprehensive fashion. Despite their apparent relevance on an intuitive level for work with groups, it is not entirely clear precisely how these new developments can be cogently applied to deepen our understanding and appreciation of the therapeutic power and potential of groups.

Several factors might account for this situation. For example, advances in object relations and self psychology have been in large measure based upon work in individual psychotherapy. Comparatively little attention has been devoted to carefully articulating the implications of this work for group therapy theory and technique. In addition, the lack of a broadly accepted single theory of object relations has impeded translation to the group context. There are, in fact, multiple theories of object relations, and it is not yet clear how they fit together. As a consequence, attempts to apply "object relations theory" (as if there were one such entity), are often confusing and piecemeal rather than comprehensive, and therefore difficult for the practicing group therapist to integrate.

With regard to self psychology, Kohut's formulation of a separate line of narcissistic development independent of and prior to psychosexual and ego development, and its implications for the changing nature of object relations and for the role of noninterpretive factors in the treatment process, has remained a controversial issue. Debate also continues as to whether Kohut's contributions can best be regarded as a two-factor or a one-factor theory. When viewed as a two-factor theory, these formulations can be applied in conjunction with, can complement, and can enlarge the scope of traditional theory, particularly with regard to treating patients with borderline and narcissistic disorders. In contrast, when viewed as a one-factor theory, these formulations appear to be intended to replace the id–ego model of psychoanalysis (Eagle, 1984). On a more concrete, practical level, the relative absence of self psychology proponents within the group therapy ranks has had a similar effect in delaying wider application of these ideas to work with groups.

Social systems notions about groups having their own inherent laws of operation, development, and change somewhat surprisingly seem to have had a much more substantial impact upon the field of family therapy than upon the work of group therapists. One reason may be that many group therapists were originally trained as individual therapists and, historically, many of the theories and techniques of group therapy were derived from clinical work with individuals.

Therefore, adopting a different level of focus, that is, observing, conceptualizing, arriving at clinical formulations, and technically framing clinical interventions at the level of the group as a whole is difficult for many group therapy trainees and practitioners. Furthermore, it has remained unclear to many how focusing and intervening on the group level can promote change efficiently in individual patients, when in fact we are not working directly with dysfunctional families, except as they exist at a representational level and therefore affect patients' current interpersonal relationships. In addition, the lexicons of social systems theories (here, too, there are several, not just one theory) often seem rather abstract and removed from the clinical situation (e.g., as in general systems theory), or the recommended techniques seem to plunge group participants (both members and leaders) into regressive reenactment of disturbing preoedipal issues that are difficult to endure as well as to conceptualize (e.g., as in the Tavistock approach).

Nevertheless, within the field of group psychotherapy there is lively interest in and involvement with understanding, evaluating, and applying these advances from object relations, self psychology, and social systems theories to clinical work with groups. The steady influx of presentations and workshops on these topics during the national conferences of the American Group Psychotherapy Association, as well as the rising tide of publications devoted to these issues, speaks to the level of interest among group therapists.

THE TASK AND ORGANIZATION OF THIS VOLUME

Our purpose here is to address the concerns we have presented. We have decided to focus on recent contributions from object relations and self psychology because we believe that they represent the cutting edge of developments in psychoanalytic/psychodynamic psychotherapy. We have included contributions from social systems theories since, in our opinion, this body of work offers the potential for developing a more integrative, metatheoretical structure for working with groups as systems. When used in conjunction with theories focusing on individual development and motivation, a social systems perspective may enable the group therapist to work most effectively with the complex, simultaneously operating multiple levels of group functioning.

This volume is organized into three parts: recent theoretical developments, clinical applications to patient care, and the role of the therapist. Within each part, a chapter is included representing each of the three perspectives: object relations, self psychology, and social systems. In addition, each section includes a summary chapter. Through this collection of previously unpublished material written by leading clinical theorists and practitioners, our intention is to assemble many of the essential ideas needed for an in-depth view of the individual in the group and the role of various complex social systems in the group therapy process. Carefully edited clinical examples that protect patients' identities are provided to explicate the conceptual and technical issues under consideration. The inclusion of each perspective in each of the three sections is designed to enable us to compare and contrast these different models. By placing these theories in a historical context, considering each in relation to a traditional psychodynamic model, and successfully pinpointing their similarities and differences, we hope to arrive at a more comprehensive and thoughtful integration of these approaches.

Finally, we approached this volume with a series of questions in mind. With regard to theoretical development, we asked ourselves, what constitutes the key concepts and premises of each model? What is unique about this perspective? How is this theory relevant for conceptualizing group psychotherapy? Is this theoretical framework particularly well suited to working with specific types of patients? How does this theory complement, enrich, or deviate from a traditional psychodynamic framework? In terms of clinical applications to patient care, how does each approach define psychopathology? What are the central concepts these clinicians use in their work? What are the implications of these concepts for the therapeutic contract, task definition, and treatment focus? How does each view the change process and the nature, timing, and level of therapeutic interventions? What therapeutic factors are at work, and how are these to be mobilized or used? What are the strengths and weaknesses of each theory for conducting group psychotherapy?

Regarding the therapist's management of self in role, we asked how clinicians frame the task, the contract, the patient's expectations, and the change process. How do therapists functioning within each of these approaches use their own experiences and relationships with both individual patients and the group during group psychotherapy? How do they use patients' experiences of them and others in the group? In what ways is countertransference defined, identified, understood, and utilized? Do these models have different implications for therapist role definition, responsibilities, strategies, and techniques?

For us, these are the critical issues to be engaged. We invite you, the reader, to think along with us as we attempt to critically evaluate, clarify, and integrate this material in terms of its theoretical importance and heuristic value for clinical practice.

REFERENCES

Anthony, E. J. (1972), The history of group psychotherapy. In: *The Evolution of Group Therapy*, Vol. 2, ed. H. Kaplan & B. Sadock. New York: Jason Aronson, pp. 1–26.

Ashbach, C., & Schermer, V. L. (1987), *Object Relations, the Self, and the Group*. New York: Routledge & Kegan Paul.

Balint, M. (1968), *The Basic Fault*. London: Tavistock.

Bertalanffy, L. von (1968), General system theory and psychiatry. In: *American Handbook of Psychiatry*, ed. S. Arieti. New York: Basic Books.

Bion, W. (1959), *Experiences in Groups*. New York: Basic Books.

Burrow, T. (1927), The group method of analysis. *Psychoanal. Rev.*, 14:268–280.

Dreikurs, R. (1956), The contribution of group psychotherapy to psychiatry. *Group Psychother.*, 9(2):115–125.

Durkin, H. (1964), *The Group in Depth*. New York: International Universities Press.

——— (1975), The development of systems theory and its implications for the theory and practice of group therapy. In: *Group Therapy: An Overview*, ed. L. Wolberg & M. Aronson. New York: Stratton Intercontinental Books.

——— (1981), The group therapies and general system theory as an integrative structure. In: *Living Groups: Group Psychotherapy and General Systems Theory*, ed. J. Durkin. New York: Brunner/Mazel.

——— (1982), Change in group psychotherapy: Therapy and practice: A systems perspective. *Internat. J. Group Psychother.*, 32:431–439.

——— (1983), Developmental levels: Their therapeutic implications for analytic group psychotherapy. *Group*, 7:3–10.

Eagle, M. N. (1984), *Recent Developments in Psychoanalysis: A Critical Evaluation*. New York: McGraw-Hill.

Ettin, M. (1988), "By the crowd they have been broken, by the crowd they shall be healed." The advent of group psychotherapy. *Internat. J. Group Psychother.*, 38(2):139–167.

—— (1989), "Come on Jack, tell us about yourself": The growth spurt of group psychotherapy. *Internat. J. Group Psychother.*, 39(1):35–57.

Ezriel, H. (1950), A psychoanalytic approach to group treatment. *Brit. J. Med. Psychol.*, 23:59–74.

—— (1952), Notes on psychoanalytic therapy: II, Interpretation and research. *Psychiatry*, 15:119–126.

—— (1957), The role of transference in psychoanalytical and other approaches to group treatment. *Acta Psychother.*, 7(Suppl. 2):101–116.

—— (1973), Psychoanalytic group therapy. In: *Group Therapy 1973*, ed. L. R. Wolberg & E. K. Schwartz. New York: Intercontinental Medical Books, pp. 183–210.

Fairbairn, W. R. D. (1954), *An Object Relations Theory of the Personality*. New York: Basic Books.

Foulkes, S. H. (1964), *Therapeutic Group Analysis*. New York: International Universities Press.

Freud, S. (1915), Instincts and their vicissitudes. *Standard Edition*, 14:109–140. London: Hogarth Press, 1958.

—— (1922), *Group Psychology and the Analysis of the Ego*. New York: Liveright, 1967.

Ganzarain, R. (1959), Study of the effectiveness of group therapy in the training of medical students. *Internat. J. Group Psychother.*, 9:475–487.

—— (1977), General systems and object relations theories: Their usefulness in group psychotherapy. *Internat. J. Group Psychother.*, 27:441–456.

—— (1990), *Object Relations Group Psychotherapy: The Group as an Object, a Tool, and a Training Base*. Madison, CT: International Universities Press.

Glatzer, H. T. (1960), Discussion of symposium on combined individual and group psychotherapy. *Amer. J. Orthopsychiat.*, 30:243–246.

—— (1962), Narcissistic problems in group psychotherapy. *Internat. J. Group Psychother.*, 12:448–455.

—— (1975), The leader as supervisor and supervisee. In: *The Leader in the Group*, ed. Z. A. Liff. New York: Jason Aronson, pp. 138–145.

Greenberg, J. R., & Mitchell, S. A. (1983), *Object Relations in Psychoanalytic Theory*. Cambridge, MA: Harvard University Press.

Grotjahn, M. (1971), The qualities of the group therapist. In: *Comprehensive Group Psychotherapy*, ed. H. Kaplan & B. Saddock. Baltimore: Williams & Wilkins.

Guntrip, H. (1969), *Schizoid Phenomena, Object Relations and the Self*. New York: International Universities Press.

Hartmann, H., Kris, E., & Lowenstein, R. M. (1946), Comments on the formation of psychic structure. *The Psychoanalytic Study of the Child*, 2:11–38. New York: International Universities Press.

Horwitz, L. (1971), Group centered interventions in therapy groups. *Comprehen. Group Studies*, 2:311–331.

—— (1977), A group-centered approach to group psychotherapy. *Internat. J. Group Psychother.*, 27:423–440.

—— (1983), Projective identification in dyads and groups. *Internat. J. Group Psychother.*, 33:259–279.

Jacobson, E. (1964), *The Self and the Object World*. New York: International Universities Press.

Kauff, P. F. (1979), Diversity in analytic group psychotherapy: The relationship between theoretical concepts and technique. *Internat. J. Group Psychother.*, 29:51–66.

Kernberg, O. F. (1975), *Borderline Conditions and Pathological Narcissism*. New York: Jason Aronson.

Kibel, H. D. (1981), A conceptual model for short-term inpatient group psychotherapy. *Amer. J. Psychiat.*, 138:74–80.

—— (1987), Inpatient group psychotherapy—where treatment philosophies converge. In: *Yearbook of Psychoanalysis and Psychotherapy*, Vol. 2, ed. R. Langs. New York: Gardner Press, pp. 94–116.

—— Stein, A. (1981), The group as a whole approach, an appraisal. *Internat. J. Group Psychother.*, 31:409–427.

Klein, M. (1932), Love, guilt and reparation. In: *Love, Guilt and Reparation and Other Works*. New York: Delacorte Press, 1975.

—— (1937), Love, guilt and reparation. In: *Love, Guilt and Reparation and Other Works*. New York: Delacorte Press, 1975.

—— (1957), *Envy and Gratitude*. New York: Basic Books.

Klein, R. H. (1977), Inpatient group psychotherapy: Practical considerations. *Internat. J. Group Psychother.*, 27:201–214.

—— (1981), The patient–staff community meeting: A tea party with the Mad Hatter. *Internat. J. Group Psychother.*, 31:205–222.

—— (1983), Group treatment approaches. In: *The Clinical Psychology Handbook*, ed. M. Hersen, A. E. Kazdin, & A. S. Bellack. New York: Pergamon Press.

—— Brown, S. L., & Hunter, D. L. (1986), Long-term inpatient group psychotherapy: The ward group. *Internat. J. Group Psychother.*, 36:361–380.

Kohut, H. (1977), *The Restoration of the Self*. New York: International Universities Press.

Lazell, E. W. (1921), The group treatment of dementia praecox. *Psychoanal. Rev.*, 8:168–179.

Lewin, K. (1951), *Field Theory in Social Science*. New York: Harper & Bros.

Mahler, M. (1971), A study of the separation and individuation process. *The Psychoanalytic Study of the Child*, 26:403–424. Chicago: Quadrangle Books.

Marsh, L. C. (1931), Group treatment of the psychoses by the psychological equivalent of the revival. *Ment. Hyg.*, 17:396–416.

Moreno, J. L. (1932), *Group Method and Group Psychotherapy*. Sociometry Monogr. 5. New York: Beacon House.

—— (1953), *Who Shall Survive? Foundations of Sociometry, Group Psychotherapy, and Sociodrama*. Beacon, NY: Beacon House.

Parloff, M. (1968), Analytic group psychotherapy. In: *Modern Psychoanalysis*, ed. J. Marmor. New York: Basic Books, pp. 492–531.

Pines, M. (1981), The frame of reference of group psychotherapy. *Internat. J. Group Psychother.*, 31:275–285.

Pratt, J. H. (1906), The "home sanatorium" treatment of consumption. *Boston Med. Surg. J.*, 154:210–216.

Rice, C., & Rutan, J. S. (1987), *Inpatient Group Psychotherapy*. New York: International Universities Press.

Rogers, C. (1970), *Carl Rogers on Encounter Groups*. New York: Harper & Row.

Rosenbaum, M. (1978), Group psychotherapy: Heritage, history and the current scene. In: *Group Psychotherapy, Theory and Practice*, ed. H. Mullan & M. Rosenbaum. New York: Free Press.

Roth, B. E., Stone, W. N., & Kibel, H. D. (1990), *The Difficult Patient in Group: Group Psychotherapy with Borderline and Narcissistic Disorders*. Madison, CT: International Universities Press.

Rutan, J. S., & Stone, W. N. (1984), *Psychodynamic Group Psychotherapy*. Lexington, MA: Collamore Press.

Sadock, B., & Kaplan, H. (1983), History of group psychotherapy. In: *Comprehensive Group Psychotherapy*, ed. H. Kaplan & B. Sadock. Baltimore: Williams & Wilkins.

Scheidlinger, S. (1964), Identification, the sense of identity and of belonging in small groups. *Internat. J. Group Psychother.*, 14:291–306.

——— (1974), On the concept of the "mother group." *Internat. J. Group Psychother.*, 24:417–428.

——— (1980), *Psychoanalytic Group Dynamics—Basic Readings*. New York: International Universities Press.

——— (1982), *Focus on Group Psychotherapy: Clinical Essays*. New York: International Universities Press.

——— (1984), Individual and group psychotherapy—Are they opposed? *Group*, 8:3–11.

Schilder, P. (1939), Results and problems of group psychotherapy in severe neurosis. *Ment. Hyg.*, 23:87–98.

Shaskan, D. (1978), *History of Group Psychotherapy: W.W. II*. AGPA Working Papers, 1–6. New York: AGPA.

Slavson, S. R. (1940), Group psychotherapy. *Men. Hyg.*, 24:36–49.

——— (1964), *A Textbook in Analytic Group Psychotherapy*. New York: International Universities Press.

Stone, W. N., & Gustafson, J. (1982), Technique in group psychotherapy of narcissistic and borderline patients. *Internat. J. Group Psychother.*, 32:29–48.

Tuttman, S. (1986), Theoretical and technical elements which characterize the American approaches to psychoanalytic group psychotherapy. *Internat. J. Group Psychother.*, 36:499–516.

Wender, L. (1936), The dynamics of group psychotherapy and its application. *J. Nerv. & Ment. Dis.*, 84:54–60.

Whitaker, D. S., & Lieberman, M. A. (1964), *Psychotherapy Through the Group Process*. New York: Atherton.

Winnicott, D. W. (1957), *Collected Papers*. New York: Basic Books.

——— (1965), *The Maturational Processes and the Facilitating Environment*. New York: International Universities Press.

Wolf, A., & Schwartz, E. K. (1962), *Psychoanalysis in Groups*. New York: Grune & Stratton.

Yalom, I. D. (1975), *The Theory and Practice of Group Psychotherapy*. New York: Basic Books.

Part I

Recent Theoretical Developments

2

Contributions from Object Relations Theory

CECIL A. RICE, Ph.D.

> As Sartre so aptly declares, it is only in turning to the Other
> that we can "apprehend who we are," and I might add, who
> we wish to become [Hedges, 1983, p. 203].

In psychoanalytic theory, relationships are often described as object
relations. The impersonal term "object" was first used by Freud (1905)
in recognition of the fact that an individual's feelings and desires can
be directed toward things as well as people. More often than not,
however, "object relations" refers to interpersonal relations, whether
external to the individual or as represented within the individual's
psyche. Inner objects are also called representations, images, or, on
occasion, models.

Object relations theory is actually a collection of theories that examine relationships from a variety of perspectives and with a number of
emphases. Two opposing perspectives are of major importance. One
argues that relationships and personality structure emerge out of the
vicissitudes of the sexual and aggressive drives; another argues that
the search for relationships is the primary motivator of human behavior, and the nature of those relationships the creator of personality
structure. Greenberg and Mitchell (1983) describe those two viewpoints as the drive/structure and relational/structure models, respectively. The former model lies within the classical psychoanalytic tradition, whereas the latter represents an emerging paradigm that seeks

I wish to express appreciation and thanks to my friends and colleagues Drs. Anne
Alonso, J. Scott Rutan, and Judy Silverstein for their suggestions and editorial help in
writing this chapter.

27

to address perceived limitations in the classical paradigm. Object relations theorists are often perceived as centering around the relational pole. In fact, however, they can be located at different points along the continuum between those two models.

Similarly, object relations theorists differ in their emphasis on inner and outer objects. At one end of this continuum lie those who consider inner objects or object representations to be of primary importance, while at the other end lie those who consider real, external relationships to be primary. It is *not* the task of this chapter to argue the merits or limitations of these varying perspectives. Rather, the aim is to discuss the primary ideas and concepts within object relations theory and apply them to the treatment of people in groups. To achieve that end, I will first examine the development of object relations theory and its major premises and concepts through synopses, in approximately historical sequence, of the work of some of the leading thinkers in the field, beginning with Freud. In addition, I will note the degree of similarity or deviance from the more classical psychoanalytic approach.

HISTORICAL ROOTS AND DEVELOPMENT OF CONCEPTS

Freud

Freud's early seduction theory fell within the relational/structure model. In it he hypothesized that hysterical disorders were the result of actual sexual seductions of the patient during childhood. When subsequent data indicated that seduction was not always present, he reconsidered that hypothesis and gradually replaced it with his drive theory, suggesting that it was something within the patient that contributed to his difficulties. According to this model, the satisfaction of the drives is primary, and relationships develop in response to drive satisfaction and frustration. In his *Three Essays on the Theory of Sexuality*, he defined the sexual drive (libido) as having a source, an aim, and an object. The source is physiological excitation in erogenous zones in the body, the aim is to reduce the libido-generated tension and so return the organism to a state of homeostasis, and the object is that (person or thing) which satisfied the libido and reduced the tension. For the infant, the major source of drive satisfaction and frustration is the mother, who thus becomes "known" and highly valued. In Freud's terms, she becomes the focus of a great deal of libidinal energy and thus is highly cathected.

Later, when Freud developed his structural submodel of id, ego, and superego, he saw the satisfactions and frustrations of the libido as the source of the ego and superego structures and of the unique relationships between them in any given individual. Additionally, he hypothesized that through identification with his parents, the child internalized them within the ego, specifically in the superego subsystem, which then became the carrier of social values and proscriptions. Finally, in Freud's system, it was actually those mental representations that were cathected and not the objects themselves. The emphasis had moved from external object relations to internal ones.

With the incorporation of the parental objects within the superego, Freud had laid the basis for future interest in inner object relations and consolidated the drive/structure model.

Melanie Klein

The next major figure in the history of object relations theory was Melanie Klein. Klein, whose work was published from 1912 to the 1960s, enlarged on Freud's drive theory, focusing especially on the aggressive drive (Klein, 1935, 1964). She also modified his drive theory by incorporating the object within the drive and set the stage for the later relational models of Fairbairn, Winnicott, and others.

In contrast to Freud, who worked mostly with adults, many of Klein's concepts grew out of her work with children. Her writings reveal a number of phases of her interests. In the early years she focused on the libido in young children, concluding that oedipal concerns occurred at a much earlier age than that suggested by Freud. In the next phase she turned her attention to the aggressive drive, and then returned to libidinal concerns with a focus on the infant's capacity for reparation. Finally, she sought to integrate her work on libido and aggression, and she developed and/or refined such concepts as splitting, projective identification, and envy.

For Klein, object relations were a complex matrix of "phantasy"[1] relations with others. As the result of slow phylogenetic processes, the infant's phantasies are comprised of an inherent set of inner objects or part-objects. The inherent objects include images of such phenomena as wombs, breasts, penises, and babies. Further, those inner objects are associated with and inextricably bound to the libidinal and

---

[1]To emphasize Klein's unique use of this term, writers have usually followed her lead and used the word "phantasy," rather than the more common "fantasy," when describing her work.

aggressive drives. In other words, the drives are directed toward inner objects from the beginning and do not become cathected to them later, as Freud argued. Thus, "drives, for Klein, are relationships" (Greenberg and Mitchell, 1983, p. 146).

The libidinal and aggressive drives represent for Klein expressions of the life-and-death instincts respectively creating within the infant a life-and-death struggle from the beginning. The infant handles that life-and-death struggle by splitting the inner objects into bad and good components. Good object components are those cathected with libido, and bad ones, those cathected with the aggressive drive; thus, the phantasies of the infant are populated with bad and good breasts, bad and good wombs, and so on. In addition, because the drives are attached to objects from the beginning, Klein's descriptions of the sexual and aggressive drives take on a personal coloring, so she speaks of love and hate rather than simply of sex and aggression.

In Klein's view, infants are active partners in their early development and not passive recipients of environmental pressures. Their relationships with others are developed through a process of fitting these outer relations to already existing inner object relations. Fitting takes place through the processes of projection, identification, and introjection. The bad and good, loved and hated inner breasts, for example, are projected onto the maternal breasts, which are thus respectively experienced as bad and good, hateful and loving. In normal development, the mother's ameliorative responses to the hateful and aggressive projections of infants are identified with by the infants and introjected into their egos. This process, known as *projective identification*, gradually modifies the internal hateful and aggressive objects and allows the infant to integrate them with the loving and libidinal ones.

Infant development reflects Klein's understanding of the object relatedness of the drives. She uses the term "positions," rather than the more traditional terms "phases" or "stages" of development. If successfully completed, these positions, while initially sequential, actually represent sets of defenses and ways of organizing experience and relations with others that are present throughout life.

The first position is the paranoid-schizoid position. Initially, infants relate to their mothers in a state of hallucinatory fusion: the schizoid side of this position. Later, as infants begin to separate, they view the world in terms of bad and good, loved and hated objects—the paranoid side of this position. After approximately six to twelve months, infants begin to accept that their mothers are both bad and good. In doing so they enter the second position, called the depressive position, in which good and bad objects are integrated, the illusion of an all-good world is regretfully given up, and people are perceived as whole objects rather than part-objects. In this position the infant is able to have concern for others, to love and hate the same person, and to experience guilt. It is similar to the resolution of the oedipal complex in classical theory, though placed developmentally much earlier. Multiple, triadic relationships with conflicts over sex and aggression are now possible.

Klein, then, follows Freud closely by placing her emphasis on the drives and on inner objects in contrast to outer objects. Arguably, she may have gone further than Freud in her emphasis on inner objects. In her model, while the mother can have a palliative effect on the infant's struggles with love and hate, that palliative effect bears little relation to how she actually behaves, or the nature of her own character structure. Rather, she is used by the infant to neutralize, modify, and eventually to integrate the loving and hating objects. However, Klein broke with Freud significantly by conceiving the drives as bound to inner objects. She thus set the stage for Fairbairn's work.

Fairbairn

Much of W. R. D. Fairbairn's work was developed in reaction to both Freud and Klein. He argued that classical theory had mistaken the means for the ends. The drives, and the bodily zones through which they are given expression, he argued, were means to establish relationships and not ends in themselves. He wrote, "libidinal attitudes are relatively unimportant in comparison with object-relationships and, . . . the object, and not gratification, is the ultimate aim of libidinal striving" (Fairbairn, 1952b, p. 103). He considered pure pleasure-seeking a breakdown in the more basic search for pleasurable relationships with others. In contrast to Freud, then, who considered the infant as initially pleasure-seeking and only later becoming directed toward reality, Fairbairn considered the infant as oriented toward reality from the beginning.

Fairbairn followed Klein's development of object relations, but placed the primary emphasis on external relationships from which, he claimed, inner objects were derived. He wrote, "Introjection is the process whereby a *mental structure* representing the external object becomes established within the psyche" (Fairbairn, 1954, p. 107). Like Klein, he considered the ego to be present from birth rather than developing later, as postulated by Freud. However, unlike Klein, he considered the ego at birth to be in pristine if undifferentiated form, having the primary task of negotiating the relationship between the self and reality, including external objects such as the mother. For

Fairbairn, the infant has no hostile, destructive desires, as in Klein's work; rather, those desires arise in response to the infant's relations with the object. According to Fairbairn, the mother is no substitute for the bliss of the womb and must inevitably frustrate the infant. To defend itself against those stresses the ego splits the internal representative of the outer object into an ideal object, representing relatively satisfying experiences with the mother, and into the rejected object, representing the intolerably frustrating and unsatisfying experiences with the mother.

The rejected object is further split into a rejecting and an exciting object. The rejecting object represents the frustrating mother, and the exciting object represents the intense yearnings associated with the enticement of a potential good relationship with the mother. The ego splits off the rejecting and enticing objects, along with their associated affects of rage and intense yearning, into what Fairbairn calls the unconscious antilibidinal and libidinal ego, respectively. The remainder of the ego remains conscious and contains the ideal object as a defense against the unconscious and intolerable objects.

This is clearly an interpersonal model of personality situated at the opposite end of the drive–relational continuum from Freud and Klein. In this model, inner objects are primarily substitutes for satisfactory interpersonal relationships. Theoretically, in a world of perfect relationships, the ego would remain whole and undivided, and free of inner objects. Conversely, pathology is the result of unhappy relationships. As with inner objects, fantasies are viewed as substitutes for relationships and do not carry the powerful, drive-related creative and destructive power of Klein's phantasies.

Development in Fairbairn's system reflects his interpersonal emphasis. He identifies two developmental stages: (1) infantile dependency, when the infant is totally dependent on others for physical and emotional survival, and (2) mature dependency, when one can establish mutually interdependent relationships. Between those two stages is a transition period in which individuals gradually separate from their primary caregivers until they are able to establish interdependent relationships.

Fairbairn's interpersonal model has many similarities to the interpersonal model developed by Sullivan in the United States at about the same time. Like Fairbairn, Sullivan rebelled against the mechanistic drive theory of classical analysis, claiming that health and pathology were determined by the individual's relationships and not by the satisfaction or frustration of pleasure-seeking drives. Whereas Fairbairn used the language of classical theory, albeit with modifications of meaning, Sullivan's concepts came from many sources, including operationalism and pragmatism, making his work seem strikingly different from classical theory.

In Britain, Winnicott, Bowlby and others followed the interpersonal route taken by Fairbairn.

Winnicott

D. W. Winnicott did not write a comprehensive theory of personality, but focused instead on specific issues, most of them revolving around the mother–child relationship and the process by which the child emerges out of that unit. His work, nevertheless, had a major impact on object relations theory (Winnicott, 1971, 1975, 1988).

Winnicott was a pediatrician before and during his career as a psychoanalyst. That dual career is reflected in his thinking about child development. He challenged a basic assumption that he perceived in the work of many of his predecessors, namely, that the infant exists as an independent person to be studied. For Winnicott there was no such thing as an infant independent of his or her mother. For him, the mother and infant were one unit out of which the child emerged. That destruction and re-creation of his predecessors' basic assumption illustrates both how Winnicott wrote and how he perceived infant development. Though he claimed orthodoxy, his reworking of aspects of his predecessors' thinking made him unorthodox. He viewed the infant as destroying the object (caretaker) once it became real—that is, was no longer a fantasy of his own creation—but the object became real precisely because it had been destroyed. Relationships and paradox were central to his thinking and writing.

A central component of child development for Winnicott was the synchrony within the mother–child unit. Infants matured effectively to the extent that their mothers related in a synchronous manner to their developmental needs. Initially the child is in a condition of scattered and unorganized bits and pieces of experiences. The child organizes those experiences in accordance with the mother's organizing of them. During the last few months of pregnancy and the first few months following birth, the mother is preoccupied with, and very attentive to, her child and to his needs and experiences. In this state of "primary maternal preoccupation,"[2] the mother reflects and names the child's experiences and provides a "holding environment" that facilitates organization of the infant self. He wrote, "an infant who has had no one person to gather his bits together starts with a handicap in his own self-integrating task" (Greenberg and Mitchell, 1983, p. 191).

---

[2]Because many of Winnicott's terms are expressed in everyday phrases and words, I have chosen to place them between quotation marks so they can be distinguished from the remainder of the sentence.

Synchrony plays a particular role in the mother's task of bringing the child into the world of others. Winnicott postulates that when the infant experiences a need, such as hunger, it comes close to conjuring up a means of satisfying that need. If at that moment the mother presents a suitable object, say, her breast, to the infant's searching mouth, the almost-conjured-up solution and the event are experienced as the same. The infant's subjective experience is of having created the solution. This is referred to as the "moment of illusion." It is also the moment when the infant connects need and object.

Though it is important for the mother to know when to introduce the object to meet the infant's need, it is equally important for the mother to know when to be present without presenting anything. Winnicott spoke of the infant's need to have space in which to be, the proper management of which enables the infant to develop the capacity to be alone. It is important that the mother be present during those moments and allow the infant to be quiescent without making any demand.

The primary maternal failures that are detrimental to the infant's development, according to Winnicott, take place when the mother fails to present the appropriate object at the "moment of illusion" and/or makes a demand when the infant wishes to be quiescent. When there is a severe and consistent loss of synchrony in this manner, the infant protects himself by the development of a "false self" that protects the "true self." The false self is the self the mother wanted the child to be as communicated through the empathic failures.

As the mother's maternal preoccupation diminishes and she becomes concerned about other matters beyond the child, she fails to match conjured-up solutions with suitable objects and is less present than before. In response, the child begins to separate and to learn the limits of what he can do. The pain of this loss of synchrony is compensated for by the infant's maturational need to separate, which, paradoxically, is yet another example of synchrony between mother and child. The "transitional object" is important to this separation process. This object, often a blanket or soft toy, is perceived by the child, and supported by the mother, as a creation of the child and simultaneously as a separate object in the real world. Thus, as the mother–child unit separates, the infant becomes more able to distinguish the subjective and the objective worlds without losing either.

Like Fairbairn, Winnicott demonstrates special interest in the role of outer object relations in child development and in the creation of health and psychopathology. However, in contrast to Fairbairn, he also emphasizes the contribution of the child to that process, demonstrating the influence of Klein. It is the synchrony or the lack thereof between the demands and needs of the child and the responses of the mother that are significant.

Bowlby

John Bowlby's primary contribution to the field of object relations was his writing and research in the areas of attachment and loss. He integrated the work of ethologists with his and others' observations of children and brought considerable evidence to bear on the importance of early relationships on human development, especially the impact of actual attachments, losses, and grief. Moreover, he concluded that the seeking of a relationship was a primary motivating factor in human relations, at least as primary as sex and aggression (Bowlby, 1969, pp. 177–209).

Bowlby was clearly in the mainstream of the interpersonal theorists. However, unlike Klein, Fairbairn, or Winnicott he paid little attention to subjective experience and spoke only briefly about inner objects, which he called models. His work focused on actual experiences, not fantasied ones, on parental losses and not on parental attitudes or projections. For Bowlby, it was actual loss and grief that on occasion left scars that "like rheumatic fever" can cause considerable difficulty later in life (Bowlby, 1980, pp. 7–39). His recognition of the importance of attachment in human development has become widely accepted within object relations theory.

THE BRIDGE THEORISTS

The growth of interest in object relations has led to a variety of modifications of the classical and relational models; some theorists, like Jacobson, Mahler, and Kernberg, have sought to include the preceding object relations theorists within the classical drive framework.

Jacobson, Mahler, and Kernberg

Like Freud, Edith Jacobson assumes that the infant's early relationship with the mother is primarily one of instinctual gratification. The experiences of satisfaction and frustration that are inevitable in this relationship lead to the development of inner representations of a good and bad mother, respectively. Jacobson adds, however, that the attitudes associated with the internal object relations later become motivating forces. That is, the drives are no longer the primary motivating forces; instead, object relations have become the motivators.

Margaret Mahler (1979), whose work preceded that of Jacobson, modifies classical theory in a similar way. While operating out of the classical drive model, she nevertheless created a developmental schema that is highly social and in which the central motivating force is that of individuation. She wrote, "Object relationship develops on the basis of, and *pari passu* with, differentiation from the normal mother–infant duality . . ." (Mahler, 1972, p. 120). According to Mahler, infants move from a period of normal autism in the first few weeks of life, when they appear oblivious to all stimulation, through a period of normal symbiosis in the third to fourth week in which there are responses to external stimulation and a dim awareness of the mother as an external object. However, from the infants' perspectives there is no differentiation between the two components of the symbiotic unit during this phase. Separation—individuation follows the symbiotic phase at about four to five months and is the phase of greatest interest for Mahler. This phase she divides into three subphases: differentiation, when infants begin to make bodily gestures of pushing away from their mothers; practicing, when they move off their mothers' laps and crawl away; and rapprochement, when infants recognize their mothers as separate and themselves as living in a sometimes threatening world, and they begin to struggle actively with the desire to be close to mother and also to separate from her. The last phase in Mahler's schema is that of object constancy, when infants develop a stable concept of self and a stable concept of others, particularly the mother.

Otto Kernberg (1980), who was influenced by Jacobson, Mahler, Klein, and Fairbairn, has arguably created the most successful and thorough integration of the interpersonal and drive models to date. Like Freud and Jacobson, he sees the initial relationship with the mother as that of instinctual gratification (and frustration) leading to the development of inner objects. He refines Klein's concept of object relations and relates the formation, splitting, and integrating of inner objects to five developmental stages based on Mahler's schema (Kernberg, 1976). During the first stage of normal autism, the private world of the infant is nonexistent and undifferentiated from that of the mother's. In the second stage of normal symbiosis, the inner images or representations of the mother and the child are undifferentiated and are referred to as a "selfobject." Next, infants begin to separate from their mothers in the separation—individuation stage, and the inner objects are broken down into a good self-image, a bad self-image, a good object-image and a bad object-image. In the following stage, as infants begin to see their mothers as whole persons, the inner objects become integrated into good and bad self-images and good and bad object-images. In the final stage of object constancy, the classical structure of id, ego, and superego become established. Some theorists argue that although Kernberg developed a thorough integration of the drive and interpersonal model, he actually broke ranks with the drive model and has created an interpersonal model that contains some remnants of the drive model (Greenberg and Mitchell, 1983, p. 340).

It is clear from the preceding discussion that object relations theory is not merely a collection of theories but also a vital process—stimulated by strong differences, creative interchanges, vivid and sometimes unclear terminology, and a variety of ideas and perspectives. It is still not clear what the end result will be. Are new ideas developing that can be added to and incorporated within classical psychoanalytic theory? Is a new paradigm emerging that may supersede the classical model? Is a new model being created which, while contradicting the classical model, nevertheless provides a way of understanding and addressing the needs of certain patients that the classical model cannot? And is the converse also true, thus giving psychotherapy its equivalent of the wave and particle theories in physics to explain light? Though the models are incompatible, each can be used to effectively explain phenomena the other cannot. Some practitioners argue, for instance, that object relations theory is valuable for understanding and treating patients with character disorders in which the concerns are primarily preoedipal, whereas classical theory is more useful in understanding and treating neurotic patients for whom oedipal issues are of primary concern (Hedges, 1983).

Given the controversy within object relations theory, it becomes clear that there is no agreed-upon set of object relations concepts to be directly applied to groups. Thus, I must not only be selective, but my selection will probably reflect my particular biases.

Despite that caveat, there are a number of object relations premises and concepts that have received general acceptance. These include the importance and centrality of relationships in human development and well-being; the reciprocity between internal and external object relations; and the developmental and defensive functions of splitting, projection, introjection, and projective identification, among others. In addition, object relations theory has modified our understanding of a number of traditional psychoanalytic concepts, such as the repetition compulsion, resistance, and transference. It has also modified our understanding of the therapeutic task by placing a greater emphasis on the curative power of the therapy relationship. Thus, while there is a broad range of understanding and intense debate about the role of the therapy relationship in healing, the classical formulation of the therapy task as making the unconscious desires conscious may be reformulated as making the inner object relations and associated desires conscious, especially as they are played out, experienced, and reexperienced in the relationship between the patient and the therapist. These and other concepts will be discussed in more detail when I apply them to group therapy.

OBJECT RELATIONS THEORY AND GROUP PSYCHOTHERAPY

Group therapy is a mode of treatment built around relationships: member-to-member, member-to-therapist, member-to-group, member-to-subgroup, and subgroup-to-subgroup relationships. Hence, it seems only natural that a theory or set of theories concerned with human relationships should have something significant to contribute to the understanding of group therapy. In applying object relations theory to group therapy, I will limit myself to the following issues: structure and group development, therapeutic process, the role of the therapist, and group composition and patient selection.

Structure and Group Development

At the formation of a group, the structure is comprised of a set of agreements between the group members and the therapist about how they shall work together. That structure includes agreements about time, place, fees, and duration of the group and about the group task, such as working on the problems that brought the members to the group, and so on. From an object relations perspective the group task is to make conscious the inner object relations of the members, both as they are played out in the members' relations with each other and with the therapist and as they are reflected in the problems that brought the members to the group. Group structure also includes a physical arrangement in which the members sit in a circle and face each other. All these manifestations of structure, once agreed to and acted on, bring the group into being and lead to a variety of interactions among the members.

Paradoxically, however, a therapy group is essentially unstructured. Within the limited parameters I have mentioned, members are free to talk about any issue or concern they choose. Further, the therapist gives no indication or suggestions regarding desirable topics but instead follows the members' lead with minimal comment.

In the beginning, the virtually structureless nature of a therapy group leads to ego regression in the members (Bion, 1961; Scheidlinger, 1968; Foulkes, 1977). This regression is a highly adaptive response through which the members attempt to organize their relationships with each other and bring structure to the group. As a consequence of this regressive response, groups follow developmental processes that are isomorphic with the phases of infant development. Those phases also embody different forms of group structure.

Structure and the Beginning Phase. The beginning phase of a group bears many of the characteristics of Klein's schizoid phase of development (Alonso and Rutan, 1984), in which mother and infant are in a state of fusion, or of Kernberg's state of normal symbiosis, with its accompanying inner selfobject organization. Bion (1961), who was strongly influenced by Klein, sees the early phase as operating on the basis of the shared assumption that the leader will provide for all the needs of the members. The leader is all-powerful and the members, through their identification with him, are also all-powerful, thus creating a fantasy-based, harmonious world in which all their needs will be taken care of. Bion called it a basic assumption dependency group. Thus, the formative moments of a group are often pleasant, despite some initial anxieties about meeting with strangers.[3] Members see each other in the most positive light, differences are minimized or ignored, and numerous commonalities are found, even if it means stretching the truth considerably. Anything that may be upsetting or annoying is ignored or denied, and the therapist is idealized. The capacities of the members to differentiate and critically evaluate seem to be operating in neutral during this period.

Just as with the mother–infant relationship, the early process of undifferentiated bonding in a group enables the members to cope with the "object anxiety" generated by meeting strangers, permits attachments to be made and allows for the development of a boundary that clearly distinguishes those who belong from those who do not. Furthermore, as in infancy, such undifferentiated attachment provides the basis for later differentiation.

---

[3]Exceptions to this generalization are found among patients who have particular difficulty in bonding with others: see this chapter, p. 44; Yalom (1975, pp. 222–235); and Rice and Rutan (1987, pp. 55–57).

Paradoxically, however, that structure also discourages differentiation among the members. Thus, every beginning group has an "unconscious" tension—that is, a tension residing in the unconscious of each member—that in time seeks expression. In the words of de Mare (1972), it is a tension between oneness and multiplicity, between the desire to belong and the desire to be separate. In the Kleinian metaphor, it is the tension between the love and hate of the fantasied "mother group," of which the therapist is the embodiment, and between the desire to be nurtured by it and the fear of being consumed by it. Bion describes the tension as being between the dependency assumption and the fight–flight assumption. Acting under the latter assumption, the members have the unconscious fantasy that there is an enemy in the group or outside it who is threatening the harmonious group and who must be avoided or fought. The fantasy enemy is created by the projection of the bad part-objects, which have been denied up to this point, onto the group.

Structure and the Protest Phase. What was unconscious in the opening phase of the group becomes active and apparent in the second phase. The therapist is no longer idealized. Rather, his competency is openly questioned and the value of the group is suspect. Experience in the group is no longer pleasant. Members bond against the leader who has disappointed them and whom they fear. Following attacks on the therapist, members may then attack and injure each other. The sense of unity is gone, and members threaten to leave or question the wisdom of their decision to join; a general uneasiness pervades the group.

In the words of de Mare, Klein, and Bion, oneness has been replaced by multiplicity, and members have begun to flee the potentially consuming or dangerous group and to fight the therapist who is perceived as threatening and as neither protecting the members nor fulfilling their fantasies. The relationships of the members to the leader, and later toward each other, reflects the inner object structures of the paranoid position, especially as later interpreted by Kernberg (1976): split good and bad self- and object-images. Good objects are embraced and bad objects are avoided.

The structure of the group is most threatened during this period, dropouts are not uncommon, and disorganization has replaced organization. If the earlier group structure was relatively impermeable and readily distinguished those within from those without, it is now highly permeable and those within feel identified with those without, largely because the good and loved part-objects have been denied and/or projected outside the group.

If the task of the first phase is the survival of the group and the development of attachment, the task of this phase is the establishment of individual identity and safety—the survival of the individual. The question is, can one belong to the group and survive as a separate person? Some may decide it is not possible and leave, while others enter a process of reparation and integration as the group moves toward the mature phase.

Structure and the Mature Phase. The process of reparation and integration is the means by which the members repair the fractured structure of the group and heal those who have been injured. It is analogous to the reparation that Klein (1935) described in the depressive position and the integration that Mahler (1972) noted in the rapprochement subphase, both of which lead to object constancy.

During this process, members show more genuine concern for each other and for the group. Injuries that may have been suffered during the protest phase are discussed and resolutions sought. Absences are cause for both concern and anger: anger because of the threat to the group, and concern because of what it may reflect about the absent member's difficulties. The uniqueness of each member begins to be recognized, and members may feel "badly" about injury they cause others.

This reparation makes possible the integration of oneness and multiplicity, of bad and good objects, of love and hate. The structure of the group also changes in the process and is no longer highly impermeable or overly permeable. It is becoming like a breathing membrane whose degree of permeability adjusts to the needs of the group and its members.

Thus, in the mature phase oneness and multiplicity are held in dynamic tension, dependency and autonomy become interdependence. The relationship with the leader is no longer idealized or fearful, but more collegial (Rutan and Stone, 1983, pp. 43–45). Members see and value each other as whole persons, and concern for each other that began with the reparation process becomes more fully developed. The structure is more firmly established, on the one hand, yet more adaptable to the needs of the individuals and the group, on the other. There are moments of common angers, fears, and pleasures, and also time and space for unique individual feelings, conflicts, and successes. In the mature phase, more than at any other time in the group, members encourage introspective analysis of each other's behavior and conflicts, not simply as they are reported to the group, but as they emerge in relationships with other members.

In the mature phase the structure of the object relations not only includes the integration of bad and good objects, and a flexible differentiation of self and other, but the object relations also become triadic and not simply dyadic, and genuine intimacy becomes possible in contrast to the illusion of intimacy at the beginning.

The Ever-Present Nature of Phases. As with Klein's developmental positions, the phases of a group are not simply arrived at and passed through (Klein, 1935). They are also always present. A group may regress into, or take the position of, any of these phases at any time. For instance, following the announcement of the therapist's vacation members will sometimes band together to express their anger and disappointment at him. Little permission is given for any member to disagree with this shared anger and attack. Once again, the therapist has become the bad object who, in this case, abandons the members. The group has reentered the protest phase and the unconscious part-objects have reemerged. The primary difference is that, in a well-established group, the threat to the structure is less severe, and the movement toward reparation and the return and integration of the good objects more rapid, including giving permission for contrary opinions. These regressions to prior stages are opportunities to re-work unresolved early developmental tasks time and again.

The Complexity of Structuring. I have described in broad terms the structure and development of a therapy group. It is, however, important to note that each member of the group plays a role in those developmental tasks. Ezriel (1950), who, like Bion and de Mare, was strongly influenced by object relations theory, placed considerable significance on the roles the members play in a group's development. The particular role a member plays, he argued, is related to his inner object relations and the shared tension of the group.

Thus, while oneness, idealization of the therapist, and lack of differentiation are important characteristics of the initial phase of a group's life, particular members of the group, in unspoken agreement with the other members, are self-selected and chosen to facilitate the process. They are usually people whose inner object relation constellations permit them to readily bond with others and/or encourage others to bond with them or around them. They become, in Redl's (1942) terms, central figures. They may, however, have little tolerance for conflict and hence will remove themselves and be removed from the central role during the protest phase. The central figure position will be taken by other members whose inner objects are more conducive to that task.

Hence, the broad structure of the group is not only modified as the group moves from phase to phase—each phase representing a particular kind of structure—but member roles, or substructures, are also generated in response to phase-related tasks. In addition, the inner object organization of the members change from phase to phase, that organization being most clearly articulated by the central figure. It becomes clear, then, that the group structure is both complex and dynamic. Therefore, it is probably most accurate to refer to the group structure as a continuous process of structuring and restructuring, set in motion by the opening agreement between the members and the therapist and enlarged and elaborated on as the group develops. This matter will be discussed further when I examine the therapeutic process.

Therapeutic Process

The therapeutic process refers to those individual and group activities that uncover and heal the members' pathology. Many individual and group activities contribute to this process (Yalom, 1975; Rutan and Stone, 1983, pp. 53–76). I will limit discussion to the roles of regression and transference. The contribution of the therapist will be addressed separately.

Regression. I have already discussed the adaptive value of regression in the formation and development of the group. I described regression in terms of levels of object relations organization and their related defenses such as projection, splitting, and denial. This discussion assumed that in an "ideal" healthy individual all levels of object relations organization are present and that any one of those levels of organization may be prevalent—that is, be the "figure," while others are the "ground"—at a particular time, depending on the task. For instance, when an individual is involved in complex business relationships, the triadic object relations organization are the figure and other levels of organization are the ground. However, when making love the individual regresses to a point where selfobject organization is the figure and the others, including the triadic organization, are the ground. After lovemaking another level of object relations organization will become the figure, and so on.

While all regression may be viewed as an attempt to adapt to certain internal or external demands, not all regression is effective, and some regression can be very limiting, even dangerous. For instance, some individuals may effectively join a group and share in the selfobject level of organization of the group members. But as the other members begin to differentiate, these individuals may run into a great deal of trouble. Due to unstable early relationships, the affective loading of the selfobject relations of these individuals may be such that any separation from the object is experienced as a loss of the self. While the regression is initially adaptive, its pathological nature becomes apparent when more complex relations are required. The reverse may also be true: Patients whose early relationships were overly engulfing may feel quite comfortable during the protest phase of a group, but may have remained on the fringe during the beginning phase because regression to the selfobject levels of organization may be threatening to their sense of self. For some it may be so threatening that they cannot enter a group in the first place, or they may need additional support, such as individual therapy, to do so.

Healthier patients, with well-established internal triadic object relations, may also have difficulties when regressing to lower levels of organization, because those lower levels contain elements of impaired object relations organization. This may be expressed in discomfort and resistance to participating in particular developmental phases or group events. By observing how members cope with the developmental phases and other group events, insight may be gained into the nature and pathology of their object relations.

The nature of those internal object relations, of course, is most clearly revealed in the transference.

Transference and the Therapeutic Process. Transference is an interpersonal, object-related phenomenon in which the members project onto the therapist and each other early internalized relationships along with their associated feelings, drives, and defenses, and then behave as though they were relating to those early objects.

In group therapy there are multiple transferences between and among the members. Different members may be unconsciously perceived by another member as representing important persons or aspects of those persons from his past and will be responded to accordingly, even though there may be objective data contradicting those perceptions. Likewise, the whole group is a frequent transference object. The group may represent one person, such as the mother, or it may represent a collective, such as the family of origin, and be responded to accordingly. Various subgroups can also become transference objects. The therapist is clearly the central transference object; that aspect of transference will be addressed at length in the next section of this chapter.

Despite the multiplicity of transferences and transference objects in a group, the transference of any individual will often focus on certain members with whom he develops very intense reciprocal relations. Sometimes a member's transference focus is the whole group, and the members collectively develop an intense reciprocal relationship with that member. Those reciprocal, transference-based relations often lead to levels of affective intensity rarely seen in individual therapy.

The object relations concept that has been used by many authors to explain this phenomenon is projective identification, an adaptive and defensive interpersonal mechanism (see p. 30) that is carried within the transference (Grotstein, 1981). More detailed discussions of this concept can be found elsewhere (Grotstein, 1981; Ogden, 1982; Horwitz, 1983). For our purposes, it is sufficient to say that in projective identification the individual, like the infant, projects onto another person a split-off, discomforting aspect of his inner objects, such as a sadistic object. The other person accepts the projection and may then act on it: For example, he may act sadistically. The individual making the projection then identifies with the projected part in the recipient, who is often surprised by the intensity of his reactions. The process is complicated in the group because the recipient often projects a complementary split-off aspect, such as a masochistic object, onto the original person, which he accepts and may also act on (that is, he may act masochistically). The "couple" then readily become locked in a sadomasochistic collusion, in which each reinforces and dramatically polarizes the other's projections, tossing back and forth, as it were, uncontained, discomforting inner objects.

Such transference-based collusions not only generate intense and sometimes painful relations among the members, but they also provide a unique opportunity for change. The nature of the members' conflicts and the unspoken assumptions out of which they act are clear for all to see. The desperate attempts the individuals make to solve inner conflicts through their relations with others and to find someone to contain what they have so far been unable to contain are made visible. In these collusions, the inner and outer objects and the past and the present are joined. The "inner" and the "there-and-then" meet in the collusive "here-and-now" relationships and are available for examination, confrontation, and interpretation.

Interpretation gives meaning and brings understanding to the collusive relationship. It makes sense out of what seems chaotic, thereby enabling all parties to begin to contain their projections and reducing the likelihood that they will act out the projections of others. A prior condition for effective interpretation, however, is the therapist's capacity to contain the many projections he may receive, a matter which will be considered in the following discussion about the role of the therapist.

The Role of the Therapist

The therapist's role is multifaceted. I will address two fundamental, closely related aspects of it: synchrony and countertransference.

Synchrony. The relationship between the therapist and the patient is a central aspect of any therapy, whether individual or group. Winnicott's description of the synchronous relationship of mother and child provides a valuable analogue for the relationship of therapist and group members (Winnicott, 1969, 1971). In brief, synchrony means being present and intervening or *not* intervening in ways that are in tune with the intrapsychic, interpersonal, and group tasks of the members.

This is *not* to suggest that the relationship of the therapist to the group members is that of a parent to children. If the relationship is truly synchronous it will be as adult to adults, with each person having a particular role to perform as therapist or group member. However much the members may regress, and however much they may act toward the therapist as though he were a parent, the relationship remains adult to adults, synchronously adjusted to address the particular vicissitudes of a regression.

Like the mother with her child at play, therapists often quietly observe the group members at their "play." But therapists are not mere observers. Like the mother, they are emotionally and psychologically involved, listening with a free-floating attention to the members and to themselves, aware of the ebb and flow of the interactions among the members and of the nature and intensity of the affect among the members and within themselves. For a therapist *not* to be present in this manner is comparable to being a physically present but emotionally absent mother. Members of a group may try, as children will, a whole series of devices to cope with that absence, from denial to leaving the group. Whatever the response, the lack of presence becomes a central factor in the group and an obstacle to its development of group identity. Lack of presence also makes it impossible for therapists to respond in a synchronous manner to the members.

Conversely, being present in the manner I have described enables therapists to be aware that a member (or a number of members) is ready for an intervention and what the nature of that intervention should be. Early in a group's life, for instance, being in synchrony means observing and listening to the members say "hello" to each other and accepting the idealizations of each other, the group, and the therapist, however unrealistic. Few interventions are needed, and any that are necessary will be made to support and clarify the task of saying "hello." Such synchronous interventions enable the members to bond and the group to develop. By contrast, to interpret the idealizations or to investigate, other than in a most cursory manner, personal revelations is to be out of tune with the group "play." Such interventions destroy an adaptive illusion and ask for personal exposure before sufficient safety has developed. The therapist has become intrusively present and the members will develop behaviors to hide their real concerns. The group will develop a "false self" identity.

Like Winnicott's description of the synchronous mother, the therapist must also be aware of when the members wish to begin other forms of play. The opening moments of a group can be so pleasant that when members begin to give up their idealistic illusions the therapist may not be ready. If being viewed as unrealistically wonderful is a little uncomfortable, being viewed as unrealistically incompetent may not be much of a substitute; hence, therapists may lose their synchrony and intervene in ways that may support unity rather than diversity and criticism.

The same process is involved when therapists decide whether to address individual, interpersonal, or groupwide issues. Although those aspects of group life are closely related, as demonstrated by Ezriel (1950) and others (e.g., Horwitz, 1977), they are not identical. Nor are they always of equal weight in the group. Hence, an orientation that suggests that only interpersonal, or groupwide, or individual interventions are valid risks limiting the therapist's capacity to be in tune with the members (Horwitz, 1977). A group pair in a collusive relationship, for instance, are more likely to benefit from interventions that address that collusion than from either individual or groupwide interventions alone.

As with interpretations, an important contributor to maintaining a synchronous relationship with group members is the therapist's capacity to contain the individual and collective projections of the group members, which are usually experienced in the transference–countertransference relationship.

Countertransference. In classical theory, countertransference was viewed as a neurotic response endogenous to the therapist, for which the patient is simply a trigger. Object relations theorists, especially those positioned toward the interpersonal (relational) in contrast to the drive end of the continuum, view countertransference and transference as interactive phenomena. From this perspective, the transference of the patient is generated by the interaction with the therapist and *not* by the patient alone. Likewise, the countertransference of the therapist is generated by the relationship with the patient and *not* by the therapist alone (Ogden, 1982, p. 81; Giovacchini, 1986, pp. 243–283).

This interaction between transference and countertransference arises from the operation of projective identification, whose role among group members was discussed earlier. Similarly, a patient will not only project particular inner objects onto the therapist, but the therapist also will play the role, or feel an urge to do so, or have fantasies about it. The projected object may be the object-image or the subject-image, along with the associated affects and defenses.

Thus, using our earlier illustration, the patient may *not* only perceive the therapist as sadistic (object-image) or masochistic (subject-image), but the therapist may become or feel drawn to become sadistic or masochistic toward the patient (Grotstein, 1981; Ogden, 1982).

The power of this communication is most apparent when working with very primitive patients. Bion (1961) described the therapist's experience of this phenomenon as living someone else's fantasy (p. 149). However, work with couples by Dicks (1967), Zinner (1976), and others has indicated that while projective identification may be most easily detected with severely regressed patients, it operates in most, if not all, intimate relationships, including those that are high functioning. The primary difference is that with lower functioning patients this form of communication is more immediate, more powerful, and all-pervasive than with higher functioning patients. With higher functioning patients there is much greater containment of inner objects and the related affects, so that projections are slower to develop.

Viewing countertransference from this perspective provides therapists with additional information by which to understand the group members and guide their interventions. As therapists examine and come to an understanding of their countertransferences, they also gain an understanding of their group members and can adjust their interventions to be synchronic with the members' needs. Additionally, by tolerating and examining inner responses, rather than acting on them, and turning them into interventions (e.g., reflections, clarifications, interpretations) that are in tune with the members' needs, the therapist contains the projections and modifies them, that is, detoxifies them. Those modified projections can then be reintrojected by the members.

Conversely, if the projections are not contained but are lived out through the therapist's behavior, a collusion can readily develop between the therapist and a group member or a number of group members that can seriously hinder the therapy. Similarly, projections initiated by the therapist can generate collusions with members of a group. Fortunately, examination of the countertransference by the therapist can also provide a means of breaking those collusions. The following example illustrates this phenomenon.

An experienced and talented therapist was meeting with a consultant about one of her groups. She was feeling particularly uneasy about the group. The group had no openings: All the members attended regularly and participated. Yet the group seemed stuck. She was particularly troubled by one woman, Mary. Mary was a woman of limited capacity who had been in the group for many years.

Mary talked a lot about the futility of her life and felt at the mercy of circumstances. She talked about wanting men in her life but considered it very unlikely, especially given her age and excess weight. She also felt that the group could *not* help her. Furthermore, she believed that people expected too much of her.

Group members tried to cheer her up. It did not work. They acknowledged that Mary had been in the group a long time and had made significant gains. Nothing changed. Following their lack of success the members became strikingly inactive for several weeks. The therapist tried to provoke the members into action by interpreting their behavior as unexpressed anger. Still nothing changed. She also began working very hard, making more interventions than she normally did. She began to despair about her group.

When the consultant asked the therapist what it would mean for her if the group could *not* help Mary, she was stunned. "I couldn't bear that," she said. "I already feel pretty helpless and hopeless about this group and about Mary in particular." The consultant suggested that that was probably what Mary and the group were dealing with: despair and hopelessness about the future, possibly related to some real limitations that Mary had to face.

The therapist relaxed, and then remembered that she had also been feeling some despair in her own life because her father was dying. Later, in the group, rather than struggle with Mary when she began complaining, the therapist simply asked what it was like to feel that there was no hope, and that she (the therapist) seemed to be of little help. Mary sobbed and talked about how hopeless and overwhelmed she felt and had felt since a child as she struggled to take care of her alcoholic parents.

Through the therapist's mutative intervention, the despair had been contained, the therapist was no longer the overwhelming "parent," Mary felt free to address her grief, and the therapist–Mary–group collusion was broken. The therapist was once again in tune with Mary and, in Winnicott's terms, a holding environment had been reestablished that enabled Mary and others to examine and begin to reorganize their inner worlds and their relationships with each other (Winnicott, 1969).

Viewing transference and countertransference as interactive phenomena also affects therapists' analyses (e.g., clarifications, confrontations, and interpretations) of individual and group events. The relationships between the inner and outer worlds and among the members, particularly those between the members and the therapist, are analyzed, rather than the inner conflicts and other intrapsychic phenomena in isolation from others. In our illustration the therapist's intervention addressed Mary's behavior in relation to herself (therapist). She may also have made the connection with Mary's mother, if Mary had not done so.

Mary's dilemma also illustrates Fairbairn's understanding of the repetition compulsion (Fairbairn, 1952b). Mary was repeating an old, self-limiting pattern established with her mother, in part because behaving in that manner helped to maintain the relationship: better to have a burdensome relationship with a "mother" than not to have any. That is, the purpose of the repetition is to maintain the original relationship.

Group Composition and Patient Selection

The literature is more clear about which patients should *not* be included in a therapy group than those who should (Rutan and Stone, 1983, pp. 77–87). Basically, patients who lack the capacity to form viable relationships are considered poor candidates for a group. This includes patients whose lack of impulse control is such that they may be dangerous to others, patients who are chronically psychotic, or those who are brain-damaged. Rutan and Stone (1983) used four exclusionary categories: (1) Patients in crisis due to external stress or in acute decompensation, (2) patients with severely limited impulse control, (3) patients whose character structure severely limits their capacity to relate to others, and (4) patients who are unable or unwilling to abide by the contract.

Categories 1 and 4 are the most reliable and most easily determined exclusionary categories. Category 1, however, does not apply to people who are already members of a group. The emergence of such a crisis in a group member of long-standing may necessitate the addition of individual therapy and/or medication to help address the crisis, but only rarely results in the member having to leave. Categories 2 and 3 are true for most outpatient groups, yet such patients often do quite well in homogeneous groups or in groups in a highly structured environment, such as a hospital (Comstock and McDermott, 1975; Rice and Rutan, 1987, pp. 87–89; Van der Kolk, 1987).

Thus, deciding on group composition and patient selection is not a clearly defined process. But several general statements can be made. Given the object-related nature of the problems that most patients bring to us, I make the assumption that most patients can benefit from group psychotherapy (Rutan and Stone, 1983; Rice and Rutan, 1987). Hence the crucial question is *not* who can benefit from group therapy, but, rather, who can benefit from what group and under what conditions? In a word, how good a fit is a particular patient with a particular group? For instance, psychotic patients, whose inner world is created of an array of part-objects, do not do well in a group of neurotic patients who have achieved object constancy, and vice versa. Each will benefit from a group with peers whose object-relatedness is more similar to their own (Day and Semrad, 1972, pp. 78–91).

The closeness of fit between the member and his peers also depends on the age of the group. A greater degree of homogeneity with regard to level of inner object relations organization is more desirable during the early phases of a group's life than it is later. The relative homogeneity enables the members to structure the group with greater consistency and success in the early phases. The fragility of the group structure at this point does not provide an adequate holding environment for a wide variance in the members' rates of entry into therapy. Patients with less well differentiated inner objects will need to spend a much longer period of time in the early developmental phases of the group than those who have attained object constancy. Patients entering at a pace significantly different from the rest of the members will most likely drop out of the group, further hindering the process of building a safe environment. However, when the group has been well established and an adequate holding environment established, differences among members can be more readily tolerated and wider ranges of object relations organization and different rates of entry into the therapy process are less likely to lead to dropouts.

SUMMARY AND FUTURE DIRECTIONS

Object relations theory, whose roots are seen in the work of Freud, is viewed by some theorists as a new paradigm arising to challenge classical psychoanalysis and by others as a set of perspectives that can be included in the classical model. Whatever the ultimate relationship of object relations theory to classical theory, it has led to a variety of concepts about human relationships and the representations of those relationships within an individual's psyche that are valuable tools for understanding and treating people in groups.

In this chapter, group structure and development were examined in the light of influential theories of infant development and the early formation of object relations. The roles of such concepts as projection, introjection, projective identification, and regression in understanding and in facilitating the therapeutic process in a group were discussed.

Those concepts and others were used to address the role of the therapist and the relationship between him and the members. Particular note was made of the object relations emphasis on the interpersonal nature of transference and countertransference and how an understanding of their interpersonal nature informs and affects the therapist's interventions and sheds light on the behavior of the members.

As the concepts and ideas of object relations theories continue to be developed, undoubtedly they will add further to our understanding of how people relate in groups and how group therapy, in turn, can be of help to people. However, I think much may be gained by encouraging a greater flow of concepts and ideas in the opposite direction, namely, from the world of the group to that of the individual. Most psychoanalytic understanding of people has developed in one-to-one relationships with adult patients and secondarily through the observation of children, again often in one-to-one relationships. Yet people spend most of their lives living and working as individuals in groups. Thus, I think group therapists, theoreticians, and researchers may contribute significantly to the understanding of individuals, and, in particular, to the object relations understanding of individuals through creative observation and research of adults and children being treated or living in groups. As every group therapist readily acknowledges, patients seen in groups reveal many insights and perspectives about themselves not as readily seen in individual therapy.

REFERENCES

Alonso, A., & Rutan, J. S. (1984), The impact of object relations theory on psychodynamic group therapy. *Amer. J. Psychiat.*, 141:1376–1380.

Bion, W. (1961), *Experiences in Groups and Other Papers*. London: Tavistock Publications.

Bowlby, J. (1969), *Attachment and Loss: Vol. 1. Loss*. New York: Basic Books.

——— (1980), *Attachment and Loss: Vol. 3. Loss: Sadness and Depression*. New York: Basic Books.

Comstock, B. S., & McDermott, M. (1975), Group therapy for patients who attempt suicide. *Internat. J. Group Psychother.*, 25:44–49.

Day, M., & Semrad, E. (1972), Group therapy with neurotics and psychotics. In: *Group Treatment of Mental Illness*, ed. H. I. Kaplan & B. Stock. New York: Jason Aronson, pp. 78–91.

de Mare, P. (1972), *Perspectives in Group Psychotherapy: A Theoretical Background*. New York: Science House.

Dicks, H. V. (1967), *Marital Tensions*. New York: Basic Books.

Ezriel, H. (1950), A psychoanalytic approach to group treatment. *Brit. J. Med. Psychol.*, 23:59–74.

Fairbairn, W. R. D. (1952a), *An Object Relations Theory of Personality*. New York: Basic Books.
——— (1952b), The repression and the return of bad objects (with special reference to the "war neurosis"). In: *Essential Papers on Object Relations*, ed. P. Buckley. New York: New York University Press, 1986, pp. 71–101.
——— (1954), Observations of the nature of hysterical states. *Brit. J. Med. Psychol.*, 27(3):105–125.
Foulkes, S. H. (1977), *Therapeutic Group Analysis*. New York: International Universities Press.
Freud, S. (1905), Three essays on the theory of sexuality: I. The sexual aberrations. In: *Essential Papers on Object Relations*, ed. P. Buckley. New York: New York University Press, 1986, pp. 5–39.
Giovacchini, P. L. (1986), *Developmental Disorders: The Transitional Space in Mental Breakdown and Creative Integration*. Northvale, NJ: Jason Aronson.
Greenberg, J. R., & Mitchell, S. A. (1983), *Object Relations in Psychoanalytic Theory*. Cambridge, MA: Harvard University Press.
Grotstein, J. S. (1981), *Splitting and Projective Identification*. New York: Jason Aronson.
Hedges, L. E. (1983), *Listening Perspectives in Psychotherapy*. New York: Jason Aronson.
Horwitz, L. (1977), A group centered approach to group psychotherapy. *Internat. J. Group Psychother.*, 27(4):423–440.
——— (1983), Projective identification in dyads and groups. *Internat. J. Group Psychother.*, 33(3):259–279.
Kernberg, O. (1976), *Object Relations Theory and Clinical Psychoanalysis*. New York: Jason Aronson.
——— (1980), *Internal World and External Reality*. New York: Jason Aronson.
Klein, M. (1935), A contribution to the psychogenesis of manic-depressive states. *Internat. J. Psycho-Anal.*, 16:145–174.
——— (1964), *Contributions to Psychoanalysis, 1921–1945*. New York: McGraw-Hill.
Mahler, M. S. (1972), On the first three subphases of the individuation process. In: *The Selected Papers of Margaret S. Mahler: Vol. 2. Separation–Individuation*. New York: Jason Aronson, 1979, pp. 119–130.
——— (1979), *The Selected Papers of Margaret S. Mahler: Vol. 2. Separation–Individuation*. New York: Jason Aronson.
Ogden, T. H. (1982), *Projective Identification and Psychotherapeutic Technique*. New York: Jason Aronson.
Redl, F. (1942), Group emotion and leadership. *Psychiat.*, 5:573–596.
Rice, C. A., & Rutan, J. S. (1987), *Inpatient Group Psychotherapy: A Psychodynamic Perspective*. New York: Macmillan.
Rutan, J. S., & Stone, W. N. (1983), *Psychodynamic Group Psychotherapy*. New York: Macmillan.
Scheidlinger, S. (1968), The concept of regression in group psychotherapy. *Internat. J. Group Psychother.*, 18:3–20.
Van der Kolk, B. (1987), *Psychological Trauma*. New York: American Psychiatric Press.
Winnicott, D. W. (1969), The theory of the parent-infant relationship. *Internat. J. Psycho-Anal.*, 50:711–717.
——— (1971), *Playing and Reality*. New York: Basic Books.
——— (1975), *Through Paediatrics to Psycho-Analysis: The Collected Papers of D. W. Winnicott*. New York: Basic Books.

—— (1988), *Human Nature*. New York: Schocken Books.

Yalom, I. (1975), *Group Psychotherapy*. New York: Basic Books.

Zinner, J. (1976), The implication of projective identification for marital interaction. In: *Contemporary Marriage*, ed. H. Grunebaum & J. Christ. Boston: Little, Brown.

3

Contributions from Self Psychology Theory

HOWARD A. BACAL, M.D.

Heinz Kohut definitively introduced psychoanalytic self psychology fifteen years ago (Kohut, 1977). Since then, an extensive literature has evolved which has had a significant influence on clinical practice. The effect has been most apparent in the area of individual work, but self psychological concepts are also being extensively employed by therapists treating families, couples, and groups.

While one can see evidence in Freud's writings that he recognized the importance of what we would now call the self and its selfobject relationships (Bacal, 1987, p. 1), he elaborated a one-body theory in which he focused on the operations of a mental apparatus that struggled with the vicissitudes of the child's instinctual life. Kohut was for many years a distinguished classical analyst, but he became increasingly concerned that traditional analytic theory and its application had wandered too far from the experience of his patients and the nature of the problems for which they sought help. While self psychology initially arose from Kohut's intent to offer a new explanation for the psychopathology of narcissistic personality disorders and to rationalize their effective treatment (Kohut, 1971, 1977; Kohut and Wolf, 1978), it has evolved into a general psychoanalytic theory that is applicable to the full range of psychological disorders.

Kohut did not see self psychology as based upon identifiable antecedents. He conceded, however, that one might find the beginnings of comparable ideas in the work of Heinz Hartmann (1939, 1950), who identified the "self" as the experiential aspect of the agencies of the mind and asserted that "primary autonomous ego-functions" (such as perception, motility, memory, language, intention, object comprehension, affect regulation, capacity for delay, cognition, reality testing, object constancy, creativity, capacity for internalization, etc.) proceeded not only on the basis of conflict between instinct and reality, but depended upon the presence of an average expectable environment. In effect, ego psychology in North America marked a shift of theoretical interest from intrapsychic conflict and the defensive functions of the ego to an examination of the ego's adaptive functions to this average expectable environment. Hartmann's (1939, 1950) view was that if this environment failed, these innate biological functions became enmeshed in conflict. Hartmann did not, however, investigate this average expectable environment, an investigation that effectively would have entailed a study of "object relations," since the notion of such an environment presupposes a relational milieu in which the organism can adapt and develop. Interest in object relations theory moved forward slowly and awkwardly in North America, developed mainly in the work of Sullivan, Mahler, and Kernberg. Quite a different scenario unfolded in Britain, however, where the contributions of Suttie, Klein, Balint, Fairbairn, Guntrip, Winnicott, and Bowlby constituted a definitive articulation of an object relational perspective. Although some of the contributors to this body of theory (notably the Kleinians—and Kernberg in America) have continued to assert that it is the pathology of drive derivatives that give people trouble in their relationships, most of them draw attention to the crucial role of other, noninstinctual problematic linkages between the individual and his object.

One simply cannot apply unmodified classical drive theory in the clinical situation and expect that the patient will feel understood. It is essential that the therapist recognize, tacitly or explicitly, the central importance of relationships. Put in another way, there has always been a considerable discrepancy between what effective classical theorists preach and what they practice. Theories of object relations have filled much of this gap—especially those elaborated by several of the British workers—as well as by Sullivan, Mahler, and Spitz in America. However, none of them except Guntrip explicitly recognized the *self* and its personal development as the legitimate *subject* of object relations and, with the exception of Bowlby, none of them attempted in a systematic or consistent way[1] to conceptualize an essential or fundamental type of object relationship that is operative throughout life.

There are four major, related characteristics that distinguish self psychology from classical psychoanalytic theory: the removal of instinctual motivation as a significant factor in development and pathogenesis; the shift from a one-body to a multibody psychology; the

---

[1]For a discussion of why John Bowlby may be regarded as an exception, see Bacal and Newman, 1990.

specification of the *self* as "the center of the individual's psychological universe" (Kohut, 1977, p. 311) and of its needs for a certain kind of essential relationship with objects; and the transformation of the traditional perspective on narcissism. The first two characteristics are shared by certain object relations theorists; the latter two are unique to self psychology.

While the notion of object relation is apparently ignored in self psychology and the stated focus is on the development of the self, the *selfobject*—which is the pivotal concept of self psychology—implies a particular kind of relationship[2] as *the* determinant of self-experience and the vehicle for self-development. That is, what is largely missing but implicit in object relations theory is the notion of the "self" and the central importance of the sustaining relationship with the essential other—the *selfobject,* and what is obvious but ignored by self psychology theory is that it tacitly regards a particular "object relationship"—namely, the relationship between the self and its selfobjects—as central for self development. The centrality of object relationship in self psychology, which I have elaborated elsewhere (Bacal, 1985a, 1990a) is most tellingly demonstrated by Kohut's perspective on narcissism. In effect, Kohut's understanding of "narcissism" recognizes it as a disturbance in the relationships between the self and its most significant objects, that is, a disturbance of *selfobject relationships.* Classical theory instructs the therapist to regard narcissistic symptoms and behavior as a selfishness or self-centeredness that reflects a stubborn retention of an immature position, and that narcissism ultimately constitutes a defense against object-love. Kohut views the narcissistic disorder as the expression of a reaction of injury to the self consequent upon the rupture of self-sustaining relationships with essential others. He regards the experience of these links between the self and the selfobject to be crucial for psychological health and growth.

The development of a perspective on "narcissistic"[3] disorders that understood its manifestations in terms of the distorted yet psychologically legitimate need to elicit selfobject responsiveness in order to preserve or restore self cohesion and promote self development was therefore ultimately delayed not only because of the continued adherence to Freud's instinct theory, but because object relations theorists also continued to regard problems of "narcissism" from a moralistic

---

[2]The abbreviated term "selfobject relationship" is commonly used instead of the more cumbersome "self–selfobject relationship."

[3]From this perspective, narcissistic phenomena may be regarded as the problematic expression of the need for selfobject responsiveness.

perspective. It was acceptable for seriously regressed patients to express intense needs to be attended to without expecting that they should also exhibit concern for the object, but this was not legitimate for others—"not realistic" was the usual euphemism that cloaked this attitude—an attitude that, for many patients, precluded the establishment of a healing relationship.

The concepts of the selfobject and selfobject relationships provide a fresh basis not only for understanding disorders of the self arising from deficit—that is, psychological deficiency states—but also for the further understanding of conflict and the problematic relationships with which they are associated. In conceptualizing the selfobject and selfobject relationships, Kohut provided a theoretical underpinning for clinical work that comes closer to what most patients actually experience and how most therapists actually work.

THE SELFOBJECT, THE SELF, AND THE SELFOBJECT RELATIONSHIP

An object is a selfobject when it is experienced intrapsychically as providing functions in a relationship that evoke, maintain, or positively affect the sense of self.[4] A comprehensive list of such functions has not been compiled, but the following are generally regarded as comprising the more important ones: attunement to affective states; validation of subjective experience—including temporary identification with the "rightness" of the child's or patient's perceptions; affect containment, tension regulation, and soothing; sustaining and organizing or restoring a weakened sense of self disrupted by selfobject failure; and recognition of uniqueness and creative potential.

While the self of psychoanalytic self psychology has been defined in one-person terms, for example, as "a unit, cohesive in space and enduring in time, which is a center of initiative and a recipient of impressions" (Kohut, 1977, p. 99), it is often conceptualized in terms of its relationships with its selfobjects. Here are just a few such definitions of the self amongst the many that have been offered by eminent self psychologists: "A self can be said to be established at that point

---

[4]Wolf's definitions are similar to mine: "Those functions of the relationship with the caretakers that evoke and maintain in the infant the experience of selfhood are defined as selfobject functions" (Wolf, 1984/85, p. 60); "Strictly speaking . . . selfobjects are neither self nor object; they are the subjective aspect of a function performed by a relationship" (Wolf, 1985, p. 271).

in analysis when the selfobjects (and their functions) have been . . . transformed into psychological structures . . ." (Kohut, 1977, p. 139). Goldberg (1982) conceptualizes the self of self psychology [as] "composed of permanent units of relationships" (p. 14) [and as] "the functionally or operationally separate focus of various relations . . ." (p. 18). Wolf (1984/85) has defined the self as a psychological structure, an enduring configuration associated with the experience of selfhood, consisting of a cluster of potentialities evoked and maintained by selfobject relations (p. 61). Insofar as the self is a "'psychological structure" and has acquired "self" maintenance capacities, these can be regarded as comprising representations, or amalgams, of a healthy self–selfobject linkage.

A selfobject relationship is one in which a relatively stable sense of the object's availability as a selfobject prevails. From this perspective, then, the *mirroring, idealizing,* and *alter ego* selfobject relationships that have come to be recognized as particularly important for the self's healthy development are aspects of the child's experience of the selfobject availability of significant caretakers. The mirroring experience, which includes much of which I have already described as constituting important selfobject functions, denotes in particular a selfobject relationship in which recognition is felt to be provided by a significant other for what one has to offer, such as one's unique capacities, talents, abilities, and personal attractiveness. An idealizing selfobject relationship denotes the experience of feeling linked to the admired other—the self, in effect, walks proudly in the shadow of his admired object.

The archaic variants of each of these have been called *merger* relationships. In fact, all selfobject relationships have been regarded as reflecting an experience between the self and the object that is to some extent undifferentiated. Thus, many self psychologists would wish to add to my definition of the selfobject that it is specially distinguishable from other objects because of its being experienced as part of the self. While the latter is certainly not uncommon, recent infant research (see especially Stern, 1985, p. 10) has questioned the existence of any confusion by the normal infant between himself and others at any phase of development. Thus, the assumption that merger is a normal archaic selfobject experience is questionable. Rather, I would suggest that the experience of the provision of selfobject function by a relatively differentiated other is characteristic of a normal, healthy self.

This view is perhaps most convincingly supported by our recognition as clinicians that a person whose sense of self is relatively strong and well demarcated will not experience severe symptoms (e.g., anxiety, depersonalization, fragmentation) in the face of separation, although he may feel sadness and a painful sense of aloneness because of the loss of a relatively differentiated important other. In the situation in which the self is prone to disintegration anxiety and fragmentation in the absence of the selfobject, we may assume the existence of a particularly vulnerable, that is, unhealthy, self that may need to experience another as part of itself in order to stay intact in the same sense that the glue that is necessary to keep the parts of a broken vase together becomes part of the vase itself.

This way of conceptualizing the selfobject experience also accords with recent discoveries about the normal infant's early capacities for self–object discrimination. Nevertheless, Kohut and Wolf's (1978, p. 414) view that "the expected control over [selfobjects] is . . . closer to the concept of the control which a grown-up expects to have over his own body and mind than to the concept of the control which he experiences over others" has a significant validity. There is a sense of ownership about the selfobject. However, this is best understood as a kind of taking it for granted—that is, behavior suggestive of a sense of relatively unquestioned, comfortable entitlement to the provision of the functions of another rather than a sense of control over an undifferentiated bit of the self. Balint described a similar archaic relationship, which he called "primary love," or "primary object-love,"—a *natural*, that is, normally occurring, early harmonious experience of the infant with the mother in which the infant feels there is no difference between his interests and hers[5] (Balint, 1937, p. 84; Bacal, 1987, p. 90; Bacal and Newman, 1990). That is, the experience of a responsive archaic selfobject environment is the initial, normal experience of the infant, and its firm internalization provides the basis for a confident expectation of appropriate selfobject responsiveness in later life. I am, in effect, asserting that the selfobject is experienced as "the self's object" and that the sense of its possession and entitlement to its functions are often quite unconscious. The ability to seek out appropriate selfobjects likely depends, to a hitherto unrecognized degree, upon the intactness of a basic sense of entitlement to the selfobject's responsiveness.

---

[5]Although Balint calls this relationship "primary love," he does not conceive of it as libidinal but rather as a primitive object-relatedness whose essence is a sense of harmony between the infant and the mother. Balint's concept is analogous to Kohut's archaic mirroring or idealizing selfobject relationships (Bacal, 1981, p. 34) and, in the light of current research on infants, none of them need be conceptualized as a "merger" state.

From the perspective of self psychology, one never "outgrows" one's needs for selfobject responsiveness. Normally, in an appropriately responsive selfobject environment, these needs decrease in intensity and urgency, along with the lessening of the requirement that the selfobjects of childhood and their current transference representatives fulfill them.

In the alter-ego selfobject relationship, which is sometimes called "twinship" or "partnering," the sense of sameness with the object, a relationship that is of particular significance during latency, constitutes the basis of the self-sustaining, self-enhancing or self-restoring functions. We now appreciate that there are other important selfobject configurations. Wolf (1980, pp. 125–126) has indicated that the boundaries of the self may be strengthened by experiences of a relationship with the selfobject as both an ally and as an antagonist against which one may mobilize self-assertion and healthy aggression. Lachmann (1986) has described a similar, "adversarial," selfobject: "[A]dversarial experiences [can] serve as selfobject functions, [and] such functions can be placed on a continuum of increasing complexity from archaic needs for self-consolidation to self-demarcation and self-enhancement" (p. 350). While recurring selfobject failure is inevitable in human relationships—and, if not traumatic, can be stimulating to self growth—basic to the experience of a selfobject relationship is affective attunement on the part of the object-world and the translation of this attunement into responsiveness that is optimal for the development of the self of that particular individual (Bacal, 1985b, p. 224; Terman, 1988).This is as valid for the therapeutic process as it is for the healthy development of the child. This perspective becomes apparent in the self psychological view of the drives, defenses, anxiety, conflict, and the oedipal situation.

SELF PSYCHOLOGY, THE DRIVES, AND THE OEDIPAL SITUATION

As I have indicated, most object relations theorists had already moved beyond Freud to consider factors other than sex and aggression as significant in development and pathogenesis (see Bacal, 1987; Bacal and Newman, 1990). Self psychologists have gone further in the same direction. They repudiate the notion of an intrinsic destructiveness or perversity that must be renounced, tamed, or sublimated, and regard the emergence of such behaviors as reflecting instability or fragmentation of self experience. The disturbance of self experience is ultimately due to significant disruption of the essential object relationship, that is, the selfobject relationship. To be able to indicate one's sexual needs, convey one's views and wishes assertively, or to become angry or even aggressive in the face of significant frustration, interference, or rejection are expressions of an intact, robust self. That is, experience and expression of healthy instincts are instrumental in the vigorous pursuit of the aims and goals of the self.

Narcissistic Rage

The injured, enfeebled, or fragmenting self is unable to mobilize potentially effective assertiveness or aggressiveness. When the self in childhood has been weakened by serious selfobject failure or has never achieved stable cohesiveness because it has hardly experienced the world as providing selfobject functioning, it will be particularly susceptible to the stresses that are specific to its vulnerabilities. It will, in effect, experience certain kinds of faulty responsiveness as a retraumatization and will be unable to answer with constructive assertiveness or anger. It is in this state that the self reacts with distorted anger—"narcissistic rage" (Kohut, 1972, pp. 360–400). While the expression of "acute" narcissistic rage can sometimes assist the reintegration of the self (Kohut, 1977, personal communication), "chronic" narcissistic rage, which is usually associated with an underlying, ongoing sense of injury, does not serve to restore the self's cohesiveness and strength. The goal now is not primarily to remove a frustration, but to stave off further disintegration and to redress the hurt in some way, which may entail retaliation against and even destruction of the perpetrator of the injury. The emergence of this isolated "drive" may constitute a compelling, even consuming motivation. It is not, however, an expression of the fundamental nature of the personality, a representation in the mind of an excessive amount of a basic instinctual force that must be modulated in the light of reality testing. It is, rather, an abnormal affect state that is the result of a pathogenic experience, an isolated drivenness that takes over when the self is seriously injured and feels a sense of helpless disconnection from its selfobjects. Self psychologists refer to it as a "breakdown product"—a product of the fragmentation of the self.

While Kohut had indicated that narcissistic rage is associated with a sense of shame (Kohut, 1977, p. 77), Morrison (1989) underscores shame as the central affect associated with "narcissistic rage." He regards shame, along with its more extreme counterpart, humiliation, as the quintessential reaction to the sense of helplessness in the face of the experience of selfobject failure. However, since these affects are so intolerable, they are quickly erased from consciousness and, at the same time, trigger the expression of narcissistic rage at the offending object. A self, however, that has become strengthened by selfobject relationships is less prone to states of "narcissistic rage."

Comparably, to fully welcome erotic desire and to enjoy sexual experience are expressions of a normal, vital self, and the distortions of sexuality reflect disorder in the self. From the perspective of self psychology, abnormal sexuality—whether inhibition, perversion, or chronic absence of satisfaction—is not regarded as primarily a disturbance in drive regulation or its sublimation, nor an indication of the retention of unmodified primitive sexual component-instincts that have not become subordinated to genital primacy. It is, rather, taken as symptomatic of a self whose selfobject needs, including those related to its developing sexuality, have not been responded to optimally in childhood and adolescence. An examination of the vicissitudes of the oedipal situation will illustrate this perspective.

The Oedipal Situation

Long before the advent of self psychology, object relations theorists had questioned the classical position of regarding the oedipal situation as central to development and pathogenesis. Rather, they recognized "preoedipal" issues as the psychological bedrock that gave shape to oedipal conflicts and significantly determined the nature and completeness of their resolution, and Kleinian theorists even placed pre-oedipal issues[6] at the center of development and psychopathology. Self psychologists do not put as much weight as other theorists on the distinction between "oedipal" and "preoedipal," as they do not regard the Oedipus as necessarily occupying a crucial psychological position in development or in the determination of psychopathology. While they recognize the validity of oedipal conflicts, they do not regard their presence as necessarily indicative of psychopathology. In effect, they regard the Oedipus as an object relationship that may have normal or pathological selfobject and instinctual-object dimensions.

Kohut embodied these two dimensions of object relationships in his distinction between an *oedipal stage* and an *oedipal complex*. The former—the oedipal stage—develops as a result of the interaction between the child's natural strivings in triangular situations and the

---

[6]Kleinian theory asserts that the Oedipus situation begins within the first few months of life.

parents' more-or-less optimal responsiveness to them; the latter—the oedipal complex—results from the interaction between these strivings and the parents' inadequate or inappropriate responses to them. If the parents react to the expression of their child's oedipal feelings as normal, playful wishes for sensual and affectionate closeness and for the opportunity to test his strength against that of the homogenital parent, the child will feel understood and will traverse the hurdles of the oedipal stage with a sense of satisfaction and pride, strengthened in his or her development. As Tolpin puts it, the expression of the child's naive sexuality, affectionateness, and assertiveness go together from the start and his experience of hurt, anger, and jealousy are to some extent inevitable in consequence of his sense of rejection of his claims for exclusive love and commitment. However, if disappointment and injury are adequately counteracted by appropriate soothing and ongoing confirmation of the child, the degree of expectation of himself and of his selfobject world become modified, and his self is thus strengthened to meet further disappointments in life. In short, the development of a sense of secure masculinity and femininity,[7] and a healthy sexuality, depend upon secure development, that is, upon the quality of the selfobject relationships between the child and his caretakers (Tolpin, 1988).

If, however, the parents view the oedipal child as wanting actual sexual relations with or as offering serious competition to the parent, he is likely to become overstimulated, anxious,[8] conflicted, and confused.[9] If, then, he is "rejected"—or met by an "acceptance" with which he cannot cope—he will become variously overwhelmed by shame and guilt, and may experience both a sense of inadequacy as well as a fear of his own strength and that of the parent. Kohut calls this situation an oedipal complex to distinguish it from its natural counterpart. It is not a normal situation in which an intact self struggles, with selfobject assistance, with expectable, universal conflicts, but an abnormal relationship in which not only the seeds of the polymorphic neurotic disturbances of the oedipal phase are sown but in which the sense of self is always affected to some degree. That is, the oedipal situation of classical analysis, along with its associated anxieties and

---

[7]Kohut did not discuss the development of masculine and feminine self structuralization as a result of differential responsivity of selfobjects. For an important contribution to this subject, see Lang (1984).

[8]Self psychologists recognize "castration anxiety," but would regard its symptomatic manifestation as indicative of oedipal *self pathology*, not as an expectable accompaniment of the engagement of the oedipal situation.

[9]Confusion is not often enough recognized as a significant deleterious effect of faulty responsiveness to the child's nonpassionate strivings toward adults (see Ferenczi, 1933).

conflicts is, in effect, regarded by self psychology as the result of the derailment of a normal object relationship and, consequently, of the sense of self, in a phase its development. In practice, one does not see examples of oedipal disturbance "in pure culture." Rather, one sees a mixture of this and other self disturbances that derive from disruptions in the total constellation of selfobject relationships between the child and its parents. It is important, of course, to recognize the specific, idiosyncratic vulnerabilities of the child—and the child in the adult patient—as well as the particular characteristics of the oedipal object when considering the determinants of an oedipal complex or, for that matter, the development of any self pathology.

Conflict and Anxiety

The oedipal complex, as I have described it, provides a good example of the perspective of self psychology on conflict: Significant psychological conflict does not occur without some effect on the self. Moreover, the basic determinants of conflict and anxiety do not emanate from the clamor for instinctual satisfaction but are the result of disturbances in selfobject relationships. An intense wish for gratification of an incestuous instinctual desire associated with its specific anxieties and conflicts is already a sign of self pathology and its underlying determinants—disturbed selfobject relations. While traditional analysis consistently views conflict in terms of the problems attending the expression of the forbidden drive, self psychology considers that the individual's subjective experience must define the nature of conflict. In the oedipal complex, the conflict entails the wish for sexual possession of the heterogenital parent associated with castration anxiety and/or loss of the love of the homogenital parent. But however prevalent conflict over instinctual wishes, along with anxiety about "castration" and loss of love may have been for the patients examined by Freud and his early followers, they do not constitute the major determinants of the problems for which patients consult us today. It is self-esteem vulnerability and the threat to the sense of self cohesion ("disintegration anxiety") that underlie their difficulties and that predispose to the development of significant conflict. This weakness and the accompanying anxiety within the self may range from simple apprehension to outright feelings of dissociation or fragmentation. They are not produced by instinctual conflict but are precipitated by a conflict over the assertion of developmental need or over the expression of disavowed affects that are associated with the frustration of those needs. They thus arise as a result of perceived failure of selfobjects to meet these needs.

This conflict, which Stolorow, Brandchaft, and Atwood (1987, pp. 52, 90) have called the "fundamental psychic conflict," is occasioned by an opposition between the needs of the self and the perceived needs and attitudes of the caretakers. This produces internal conflict between the inclination to express the needs of the true self and false compliance with another person. That is, the conflict arises when the declaration of needs is felt to threaten the links that would ensure the provision of whatever selfobject responsiveness may be available. The conflict essentially entails the risk of loss of or damage to the selfobject on the one hand or the renunciation of the sense of one's real self on the other. The pathological solutions to this conflict, such as tormenting ambivalence, defiance, and rebellion; abandonment of selfobject needs leading to self distortion and self abnegation; or depressive compliance with the emotional needs of one's caretakers (Stolorow, Brandchaft, and Atwood, 1987, p. 52), will arise whenever the child's caretakers are inflexibly responsive to the child's selfobject needs.

Guilt

A discussion of guilt is conspicuously sparse in self psychological writings. This is because self psychologists generally regard guilt as an affect that is specifically related to the expression of forbidden drives and therefore not relevant to the self psychological model. Rycroft's definition of guilt (1972, p. 59) as "the emotion which follows infringement of a moral injunction . . . [and] arises as a result of conflict between the superego and infantile sexual and aggressive wishes" would seem to support this explanation. Self psychologists believe, moreover, that what analysts often refer to as guilt is more accurately described as shame. Guilt clearly needs more examination by self psychologists. Thomson (personal communication, 1988) has proffered the opinion that guilt is a very common experience of the self and is the product of conflict between the needs of the self and the perceived values and attitudes of the internalized parents. The parents' values may or may not be inimical to the strivings of the "true self" (Winnicott, 1960). It is only in the latter situation—that is, when the parents' values *are* inimical to the needs of the true self—that guilt could be considered pathological. Markson (personal communication, 1988) regards guilt as often associated with the feeling that the subject's attempts to have its selfobject needs met are injurious to the selfobject. From this perspective, guilt is the outcome of conflict between the pursuit of selfobject needs and the sense of the suffering of the selfobject.

THE DEVELOPMENT OF MATURITY

The assertion by self psychologists of the normality of the continuing need to experience objects as selfobjects, from which the self "takes," would appear to preclude the development of a capacity for "giving" and for "concern for the other," which object relations theorists tend to regard as the hallmarks of maturity. This view of maturity reflects the traditional psychoanalytic conception of the "whole" or "true" object which is, in effect, not an object from which one expects something, but an object that one relates to with an attitude of concern—that is, with a readiness to *provide* selfobject functions. Self psychology has consistently viewed maturity as marked not by the diminution of a psychological investment in one's self nor by the replacement of a "narcissistically cathected" object by either an object of "love" or of concern, but by the maturation of selfobject relationships. As I have indicated, this does not entail renunciation of selfobject needs; one experiences them as less intense and less urgent, and their nature also undergoes transformation with development. In adolescence, for example, the peer group provides selfobject functions for the maintenance of self-esteem which, when internalized, strengthens ideals and values and helps to establish future choices of vocation and mate (Wolf, 1980, pp. 127–128). In adulthood, many important personal selfobjects remain but, insofar as the self has developed the capacity to diffuse its needs for appropriate selfobject relationships, some older personal selfobject ties are substituted by their symbolic equivalents in various meaningful affiliations (Wolf, 1980, pp. 127–130; Kohut, 1984, p. 77). Self psychology, in effect, defines maturity in terms of the self's "more mature" *usage* of others, although Ornstein (1981) recognizes that the increasing strength of the self enables it to become "a relatively independent center of initiative . . . [and then] . . . capable of recognizing the relatively independent center of initiative in the other—the 'true object' of the classical framework," and that a healthy self will fluctuate flexibly between these two modes of relating (p. 358).

The paucity of theoretical discussion by self psychologists of how these capacities develop, however, is all the more striking if one considers that self psychologists tacitly regard giving, in the form of providing selfobject function, to constitute perhaps the most mature function of all, as evinced, for example, by the ministrations of a good parent, or a good analyst. Possibly it arises from their wish to avoid the "maturity-morality" that tends to pervade traditional analytic theories (including object relations theory). But this need not present a problem for self psychological theory if one assumes, with Suttie (1935), an *inherent* capacity and a wish to give on the part of the infant. In addition, the experience of having been generously given to will naturally move one to treat others in a comparable way. In fact, this is implicit in Wolf's (1980) idea of a complexity of *virtual reciprocal selfobject relations* that characterizes the early interactions between the infant and the mother (pp. 119–123). One might then legitimately regard the infant, in his contribution to this interaction, as displaying phase-appropriate "maturity." I would thus suggest that the basic sense of entitlement to selfobject relationships that consolidates as a result of such interactions in which the responsiveness of a reliable archaic selfobject is taken for granted is also paradoxically the basis for the development of the capacity for concern. As the self becomes strengthened through appropriate selfobject responsiveness, it also becomes more solid about this sense of entitlement to selfobject needs. The consolidation of this development enables one's *inherent capacity for giving* to be mobilized without anxiety by the needs of others, to whom one may then naturally offer oneself as a selfobject. Maturity then becomes characterized by the development of a strong and joyful self that enables one to actively pursue one's own interests and by the ability to make comfortable and mutually enriching reciprocal selfobject relationships with others. The traditional criteria of emotional maturity—the capacity to love and to work and to enjoy sexual relationships—would therefore be regarded by self psychology not as the final outcome of healthy development but as two of the more significant capabilities of a strong and vital self.

DISORDERS OF THE SELF

It is, of course, inevitable that the child will experience frustrations, disruptions, and conflicts associated with selfobject relationships but, to borrow another term from Winnicott, if the latter are "good-enough," psychological disorder will not occur. If, however, the selfobject world is experienced as predominantly unreliable or unavailable, the child's self will become weakened or fragmented and will be vulnerable to the development of self pathology. From the perspective of self psychology, then, disorders of the self derive from the child's experience of faulty interactions between himself and his caretakers. Stolorow, Brandchaft, and Atwood (1987, p. 132) have refined this perspective and regard psychopathological symptoms as concrete symbols[10] of the experience of the serious disruptions that arise in specific intersubjective contexts; that is, symptoms are the concretization of the need to objectify disruptive experience that cannot be otherwise represented. While I believe that this view is valid, self psychology has yet to take into account the varying strength of the self in different individuals that is constitutionally determined. This variability contributes to differential vulnerability and resilience and may significantly determine different reactions to the efforts of caretakers, as well as of therapists (Fajardo, 1988).

Kohut's struggle to understand and treat more effectively the "narcissistic personality disorders" initially constituted the *via regia* to his psychology of the self. However, as I have indicated, self psychologists now regard the latter as applicable to the full range of psychopathology. Kohut and Wolf (1978) and Wolf (1983) view the etiology of the common varieties of psychological illness according to the nature and degree of the injury or impairment sustained by the self in its contact with objects that seriously fail to provide needed selfobject functions. Here, I will précis Wolf's recent (1983, 1984/85) summaries of those most commonly encountered in clinical practice, and I would recommend Kohut and Wolf's 1978 article for a more thorough discussion. In *schizophrenia*, the effects of seriously deficient early mirroring in combination with constitutional factors produce an illness in which self fragmentation is pervasive. Other organic factors in association with the specific and pervasive absence of joyful selfobject responsiveness predispose to *empty depression*. In *mania* or *guilt depression*, psychologically predisposing factors comprise an absence of adequate self-soothing or self-supportive structures that result from the lack of association with steady and calm idealized selfobjects.

Wolf does not specify the underlying determinants of the narcissistic and borderline personality disorders, but self psychological theory generally regards these as comprising a complexity of selfobject failure entailing varying degrees of lack of empathic attunement and personal validation on the part of caretakers in concert with the susceptibility of constitutionally vulnerable children. According to Wolf, the damage to the self in *borderline disorders* may be of comparable severity to that of psychotic disturbances but is covered over by complex defenses. The defenses that the borderline self uses to protect its vulnerable self structure against further damage that may attend the stresses of ordinary social intercourse are mainly schizoid and

---

[10]Their term is "concretization," which they define as "the encapsulation of organizations of experience by concrete, sensorimotor symbols" (Stolorow, Brandchaft, and Atwood, 1987, p. 132).

paranoid in nature. Schizoid defenses serve to prevent deep involvement, and paranoid defenses build a protective aura of suspicion and hostility around the self to keep potentially injurious objects at a safe distance. In the *narcissistic behavior disorders*, the damage to the self is less severe. These people characteristically attempt to shore up their fragile self-esteem by engaging in addictive, perverse, or delinquent behavior. Self-damage in the *narcissistic personality disorders* is regarded as even less severe,[11] and seems particularly to predispose the sufferer to problems in self-esteem regulation. Subjective disturbances characteristically associated with this condition include hypersensitivity to slights and perceived failures, inability to forgive, difficulties in appropriate self assertion, lack of zest, and unsatisfying personal relationships. Common symptoms, among many others, also include irritability, hypochondria, depression, insomnia, difficulties in concentration, loneliness, general unhappiness, a lack of a sense of accomplishment, and perhaps even a sense of meaninglessness or absence of direction in life.

Self psychologists take the view, as I have already indicated, that beneath the polymorphic disturbances that comprise the *psychoneuroses*—such as hysterical, obsessive–compulsive, phobic, and anxiety symptom neuroses (which are infrequently seen as such today but are more usually manifest in ways that suggest an accompanying narcissistic personality disorder)—lie a variety of disruptive experiences between the self and its selfobjects (Wolf, 1984/85, pp. 65–66). To the extent that they arise from a pathological oedipal situation, they constitute defensive organizations that protect a self adversely affected through faulty responses by oedipal selfobjects from further injury—a self that may or may not have already been affected by earlier selfobject failure. An appreciable proportion of those people who are initially diagnosed in these ways turn out to be suffering from more severe disorders of the self—usually narcissistic personality disorders—but not infrequently, from even more severe disorders of the self, such as borderline disorders or even psychoses. In a small number of patients, the vulnerability of the self may be a minor factor and the manifest picture of the psychoneurotic disorder derives predominantly from the neurotic conflicts associated with oedipal complex pathology.

---

[11]Dr. Evan Brahm (personal communication, 1988) has suggested that people with borderline disorders may not have sustained more self damage than those with narcissistic personality disorders, but simply have different ways of expressing the damage, which is determined by experiences of self disruption at different nodal points in their self development.

IMPLICATIONS FOR TREATMENT

The application of self psychology theory to clinical work does not entail any alteration in the framework of the particular modality of treatment in which it is used. Thus, when applied to group psychotherapy, it implies no change in such parameters as group size, composition, structure, or selection of patients.[12] However, its application is inevitably accompanied by a significant difference in the climate or atmosphere of the therapeutic work, whatever the modality or setting in which it is employed. This difference is mainly due to the different perspective that self psychology brings to transference, defense, and resistance.

Selfobject Transference and Selfobject Relationship

Kohut's most striking contribution to the therapeutic process that follows directly from his theoretical views is the abandonment in the treatment situation of the attitude that maturation must entail a decreasing interest in the needs of one's self. Kohut's new perspective, in effect, constitutes a "de-moralization" of narcissism and a tacit invitation to the patient to establish, or reestablish, as the case may be, a sense of psychological entitlement to significant others as selfobjects.

When someone becomes a patient in a group, he is legitimately expressing the expectation that the responses of his therapist and other group members will enable him to experience missing selfobject functions and relieve the pathological effects of inimical experiences. This is the *selfobject transference*, which Stone and Whitman (1977) first described as operating in the setting of group psychotherapy, and which has since been elaborated by Harwood (1983), Schwartzman (1984), Bacal (1985a), Detrick (1985, 1986), and Weinstein (1987). In my view, however, selfobject transference is more properly understood as selfobject *relationship*. In my article (1985a), I contrasted the group therapy process that is based on a traditional object relations approach with one that is informed by self psychology. In the former,

---

[12]Some therapists, however, such as Harwood (1983) and Weinstein (1987), are careful not to introduce patients with significant self disorders into group treatment until a selfobject relationship has first consolidated in individual sessions with the prospective therapist. Harwood will see these patients individually if they are traumatized in the group setting, and Weinstein describes a self psychological approach of combined group and individual therapy.

the therapist works through the defenses and anxieties of the members that are associated with the expression of their wishes for unacceptable forms of relationships with others in the group, that is, those that are related to unconsciously warded-off instinctual drives. In contrast, the therapist whose work is informed by self psychology addresses the defenses and anxieties associated with the expression of developmentally phase-legitimate selfobject needs.

In practice, as Harwood (1983), Schwartzman (1984), and Weinstein (1987) have beautifully illustrated, the group therapeutic process essentially entails the experience by the members of sustained selfobject-relatedness with others as well as experiences of its restoration following disruption. The working through of selfobject disruptions and the associated resumption of the selfobject bond with the therapist and with other group members will strengthen the patient's sense of self, render him less vulnerable, and help him to resume his interrupted development.

In 1976, Kohut (Kohut, 1976, pp. 837–838) introduced the idea of the "group self," which he saw as embodying both the group's ambitions and ideals; that is, he regarded the group self as a container of both the individual's sense of grandiosity[13] and idealized values. Meyers (1978) emphasized the importance, for group cohesion, of the group members' idealizing selfobject experience of the therapist and, by extension, of the group as a whole. According to Meyers, the idealizing selfobject transference becomes mobilized by the initial feelings of relative helplessness, disquiet, and narcissistic imbalance experienced by patients on entering the group and by the regressive pull of the group that causes a loosening of character defenses. Weinstein (1987) has also observed that the group as a whole tends to become an idealized selfobject, and has emphasized the importance of this in sustaining the individual during periods of selfobject disruption. Detrick (1985, 1986), however, maintains that the group has an essentially unipolar structure; in effect, the alter-ego dimension of experience among group members constitutes the core of the group self. In other words, according to Detrick, group members' experience of essential sameness is felt to guarantee the cohesiveness of the group.

---

[13]"Grandiosity," in my view, is not always an appropriate designation for the self state that it refers to. I believe that what Kohut meant by this term would better be separated into two ideas. The one would reflect the sense of personal conviction of one's unique importance. This would be a self percept that presumably arises out of optimal experiences of mirroring by selfobjects. It is affectively toned in a healthy way. The other, which would be closer to the traditional notion of "grandiosity," would reflect a self percept that is inflated beyond what the individual would normally experience. This may properly be regarded as a pathological self state, and it is associated with a disavowed sense of low self-esteem.

More experience of group work utilizing a self psychological perspective will be required before it can be determined which of these views is correct. My own opinion is that the particular preference, or valence, of the leader for a particular group ethos (of which the leader may not be completely aware) significantly influences the degree to which mirroring, idealizing, or alter-ego dimensions of selfobject relationships will prevail. The group situation, however, does offer more opportunity than dyadic therapy for working through the full range of selfobject experiences. In addition to enabling the experience of mirroring and idealizing selfobject relationships with other group members, the therapist, and the group as a whole, the group setting tends also to facilitate the development of alter-ego selfobject relationships more readily than dyadic therapy, since patients more naturally experience other group members as peers. The valuable dimension of therapeutic experience afforded by the alter-ego selfobject relationships and the working through of their disruptions is not readily available in individual therapy, especially in the analytic situation, where the patient's transference regression as well as the therapist's preference or valence favors experiences of discrepancy and thus the prevalence of mirroring and idealizing selfobject relationships.

The patient's readiness to engage in selfobject relationships with others to relieve his suffering and help him grow presupposes a certain confidence that he can expect others' attention as selfobjects, but his sense of entitlement to this will be unstable in varying degrees, depending upon the degree of self injury he has sustained. Significant disruption in childhood of any of the selfobject relationships will comparably influence how they are experienced and expressed in relation to others. The appreciation of this can be helpful in understanding urgent, intense needs for merger and the sometimes clamorous, controlling, and extravagant expressions (from the therapist's perspective) of "entitlement," as well as their defensive opposite—a more or less studied avoidance of a close relationship, or the reticence of the patient who dares not expect anything from others. I draw attention to this kind of early disturbance and some of its manifestations not because I regard it as the central issue in all cases but because it usually plays a role to some degree in all instances of self pathology and because it tends to emerge in regressive climates that can become activated in the group.

I have recently stressed the therapeutic usefulness of being aware of the patient's contribution to his selfobject experience that arises from the creative phantasies he generates about others that depict them as selfobjects that will justify this trust[14] (see Bacal, 1985b; Bacal and Newman, 1990). While analysts have traditionally associated phantasy with the mental representation of the instincts, phantasy is by no means limited to this activity. In the process of becoming a patient, one is already beginning to weave hopeful phantasies of the therapist and other members of the group as figures who will respond to selfobject needs. That is, conscious and unconscious elaborations in phantasy of positive images of the object contribute to its being experienced as a selfobject and, in this way, become integral components of the selfobject experience. In this sense, of course, all selfobjects are to some extent "phantasy" selfobjects.[15] However, the term *phantasy selfobject* is worth retaining, I believe, to designate one end of a continuum where the experience of selfobject relationships is minimally influenced by actual experiences of caretakers, but predominantly determined by the elaboration of phantasy. Put in another way, the phantasy component of the selfobject experience is similar to the exercise of an idealizing capacity but is based to a minimal degree on idealizable aspects of the object. These phantasy selfobject relationships are, in effect, constructed as psychologically lifesaving responses to otherwise unmanageable trauma. They can become a survival tool for some people when an adequate selfobject milieu is unavailable or in the presence of a seriously disillusioning selfobject world or a traumatically interfering world of objects that have never been experienced as selfobjects. In such a situation, the creative, or phantastic element in the selfobject experience will predominate, rather than the assimilated optimal responses of caretakers, and the patient may be especially vulnerable to selfobject failure.

Defense, Resistance, and Intersubjectivity

Resistance, from a classical perspective, reflects an opposition to the efforts of the analyst and the analytic process occasioned by the threat of free association to the inner balance between drives and defenses.

---

[14]Markson (personal communication, 1988) has observed that if the patient cannot generate such phantasies serious therapeutic difficulties will arise. We may also consider whether the absence of this capacity may account for the inability of certain people to follow through with therapy or to undertake therapy at all.

[15]Paul Ornstein and Anna Ornstein (1977, pp. 338–339) introduced the concept of the "curative fantasy," which refers to the patient's conscious and unconscious expectations or wishes for help from the therapist. We would regard this concept as similar to the concept of the phantasy selfobject. The curative fantasy may or may not, however, constitute a selfobject experience.

In addition, prior to Kohut's recognition of the psychological legitimacy of selfobject needs throughout life, most analysts treated "narcissistic" manifestations solely as defense. Many, though not all, classical analysts continue to do this. Examples of this perspective are the viewing of the idealizing selfobject transference as a defense against a basic underlying contempt or hostility, and regarding the mirror transference as a defense against "object-love." These attitudes stand in contrast to the view of self psychology that such transferences represent attempts to reinstate an aborted developmental process.

From the classical analytic perspective, it is expected that the patient will enact his opposition to therapeutic work not only by employing a variety of defense mechanisms but also by carrying out enactments of one sort or another in order to avoid the anxieties associated with the awareness of drive derivatives in relation to the therapist. The job of the classical therapist—again, regardless of the therapeutic modality in which he is working—is ultimately to modify the patient's defenses so that some measure of safe expression of drive-wishes is felt to be possible. Insofar as the operation of defense and resistance is also regarded by the therapist as associated with the patient's distorted view of some aspect of reality, the therapist's expectation is that the patient will ultimately repudiate what is infantile and unreasonable in the drive-wishes, and grow up. A good deal of "resistance" in a classically informed therapy could thus intelligibly be understood as the expression of the patient's experiencing some anxiety or conflict about meeting the therapist's expectations. This maturity-morality tends to create an adversarial climate in the therapy situation insofar as the patient is seen as opposing the momentum of this developmental thrust.

The self psychological view of defense and resistance to the therapeutic process arises from the recognition that the self—viewed not as a component of a mental apparatus, but as the core of the personality—needs to protect itself, not against the emergence of dangerous drives and wishes, but against the possible repetition of significant psychological injury, especially against traumatic assaults on self-esteem incurred in childhood, to which the self might be particularly vulnerable. That is, patients defend against the dangers of expressing their selfobject needs in relation to others. As Kohut (1984, pp. 111–151) puts it, defenses and resistances are employed to safeguard what remains of a healthy self, especially against the experience of painful and disruptive affect states (Newman, 1980, p. 263), so that the patient may resume his interrupted growth under conditions that are now felt to be safe. This view of the therapeutic process inevitably results in a more collaborative, rather than confrontative or adversarial, treatment climate, and tends to promote the development of selfobject ties.

When a person has experienced serious selfobject failure, his sense of self becomes weakened and prone to fragmentation. He may experience his selfobject needs consciously and with a sense of immediacy, or he may protect himself against their emergence into consciousness with defensive organizations. The patient's anxiety that the therapist or others in the group may not provide him with conditions under which he may feel safe to form a selfobject relationship with them, as well as his actual experiences of faulty attunement and responsiveness from others once selfobject relationships have formed, will occasion his defensiveness, or "resistance," to therapeutic work. The patient is also afraid that his negative affective reactions (such as anger and withdrawal) to the frustration of these essential selfobject needs will evoke retaliation and rejection. In short, the patient's "defensiveness" is due to his dread of being retraumatized by his bad objects as represented by the therapist and others in the group, as well as a fear of losing his good objects, that is, selfobjects, altogether. Protracted resistance to therapeutic work, or *negative therapeutic reaction*, is due to the patient's experience of significant others' persistent empathic "out-of-tuneness" with his primary self disorder and selfobject needs (Bacal, 1979; Brandchaft, 1983).

Meyers (1978) has described three resistances to the formation of sustaining idealizing transference relationships in the group:

1. The reluctance to relinquish the need for the mirroring of . . . [an individual's] grandiosity out of fear that the unmirrored self will lose its cohesion and fragment.[16]
2. The reluctance to relinquish one's own idealized values in order to gain acceptance by the group and the therapist.
3. The fear of loss of self through merger with the group and the idealized therapist.

Meyers indicates that the therapist can assist the group members in working through these resistances by conveying his understanding

---

[16]Meyers has referred in this context to my observation (Bacal, 1985a) that conflicts can arise between the various needs for selfobject relationship (such as the conflict between the need for an idealizing selfobject relationship and a mirroring selfobject relationship or a partnering [alter-ego] selfobject relationship). I have also indicated that this problem may be more easily resolved in group therapy than in dyadic therapy due to the opportunity, in the former, to direct one's selfobject needs to different people in the group, as well as, I would now add, to the group as a whole, as selfobject.

that they serve the important function of protecting members from a sense of precipitous loss of their sense of grandiosity (see n. 13).

Insofar as the therapeutic work of the self psychologist is intersubjectively informed, patients and therapists may be regarded as together constituting "an indissoluble psychological system" (Stolorow, Brandchaft, and Atwood, 1987, p. 1, quoting Atwood and Stolorow, 1984, p. 64). From this perspective, the problem of defensiveness or resistance takes on a different shape; in effect, it becomes an issue of the discrepancy between the patient and significant others. You will have noted that, in my discussion of transference, I did not mention the notion of "distortion" of perception. While traditional analysts tend to focus on the patient's unrealistic attitudes or distortions, self psychologists address themselves to the patient's subjective experience and his struggle to feel his experience as valid. They tend to regard transference not as a product of the patient's regression, displacement, projection, or distortion from his childhood experience, but as "an expression of the *continuing influence* of organizing principles and imagery that crystallized out of the patient's early formative experiences" (p. 36). When the therapist regards transference not as distortion but as the *organization of subjective experience* (Stolorow, Brandchaft, and Atwood, 1987, pp. 28–46) and thus as the psychologically understandable expression of selfobject needs, he will foster an inter- subjective perspective on interaction. This perspective is particularly applicable to group psychotherapy, where the therapist is in an excellent position to attend to the effect of the interplay between the differently organized psychological worlds of interacting individuals—in this situation, both among patients and between patients and himself. The working through of subjectively experienced disjunctions in self- object relationships in patient–patient and patient–therapist interaction then constitutes the central task of the therapeutic group.

When a group of people meets for the purpose of therapy, there is a natural inclination to explore and to confront problems that the individual encounters when he reacts inappropriately from the point of view of the needs and expectations of others. Less emphasis and less legitimacy are accorded to the individual's selfobject needs in relation to others and to the group as a whole. Put in another way, interactions between members of the group, whatever their content and however defended and disguised they might be, are, formally speaking, expressed in two modes, which I have called *reactiveness* and *responsiveness* (Bacal, 1991). Reactiveness tends to be the more prevalent one.

Reactiveness and responsiveness reflect different modes of listening to others. Reactiveness is a way of communicating and relating that reflects a listening perspective that is relatively experience-distant, and responsiveness is a way of communicating and relating that is relatively experience-near. When reactiveness is operating, the experience of others is registered in terms of a sense or understanding of how it affects one's self. The Tavistock groups that were conducted by Bion and Ezriel and their colleagues exemplified this mode of relating, since the leader's communications to the group consistently reflected an understanding of the group process primarily as it affected him (see Heath and Bacal, 1968). In effect, many other therapy group leaders wittingly or unwittingly tend to foster the use of reactiveness as the predominant communicative mode in the group, even though they may not relate to the group as remotely as the "classical" Tavistock consultant does.

Reactiveness as a way of communicating makes sense in its correspondence to the legitimate expectations that the family group has of the child; that is, it is based on widely accepted norms within the subculture as to how people should behave. In addition, these norms have come to reflect more or less traditionally established psychodynamic theory that addresses itself to the explanation of psychopathology, maintaining that psychological troubles are, at base, determined by the persistence of instinctual drives in their archaic forms, or by "narcissistic" needs of one sort or another that the chronological adult has not outgrown. What naturally follows from this emphasis is that the therapy group should ultimately enable the individual patient to renounce or at least modify these primitive ways and grow up. When such a maturity-morality dominates the group ethos, group members are tacitly encouraged to *react* personally to other group members' repetition of pathological childhood interpersonal relationships in current interaction. The task of the therapist, apropos, is to unravel these transference distortions between the group members and between them and himself.

It is this theory of therapy—where transference is regarded as a repetition or projection of early pathological relationships and distorted perceptions that determine interpersonally maladaptive behavior—that underlies and that inevitably gives rise to the sort of interpersonal communication that I have called reactiveness. The messages conveyed, whether from therapist or patient—more spontaneously from other patients, more "understandingly" from the therapist—are inevitably going to imply, and sometimes accurately identify, psychopathology, distortion of reality, and an expectation of change. Little or no empathy is required, and the use of experience-distant reactiveness as a communicative mode is consistent with this perspective. We would certainly not wish to deprive our patients of the value of the spontaneous expression of their feelings toward each other—which, in addition to providing grist for the mill of understanding, may constitute, at times, "optimal responsivity" for the individual. However, it is important that the therapist convey to the members of the group his regard for the therapeutic value of responding also on the basis of their empathically informed perceptions of others' needs for selfobject functioning. This kind of optimal responsivity is always necessary for psychological survival; the development of a more or less reliable *expectation* of it is essential for psychological health. However, problems in mutual understanding that occur at the intersection of the different subjectivities of participants in a therapy group are the order of the day, and experiences of selfobject disruption—frustrating and, at times, enraging—are frequently experienced at these interfaces. The repair of these disruptions, and understanding of them when harmony cannot be restored, will also constitute significant therapeutic experiences for the members of the group. The setting of group psychotherapy, in effect, presents multiple and varied opportunities for the development of selfobject ties as well as for experiences of repair of their disruption, thus providing rich possibilities for therapeutic experience and psychological growth.

In contrast to the classical analytic and object relations perspective, self psychology explains the emergence of destructive phantasy or enactment in treatment not as due to the emergence of primitive instinctual drives but rather as being triggered by the threat or experience of earlier inimical relationships—in effect, with bad objects or with failing selfobjects—through comparably experienced situations in the here-and-now. It is these experiences and their significance that are interpreted. In this connection, the therapist's experience of what the Kleinians describe as projective identification of bad experiences and bad parts of the self may constitute a lag in attunement with the patient's need to rid himself of intolerable links with unempathic objects in the present that reactivate comparable experience with bad objects in the past (Bacal, 1987)—including the therapist who, at that moment, may not be aware of the extent to which his lack of optimal responsiveness has contributed to the patient's internal "bad-object-relational" experience. The therapist's "impossible" task, which he nonetheless must attempt during every treatment, and help other group members to do the same, is to both contain this experience as well as to "decenter" from the patient's attribution that the group members and therapist are the embodiment of the patient's bad objects, and therefore personally responsible for his misery. Brandchaft and Stolorow (1988) have also challenged the concept of projective identification as described by Klein (1955, p. 310; see also 1952, p.

207). Their criticisms are that the concept constitutes a presumptive questioning on the part of the therapist of the validity of the patient's perception of him and an unjustifiable attribution of the therapist's "own unwanted or disruptive affective reactions to the hidden intention of the patient" (Brandchaft and Stolorow, 1988, p. 38). I would agree that this occurs in many instances, and that it is usually precipitated by the therapist's rigid lack of attunement to the patient; however, I think it is also experientially valid that the patient may need the therapist—as well as others, in the group therapy situation—to hold and detoxify his unbearable feelings and that he does, so to speak, hand them over to the therapist and to others for this purpose (Meltzer, 1984).

Deficit and Conflict and the Therapeutic Process

Problematic object relations are experienced both in terms of "deficit" and "conflict." As Wallerstein has pointed out (1981, 1983, 1985), it is commonplace in practice to encounter both, and Stolorow, Brandchaft, and Atwood (1987, p. 26) point out that conflict and deficit operate as dimensions of experience in object relationships, at times as "figure," at other times as "ground." Conflict over instinctual drives is, however, not regarded by self psychology as the primary determinant of psychopathology. Markson and Thomson (1986, p. 34) assert that "there is no conflict of clinical dimension without underlying deficit." This view is affirmed by Stolorow, Brandchaft, and Atwood (1987, p. 26), who state that the formation of inner conflict always occurs in the context of the patient's subjective experience of the analyst's selfobject failures. I have already discussed the sequence that determines this.

Here is a paradigmatic, composite summary of the elements of significant conflict from the self psychological perspective: On the one hand, the patient struggles to contact and express his selfobject needs, as well as disavowed negative affects that were occasioned by the experience of the frustration of these needs by childhood caretakers and which now may be triggered by the anticipated or experienced reactions of others. On the other hand, the patient not only fears rejection and retaliation from the therapist and from others and the frightening affects with which these are associated, he also wants to preserve his sense of significant others as good or idealized figures that he desperately needs to internalize in order to shore up a self that is weakened and injured by selfobject failure. Such conflicts are exacerbated when the selfobject figure of these significant others is felt to be unidealizable or when the patient's idealization is in large measure the product of his phantasy.

How Therapy Cures

Kohut has asserted that the outcome of successful treatment entails both strengthening the self and acquiring the ability to establish developmentally appropriate relationships with available selfobjects (Kohut, 1984, p. 77). In effect, we may regard the one as having a reciprocally reinforcing effect on the other: The development of the capacity for mature selfobject relations increases the strength of the self, and a stronger self is more capable of effectively engaging progressively more mature selfobject relationships.

According to Kohut (1984), therapeutic effect is mediated through the patient's experience of multiple, manageable "optimal frustrations" of selfobject needs, the result of which is that the patient takes over, or internalizes—via transmuting internalization—the analyst's selfobject functions for his own use. I have taken issue with Kohut's view and have suggested that the concept of "optimal responsiveness" is more relevant in explaining therapeutic gain. Thus, I am, in effect, in essential agreement with Marian Tolpin (1983) that the internalization of the cohesion-fostering selfobject tie constitutes the essence of what is therapeutic. The therapeutic process is legitimately understood as a "corrective selfobject experience," the elements of which are the transference of needs that incline the patient to put others in the role of selfobject; the residue of the individual's archaic, basic sense of natural entitlement to the functions of the caretaker of earliest childhood—that is, the derivatives of felicitous early experience; the patient's capacity for creative, or phantasy, elaboration of a selfobject; and the optimal responsiveness of others to the individual's selfobject needs. The corrective selfobject experience should be distinguished from the provision of "gratifications." While no moral constraint need be applied to gratification, a selfobject experience may or may not affect a patient in this way.

If the anxieties and defenses associated with unmet needs and conflicts and their disturbing affects are adequately understood in an intersubjective context, and significant others' perceived failures are balanced by one's experience of them as providing optimal responsiveness, selfobject relationships will reestablish themselves following (inevitable) selfobject rupture. This way of understanding the current self psychological view of the curative process is as valid for one modality of therapy as another. The self psychological view that the significant element in the curative process entails the experience of the relationship—in contrast to the traditional analytic view that insight is the major therapeutic factor (see also Bacal, 1990b)—implicitly ascribes to the group a unique therapeutic potential: There is much more opportunity for the impact of one personality on another in the group therapy situation. There is also a greater potential threat to the therapeutic experience of any individual: While, as we have noted, group therapy offers the patient the possibility of experiencing diverse selfobject relationships due to the differential responsiveness of group members to selfobject need, a particular group culture may also become organized in such a way that the reactiveness of the members is recurrently traumatic to an individual patient. While in such an instance the patient can be regarded as a "deviant," one may also regard the culture of that group as inimical to the self development of that particular individual. There is no therapist and certainly no group whose responses are so "optimal" as to preclude the patients' recurrently experiencing frustrating and hurtful discrepancies between what they are after and what they get from the therapist and the other group members.

However, if these inevitable disruptions are not traumatic, they are potentially of considerable therapeutic value, since the repeated reestablishment of selfobject relationships following disruption strengthens the self and promotes a sense of entitlement to, and a confident expectation of, being listened to and understood and having one's essential psychological needs met. From this perspective, the group provides a situation in which a diversity of reactivity by other patients can lead to the experience of a wider spectrum of selfobject disruptions that are pathognomonic of the patients' earlier significant discord, thus constituting a broader base for encountering these issues. One of the central tasks of the group therapist, therefore, is to promote a climate in the group that allows for an optimal mixture of reactiveness and responsiveness. This will then provide the group members with an optimal balance of the therapeutic dimensions of both selfobject relationship and the working through and repair of their disruptions.

REFERENCES

Atwood, G., & Stolorow, R. (1984), *Structures of Subjectivity*. Hillsdale, NJ: Analytic Press.
Bacal, H. A. (1979), Empathic lag in the analyst and its relation to "negative therapeutic reaction." Paper presented at the 31st International Psychoanalytical Congress in New York.

———— (1981), Notes on some therapeutic challenges in the analysis of severely regressed patients. *Psychoanal. Inq.*, 1:29–56.

———— (1985a), Object-relations in the group from the perspective of self psychology. *Internat. J. Group Psychother.*, 35:483–501.

———— (1985b), Optimal responsiveness and the therapeutic process. In: *Progress in Self Psychology, Vol. 1*, ed. A. Goldberg. New York: Guilford Press, pp. 202–226.

———— (1987), British object-relations theorists and self psychology: Some critical reflections. *Internat. J. Psycho-Anal.*, 68:81–98.

———— (1990a), Does an object relations theory exist in self psychology? *Psychoanal. Inq.*, 10:197–220.

———— (1990b), The elements of a corrective selfobject experience. *Psychoanal. Inq.*, 10:347–372.

———— (1991), Reactiveness and responsiveness in the group therapeutic process. In: *Psychoanalytic Group Theory and Therapy: Essays in Honor of Saul Scheidlinger*, ed. S. Tuttman. Madison, CT: International Universities Press, pp. 309–318.

———— Newman, K. M. (1990), *Theories of Object Relations: Bridges to Self Psychology*. New York: Columbia University Press.

Balint, M. (1937), Early developmental states of the ego. Primary object love. In: *Primary Love and Psycho-Analytic Technique* (new, enlarged ed.). London: Tavistock Publications, 1965, pp. 74–90.

Brandchaft, B. (1983), The negativism of the negative therapeutic reaction and the psychology of the self. In: *The Future of Psychoanalysis*, ed. A. Goldberg. New York: International Universities Press, pp. 327–359.

———— Stolorow, R. (1988), On projective identification: A reply. *Los Angeles Psychoanal. Bull.*, Summer:35–38.

Detrick, D. (1985), Alterego phenomena and the alterego transferences. In: *Progress in Self Psychology, Vol. 1*, ed. A. Goldberg. New York: Guilford Press, pp. 240–256.

———— (1986), Alterego phenomena and the alterego transferences: Some further considerations. In: *Progress in Self Psychology, Vol. 2*, ed. A. Goldberg. New York: Guilford Press, pp. 299–304.

Fajardo, B. (1988), Constitution in infancy: Implications for early development and psychoanalysis. In: *Progress in Self Psychology, Vol. 4*, ed. A. Goldberg. Hillsdale, NJ: Analytic Press, pp. 91–100.

Ferenczi, S. (1933), Confusion of tongues between the child and the adults. *Internat. J. Psycho-Anal.*, 30:225–230.

Goldberg, A. (1982), The self of psychoanalysis. In: *Psychosocial Theories of the Self*, ed. B. Lee with K. Smith. New York: Plenum Press, pp. 3–22.

Hartmann, H. (1939), *Ego Psychology and the Problem of Adaptation*. New York: International Universities Press, 1958.

———— (1950), Comments on the psychoanalytic theory of the ego. In: *Essays on Ego Psychology*. New York: International Universities Press, 1964, pp. 113–141.

Harwood, I. (1983), The application of self-psychology concepts to group psychotherapy. *Internat. J. Group Psychother.*, 33:469–487.

Heath, S., & Bacal, H. (1968), A method of group psychotherapy at the Tavistock Clinic. *Internat. J. Group Psychother.*, 35:21–30.

Klein, M. (1952), Some theoretical conclusions regarding the emotional life of the infant. In: *Developments in Psycho-Analysis*, by M. Klein, P. Heimann, S. Isaacs, & J. Riviere. London: Hogarth Press, 1970, pp. 198–236.

———— (1955), On identification. In: *New Directions in Psycho-Analysis*, ed. M. Klein, P. Heimann, & R. Money-Kyrle. New York: Basic Books, pp. 309–345.

Kohut, H. (1971), *The Analysis of the Self*. New York: International Universities Press.

———— (1972), Thoughts on narcissism and narcissistic rage. In: *The Psychoanalytic Study of the Child*, 27:360–400. New York: Quadrangle Books.

———— (1976), Creativeness, charisma, group psychology. In: *The Search for the Self: Selected Writings of Heinz Kohut, 1950–1978*, Vol. 2, ed. P. Ornstein. New York: International Universities Press, pp. 793–843.

———— (1977), *The Restoration of the Self*. New York: International Universities Press.

———— (1984), *How Does Analysis Cure?*, ed. A. Goldberg & P. Stepansky. Chicago: University of Chicago Press.

———— Wolf, E. (1978), The disorders of the self and their treatment: An outline. *Internat. J. Psycho-Anal.*, 59:413–425.

Lachmann, F. (1986), Interpretation of psychic conflict and adversarial relationships: A self-psychological perspective. *Psychoanal. Psychol.*, 3(4):341–355.

Lang, J. (1984), Notes toward a psychology of the feminine self. In: *Kohut's Legacy*, ed. P. Stepansky & A. Goldberg. Hillsdale, NJ: Analytic Press, pp. 51–69.

Markson, E., & Thomson, P. (1986), The relationship between the psychoanalytic concepts of conflict and deficit. In: *Progress in Self Psychology, Vol. 2*, ed. A. Goldberg. New York: Guilford Press, pp. 31–40.

Meltzer, D. (1984), "What is an emotional experience?" Paper presented at the Seventh Annual Self Psychology Conference, Toronto, Canada.

Meyers, S. (1978), Group therapy and the disorders of the self: Theoretical and clinical considerations. *Group*, 2:131–140.

Morrison, A. P. (1989), *Shame: The Underside of Narcissism*. Hillsdale, NJ: Analytic Press.

Newman, K. (1980), Defense analysis and self psychology. In: *Advances in Self Psychology*, ed. A. Goldberg. New York: International Universities Press, pp. 263–278.

Ornstein, P. (1981), The bipolar self in the psychoanalytic treatment process: Clinical-theoretical considerations. *J. Amer. Psychoanal. Assn.*, 29:353–375.

———— Ornstein, A. (1977), On the continuing evolution of psychoanalytic psychother-apy: Reflections and predictions. In: *The Annual of Psychoanalysis*, Vol. 5. New York: International Universities Press, pp. 329–355.

Rycroft, C. (1972), *A Critical Dictionary of Psychoanalysis*. New York: Penguin Books.

Schwartzman, G. (1984), The use of the group as selfobject. *Internat. J. Group Psychother.*, 34:229–241.

Stern, D. (1985), *The Interpersonal World of the Infant*. New York: Basic Books.

Stolorow, R., Brandchaft, B., & Atwood, G. (1987), *Psychoanalytic Treatment: An Intersub-jective Approach*. Hillsdale, NJ: Analytic Press.

Stone, W. N., & Whitman, R. H. (1977), Contributions of the psychology of the self to group process and group therapy. *Internat. J. Group Psychother.*, 27:343–359.

Suttie, I. D. (1935), *The Origins of Love and Hate*. London: Kegan Paul, Trench, Trubner.

Terman, D. (1988), Optimum frustration: Structuralization and the therapeutic pro-cess. In: *Progress in Self Psychology, Vol. 4*, ed. A. Goldberg. Hillsdale, NJ: Analytic Press, pp. 113–125.

Tolpin, M. (1983), Corrective emotional experience: A self psychological reevaluation. In: *The Future of Psychoanalysis*, ed. A. Goldberg. New York: International Universities Press.

——— (1988), *The Psychology of Women*. Unpublished manuscript.

Wallerstein, R. S. (1981), The bipolar self: Discussion of alternative perspectives. *J. Amer. Psychoanal. Assn.*, 29:377–394.

——— (1983), Self psychology and "classical" psychoanalytic psychology: The nature of their relationship. *Psychoanal. Contemporary Thought*, 6:553–595. Rpt. in: *The Future of Psychoanalysis*, ed. A. Goldberg. New York: International Universities Press, pp. 19–63.

——— (1985), How does self psychology differ in practice? *Internat. J. Psychoanal.*, 66:391–404. Rpt. in: *Progress in Self Psychology, Vol. 2*, ed. A. Goldberg. New York: Guilford Press, pp. 63–83.

Weinstein, D. (1987), Self psychology and group therapy. *Group*, 11:144–154.

Winnicott, D. W. (1960), Ego distortion in terms of true and false self. In: *The Maturational Processes and the Facilitating Environment*. London: Hogarth Press, 1965, pp. 140–152.

Wolf, E. (1980), On the developmental line of selfobject relations. In: *Advances in Self Psychology*, ed. A. Goldberg. New York: International Universities Press, pp. 117–130.

——— (1983), Selfobject relations disorders. In: *Character Pathology: Theory and Treatment*, ed. M. Zales. New York: Brunner/Mazel.

——— (1984/85), Self psychology and the neuroses. In: *The Annual of Psychoanalysis*, Vol. 12/13. New York: International Universities Press, pp. 57–68.

——— (1985), The search for confirmation: Technical aspects of mirroring. *Psychoanal. Inq.*, 5:271–282.

4

Contributions from Social Systems Theory

EDWARD B. KLEIN, Ph.D.

This chapter, which details the contributions of Tavistock social systems theory to group psychotherapy, has been divided into two major sections. The first, a *theory* section, begins with a description of Melanie Klein's individual psychology that focuses on the defenses developed in the first year of life by the infant in interaction with mother. Bion, expanding on Kleinian concepts, draws an analogy between the infant and mother and the group and the leader. He then describes the differences between the work and the basic assumption groups. The organizational/systems psychology of Rice, focused on task, boundary, leadership, authority, social defenses, culture, role, and comparisons to other systems theories, concludes the first section. The second, *applied* section begins with discussion of the practical use of Tavistock theory in treatment groups and the application of social systems theory in group psychotherapy and consultation. Then a selective overview of group research conducted from a systems perspective is presented. The chapter concludes with a discussion of implications for the future.

THEORY

Individual

The Tavistock systems approach to group psychotherapy developed in London, England. It evolved from the object relations school initiated by Melanie Klein (1959), who primarily treated young children.

When Klein started her work with children in the 1920s, she assumed that Freud's methods could be applied with minor modifications. But, in contrast to the oedipal focus of traditional Freudian theory, Klein conceptualized a preoedipal developmental line of defense mechanisms, which she felt was necessary in understanding children. She noted that in the first year of life (Freud's oral phase) there are two positions (developmental stages), the paranoid-schizoid and the depressive, with associated primitive anxieties.

In the first few months of life the self is vulnerable to both real and imagined harm from parental neglect, overstimulation, and aggressive internal drives that, ideally, are attenuated by a loving, giving mother. Klein (1959) proposed that the infant imagines being attacked by "bad objects" that evoke persecutory anxiety. "Good objects," associated with protective, comforting, and rewarding experiences, are used by the infant to defend against such negative feelings. The objects in the paranoid-schizoid stage are called part-objects because of their connection to powerful affects and body parts (e.g., the mother's breast). (Experiencing the mother as a whole object, that is, as an external person who is, to some extent, independent of the infant's needs, does not occur until the depressive stage.)

Infants use the defense mechanism of splitting to cope with the powerful affects they experience. Klein (1959) viewed splitting as essential to understanding the infant's early anxieties. She saw life as a struggle between the Freudian life and death instincts, and therefore viewed splitting as necessary for emotional survival in the first months of life. Splitting enables the infant to separate good from bad, love from hate, and to preserve positive experiences, affects, and objects free from contact with their negative counterparts. The prototypical experience is nursing. Feeding engenders a positive sense of self (satisfied infant), a positive experience of the object (the attentive mother), and positive affect. Hunger evokes a negative experience of the self (frustrated infant), an inattentive object (the unavailable mother), and negative affect (anger). Thus, splitting arises because the infant's experiences with the mother are both nurturing and frustrating. The infant's problem is how to respond to a good mother who causes bad things to happen. The solution is to split the experience with the mother into two objects. There is a good mother (with a denied bad mother) and eventually a good self (with a denied bad self). Over time, the infant integrates the good and bad into a single mother and single self.

A second major defense mechanism the infant uses to deal with persecutory anxiety during the paranoid-schizoid position (birth to six months old) is that of projective identification, an intrapsychic process in which the infant projects internal material onto mother and, at the same time, unconsciously identifies with the projected material. The infant deposits unwanted feelings into the mother's feeling system. The mother thus becomes a container being filled up with projected material. The infant, wishing to get rid of these unwanted feelings, then treats the mother *as if* she were indeed experiencing the projected feeling state. Projective identification aids the infant's learning and is defensive. By projecting into the mother, the infant learns to tolerate discomfort and how to comfort himself. It is also defensive since it protects the infant from discomfort until he is more able to manage it himself. The process moves toward closure with the infant's reintrojection of neutralized metabolized projections, in relation to the mother. The process of projective identification may form the basis for empathy in adulthood (Grotstein, 1981).

These early defenses are normal since they aid the infant in distinguishing between good and bad (splitting) and in developing affective communication (projective identification). In sum, splitting and projective identification are related mechanisms that provide a basic mode of organizing early life experiences. The loved mother can be separated from the hated mother, while the infant's hating self can be separated from the loving self. These mechanisms allow the infant to feel safe without fear of intrusion from negative self or object representations. These defenses prevent the good from being destroyed by the bad and allow the infant to experience disturbing aspects of the self and others at a safe distance until he is psychologically ready for the task of integration.

With "good-enough" mothering (more positive than negative experiences with the mother), the infant moves on to the next stage. During the depressive position (seven to twelve months) the infant makes a major maturational step signaled by an increased awareness of the mother. The infant progresses from self preoccupation to concern for mother as a separate person. There is a beginning integration of the good and bad aspects of mother. The infant is aware of separation, loss, envy, and guilt. The infant can distinguish me from not-me (self from the rest of the world) and experiences depressive anxiety over its developing internal psychology and fear of loss.

In the paranoid-schizoid position the infant has no concept of a whole person. He relates to part-objects and experiences no ambivalence. An object is split into an ideal and a persecutory one; the fear is that persecutors may invade and destroy the self and the ideal object. In contrast, the depressive position involves integration and recognition of mother *not* as a collection of anatomical parts—breasts that feed, hands that tend, eyes that smile or frighten—but as a whole person with an independent existence of her own, who is a source of *both* good and bad experiences. He then gradually realizes that it is the same infant, himself, who both loves and hates the same person, mother. The infant now experiences ambivalence, which, developmentally, replaces splitting. His anxieties now are about his own aggression toward his ambivalently loved object, mother. That is, his anxiety has changed from a paranoid to a depressive one (Segal, 1973).

For Klein, development involves the movement of the psyche through these two stages. In the paranoid-schizoid position the task is to preserve the emerging self from danger; in the depressive stage the task is to protect the love object (mother) from the infant's own aggression. This latter task is facilitated by a greater reality orientation (recognition of self, mother, and father as whole, separate persons) and increased integration of the infant's personality. Therefore, some aspects of the oedipal situation (envy at the relations between father and mother that exclude the infant) and an emerging superego (guilt) occur in the very first year, much earlier than in the traditional Freudian view.

The working-through of the depressive position in normal development depends on the capacity to make reparation. When the infant feels that he has destroyed both his good external and internal objects, he experiences guilt and a longing for the lost harmony. This reparative drive is an important source of growth and creativity. A successful working-through is essential for mental health. In the process, the ego becomes integrated, capable of reality testing and sublimation, and it is enriched from the introjection of good objects. This in turn lessens the infant's omnipotence, guilt, and fear of loss. Throughout life a person oscillates between these two positions on a continuum. At one end is a schizophrenic patient who rarely reaches a depressive integration, at the other end is a mature adult with a well-integrated inner world, who has mostly overcome depressive anxiety, with trust in a good inner object and his own creative potential.

Group

Bion (1959), who was analyzed by Klein, applied many of her ideas to groups when he was directing a rehabilitation center in a British military psychiatric hospital during World War II and again, later, at the Tavistock Clinic in London. He also used the work of other British object relations theorists to understand covert group process. From Ezriel (1950), he used the concept of common group tensions: the common denominator of the dominant unconscious fantasies of all patients with required, avoided, and calamitous relationships. The group politely listens to my interpretations (required), but assiduously ignores them (avoided), because of your fear of abandonment (calamitous). Ezriel noted that every patient plays a role according to the particular unconscious fantasy group relations that he entertains. By analyzing the role that each patient assumes in dealing with the common tension, the therapist can demonstrate particular defense mechanisms in the same manner as in psychoanalysis, but with comments connecting the patient to the group as a whole.

In addition, Bion used Winnicott's (1952) work on the transitional object, the child's first "not-me" possession (i.e., a toy, a blanket), which has fantasy and reality components. With the transitional object the infant uses his imagination to feel safe in the absence of his mother. The infant substitutes an inanimate object for the mother and uses it for comfort and to integrate reality and fantasy.

Bion (1959) incorporated these insights from the work of Klein, Ezriel, and Winnicott in his model for understanding group processes in dynamic psychotherapy by drawing an analogy between the relationship between infant and mother and the relationship between the group as a whole and the leader. For instance, Bion used the concept of projective identification in his description of unacceptable impulses or wishes being disowned and poured into the therapist or the group, like the infant pours unwanted feelings into the mother.

Bion posited two levels that simultaneously occur in any group. First, the *work group* pursues the explicitly stated primary task by having an agenda, time frame, and leadership. The leader is not the only one with skills; he leads as long as he serves the group task, while members contribute as separate individuals. Second, the emotional aspects of groups, which Bion called *basic assumption* life, are stimulated by shared anxieties. Basic assumptions are collective, usually unconscious, stances groups take to avoid dreaded relationships and/ or in reaction to the authority of the leader. Basic assumptions are not directed outward toward reality, as in the work group, but inward toward fantasy and are uncritically enacted. When basic assumptions hold sway there is a lack of a time frame, members are anonymous, vicarious aspects predominate and there are constant attempts to seduce leaders away from the group task. The group acts "as if" some untested tacit assumption is true. Participants experience the group as a magical entity. It has a purpose and a life independent of the collaborative efforts of its members. Basic assumption behavior expresses the members' wish that they might create a wonderful world without work. When the work task promotes anxiety, basic assumption life enables participants to limit their feelings of isolation.

Bion identified three, among many possible, basic asssumptions: dependency, fight–flight, and pairing. The *dependency group* aims to attain security. Participants act "as if" they are inadequate and imma- ture, and the leader, by contrast, is omnipotent and omniscient. This kind of group orientation may arise among, for example, a group of inpatients and a wise hospital group therapist. The wisdom of the clinician is not tested. Patients do not need to give her information about their difficulties for she knows all and plans for the collective good. In this emotional state patients insist on simple explanations and believe that the therapist can solve all difficulties. She is idealized and made into a mother who will take care of her children. A major concern in this group is greed; with childlike dependency, each per- son demands more than his share of parental care. The outside world looks cold and unfriendly in comparison to the warmth of the com- fortable and secure dependency group.

The basic assumption among members of the *fight–flight group* is that they should behave "as if" there is an enemy against whom they must defend themselves or from whom they must escape in order to preserve the group. Members see the environment as extremely dangerous; people are not trustworthy. Self reflection and insight are lacking. Misfortunes are not due to one's behavior: Others are to blame. Hostile impulses are externalized and projected; therefore, the leader's role is to mobilize for immediate action—flight or fight. Leaders are very important, individuals do not count. The dominant emotions are anger, hate, fear, panic, suspicion, and paranoia. The leader needs certain characteristics, such as the ability to rally the troops when spirits flag and to locate a danger even when none is conveniently available. A touch of paranoia often helps in leading a fight–flight group.

The *pairing* basic assumption is that the group should act "as if" it has met for purposes of reproduction, to bring forth a messiah. Two people need to get together to carry out the task of creation. When pairing is in the air an atmosphere of eager hopefulness pervades the group. Participants are living in the hope of the creation of a new leader or thought which will bring forth Utopia. In order to maintain hope, the leader must be *unborn*. A prevailing and powerful feeling of hope is evidence that the pairing group exists. Participants enjoy the group optimism, with soft and agreeable feelings predominating. The unborn leader will save the group from feelings of helplessness, hatred, destructiveness, and despair.

There are more than three assumptions, as Bion (1959) noted. Turquet (1975) discussed another basic assumption, fusion: an over- powering, often mindless, oneness in which individual differences of attitude, occupation, gender, and race are assiduously denied. Other basic assumptions will be uncovered as researchers study dynamic small-group processes.

Bion noted that members have a built-in valency (a predisposition) toward basic assumption life and a predominance toward a particular basic assumption. For example, some members are particularly prone toward flight, leading the discussion away from any loaded intragroup topic back to the outside world. The basic assumption mode can provide emotional energy and vitality in the group but constantly seeks to suffuse and take over the work group. Basic assumptions can therefore facilitate or impede the work of a group. The former happens when a group or organization mobilizes its collective psychology to accomplish a work task. In the mature work group, which uses the basic assumptions for task accomplishment, when dependence is operating, the leader is dependable; when fighting, the leader is courageous, and when engaging in pairing, the leader is creative (Rioch, 1970). Or as Bion (1959) noted about "good group spirit," the group has a common purpose; there is recognition of boundaries, a capacity to absorb and lose members; individuality is recognized; and there is a capacity to cope with dissent among members. On the other hand, basic assumptions impede the work of the group when there is regression to more primitive functioning as the group relates to the authority of the leader/therapist and tries to manage its collective anxiety. Basic assumptions are an interference with the work task, just as primitive impulses may interfere with the work of the mature adult. Members use splitting between the good and bad leader or between work and basic assumptions as a way to reduce the contradictory feelings and ambivalence that mark group life. Splitting can dissipate anxiety and manage regression in order to make the group more comfortable. Splitting, which is the developmentally earlier line of defense in the individual, probably occurs before projective identification in groups.

Bion expanded on M. Klein's (1959) concept of projective identification, formulating the concept of container–contained to enhance understanding of the individual and the group. The mother, by forming a "thinking couple" with the infant, aids in making sense out of the overwhelming stimuli which affect the infant. This kind of thinking originates in an interpersonal process with the mother who makes available her ego to the infant, who then begins to organize experiences into patterns. Although this idea comes from the infant–mother interaction it can be seen as a way the group acts as a container for group participants. Disavowed anxiety may be contained as a basic assumption, a pair of patients may be a container for the hope of the group. Members can therefore discuss and work on difficult tasks in an organizational setting (e.g., address management's purposeful use of ambiguity to foster staff uncertainty and passivity) and patients can say what they think in a therapy group (e.g., the difficulty of leaving the dependent patient role). Having thoughts contained, understood, and validated in a treatment group can help to prevent madness, just as it aids collaboration in an organizational work group.

Individuals often fear being overwhelmed by group forces, but interpretation of the basic assumptions gradually brings these forces into consciousness and, over time, they lose some of their threatening quality. To consciously experience the work group depends on the developing ability of each of the participants to use their skills responsibly in the service of the common task. Bion is not talking about closeness to ward off fear of aloneness but using one's authority to accomplish the group's stated task. The group-as-a-whole view aids patients in examining how they use and are used by others via projective identification. To look at the devalued parts of ourselves we ask other group members to carry requires courage and hard work.

Social Systems

The preceding ideas and concepts were utilized by A. K. Rice, who was a member of a training group led by Bion in 1947, and others affiliated with the Tavistock Institute in applying individual and group theory to the working of complex social systems. Starting from Bion's work, they investigated task performance and authority relations as they were experienced in a group. Emphasis was placed on understanding group behavior and the influences of the social structure on individuals. Here we will review nine concepts developed in organizational work—primary task, open systems, boundary, authority, leadership, sociotechnical systems, social defenses, culture, and role—and their usefulness in group treatment.

A major Tavistock concept is the *primary task*: the work that an organization has to do to survive in its environment (Rice, 1963). The Tavistock approach emphasizes the primary task with group-level interventions. In this way of organizing work, employees form autonomous groups, exchange assignments, and are paid as a group, rather than as individual contributors. For instance, Trist and Bamforth (1951) studied a British coal mine that used two different work systems. The long-wall method minimized interpersonal and group relations; workers were assigned to specific tasks and paid on an individual basis, which led to low performance, passivity, and high absenteeism. A more social group approach was introduced (the composite long-wall method) leading to higher morale, productivity, attendance, and safety (Emery and Trist, 1960; Trist, Higgin, Murray, and Pollack, 1963). A literature review (E. B. Klein, 1978) found that there are additional desirable results: Workers report a heightened sense of cohesion, greater use of skills, and a decrease in intergroup battles.

In psychotherapy the primary task of personal change is often confusing because it involves learning about oneself through the examination of feelings and relationships both inside and outside of the group. But as Garland (1982) noted, a working psychotherapy group is one in which patients become less interested in their individual presenting problems and more concerned with *group* interactions, which they initially saw as a nonproblem or as irrelevant to their needs. This shift means that the therapist helps members see that the *primary task* can best be pursued by focusing on the here-and-now, thereby enabling patients to deepen and expand their views of feelings and relationships in life and more fully understand their initial presenting problems as these are reflected and reactivated in the group process.

Any enterprise may be seen as an *open system*, which has characteristics in common with a biological organism. An open system exists, and can only exist, by exchanging materials with its environment. It imports materials, transforms them by means of conversion processes, consumes some of the products of conversion for internal maintenance, and exports the rest. Directly or indirectly, it exchanges its outputs for further intakes, including further resources to maintain itself. These import–conversion–export processes are the work the enterprise has to do if it is to survive (Miller and Rice, 1967). For instance, Levinson and Astrachan (1974) noted that the entry system of a community mental health center (CMHC) is a boundary region between the community and the center. If difficulties arise on intake, the course of individual and group treatment, and particularly termination, becomes highly problematic. On the other hand, if the system functions well, community members will use the services and support the CMHC with referrals and positive votes on mental health tax levies.

A critical Tavistock concept is *boundary*—the region that separates the individual from the group or the group from the rest of the environment. Boundaries have temporal, spatial, and geographic aspects (Miller, 1959). An enterprise can survive only by an ongoing interchange of materials with its environment. The boundary across which these materials flow separates the enterprise from its environment. But because of continuing changes, which mark all living systems, the boundary is a region, not a line. The inner boundary interfaces with the internal subsystems, the outer boundary with the related external systems. Leaders in this boundary region protect the internal subsystem from the demands of the environment, yet also promote internal change so that the organization is adaptive in relation to the larger environment. Miller (1985) describes the internal part of the boundary as the *inline* under the control of the person, group, or organization. The external part of the boundary is the *outline*, or how others see the person, group, or organization. To the extent that the inline and outline are broadly *congruent*, there is a shared frame of reference and good communication. If there is a lack of a frame of reference, there may be a breakdown in the relationship between two people or between a group and the larger environment.

As an example, Rice and Rutan (1987), when discussing inpatient group psychotherapy, note the need to have two contracts, one for the outside boundary to the hospital and one for the inside boundary to the group. The outside contract, negotiated by the group therapist with the administration, needs four ingredients: group therapy consistent with the hospital's overall program; group as a primary treatment mode; group boundaries respected by patients and staff; and all patients to participate in group. The four ingredients of the inside contract, negotiated between the therapist and patients, are the following: Members attend all sessions; patients do not discuss information revealed by other members with non–group patients; patients bring all non–group member discussions back to the group; and communication is by talking only. For group therapy to be effective these contracts must be *congruent*.

Related to the concept of group boundary is the issue of the leader's *authority*. In Rice's (1969) last published paper, before his early death at the age of sixty-one, his basic propositions were that (1) the effectiveness of every intergroup relationship is determined by how much groups have to defend against uncertainty about the integrity of their boundaries, and that (2) every relationship—between individuals, within small groups and within large groups, as well as between groups—has the charcteristics of an intergroup relationship. A corollary of the first proposition is that any intergroup relationship carries with it the possibility of a breakdown in *authority*, the threat of chaos and the fear of disaster. Rice worked throughout his life, in his writings, organizational consultations, and group training conferences to endorse the authority of the leader to manage group and organizational boundaries. In outpatient clinical work, therapists often deny or refuse to discuss the basis of their authority. Such a stance produces unclear boundaries around the treatment and prevents additional learning and change on the part of patients (Newton, 1973). Similarly, trainees in many hospital settings have little authority over their therapy group (patients do not attend and/or are called out of sessions for individual treatment), thus making group therapy a less effective vehicle for learning and change.

With regard to *leadership*, the focus has been primarily on external boundary management. An important aspect of the executive function is to maintain a position on the external boundary of the group, importing supplies, exporting products or services, relating the group/organization to the external world, and protecting the organization from environmental stresses. The leader uses his authority to control and protect the boundary by monitoring the forces that intrude on the work group/organization. Without a well-managed external boundary, an organization cannot survive for long, nor can a psychotherapy group treat patients within a coherent and predictable environment. Therapists, in their leader roles, have to develop a good flow of referrals, use appropriate screening, and negotiate contracts with different clinical agencies.

The *leader* is seen as "Janus-like," looking inward and outward, dealing with pressure from both directions. Rice's (1965) emphasis upon the mutual dependency and hostility residing in followers and leaders is noteworthy because hostility is often ignored by other systems approaches. The difference is due to the level of systems analysis. Tavistock writers focus more on the external boundary management of top leaders, not the needs of middle managers or workers. Rice wished to enable leaders to develop insights that would allow them to stand amid the multiple cross-pressures accompanying their roles. In a university-affiliated community mental health clinic, Johnson and Howenstein (1982) note that for a group psychotherapy program to be effective it must be endorsed by *top* management (academic and administrative), have credibility in the eyes of outside referral sources, staff, and patients, and have a *leader* with organizationally sanctioned authority. Kernberg (1975) notes that accurate group *leader* interventions require clarity about the primary task, systems knowledge, and tolerance of conflicts (psychological, social, technical, cultural, and systems). He feels that the worst type of group leaders are those who combine severe narcissistic features with depreciation of learning, emotional depth, and moral convictions.

Tavistock social scientists proposed the concept of a *sociotechnical* system, a concept that points to the interrelatedness of technical and sociopsychological factors in production enterprises. The thrust of this work has been to call into question the salience of technology as *primarily* determining social, political, and other relationships within enterprises. Organizational *choice* is possible by designing forms of work organization that optimize the best *fit* among social, psychological, technical, political, and economic factors. In a hospital setting, the therapist needs to have a clear contract with the administration so that there is a flow of appropriate patients who will *fit* into the treatment group (Rice and Rutan, 1987). In outpatient settings, the director of a group program needs to obtain agreement with the admissions staff and the emergency room service so that patients who can benefit from group psychotherapy are referred for treatment, not dumped because there is an overflow of patients (Johnson and Howenstein, 1982).

Tavistock authors seek congruence between the system tasks and the structure utilized to enable those tasks to be completed. An important aspect of this work is its emphasis on *unconscious* motivation and hypotheses for relating organizational structures to individual ego-defensive processes. For instance, Menzies (1960) studied a hospital and found that the organizational structure formed a *social defense system* (drugs administered regardless of need, frequent rotations, and identical uniforms) which operated to eliminate activities and relationships with very sick or dying patients that evoke nursing staff anxieties. A study by Jaques (1955) showed that the negotiation of wage rates by management and labor in the Glacier Metal Company was affected by unconscious mechanisms for dealing with paranoid and depressive anxieties.

Two examples of treatment programs that met staff needs more than patient care further illustrate the social defense system. In a local hospital, frustrated female staff started a women's group, which was well received. Shortly afterward, envious male staff started a men's group. Interviews with staff revealed that both genders realized that a focused group moving patients toward discharge (as described by Yalom, 1983) would be more helpful to members. The single-sex groups met staff political needs and were a social defense against anger with the hospital administrator and staff intergender competition. Another example is a CMHC group treatment program where all teaching, training, and supervision focused on therapy with neurotics, which was a *defense* against acknowledging the changing patient population, which was becoming primarily borderline or psychotic.

Kets de Vries and Miller (1985) illustrate how organizational *culture* is powerfully influenced by common group fantasies. They studied three types of organizational cultures: fight–flight, dependency, and utopian (pairing). Fight–flight businesses assume there is an enemy, project hostile feelings, are suspicious, short-sighted, and impulsive, have explicit means but poorly defined goals, and have an insular management style. Dependency organizational cultures assume a nourishing and protective leader, are depressive, envious, and guilty, have a present-time perspective, specified goals, and a charismatic management style. The utopian organization has enthusiasm, a future-time perspective, a highly deliberative style, defined goals, but no means, and a democratic/participative management.

I taught a weekly group psychotherapy seminar for two years at a well-managed, patient-oriented small private hospital. The seminar focused on group therapy, discussed staff members' ongoing therapy groups (most group leaders were women), and supported the group enterprise and the therapist's authority. At the first session after a two-month summer break, the group themes were prostitution, violence, and rape. It turned out that during the summer break the hospital had been bought and sold three times! The hospital went from being a well-run institution with a somewhat utopian culture and a strong local medical and administrative staff, to being "in play" in the marketplace, with resulting systems anxiety. The therapy group themes thus reflected staff and patient anxieties about feeling out of control, being hurt, and selling one's body and soul. The women staff in particular felt bereft of strong, supportive male directors. The *culture* was now one of buy and sell, watch the bottom line, and be on guard: in short, a fight–flight mentality.

A social-psychological concept emphasized by Tavistock writers is *role*. There are both task and social roles. Organizations function only when leaders, in their task roles, draw and maintain appropriate boundaries between the enterprise and the larger environment. Such boundaries determine where responsibilities and authority start and stop. Today, with rapid societal changes, boundaries also create anxieties and fears that lead to withdrawal from the boundary back into the core of the organization. By working in one's organizationally sanctioned *role* and developing task-appropriate skills, people can stay at the boundary because the value of their work may contain such fears (Hirschhorn, 1988). In a Tavistock study group that provides members with opportunities to study their reactions to authority, the consultant in his *task role* sits on the boundary, sufficiently in the group to share common attitudes and feelings, while separate enough to observe the group. Metaphorically, the consultant sits behind his own "face" and allows the members to experience relationships intensely to a distant, "rational" authority figure (E. B. Klein and Astrachan, 1971).

The preceding nine social systems concepts have productive application to group therapy settings. Astrachan (1970) described three group therapeutic approaches: the analytically oriented patient-to-psychotherapist group, the member-to-member group, and the Bion-ian group-to-therapist orientation. In a systems model, encompassing these three approaches, the therapist is in the *role* of the central *regulator* who defines and maintains the boundary between the group and its environment. Thus, he defines what is in and what is outside, and what is relevant for the group's work. Such a definition tends to focus the group on either the patient's past, current member-to-member relationships, or group reactions to the therapist's authority. In the regulator role, therapists need an awareness that patients live in many systems (e.g., family, neighborhood, school, and work) that influence the relatively open treatment group. Also, therapists need some systems knowledge to assess whether the institutional setting (e.g., a private hospital, VA, or CMHC) facilitates or inhibits the therapy group.

Another factor influencing organizations and therapy and training groups is prior social relations. Organization members know each other through formal work, authority relations and/or through social contacts. These social dimensions are termed *sentient* relations, meaning a connection of mutual choice and commitment not necessarily prescribed by institutional roles (Rice, 1970). Such sentient links, supportive interpersonal ties, or *social roles* affect how members feel in groups and organizations. Indeed, prior social relations between two patients will have an impact on their behavior in an intense therapy group. For instance, because of therapist vacation and travel, patients may meet during the regular hour at a nearby restaurant, replacing their task roles for social roles. If there is a mutually agreed-upon contract explicitly stating that patients will not have their own meeting, doing so may be acting out against the clinician and the rules. Without such a contract, the patients may have done some good work on both social and task issues. Recently, a group met for two sessions while I was away and provided support for a member going through an unexpected crisis.

In sum, most of the European social systems work has occurred in *industrial* settings. Tavistock consultants have worked with labor, management, business, and government groups for over forty years. Sociotechnical interventions have increased productivity at Shell UK Limited in England (Hill, 1971) and decreased alienation in projects with workers, employers, and the Norwegian government (Thorsrud, 1969; Trist, 1970). Nevertheless, the social systems insights they have obtained are relevant to the workings of groups formed for clinical purposes.

Tavistock in America

The Tavistock approach was brought to the United States in 1965 at the first group relations conference cosponsored by the Washington School of Psychiatry and the Psychiatry Department of Yale Medical School. The involvement of the original clinical sponsors (plus other mental health organizations such as the Menninger Foundation) led to an emphasis on the training of clinicians and organizational consultations and research with hospital and CMHC staffs (E. B. Klein, 1978). The contributions in Colman and Geller's (1985) volume *Group Relations Reader 2* continue this clinical trend.

Traditionally trained therapists have used a Tavistock orientation to enhance understanding of administrative and organizational issues. Kernberg (1978) noted that the relationship between an organization and the environment induces regression in the group and then in the leadership. Menninger (1985) recognized a system-wide positive impact from the attendance of 142 staff at various group relations conferences over a ten-year period. Thus, Tavistock has been used to alert clinicians to administrative and organizational issues, thereby increasing their sensitivity to group process and perhaps also improving the potency of therapy groups. This work has been carried out at three levels.

At an *individual* level, Newton (1973) formulated both family and psychoanalytic psychotherapy within a social systems framework. He focused on the division of authority among father, mother, and child in the family and between the analyst and patient in therapy. Father and mother respectively manage the external and internal boundaries in the traditional family, while the therapist manages both boundaries in psychotherapy. Without a well-managed external boundary it is difficult to socialize the child in the family or do the internal therapeutic work in the treatment setting. Newton demonstrates the social-structural aspects of the psychotherapy situation that reactivate early experiences from the family system. Newton's social systems approach increases the possibility of patient and therapist being clear about (1) the realistic elements (authority and power relationships) in therapy, and (2) the transferential aspects, which are stimulated by the social structure of psychoanalytic psychotherapy. Newton demystifies transference by showing how managing the external boundary (fees, scheduling, etc.) leads to paternal transference, while being empathetic stimulates maternal transference. Therefore, therapists can stimulate maternal *and* paternal transference according to which boundary they are managing at any moment in the group.

At a *group* level, Singer, Astrachan, Gould, and Klein (1975) traced the influence of social systems thought on understanding training and therapeutic groups. They conceptualized group events as temporary institutions in which a variety of tasks are pursued, with the leader having managerial authority and responsibility for the group boundary. An accurate diagnosis of organizational needs is necessary for the proper design of a group event and a clear *contract* between leader and patients is necessary for optimal outcome. They felt that many group leaders assiduously deny boundary management and administrative issues. The authors provided guidelines so both patients and therapists could be clear about contractual understandings and the *roles* involved in treatment groups.

At a *systems* level, Rice and Rutan (1987) note the impact of the hospital as a system on a dynamically oriented therapy group. A change in staffing affects the ward, just as a therapist's vacation affects the treatment group. On the latter occasion, a split will occur, with some patients voicing pleasure about the therapist's vacation while others remain silent and feel angry at being abandoned. When both aspects of the split are expressed, patients are more able to contain the ambivalence within themselves and moved on from the issue. Gabbard (1989) also notes aspects of splitting in hospital treatment. A borderline patient unconsciously perceives two staff members in dramatically different ways, usually his therapist as an idealized figure and a ward nurse as insensitive and punitive. The staff members react, through protective identification, as though they actually were the projective aspects of the patient by assuming highly polarized positions which disrupt treatment meetings. He calls for clearer conceptual understanding of splitting in the hospital to allow for early detection and the development of strategies to manage patient and staff splitting.

Much of the clinical work in America has focused on how the dynamics of the psychiatric unit and hospital are reflected or mirrored in the small therapy group. This work has examined in a systematic way a total treatment approach combining three levels: the intrapsychic aspects of the patient, the interpersonal and group-as-a-whole forces of the psychotherapy group, and the dynamics of the larger ward and hospital (R. H. Klein, 1977, 1981; Kibel, 1981; R. H. Klein and Kugel, 1981). In addition, Newton and Levinson (1973) studied a psychiatric research ward that had competing tasks (biological research and clinical care). They showed how ambiguity and covert dissension interfered with patient care and negatively affected staff morale.

In sum, Melanie Klein has provided the underlying psychology at the *individual* level. Bion has applied her ideas and those of other object relations theorists to the functioning of small treatment and training *groups*. Rice has used these individual and group concepts in explicating the dynamics of larger social *systems*. Many of the authors cited above have applied these ideas to the functioning of complex industrial systems in England and other European countries. Because of the prestige of the original clinical sponsors in the United States, most of the systems work has taken place in health-care organizations. Another difference in application is that social systems *training* conferences have focused more on gender and race in America than in England, reflecting larger cultural dynamics (E. B. Klein, 1978).

Other Systems Theories

There are two other American social systems theories that inform our view of group treatment: the National Training Laboratories (NTL) and General Systems Theory (GST). NTL was influenced by the social psychologist Lewin (1936, 1950) and the Interpersonal Psychiatry of Sullivan (1953). Although there is diversity in analytic group psychotherapy (Kauff, 1979), it tends to stress *individual* transference to the therapist (Slavson, 1964). In Tavistock, learning occurs through insights into *shared* responses to authority (E. B. Klein and Astrachan, 1971). NTL does not explore fantasies or authority; rather, *peer* relations are highlighted. Trainers promote norms of trust, openness, and risk-taking by modeling such behavior. Change occurs not through insight, but by feedback (consensual validation) about one's behavior and by experimenting with *new* behavior. In clinical work, developing interpersonal skills is at least as important for many patients as dealing with staff authority. The group therapist most identified with this viewpoint is Yalom (1975), who sees the goals of psychotherapy as symptom relief and characterological change, with emphasis on patients' interpersonal relationships. Building on Sullivan and NTL, Yalom emphasizes peer relations, but historically has minimized systems issues such as the influence of hospital culture on the therapy group.

NTL is more positive than Tavistock in its assumptions about the foundation and the potential of human nature, as the following examples illustrate. Maslow (1965) wrote of a society of self-actualizers. McGregor's (1960) Theory Y is a management philosophy oriented toward higher order needs (i.e., self-actualization). Argyris (1957, 1964, 1968) aided employees of large organizations by focusing on competence acquisition, not unconscious processes. Alderfer and Klein (1978) noted that McGregor addressed internal issues of leadership in order to reduce the distance between leaders and followers.

In an equally positive view, Bennis and Shepard (1956) found that small groups evolve from dependency on the trainer to interdependence and consensual validation. Training groups usually move, often through a rebellious act (Slater, 1966), from dependent authority relations to collaborative peer relations. NTL consultants use Katz and Kahn's (1966) open systems theory, which emphasized organizational structure, interests of employees, and the relationship between the organization and its environment. The underlying psychology is positive, interpersonally focused, and process-oriented, minimizing distance between leaders and followers and stressing peer rather than authority relations.

General systems theory (GST) has its roots in biology's open systems theory, developed by von Bertalanffy (1950, 1968). The basic characteristics of open systems are as follows. (1) Cycles of energy from the environment are transformed into a product which feeds back into the environment. (2) More energy is imported into the open system than is used. It is stored to counter entropic (decaying) forces. (3) Information is processed by the system to maintain awareness of the total environment. (4) If one element changes in the system, others change proportionally. (5) There is an increase in complexity over time. (6) The final state can be reached in several ways from one initial state, and similar initial states may lead to different final states (equifinality). A committee of the American Group Psychotherapy Association worked to apply GST to the practice of group psychotherapy. J. Durkin (1981) discussed GST as a living system in which processes autonomously cause themselves. This occurs through the closing of boundaries to distinguish a system from the environment and the opening of boundaries to the outside world in order to transform system structure.

GST authors do not focus on external boundary, authority, and hierarchical relations, as do Tavistock theorists, nor on internal boundary and peer and interpersonal relationships, as do NTL writers. For instance, Swogger (1981) noted that the group therapist is more *in* the group than on the boundary like Tavistock consultants or in a neutral role like traditional psychoanalysts. Kissen (1980) noted that moving between cognition and emotion led to enhanced learning and personal growth. When groups move between open and closed boundaries—systeming and summing (J. Durkin, 1980)—they can act like a collaborative group or like one person. For instance, a basic assumption group may at first be marked by a fused oneness, and then, after a consultant's intervention, by clearer boundaries. GST writers suggest that therapists focus on a number of dimensions rather than confining themselves primarily to authority or peer relations, as do Tavistock or NTL-oriented leaders. Therapists should

TABLE 1
Some Characteristics of Three Social Systems Theories

Dimensions	Tavistock	NTL	GST
Boundaries	Outer	Inner	Move between Both
Level of Intervention	Group as a Whole	Interpersonal	Intrapersonal, Interpersonal, and Group
Emphasis on Authority	High	Low	Medium
Focus	Leader	Peer Relations	Leader and Peers
Theory	Conflict	Growth/Change	Growth/Change
Unconscious Processes	Yes: Group	No	Yes: Individual

actively manage the opening and closing of boundaries, not emphasize the external *or* internal boundary. GST-oriented clinicians should use a growth or autonomy model, not a conflict model. Finally, therapists should not maintain either a distant or close relation with group members but should move back and forth as called for by ongoing dynamic interactions.

GST authors tend to be more flexible, advocate an "experience-near" psychology, and focus on what is being expressed rather than what is being concealed. These writers are closer to self and humanistic psychology than to traditional psychoanalytic views of group therapy. At first this may seem strange, but Kohut has succeeded in integrating many of Rogers's concepts of humanistic psychology into his version of psychoanalysis (Kahn, 1985). Both Kohut and Rogers were concerned with creating an understanding, empathetic relationship rather than maintaining the neutral stance of traditional analysts.

Table 1 summarizes some characteristics that distinguish between these three social systems theories as applied to group therapy. Tavistock stresses the outer boundary, employs group-as-a-whole interventions, highlights authority relations by focusing on the leader, and uses a conflict theory that stresses unconscious process at a group level. In contrast, NTL emphasizes the inner boundary with interventions on the interpersonal level, minimizes authority, and stresses peer relations by using a growth/change theory that ignores unconscious processes. GST tends to be in the middle, moving between the inner and outer group boundary, focusing both on leaders and peers, advocating moderate leader authority, intervening at all three levels, and using a growth/change theory that tends to recognize unconscious processes at an individual level only. The latter may possibly be due to the previous training of GST authors.

Systems Theories and Group Therapy

All systems theorists agree that every group has a boundary that distinguishes it from the environment. The leader's role involves boundary identification and regulation. Since a group is an evolving social system, if a person or subsystem changes, it affects the total group. Indeed, such changes tend to be mirrored within all levels of a system (E. B. Klein and Gould, 1973). There is a constant interaction with the environment, which can be understood as a "throughput" process with input, conversion, and output phases. Moreover, the group is affected by society in terms of values, norms, roles, and other social characteristics (i.e., gender, age, and race).

Systems theorists agree that members play roles, influenced by the larger society, but can move toward individual authority, autonomy, and growth (Bennis and Shepard, 1956). This takes place as groups go through various stages of development involving group formation, dependency, authority, intimacy, and independence. Systems theories suggest that four levels of analysis are needed to account for group life: intrapersonal, interpersonal, group-as-a-whole (Singer et al., 1975), and intergroup (Rice, 1963; Alderfer, 1970) or superordinate frame (H. Durkin, 1981). The fourth level is important in understanding an interdependent treatment group embedded in a larger culture. Indeed, group therapy would seem to be an antidote to the domestic disorder of our age: a fragmented ability to relate (Rutan and Stone, 1984).

Systems theory has become more widely discussed and integrated into training and educational events, and as a consequence group therapists are more likely to focus on intrapersonal, interpersonal, and group levels, than when Singer and his colleagues (1975) wrote their paper. In the last decade and a half, societal changes and the resulting narcissism and envy (Kahn, 1985) have encouraged clinicians to become both more eclectic and systematic in their thinking and practice. Dynamically oriented group therapists are more likely to explore defenses, resistances, and object relations at personal, peer, and group levels. They are more aware of changes in boundaries as treatment progresses through various developmental stages. Ashbach and Schermer (1987) note that clinicians from various traditions are more willing to explore *group* myths to estimate the nature of inner objects (Kleinians), the structure of the self (Kohutians), and unconscious fantasies (Freudians).

Most systems theorists would agree that after a clear contract and outer boundary are established by the therapist, patients can then take up their roles and the group can become less focused on authority and more on intermember concerns. As patients do the work of understanding individual, interpersonal, and group dynamics, thus working on the inner boundary, some affect is withdrawn from the clinician and patients can become more autonomous individuals. Over time, patients can become less passive and may develop into the role of group problem-solvers. As patients understand and accept the complexity of group life they are better able to integrate fantasy and reality, shift from unconscious to conscious processes, and move from the warmth of small-group life to thinking about and then crossing the boundary to the cold outside world. This tends to occur as members pair or identify with the work leadership of the therapist, process conflicts, and then move on to growth and change. The preceding developmental process takes time; it happens as patients experience a well-managed group boundary by the therapist and internalize a *work group role* by mastering observing and communicating skills. When the members are capable of insights into their own processes, they realistically are less dependent on the clinician. As noted by Ashbach and Schermer (1987), when the group has introjected the therapist's interpretative functions, treatment becomes psychotherapy *by* the group.

Currently, clinicians tend to be in dual roles as therapists and group dynamics experts (Yalom, 1975). As clinicians explicate different processes, they aid the group's development. These interventions can be understood as a teaching device that helps patients learn about individual, peer and collective dynamics. As patients become more knowledgeable, they become less dependent and feel more adult, responsible, independent, and authoritative. Like members in training groups, outpatient group therapy patients become more sophisticated about individual, interpersonal, group, and intergroup processes. Thus they are more ready to change and able to take up their societal role and drop their patient/member role (E. B. Klein, 1977).

One of the best papers on systems theory and group therapy is by Johnson and Howenstein (1982) who reported a case analysis of an ailing group psychotherapy program at the Connecticut Mental Health Center (CMHC). Using social systems concepts, they studied the organizational structure, distribution of resources, flow of patients, and the larger culture and then implemented interventions that revitalized this outpatient group treatment program. The authors started by noting the difficulties which face many group psychotherapy programs, the belief that group is second-class treatment. They found a set of three interrelated conditions which underlay the weaknesses in the group program: inappropriate utilization, widespread devaluation, and inadequate organization. *Inappropriate utilization* resulted from deficiencies in the admission process, interprogram conflicts, and inadequate matching of group treatment with patient characteristics. To address these problems, they started an orientation group with the unit chief as cotherapist, participated in a divisionwide patient placement committee, and extended group therapy to include borderline and psychotic patients, who are most of the clients of the CMHC. There were three aspects of the *devaluation* of group psychotherapy: the larger cultural emphasis on individualism, fear of group treatment (trainees being seen as "sick" or incompetent) and the low academic status of group psychotherapy. Responses included recognition of biased cultural attitudes, adopting policies to overcome trainee fears of group psychotherapy, providing relevant teaching, and initiating research projects. *Inadequate organization* included weak leadership with insufficient authority and a fragmented service structure. To improve the service, a committed, well-trained group psychotherapist leader who maximized formal and personal authority was hired. New group forums and communication channels were used to shore up the fragmented structure.

Johnson and Howenstein (1982) note that the unhealthy state of group psychotherapy programs will not be improved until group treatment is used and valued by the clinical community. For group psychotherapy to rise above its image as second-class treatment, organizational support must be improved. Clinicians need to become convinced of the values of group treatment: interaction with others with similar problems, the chance to give and receive help, a safe place for experimenting with new, more constructive behaviors, and the healing qualities of a cohesive group.

In systems terms, the *primary task* for revitalization of the program was recognized as treatment of sicker patients; the *open systems* aspects of referrals and patient flow were rationally addressed; *boundaries* were better managed; a strong, committed unit *leader* was appointed and his *authority* was endorsed from above, causing group therapists to feel more authorized to do their work. *Sociotechnical* aspects were highlighted by negotiating a contract which fit both the setting and treatment of sicker patients; the systems *defense* against recognition of the changing patient population was addressed by focusing on borderline and psychotic symptomatology in teaching and supervision; the *culture* became more supportive, going from flight to hope as these changes occurred, and group therapists experienced *role* enhancement and higher morale.

APPLICATIONS

This section reviews a number of applications of systems theory to selection criteria, a group therapy session, consultation, research, and future directions. A unique application of social systems theories to group psychotherapy is the intergroup level of analysis. It is a reminder of the embeddedness of the treatment group in the larger professional world of the clinician and the social matrix of patients. What the therapist and patients bring to the clinical enterprise will clearly affect who and what gets into the group. Because societal boundary relations are more permeable today, therapy reflects these changes by greater inclusion than exclusion of patients for group treatment. The therapist's role as boundary manager/regulator (Astrachan, 1970) is illustrated with regard to planning a group and taking into account role, gender, and age. The following discussion is an attempt to illustrate how social systems theory, particularly the concept of role, can guide clinical practice or stimulate research, not to exhaustively review such complex topics.

Group Therapy Selection Criteria and the Concept of Role

Yalom (1975), historically the most influential writer on group psychotherapy, suggested the inadvisability of group treatment for boring, monopolist, self-righteous moralists, "help rejecting complainers," and silent patients. Most systems authors would contend that these categories are group *roles* that patients enact for their own and the group's "benefit." Therefore, such roles can be explored, understood, and changed in a therapeutic group setting. From a systems perspective, one can treat these patients in group therapy by focusing on what the patient and the other group members get out of such *role* enactment, and what can be gained by changed behavior for all the clients.

Bogdanoff and Elbaum (1978) noted that successful group psychotherapy is marked by the achievement of role fluidity. When patients get trapped in a position, they experience role lock, a condition that fosters stereotyped behavior, increases dependency on the therapist, and limits growth. Focal-conflict theory (Whitaker and Lieberman, 1964) holds that the group's basic wish is countered by a fear, leading to a focal conflict. Bogdanoff and Elbaum (1978) see role lock as a compromise solution to a focal conflict. For instance, when the group wishes for control but fears domination, a monopolizer arises who seeks control by excessive talking. Only patients with role-congruent dynamics are "selected"; monopolizers are often diagnosed as obsessive and manic. While the monopolizer deals with his anxiety by continually talking, the group values him because he relieves members of their own anxiety and responsibilities.

Interventions need to come from both the therapist and members, and be directed at the monopolizer *and* the group support system, since he can only "get away" with such behavior with the group's support. Members rarely acknowledge their behavior; instead, the monopolizer is scapegoated. At this point the therapist can intervene: "I notice that Sally is doing most of the talking; I wonder if this solves the problem for the others?" To be effective, the therapist needs to understand the dual nature of the lock (individual dynamics and group support system), recognize the group wish and fear, and intervene appropriately so the group will stop pressuring the monopolizer and she can get out of the role lock.

Horwitz (1983) broadens our understanding by noting that projective identification has both intrapsychic and interpersonal aspects that energize role-suction, mobilizing the spokesman and scapegoat roles. Arsenian, Semrad, and Shapiro (1962) and Redl (1963) observed that groups need role occupants and draft their most likely candidates to fulfill the needed functions. Group forces pressure or suck a member into the needed role, and that patient then becomes the repository of other members' projections. Members also pick out a spokesperson to express the dominant group theme. Groups learn members' valency (Bion, 1959) toward the basic assumptions (dependency, pairing, fight–flight) and other affects and use their knowledge (consciously or unconsciously) to further their aims. A therapist knows this is happening when a patient who is "speaking for the group" is given lots of air time and is not sidetracked; when the same patient is speaking "only for himself," there is little interest or support, and often the subject is changed.

Scapegoating is expressed in two ways: (1) displacing aggressive impulses felt toward the therapist (who is not a safe target) onto a patient, or (2) projecting desired but threatening impulses onto one patient because of the group need to repress such feelings. The patient goes along with the suction since it meets his internal needs and since he is being manipulated as the group's projections exaggerate his behavior. Therefore, there is always a collusion between the patient's character style (valency) and the group's dominant need. From a systems view, the therapist needs to interpret *both* the patient's and group's contribution to the process to make it conscious, facilitate discussion, and stop the suction process and scapegoating so that patients are seen as persons, *not* just roles.

With regard to gender, therapists should not allow a token woman as a patient (Kantor, 1977). Such a patient will be seen and treated as a role, "The Woman," rather than as a complete person. Rutan and Stone (1984) noted that groups should have at least three members of each gender, but that is not always possible. No matter what the gender proportions, the psychosexual dynamics of the larger culture will be enacted in the treatment group. The clinician, therefore, has to monitor his own gender feelings (countertransferences) in order to maintain the boundary of the group. The therapist also needs to be on guard so that a single patient, or a pair of either gender, is not made into a stereotyped object for unwanted feelings by processes of splitting and projective identification. These processes lead to gender stereotypes, such as "All women are bitches" or "All men are controlling and dominant."

With regard to age, Yalom (1975, 1985) has argued for group homogeneity, suggesting that one older or younger patient in a group would be stereotyped, seen in the role of "The Youth" or "The Elder," not as an individual. However, research suggests that age may not be the only issue; rather, the *stage* of adult development is also important. Stage refers to the altering transitional (age thirty and midlife transitions) and stable (settling down) periods, as described in the work of Levinson, Darrow, Klein, Levinson, and McKee (1977) on male adult development. For instance, Smith, Cardillo, and Choate (1984) reported that over 300 men in brief inpatient treatment responded more positively to therapy during transitional periods than in stable stages. At least for male patients, treatment while in an adult transitional stage appears more predictive of positive outcome than chronological age per se. The finding that patients in transitional life stages make more changes in therapy may be due to their role boundaries and relationships being more flexible and permeable, and, therefore, subject to reevaluation/change during such periods of development.

In his inpatient book, Yalom (1983) modified the term "curative" factors to "therapeutic" factors. This modification may illustrate the influence of the mental hospital *system* on treatment. That is, treating more disturbed patients in shorter periods of time (as decided often by third parties) with less control experienced by the group therapist may have led to modifying the "curative" label derived from outpatient therapy. Inpatient work may have also influenced Yalom (1983) to be more inclusive in his group composition and treatment criteria for inpatients and also, to some extent, for outpatients (Yalom, 1985). Since society has become more open it makes systems sense that selection criteria should become more inclusive with regard to role, gender, age, and diagnosis.

A Group Therapy Session

The following is an illustration of a group boundary violation and its impact on members' core conflicts around intrusion and loneliness. An outpatient psychotherapy group for chronic mentally ill patients has been meeting weekly at a community mental health center for the past ten years. Patients vary in diagnosis: borderline, recurrent major depression, and schizophrenia, often complicated by physical illnesses. All are on medication. They range in age from the mid-thirties to the late sixties. Most are poor or lower middle class, and none are presently employed primarily due to their psychiatric illnesses. I have been the therapist for two and one-half years. Of the eight current patients, five are women and three of the eight patients are married.

The meeting began with my asking Martin to check with the office about his bill. He said that he would take care of it. This was followed by discussion of another bill that Martin received. John and Judy were surprised about the amount. There was then a discussion of the difficulty in obtaining a medical card. I asked what was required to get this card. Judy and Martin said that you had to have copies of rent receipts, medical bills, and telephone bills.

At this point, Florence, who had not attended a meeting for about a year, came in dressed sexily. She appeared a little hyperactive, and said she wanted to stay for ten minutes. Florence wondered if I had dismissed her from the rolls. I said yes. At that point her daughter came in and said, "Come on mama," and although Florence wanted to stay, she left with her daughter.

John commented about having seen a woman whose name he couldn't remember; she had been in the group, talked a great deal, and had to be told to be quiet. She had dropped out and gone to a day treatment center. Martin talked about Larry, his brother, who should be going to a day treatment center. Larry is a chronic schizophrenic who stays at home with their mother and won't even take out the garbage. Martin goes over and makes certain the garbage cans are out. Martin talked about his mother just being a block away.

Mother doesn't want people intruding on her, he said. Judy talked about her daughter, who had finally moved out with her four kids. Judy was greatly relieved. "I couldn't stand to have them around."

I commented, "I wonder if people are reacting to Florence coming in, talking a lot, and intruding." Judy said, "Yes, I hadn't liked it. I felt nervous. I really wanted to be alone." This was followed by "I do sometimes need people." I said, "This is a problem that everyone struggles with; both wanting to have privacy and wanting to be around people." Judy told a story of being invited to a birthday party, a situation that she didn't handle well. She hadn't wanted to go and got very nervous. She had to leave before the food was served. Martin asked whether there wasn't some sort of illness that people had because they were afraid to be around others. I wondered, "Are you talking about how you feel here in the group with others present?" Judy said that she felt good here, but the moment she left she began to get nervous. Sally (the youngest member) complained about her mother-in-law controlling her. Kris felt intruded on by a grandchild dumped on her doorstep by her unmarried daughter. Martin talked about wanting to be alone. He said his daughter and her boyfriend were over at the house and a woman he had known previously called. He blew up because his daughter had given his unlisted phone number to her. Martin has an unlisted phone number because he feels he gets so angry he doesn't want to be intruded on. Toni, who often complained about no one being available, said she had an unlisted phone. Judy said she also has an unlisted phone number and that she doesn't want anybody intruding on her. Martin said that this is a problem because he needs friends, and yet he gets angry, which drives people away, and he is afraid that there won't be anybody available.

This was the most clear-cut discussion of the emotional dilemmas these patients deal with in their daily lives. Members are basically struggling to maintain their personal boundaries and, in the process, make them so tight that nobody can engage them. This state is expressed as a fear of intrusion and loneliness, an equally painful affective condition. However, the tightly drawn boundaries are the cause of the isolation. In the session, the reality of Florence's entry evoked associations and helped members look at their conflicts involving their personal boundary integrity. At one level patients know that although they say they would like to be alone, their behavior, their very presence in the group, says something different. The inevitable variety of experiences in the group helps bring such conflicts into the open where members can begin to collectively address these issues.

In *systems* terms, the group started with *external* administrative, financial issues. The dramatic *boundary violation* by Florence and her daughter brought family relations *into* the group, stimulated richer personal/family associations, greater member participation, and more interpersonal conversation, and led to the sharing of secrets. For instance, I did not know that any of the group members had unlisted telephones. Given their lack of financial resources, I was very surprised. On reflection, I realized it ties into the group's preferred interpersonal style: avoiding the world. The problem with having such tight personal boundaries is that it carries a very high price: loneliness.

Sharing these concerns made them group-as-a-whole issues; universality (Yalom, 1975) came into play, and members felt less deviant or odd. Covert issues became more conscious and peer relations were enhanced. Although the associations may, at first, seem unconnected, they speak to *groupwide* concerns having to do with abandonment and loneliness. Sharing helped patients to be more *task-oriented*, experience their own feelings with some sense of *authority*, and be in a more understanding problem-solving role.

My focusing on the group's reaction to the *boundary violation* freed patients to express and share their emotional dilemmas in a fashion that acknowledges their roles in their problem without being dependent on me to offer a "magical" solution. That is, a few patients, *speaking for the group*, adapted a *work stance*, minimized basic assumption *dependence*, and *paired* with me to enhance understanding of individual and common group concerns.

Consultation

Systems training and consultation should be available for mental health professionals because it offers a broad, non–self-blaming perspective on clinical/organizational work. It reminds trainees of how the organization affects the treatment in powerful ways that they need to understand in order to be effective clinicians. For instance, a VA patient may make limited progress since greater improvement may endanger VA benefits. Or a patient may choose to remain on welfare and receive medical benefits, although he could obtain a minimum wage job without health benefits. At the least, systems training helps counterbalance trainees' exclusive focus on a psychodynamic or behavioral orientation. This added perspective provides an explanation for problematic treatments other than exclusively attributing such problems to trainees' personal inadequacies. While some trainees may need more treatment, they also may be ignorant of the organizational context in which behavior occurs.

For example, I was called in as a consultant to help an educational system understand why students had stopped going to a highly valued group psychotherapy supervision seminar and were withdrawn, sick and/or depressed. In the past, the instructor had always received the highest teacher evaluations, and his was the most popular course in the institute. The administration was baffled by this sudden turn-around in attendance and the low morale among students and faculty.

When doing consultation, I use an open-systems organizational stance, paying attention to intrapersonal, interpersonal, group, and intergroup levels. When visiting the Institute, I found that it had a three-year program, with training in individual, group, and family therapy. There was an *unwritten* understanding that all students were expected to spend *only* one year in each treatment modality seminar and then move on to the next course. Since the consultation was endorsed by management and resources were provided, I conducted interviews at all levels in the organization. They revealed that the group therapy instructor was a "wonderful, charismatic" teacher who involved students by using seminar process to illuminate group treatment issues. The attendance problem occurred in this senior teacher's seminar, in which, because of his own "narcissistic needs," he manipulated the students to request and obtain a second year of group supervision.

When other faculty discovered that students had been granted a second year of group supervision with this senior teacher, they were enraged and made biting comments about the group program's "imperialism." Students were then caught in the middle between a popular group instructor and angry faculty, particularly the family therapy teachers, who lost all of the trainees. Students resolved the systems tension by becoming sick and/or dropping out of the group seminar one at a time until the course had to be canceled. In general, there was a lack of discussion of the whole incident, until the cancellation.

My consultation was about the need for better boundary management. Clearly, the instructor broke the unwritten contract with the collusion of the students. Subsequent faculty anger led to student sickness or withdrawal and the cancellation of the course. After separate meetings with the individual, group, and family therapy faculties, and with students and senior administrators, there now is a clearly *written* policy about course sequences and time *limits* on each treatment modality. There is also less capitulating to student wishes and a clearer functioning faculty group (who had historically denied their own competitiveness but unconsciously encouraged students to act it out on their behalf). Regular bimonthly meetings between administrators, faculty, and students have been instituted.

These changes occurred after focusing on individual (charismatic instructor), interpersonal (faculty competitiveness), group (dependent student culture) and systems (student/faculty and administration/faculty) issues. The group instructor and students were not viewed by me as pathological, but rather as "speaking for" or enacting unresolved systems difficulties. By not personalizing these issues, students, faculty, and administration were able to work on them in a more open fashion. In a follow-up visit, communication has increased and sick days among institute students and faculty has decreased.

Research

A social systems perspective is useful in conducting research on group therapy since it considers the broader cultural, attitudinal, and institutional factors that influence treatment. Greene, Abramowitz, Davidson, and Edwards (1980) found that referrals to groups were influenced by myths and irrational ideas about group therapy. This happened when clinical settings were marked by a lack of understanding of group therapy on the part of staff, who shared an assumption that group is a second-class or nonpreferred treatment modality. Clearly such social *systems* issues impact on which patients will be referred, the status of the therapy and the therapist, and the likelihood of conducting a "successful" treatment group. Similarly, Johnson and Howenstein (1982) had to address systems issues of authority, leadership, boundary management, and the larger culture before revitalizing an ailing group psychotherapy program.

Most of the empirical research has been done with training groups, not therapy groups. The two groups differ in many ways: learning versus change as the primary task; trainee versus patient role; short- versus long-term commitment; massed versus spaced sessions; and different cultures. Nevertheless, since both are open systems there are similarities in boundary, authority, leadership, and social defense issues. But given these differences, implications drawn from research done on training groups have to be qualified when applied to psychotherapy groups.

Research about social systems variables has been conducted mostly with groups done in the Tavistock tradition. These studies have involved members' self-report of learning three months after participation in dynamically oriented group relations conferences focused on unconscious processes and authority relations. In a series of studies, it was found that residential training, where boundaries between the conference and the participants' ordinary activities are easier to manage and regulate, leads to more learning than nonresidential conferences (E. B. Klein, Stone, Correa, Astrachan, and Kossek, 1989). Strong organizational support (the outside social system), as evidenced by sponsorship of training events, authority and sentient links between staff and members, and an open environment, facilitate member learning (E. B. Klein, Correa, Howe, and Stone, 1983). In addition, men and women participants report more learning with female than male small-group leaders (Correa, Klein, Stone, Astrachan, Kossek, and Komarraju, 1988). The authors proposed that this finding is in part a consequence of the novelty of women in leadership/authority roles in members' adult lives. The meaning of this novelty effect for therapy groups is less clear where women have had a more central role in the clinical community.

The implications of these Tavistock systems studies for therapy are that patients may benefit most from groups that are strongly endorsed by powerful institutions valuing such treatment programs. Institutions open to new ideas and approaches will be more supportive of group therapy. Patient familiarity with the therapist, by reputation or from previous therapy experiences, should enhance effective treatment. Malan, Balfour, Hood, and Shooter (1976) found that patients at the Tavistock Clinic in London who benefited the most from group therapy had prior psychotherapy and were familiar with the treatment format and the therapist stance.

There have been some empirical studies contrasting Tavistock and NTL small groups. Tavistock consultants focus on group-as-a-whole process and authority relations, whereas NTL trainers focus more on peer relations. As predicted, Tavistock consultants produced more "transferential" reactions than did NTL group trainers (E. B. Klein, 1977). In this study it was also found that Tavistock, well-bounded small groups go through seven stages: becoming a member (giving up one's societal role); fusion; dependency; fight; flight; pairing (in a sophisticated work stance with the consultant); and leaving the group or giving up the member role.

To broaden the scope of this section, let us briefly note other relevant work. Clinical/descriptive, nonempirical papers on inpatient groups show the effects of systems issues on treatment. R. H. Klein (1981) identified the intergroup nature of the patient–staff community meeting; Kibel (1978) noted how the dynamics of the unit affect group psychotherapy; and Rice and Rutan (1987) highlight the importance of a contract with both the hospital administration and group members. The limited small-training-group research and descriptive systems work suggest the central importance of a clear contract between the therapist and the institution and/or group, and boundary identification, control, and regulation. It is only with a well-negotiated contract and managed boundary that patients can feel safe and trusting, so they can engage in treatment. A well-bounded therapy group can explore patients' authority reactions to the therapist, and then peer relations. One hypothesis is that clear developmental stages may be linked to clarity and control of group boundaries. In clearly bounded groups, after an initial fused or dependent stage, when patients are focused on the therapist, the basic assumptions occur. There will be marked splitting if the boundary is not regulated or if patients feel out of control. A later stage involves sophisticated pairing with the therapist to work on understanding individual, interpersonal, and group processes that lead to members giving up the patient role and leaving the group. This process may engender more affect and possibly be more effective with female than male group therapists.

Implications for the Future

Astrachan and Astrachan (1989b) state that over a quarter of physicians are employed by organizations (such as hospitals, CMHCs, and HMOs), often ones over which their profession once exerted control. The authors note that this has led to a shift in locus of autonomy over practice from the individual to the group. This process is uncomfortable for physicians. The writers observe that organizational structures impact autonomy and overall effectiveness. We spend billions of dollars yearly on health care delivered in organizational settings, yet medical schools do not take the understanding of organizations seriously or as worthy of scholarly investigation. This argument can easily be extended to other health-care professionals who increasingly find themselves working in multitiered complex organizations. In order for mental health workers to understand their primary task, roles, and boundary management responsibilities in changing, controlled, and hierarchical organizations, they need an understanding of social systems. In addition, since group therapy is more complex than individual treatment, group psychotherapists in particular will require sophisticated social systems training to be effective in ever more complex health systems.

Astrachan and Astrachan (1989a) also describe how the rapid growth in private hospital practice, increased connections between public and private sectors of care, managed health care programs, and the growth of the insurance industry act to restrict psychiatric care. These four forces have created a two-tiered system. The authors conclude that we need to advocate vigorously for the adequate and equitable support of psychiatric services for the poor, the elderly, and the disabled, in the face of demands for organizational profit. A social systems model may prove particularly useful for those clinicians working with various societally disenfranchised, politically underrepresented or ostracized groups—for example, the chronically ill, AIDS patients, children and adolescents, victims of abuse, and the poor. A systems perspective may be combined with other motivational psychologies (behavioral, humanistic, analytic, object relations, and self psychology) to arrive at a more powerful and comprehensive understanding of therapy groups as bounded social systems. Indeed, it may be intergroup (including social class) issues that interfere with chronically ill hospitalized patients being treated and then accepted back across the boundary into the community. The wish to split off and isolate such patients is powerful; much systems-based work, which is broad in scope and nonblaming, is needed if the treatment of the previously mentioned client groups is to be successfully addressed.

Ideally, more systems-oriented research on group therapy in both inpatient and outpatient settings will be done in the future. Research should evaluate how role, gender, stage of adult development, and social-class factors influence group treatment. A social systems approach will allow tomorrow's mental health professionals to combine it with whatever clinical/theoretical orientation they prefer in order to be more effective group psychotherapists.

REFERENCES

Alderfer, C. P. (1970), Understanding laboratory education: An overview. *Monthly Labor Review*, 93:18–27.

——— Klein, E. B. (1978), Affect, leadership and organizational boundaries. *J. Pers. Soc. Systems*, 1:19–35.

Argyris, C. (1957), *Personality and Organization*. New York: Harper & Row.

——— (1964), *Integrating the Individual and the Organization*. New York: Wiley.

——— (1968), Conditions for competence, acquisition and therapy. *J. Appl. Behav. Sci.*, 4:147–177.

Arsenian, J., Semrad, E. V., & Shapiro, D. (1962), An analysis of integral functions in small groups. *Internat. J. Group Psychother.*, 12:421–434.

Ashbach, C., & Schermer, V. L. (1987), *Object Relations, the Self, and the Group: A Conceptual Paradigm*. London: Routledge & Kegan Paul.

Astrachan, B. M. (1970), Towards a social systems model of therapeutic groups. *Soc. Psychiat.*, 5:110–119.

——— Astrachan, J. H. (1989a), Economics of practice and inpatient care. *Gen. Hosp. Psychiat.*, 11:313–319.

Astrachan, J. H., & Astrachan, B. M. (1989b), Medical practice in organized settings: Redefining medical autonomy. *Arch. Internal Med.*, 149:1509–1513.

Bennis, W. G., & Shepard, H. A. (1956), A theory of group development. *Human Rel.*, 9:415–437.

Bertalanffy, L. von (1950), The theory of open systems in physics and biology. *Sci.*, 3:23–29.

—— (1968), *General Systems Theory: Foundations, Development, Applications.* New York: Braziller.

Bion, W. (1959), *Experiences in Groups.* London: Tavistock Publications.

Bogdanoff, M., & Elbaum, P. L. (1978), Role lock: Dealing with monopolizers, mistrusters, isolates, helpful Hannahs, and other assorted characters in group psychotherapy. *Internat. J. Group Psychother.*, 28:247–262.

Colman, A. D., & Geller, M. H. (1985), *Group Relations Reader 2.* Washington, DC: A. K. Rice Institute.

Correa, M. E., Klein, E. B., Stone, W. N., Astrachan, J. H., Kossek, E. E., & Komarraju, M. (1988), Reactions to women in authority: The impact of gender on learning in group relations conferences. *J. Appl. Behav. Sci.*, 24:219–233.

Durkin, H. (1981), The group therapies and general systems theory as an integrative structure. In: *Living Groups: Group Psychotherapy and General Systems Theory,* ed. J. Durkin. New York: Brunner/Mazel.

Durkin, J. (1980), Boundarying: The structure of autonomy. Seventh Annual Ludwig von Bertalanffy Memorial Address. Society for General Systems Research, San Francisco.

—— (1981), *Living Groups: Group Psychotherapy and General Systems Theory.* New York: Brunner/Mazel.

Emery, F. E., & Trist, E. L. (1960), Sociotechnical systems. In: *Management Sciences: Models and Techniques,* ed. C. W. Churchman & M. Verhulst. New York: Pergamon.

Ezriel, H. (1950), A psychoanalytic approach to group treatment. *Brit. J. Med. Psychol.*, 23:50–74.

Gabbard, G. O. (1989), Splitting in hospital treatment. *Amer. J. Psychiat.*, 146:444–451.

Garland, C. (1982), Group analysis: Taking the non-problem seriously. *Group Analysis*, 15:4–14.

Greene, L. R., Abramowitz, S. I., Davidson, C. U., & Edwards, D. W. (1980), Gender, race, and referral to group psychotherapy: Further empirical evidence of countertransference. *Internat. J. Group Psychother.*, 30:357–364.

Grotstein, J. S. (1981), *Splitting and Projective Identification.* Northvale, NJ: Jason Aronson.

Hill, P. (1971), *Towards a New Philosophy of Management.* New York: Barnes & Noble.

Hirschhorn, L. (1988), *The Workplace Within: Psychodynamics of Organizational Life.* Cambridge, MA: MIT Press.

Horwitz, L. (1983), Projective identification in dyads and groups. *Internat. J. Group Psychother.*, 33:259–279.

Jaques, E. (1955), Social systems as defense against persecutory and depressive anxiety. In: *New Directions in Psychoanalysis,* ed. M. Klein, P. Heimann, & R. Money-Kyrle. London: Tavistock Publications.

Johnson, D., & Howenstein, R. (1982), Revitalizing an ailing group psychotherapy program. *Psychiat.*, 45:138–146.

Kahn, E. (1985), Heinz Kohut and Carl Rogers: A timely comparison. *Amer. Psychol.*, 8:893–904.

Kantor, R. M. (1977), Some effects of proportions on group life: Skewed sex ratios and responses to token women. *J. Sociol.*, 82:965–990.

Katz, D., & Kahn, R. L. (1966), *The Social Psychology of Organizations*. New York: John Wiley.

Kauff, P. F. (1979), Diversity in analytic group psychotherapy: The relationship between theoretical concepts and techniques. *Internat. J. Group Psychother.*, 29:51–65.

Kernberg, O. F. (1975), A systems approach to priority setting of interventions in groups. *Internat. J. Group Psychother.*, 25:251–275.

——— (1978), Leadership and organizational functioning: Organizational regression. *Internat. J. Group Psychother.*, 28:3–25.

Kets de Vries, M. F. R., & Miller, D. (1985), *The Neurotic Organization*. San Francisco: Jossey-Bass.

Kibel, H. D. (1978), The rationale for the use of group psychotherapy for borderline patients in a short-term unit. *Internat. J. Group Psychother.*, 28:339–358.

——— (1981), A conceptual model for short-term inpatient group psychotherapy. *Amer. J. Psychiat.*, 138:74–80.

Kissen, M. (1980), General systems theory: Practical and theoretical implications for group intervention. *Group*, 4:29–39.

Klein, E. B. (1977), Transference in groups. *J. Pers. Soc. Systems*, 7:53–63.

——— (1978), An overview of recent Tavistock work in the United States. In: *Advances in Experiential Social Processes*, ed. C. L. Cooper & C. P. Alderfer. New York: John Wiley.

——— Astrachan, B. M. (1971), Learning in groups: A comparison of study groups and T-groups. *J. Appl. Behav. Sci.*, 7:659–683.

——— Correa, M. E., Howe, S. R., & Stone, W. N. (1983), The effects of social systems on group relations training. *Soc. Psychiat.*, 18:7–12.

——— Gould, L. J. (1973), Boundary issues and organizational dynamics: A case study. *Soc. Psychiat.*, 8:204–211.

——— Stone, W. N., Correa, M. E., Astrachan, J. H., & Kossek, E. E. (1989), Dimensions of experiential learning at group relations conferences. *Soc. Psychiat. & Psychiat. Epidemiol.*, 24:241–248.

Klein, M. (1959), Our adult world and its roots in infancy. *Human Relations*, 12:291–303.

Klein, R. H. (1977), Inpatient group psychotherapy: Practical considerations and special problems. *Internat. J. Group Psychother.*, 27:201–214.

——— (1981), The patient–staff community meeting: A tea party with the Mad Hatter. *Internat. J. Group Psychother.*, 31:205–222.

——— Kugel, B. (1981), Inpatient group psychotherapy from a systems perspective: Reflections through a glass darkly. *Internat. J. Group Psychother.*, 31:311–328.

Levinson, D. J., & Astrachan, B. M. (1974), Organizational boundaries: Entry into the mental health center. *Admin. Ment. Health*, 1:1–12.

——— Darrow, C. M., Klein, E. B., Levinson, M. H., & McKee, J. B. (1977), *The Seasons of a Man's Life*. New York: Alfred A. Knopf.

Lewin, K. (1936), *Principles in Topological Psychology*. New York: McGraw-Hill.

——— (1950), *Field Theory in Social Science*. New York: Harper Bros.

Malan, D. H., Balfour, F. H. F., Hood, V. G., & Shooter, A. (1976), Group psychotherapy: A long-term study. *Arch. Gen. Psychiat.*, 33:1303–1315.

Maslow, A. H. (1965), *Eupsychian Management*. Homewood, IL: Dorsey Press.

McGregor, D. (1960), *The Human Side of Enterprise*. New York: McGraw-Hill.

Menninger, R. (1985), A retrospective view of a hospital-wide group relations training program: Costs, consequences and conclusions. *Human Relations*, 38:323–339.

Menzies, I. E. P. (1960), A case-study in the functioning of social systems as a defense against anxiety. *Human Relations*, 13:95–121.

Miller, E. J. (1959), Technology, territory, and time: The internal differentiation of complex production systems. *Human Relations*, 12:243–272.

—— (1985), The politics of involvement. In: *Group Relations Reader 2*. Washington, DC: A. K. Rice Institute.

—— Rice, A. K. (1967), *Systems of Organization*. London: Tavistock Publications.

Newton, P. M. (1973), Social structure and process in psychotherapy: A sociopsychological analysis of transference, resistance and change. *Internat. J. Psychiat.*, 11:480–512.

—— Levinson, D. L. (1973), The work group within the organization: A sociopsychological approach. *Psychiat.*, 36:115–142.

Redl, F. (1963), Psychoanalysis and group therapy: A developmental point of view. *Amer. J. Orthopsychiat.*, 33:135–142.

Rice, A. K. (1963), *The Enterprise and Its Environment*. London: Tavistock Publications.

—— (1965), *Learning for Leadership*. London: Tavistock Publications.

—— (1969), Individual, group and intergroup processes. *Human Relations*, 22:565–584.

—— (1970), *The Modern University: A Model Organization*. London: Tavistock Publications.

Rice, C. A., & Rutan, J. S. (1987), *Inpatient Group Psychotherapy: A Psychodynamic Perspective*. New York: Macmillan.

Rioch, M. J. (1970), The work of Wilfred Bion on groups. *Psychiat.*, 33:56–66.

Rutan, J. S., & Stone, W. N. (1984), *Psychodynamic Group Psychotherapy*. New York: Macmillan.

Segal, H. (1973), *Introduction to the Work of Melanie Klein*. New York: Basic Books.

Singer, D. L., Astrachan, B. M., Gould, L. J., & Klein, E. B. (1975), Boundary management in psychological work with groups. *J. Appl. Behav. Sci.*, 11:137–176.

Slater, P. E. (1966), *Microcosm: Structural Psychological and Religious Evolution in Groups*. New York: John Wiley.

Slavson, S. R. (1964), *A Textbook in Analytic Group Psychotherapy*. New York: International Universities Press.

Smith, A., Cardillo, J. E., & Choate, A. O. (1984), Age-based transitional periods and the outcome of mental health treatment. *Evaluation and Programs Planning*, 7:237–244.

Sullivan, H. S. (1953), *The Interpersonal Theory of Psychiatry*. New York: Norton.

Swogger, G. (1981), Human communication and group experience. In: *Living Groups: Group Psychotherapy and General Systems Theory*, ed. J. E. Durkin. New York: Brunner/Mazel.

Thorsrud, E. (1969), A strategy for research and social change in industry: A report on the industrial democracy project in Norway. *Soc. Sci. Info.*, 5:65–90.

Trist, E. L. (1970), A socio-technical critique of scientific management. Paper presented at the Edinburg Conference on the Impact of Science and Technology. Edinburg University.

———— Bamforth, K. W. (1951), Some social and psychology consequences of the long-wall method of coal getting. *Human Relations*, 4:3–38.

———— Higgin, F. W., Murray, H., & Pollack, A. B. (1963), *Organizational Choice: Capabilities of Groups at the Coal Face Under Changing Technologies*. London: Tavistock Publications.

Turquet, P. M. (1975), Leadership: The individual and the group. In: *The Large Group: Dynamics and Therapy*, ed. L. Kreeger. London: Constable.

Whitaker, D., & Lieberman, M. (1964), *Psychotherapy through the Group Process*. New York: Atherton Press.

Winnicott, D. W. (1952), Anxiety associated with insecurity. In: *Through Paediatrics to Psychoanalysis*. London: Hogarth Press.

Yalom, I. D. (1975), *The Theory and Practice of Group Psychotherapy*, 2nd ed. New York: Basic Books.

———— (1983), *Inpatient Group Psychotherapy*. New York: Basic Books.

———— (1985), *The Theory and Practice of Group Psychotherapy*, 3rd ed. New York: Basic Books.

5

Summary: Recent Theoretical Developments

HAROLD S. BERNARD, Ph.D., ROBERT H. KLEIN, Ph.D., and
DAVID L. SINGER, Ph.D.

Important points of both convergence and divergence can be identified among the three theoretical perspectives represented in this volume. This chapter will review each perspective briefly and draw comparisons between and among them.

CENTRAL CONCEPTS

Theory of Normal Development

It is difficult to summarize the central concepts of object relations theory because, as Dr. Rice points out, it is really not a single theory but rather a set of theories with some overarching commonalities. One of these commonalities is that the central determinant of the course of development is the quality of early relationships with significant others, especially parents or parent-substitutes. Dr. Rice writes generally about the need for the mother to provide "ameliorative responses to hateful and aggressive projections of infants" and the possibility that she can have a "palliative effect on the infant's struggles with love and hate," without specifying exactly what is involved. Clearly, the individual's first and foremost connection is with the mother, and the mother's freedom from psychopathology is critical for the normal development of the child. A healthy mother can help a child contain, neutralize, and find healthy modes of expression

125

for basic impulses as well as be a healthy object with which the child can identify. A positive mother–child relationship can serve as a prototype for healthy bonding and attachment.

While Dr. Rice does not flesh out the details, what is noteworthy is that the framework for object relations theory is clearly developmental. All object relations theorists, beginning with Melanie Klein, construe human development as proceeding through a series of identifiable developmental stages (Greenberg and Mitchell, 1983). Of course, traditional instinct theory posits a series of developmental stages as well. However, according to object relations thinkers, it is not the structural conflicts between instinctual wishes and superego demands that determine one's progress through developmental phases, but rather the nature and quality of attachments that are forged. Another way of saying this is that according to the object relations perspective, the basic "instinct" or "drive" is to connect with other objects.

Self psychology, on the other hand, is quite explicit about what is required for normal development. Its most central construct is that of the selfobject, a role occupied by different people in the individual's life at different times. It is the relationship between the self and the selfobject that is crucial. In this respect self psychology is also a theory of object relations. Development proceeds benignly when the individual is well responded to by the central selfobjects in his life. Self psychologists are explicit about what constitutes adequate responsivity: It includes such things as empathic attunement, validation, and recognition of uniqueness. When this occurs, a self which is vital, strong, flexible, and resilient develops and matures.

Kohut began by reconceptualizing the so-called "narcissistic personality disorders." He posited a separate line of development for narcissism, presumably coexisting with the Freudian developmental stages (Kohut, 1971). However, as the work of Kohut and his colleagues progressed, they began to assert that their notions have wider relevance than they first proposed. As Dr. Bacal puts it, "self psychologists now regard (the psychology of the self) as applicable to the full range of psychopathology."

Adherence to the self psychology perspective does not necessarily imply a rejection of traditional instinct theory. Some self psychologists believe that traditional theory and the psychology of the self constitute complementary perspectives about the same set of phenomena. Other self psychologists hold the view that traditional theory is explanatory for a circumscribed area of psychopathology: namely, the "structural neuroses." A third group construes the psychology of the self as replacing traditional theory across the entire range of developmental and pathological phenomena.

Dr. Bacal represents the latter position, with respect to both theory and technique. Specifically, he asserts that the "basic determinants of conflict and anxiety do not emanate from the clamor for instinctual satisfaction but are the result of disturbances in selfobject relationships." At another point he asserts that "one simply cannot apply unmodified classical drive theory in the clinical situation and expect that the patient will feel understood." From this perspective, the basic issues in development do not pivot around the conflict surrounding instinctual wishes, between id and superego. Normal development, instead, is seen as hinging on the emergence of an intact and cohesive self characterized by a clear sense of identity, by the capacity to relate effectively with others in the world, and by the ability to pursue one's talents and ambitions as mediated by the development of deep and sustaining values, goals, and ideals (Eagle, 1984).

Social systems theory is not a motivational theory as such, and does not specifically address the process of normal individual development. However, its historical roots derive from the work of Melanie Klein, who clearly concerned herself with normal individual development. She posits developmental stages which, if successfully traversed, presumably lead to normal functioning. These stages (the paranoid-schizoid stage and the depressive stage) are described very clearly in her work (Klein, 1964), and she highlights the fact that it is normal to utilize the defenses of splitting and projective identification as one progresses through them. In general, development progresses from simple and undifferentiated to complex, differentiated, bounded and hierarchically organized.

Theory of Pathology

Once again object relations theory is difficult to succinctly characterize. In a general sense, if early experiences with key objects (primarily the mother) are not benign, one's internalizations will be such that pathology of one sort or another is likely to develop. The defenses that object relations theorists most prominently focus upon (splitting and projective identification) are critical to the object relations theory of pathology, which maintains that if one's early relationships go awry, for whatever reason, one will not be able to construe the self and objects in their appropriate complexity (good-and-bad rather than good-or-bad), and one will not be able to acknowledge all of one's parts without projecting them into and onto available and willing recipients. Another way to say this is that one's view of reality, both internal and external, will be distorted rather than accurate. These distorted views of self and others are then reenacted in all subsequent relationships.

The self psychology perspective holds that pathology emanates from faulty interactions, usually early in life, between one's self and its selfobjects. Such faulty interactions occur because the selfobject is experienced as unavailable or unreliable in some way. Dr. Bacal contrasts "reactiveness" with "responsiveness" to illuminate what is required from a selfobject. "Reactiveness" refers to experience-distant listening in which the listener understands in terms of how it affects him. "Responsiveness" refers to experience-near listening in which the listener understands in terms of how it affects the individual to whom he is listening. Put more simply, responsiveness is genuinely empathic while reactiveness is not. Psychopathology emerges when the child's selfobjects repeatedly interact reactively rather than responsively. As a result, the development of a stable, cohesive self is at least compromised, and may be permanently thwarted.

With respect to psychopathology, social systems theory again is focused on groups rather than individuals. However, A. K. Rice (1969) argued persuasively that there are parallel processes operating at the individual, group, and intergroup levels that profoundly influence individual development. More specifically, healthy ego functioning at the individual level is analogous to work group functioning, in which boundaries are well defined and monitored and task-oriented work predominates at the group level. The analogue to the intergroup level is when the representatives of the group in question are clear about the nature of the authority that has been delegated to them, and work comfortably and consistently from that base on intergroup tasks without either jeopardizing their loyalties and ties to the groups they represent, or unnecessarily compromising their group's specific interests.

A central focus in social systems theory is the concept of boundaries, which Dr. Klein defines as "the region that separates the individual from the group or the group from the rest of the environment." Any well-functioning enterprise, whether an individual in the world or a group or a system of some sort, needs a set of boundaries that are clearly articulated, well maintained, and permeable enough for productive exchanges to take place between that enterprise and the larger environment within which it exists. Conversely, when boundaries are not clearly articulated and maintained, or are either too permeable or not permeable enough, some form of pathology inevitably develops.

Theory of Groups

Object relations theory posits that individuals develop internalized representations of the key objects and key relationships in their lives. These representations in turn have great influence on the nature of all subsequent relationships, including relationships with other individual members of groups with which they are involved and with groups as a whole. These repetitious and unconscious reenactments lead individuals to play out particular roles in groups and to find others who will assume the necessary reciprocal roles that allow for the externalization of their internal dramas. Object relations theorists tend to emphasize the mechanisms of projection, identification, splitting, and projective identification in their consideration of what transpires in groups.

As mentioned above, self psychologists focus primarily on the notion of the selfobject. Thus, what occurs in groups is a function of unfolding dynamics between selves and their selfobjects. Presumably, when selfobjects are being "responsive" to self needs, things proceed comfortably. However, when they are being "reactive" there are disturbances of various kinds. Such disturbances are evidenced by the reenactment of failed self–selfobject relationships. People search for selfobjects who can provide what they need. When the individuals in question suffer from pathology of some kind, they tend to fail to find what they are looking for. They experience current failures in the group context as echoes of unresolved past disappointments suffered at the hands of faulty selfobjects. In this respect self psychology is an object relations theory. As such, the same basic mechanisms of group life are emphasized: splitting, projective identification, and so forth.

Social systems theory postulates an elaborate theory of group functioning. It is a "sociotechnical" theory: That is, it emphasizes the interplay of technical and social-psychological factors in group life. It assumes that groups have tasks (sometimes clear, sometimes covert), and that group functioning is in part determined by the congruence between a group's task and its structure. It focuses on the ways in which group members exercise their own authority and relate to designated authority. The nature of the so-called "authority relations" that emerge determine how effectively a group is able to work toward the accomplishment of its task(s). Social systems theory underscores the importance of the concept of boundaries and postulates that a great deal of what occurs in groups can be explained by how various boundaries are defined and then either maintained or violated in the life of the group.

Finally, social systems theory emphasizes the notion that individuals take up, or are assigned, socioemotional "roles" in groups and frequently become repositories for affects or motives that exist in others. The roles that particular individuals take up are determined in part by their "valences," or predispositions. Presumably, such valences are not inborn; rather, they develop out of early interaction with significant others. This perspective is obviously consistent with object relations principles.

Theory of Therapeusis

Once again, because object relations theory is really a set of theories with some overarching commonalities, it is difficult to clearly articulate its theory of therapeusis. However, object relations approaches clearly emphasize the healing power of therapeutic relationships. Object relations theorists posit that the drive to establish connections with other objects is primary rather than derivative; as such, they believe that when this process has gone awry, it can be corrected by a relationship with a therapist (and/or fellow group members) that is corrective and therefore curative. Some object relations theorists describe this process in traditional terms, such as "the resolution of transference distortions." Others are more vague about just what the therapeutic process entails, focusing instead on the necessary *conditions* for change: for example, Winnicott's (1965) emphasis on the holding environment, in which the therapist serves as a "container" for unacceptable parts of members' selves, and the group serves as a transitional object in which members recapitulate and rework distorted internalized representations in an empathic context.

By way of contrast, self psychology has a very clearly agreed-upon view of how therapy works. When therapy is effective, selfobject disruptions are worked through and selfobject bonds are either resumed or newly established. When a therapist (or group) is responsive rather than reactive, the individual moves toward taking over the therapist's (or group's) selfobject functions, thereby strengthening the self. Thus, self psychology also emphasizes the curative power of therapeutic relationships, whether they be with one's therapist, one or more fellow group members, or the group as a whole. In contrast to the traditional notion that resolution of conflict is the central element in therapeutic change, self psychology focuses on helping the individual make up for deficits by gradually acquiring new capacities for living successfully.

This analysis highlights a critical difference between self psychology and those perspectives that emphasize the interpretation of unconscious structural conflict: In self psychology the emphasis is on the provision of necessary but previously unavailable selfobject functions, primarily by the therapist. The crucial tool utilized to accomplish this provision of functions is *empathy*. Presumably what occurs is that the patient takes on those functions initially supplied by the selfobject, and they eventually become integrated into the patient's self. The process by which this occurs is called "transmuting internalization" by self psychologists, which is akin to what traditional theorists call "internalization" and/or "identification."

Social systems theory does not put forth an explicit theory of therapeusis for individual change. In a general way, its major tenets suggest that the exploration of roles and boundaries, and the emphasis on projective processes (with the hoped-for reowning of projections) is what is curative about the therapeutic enterprise. More specifically, as a result of clarifying work and regulatory transactions of the various boundaries that define the individual in relation to his context, there is increased differentiation and complexity of functioning. The individual is able to exercise his authority in increasingly effective ways as impediments to this process are overcome. Finally, the individual is able to recover split-off parts through increased understanding of roles, values, and projective processes, resulting in increased integration, complexity and wholeness of functioning. Social systems theory does, however, address issues of developmental sequences of individuals and groups which have relevance for how therapeutic change occurs. Specifically, development and growth proceed from relatively simple and fused to increasingly complex and differentiated. In the context of treatment, the primary tool used to bring about this evolution is interpretation.

Inferences about individual change can be drawn from social systems notions about group change. Just as groups can learn to increasingly operate in a productive work mode, so the individual ego can gradually expand its domain of function and control as an outgrowth of successful treatment. Thus, the ego is the equivalent within the individual psyche to the work mode at the group level, just as the id is the individual equivalent to a group's various basic assumption modes.

Historical Roots

The genesis of all psychodynamic theories can be traced back to Freud. The developmental lines that different theories have taken since Freud vary considerably. Freud posited a drive psychology based upon the expression of inborn sexual and aggressive instincts, as modified by the ego's efforts to mediate between the impulses of the id and the constraints of the superego (Freud, 1923).

Melanie Klein, generally considered the progenitor of object relations theory, modified Freud's approach substantially. Instead of thinking of the object as incidental to the experiencing and expression of drives, she regarded the object of the drive as central (Klein, 1964). As such, she set the stage for all relational theories. However, her focus was more on inner object representations than on real relationships. Fairbairn (1952) was the first theorist to view drives as a means to the end of establishing actual relationships.

Thus, in contrast to the traditional view, Klein and those who followed her did not place instinctual discharge at the heart of their view of the human condition. Rather, it is the need to establish connections with others that is seen as central.

Dr. Bacal traces the origins of self psychology theory back to Freud as well, but he sees the evolution as moving from him to Hartmann, Guntrip, and others. They marked the shift from a focus on intrapsychic conflict to an emphasis on the ego adaptive functions in an average expectable environment (Hartmann, 1939; Guntrip, 1961). Because this latter concept presupposes a relational milieu, this evolution marked the movement from an intrapsychic, single-person perspective to an interpersonal, multiperson perspective.

The importance of this evolution cannot be overemphasized. Instead of focusing on the unfolding dynamics *within* the individual, and viewing the significant others in the individual's world as incidental, the focus of self psychologists is on the *individual-in-relation-to* the significant others in his life. The role of the "other" is construed as central, not incidental. This change of perspective has important implications for technique, even in dyadic treatment: The examination of the "real" relationship between the individual and others in the treatment setting (the therapist in dyadic treatment, the therapist and fellow group members in group treatment) becomes much more important in the treatment process, since it is the nature of *relationships* that provides important clues about the deficits arising from faulty self–selfobject ties.

Social systems theory incorporates the group dynamics perspective developed by Bion into the social-structural constructs propounded by Miller and Rice (1969). Bion's (1961) concepts can be traced back to Melanie Klein's notions about the primitive defenses developed in the first year of life, and even further back to Freud. Miller and Rice's perspective developed out of the social psychological perspective of Lewin (1936), as well as the work of theorists who focused on the properties of open living systems in interaction with their environments (von Bertalanffy, 1968).

Thus, all of the approaches explored in this volume can ultimately be traced back to Freud's vast contributions. However, they took very different directions thereafter. What they have in common is that they represent the movement toward multiperson, relational thinking concerning what makes people behave as they do, in groups and elsewhere.

Relationship to Traditional Theory

What can be said about the relationship of each of these theories to classical psychoanalytic theory? To begin with, there continues to be considerable disagreement as to just how much object relations theory deviates from the classical psychoanalytic point of view. Some see it as falling within the rubric of the classical mode, while others construe it as a challenge to that model. In the former category are those who see object relations theory as addressing the pathology of drive derivatives that create difficulties in interpersonal relationships. In the latter category are those who believe that object relations theory construes humanity not as primarily instinctual, but rather as primarily object-seeking.

Is this a meaningful debate, or just a semantic argument? We think it is meaningful in that a view of humanity as object-seeking is a basically different conception of the human condition in the following sense: The unit of analysis is a multiperson relational field rather than a single individual who is governed by internal drives and defenses against those drives. The focus is on unconscious object and relationship representations, not drive derivatives.

Self psychology also removes instinctual motivation as the central factor in development and pathogenesis. While the self is at the center of individual psychology, the emphasis is on the self's need for certain kinds of essential relationships with objects. Thus, like object relations theory and unlike classical theory, self psychology is a multiperson psychology. At its core it is a deficit model of pathogenesis, and as such it takes a basically different stance in relation to such core treatment phenomena as resistance and transference. When these phenomena manifest themselves in the treatment situation, they are seen as indications of functions or capacities the individual has failed to develop through his formative relationships, not as evidence of unresolved intrapsychic conflict.

Social systems theory is in some ways closely aligned with classical theory, but in other ways it differs fundamentally. It takes the view

that the projections and distortions manifested in the treatment setting are most often a function of both the individual's and the group's
dynamics. Through application of the principle of therapeutic abstinence, social systems theory promotes regression and the analysis of
transference and resistance. However, it, too, is a multiperson model.
All of its central constructs (tasks, roles, boundaries, authority, and
leadership) presuppose an interpersonal field. In fact, social systems
theory goes beyond the other two theories explored in this volume in
one respect. In object relations theory and self psychology, the primary level of analysis is interpersonal: what transpires between the
individual and significant others in his or her life, whether inside or
outside the group. Social systems theory is farther removed from the
classical approach, as its primary foci are the group-as-a-whole level
and, at times, the intergroup level of analysis.

RELEVANCE TO GROUP THERAPY

Role of the Therapist

Although this issue is the focus of the third section of this volume,
there are many implications for what the group therapist does that
emanate from each of these theories, so they will be briefly addressed
here.

As presented by Dr. Rice, object relations theory does not offer a
specific prescription about how the group therapist should work, but
does provide some general guidelines. In the classical psychoanalytic
approach to treatment, the therapist is a neutral observer, a blank
screen upon which individuals (or groups) project their unconscious
conflicts, which then become the subject for analysis. While transference analysis inevitably involves interpersonal/relational considerations, the primary focus remains the patient's uresolved intrapsychic
structural conflicts that are being re-created and expressed in the
context of the therapy. By way of contrast, object relations therapists
consider the unit of analysis the patient–therapist (or group–therapist) dyad. Whether one focuses on internalized objects or real objects,
the emphasis is on the patient's (or group's) relationships and transactions with others.

It is significant that nowhere in Dr. Rice's chapter does he specifically articulate an object relations–based theory of therapeusis. At
least in part this may be because there are so many theoreticians, both

British and American, associated with the object relations approach that no single integrated set of principles adequately characterizes all of these perspectives. However, there does seem to be unanimity that the role of the therapist is to establish a holding environment with a suitable set of structures and norms within which distorted internal dramatizations can be enacted and examined. In addition, the role involves interpretation of unconscious conflicts among internal objects as they are enacted or expressed, so as to foster recovery of disowned and distorted aspects of the self and to thereby modify internal and external object relations.

The role of the self psychology practitioner is much easier to characterize. Self psychology theory is explicitly a deficit model; as such, the therapist's job is to supply (or to help the group supply) what the patient has needed and not received up until the time of treatment. Specifically, Kohut talks of the selfobject supplying the mirroring, idealizing, or alterego needs of the patient. The goal is for the selfobject to be optimally responsive to the patient's selfobject needs. It is an "experience-near" form of treatment in which the most important thing the therapist or other selfobject can bring to bear is accurate empathy. The reparative process results in "transmuting internalizations": Patients emerge with capacities they did not have when they began treatment. Presumably, this occurs in a fashion similar to that which occurs in traditional psychotherapy, namely, via imitation, introjection, and identification. As a result of these processes, the missing parts or functions supplied by the external selfobject gradually become part of the self.

What makes social systems theory difficult to characterize in this regard is that it was not developed as an approach to treatment per se. Nevertheless, some things can be said about the role of the therapist who operates out of a social systems perspective. Of the three approaches to treatment explored in this volume, it is closest to classical psychoanalytic treatment in its emphasis on abstinence and technical neutrality, which lead to regression, and the interpretation of transference and countertransference distortions that subsequently emerge. The focus is on the ways the group as a whole relates to the therapist, and how individual members interact with each other: the roles they adopt, the boundaries they honor or violate, the tasks they pursue, the cultures and structures they develop, and so on. With regard to individual members, the particular roles they adopt and how the group deploys and uses them can all be explored. The social systems approach is an "experience-distant" form of treatment in which the therapist, through the use of interpretation, focuses primarily on how the group as a whole is relating to him or her, rather than on being accurately empathic. The emphasis is on the repetitive, unconscious transactions between the group and the therapist; more specifically, on what the patients are doing to, and thereby eliciting in, the therapist. The social systems approach is a conflict model of treatment: It is the resolution of conflicts through interpretation to the group as a whole that leads to such outcomes as the integration of fantasy and reality, and the shift from unconscious to conscious processes.

Transference–Countertransference

As multiperson approaches, object relations theory and self psychology take a stance in relation to transference and countertransference phenomena that deviates from the classical approach. The focus is not on the patient as an entity unto himself; rather, it is on the patient in relation to others. Thus, transference and countertransference emanate out of the *relationship* between patient and therapist, each with his own unconscious structural conflicts, not out of the patient and therapist as separate entities.

Object relations theory, in particular, emphasizes the total relationship between patient and therapist, which includes not only the unconscious aspects contributed by both interacting participants, but also their respective objective aspects. Sullivan, a prominent object relations contributor, described the therapist role as that of "participant observer," which was his way of emphasizing the importance of the "real relationship" between therapist and patient (Sullivan, 1953). Winnicott (1965) alerted us to the importance of "synchrony" between therapists and patients. While the concept of "synchrony" is most directly applicable to the mother–child interaction, it can be applied to the treatment situation. In essence, and like the mother, the therapist must do enough but not too much to promote the patient's growth. If the therapist does either too much or too little, growth will be inhibited rather than facilitated.

Similarly, self psychology focuses on the total relationship between patient and therapist. The therapist's most important responsibility is to be accurately empathic with his patients. When patients feel hurt in the therapeutic setting, the therapist does not assume that they likely are reacting in a distorted way, but rather that it is their way of organizing their subjective experience. This view of transference reactions leads to what Dr. Bacal describes as an "intersubjective perspective on interaction." As he goes on to say, the exploration of subjectively experienced dysjunctions in selfobject relationships in pa-tient–patient and patient–therapist interaction constitutes the work of the therapy group.

Once again, social systems theory takes a more traditional view of transference and countertransference phenomena. The therapist is construed as a blank screen into and onto whom are projected pa-tients' distorted feelings, impulses, and fantasies. Therapists use the feelings induced in them via projective identification, projection, and splitting—mechanisms that are engendered in the regressive situation of the group—to understand patients' collective experience. This un-derstanding is presumably less accurate if countertransference mani-festations intrude. Dr. Skolnick addresses this issue in Chapter 12 in this volume.

Nature of Clinical Data Utilized

Both object relations theory and self psychology focus on the full range of conscious, preconscious, and unconscious material. Object relations theory places special emphasis on the unconscious reen-actment of distorted self–other relationships, which then become the subject for interpretation, thereby promoting conscious exploration and relearning.

In self psychology the initial emphasis is on what patients do and express. However, the aim is to use this material to learn what each patient unconsciously needs from others to make up for the past failures of important selfobjects in that individual's life. Such under-standing can be used to assist patients to deal more effectively with these old injuries to the self and the impact these injuries have had upon self coherence, self-esteem, and object ties.

Social systems theory, like object relations theory and self psychol-ogy, begins with what patients bring to the treatment, but it, too, uses this material to make inferences about unconscious needs, wishes, and dispositions. Because most social systems practitioners subscribe to the basic tenets of Melanie Klein's developmental schema, social systems practice usually attempts to access early life experiences that are largely preoedipal and, in fact, preverbal. The emphasis on therapist abstinence, which fosters regression and elicits levels of experience that are usually difficult to access, emerges from this emphasis. Real relationships, both within and outside the group, are less important than the fantasy and other primitive material that is inevitably evoked in groups run by therapists who adhere to the social systems per-spective.

In summary, all three approaches considered here are character-ized by their emphasis on pregenital material. As multiperson ap-proaches, they are all concerned with the basic issues of attachment and loss. In Eriksonian terms, matters of trust and autonomy are the primary foci (Erikson, 1968). This is an important point of congru-ence among the three perspectives. Although there are, of course, a number of important differences among the three theories repre-sented in this volume, what they have in common is that they are multiperson theories concerned with early life experience that at-tempt to make sense of the human condition and to help people change by focusing on the individual in relation to others in his life, both within the group (therapist and fellow patients), within himself (internalized objects), and in his past and present life (significant oth-ers). Group treatment is the logical modality in which this work can be most effectively undertaken.

REFERENCES

Bertalanffy, L. von (1968), *General Systems Theory: Foundations, Development, Applications.* New York: Braziller.

Bion, W. R. (1961), *Experiences in Groups.* London: Tavistock Publications.

Eagle, M. N. (1984), *Recent Developments in Psychoanalysis.* Cambridge, MA: Harvard University Press.

Erikson, E. H. (1968), *Identity: Youth and Crisis.* New York: Norton.

Fairbairn, W. R. D. (1952), *An Object Relations Theory of the Personality.* New York: Basic Books.

Freud, S. (1923), The ego and the id. *Standard Edition,* 19:19–27. London: Hogarth Press, 1961.

Greenberg, J. R., & Mitchell, S. A. (1983), *Object Relations in Psychoanalytic Theory.* Cambridge, MA: Harvard University Press.

Guntrip, H. (1961), *Personality Structure and Human Interaction: The Developing Synthesis of Psychodynamic Theory.* New York: International Universities Press.

Hartmann, H. (1939), *Ego Psychology and the Problem of Adaptation.* New York: Interna-tional Universities Press.

Klein, M. (1964), *Contributions to Psychoanalysis, 1921–1945.* New York: McGraw-Hill.

Kohut, H. (1971), *The Analysis of the Self.* New York: International Universities Press.

Lewin, K. (1936), *Principles in Topological Psychology.* New York: McGraw-Hill.

Miller, E. J., & Rice, A. K. (1969), *Systems of Organization.* London: Tavistock Publica-tions.

Rice, A. K. (1969), Individual, group and intergroup processes. *Human Relations,* 22:565–584.

Sullivan, H. S. (1953), *The Interpersonal Theory of Psychiatry.* New York: Norton.

Winnicott, D. W. (1965), *The Maturational Process and the Facilitating Environment.* New York: International Universities Press.

Part II

Clinical Applications to Patient Care

6

The Clinical Application of Object Relations Theory

HOWARD D. KIBEL, M.D.

A discussion of the origins of object relations theory as it applies to the analysis of dynamic processes in groups is a prerequisite for an examination of the clinical application of this theory. In particular, Bion's fundamental contributions to group psychotherapy will be noted. The traditional application of his work, in particular, and object relations theory, in general, has focused on group-as-a-whole or holistic phenomena, wherein each member's contribution to the process is viewed as being in the service of unconscious motives that unite the group. However, viewing collective phenomena merely as reflecting shared themes or, more specifically, functioning as a common denominator for members' conflicts unduly restricts the understanding of group process. Group-level fantasies have other roots, which will be described.

The position taken here is that group-level processes are always operative, but that each member's contribution is unique and each one's role in the product differs, as does his or her investment in it. The group inevitably serves as the arena for the expression of the internal object relations of its members. This happens for a very specific reason. Fantasies in a group are intrinsic to its organization. They derive from the projection of early introjects. They are the means whereby the group takes shape, develops its characteristics, and functions. Just as fantasies organize intrapsychic life, provide structure, shape the individual, and facilitate the executive functions of the ego, so collective fantasies organize the group's functioning and determine its latent structure. The relationship of group-level processes to each member's contribution to such holistic phenomena is exceedingly complex, since each person's influence on the result is diverse. For some, a particular group-as-a-whole reaction will reflect central aspects of their psychopathology, while for others it will be nonspecific.

The bond that members develop to the group entity permits their internal object relations to be reenacted in a controlled and supportive way. These notions have important implications for technique. Group interventions and therapeusis will be discussed from an object relations vantage point. Projective mechanisms are noted to be the cornerstone of this view of group process. But the reintrojection of projected fantasies is the bedrock of change. All this puts group interactions and feedback into a new context, one that is relevant to the psychology of ego structures.

BIRTH OF THE THEORY

Object relations theory began with Freud's essays on narcissism and melancholia, which identified the existence of a reciprocal relationship between the ego and the object, whereby the ego modifies an internal representation of the object through introjection and is then modified in turn through identification (Ashbach and Schermer, 1987). His structural theory was first elaborated in "The Ego and the Id" (Freud, 1923). In that work he noted that the character of the ego is a precipitate of abandoned object cathexis and is shaped by early object choices, and that the earliest identifications made in childhood are profound and lasting (Kernberg, 1976).

Contributions to theory came from interpersonal psychoanalytic theory, ego psychology, and the so-called "British psychoanalytic school" of Melanie Klein, Fairbairn, Winnicott, and others. Central to its development were Fairbairn's (1952) claims that a pristine whole ego existed at birth and that it was object-seeking, as opposed to satisfaction-seeking. This notion transformed psychoanalytic thinking by turning investigation away from an exclusive focus on instinctual development and toward the study of the nature and origin of interpersonal relationships. Subsequently, object relations theory, in its broadest sense, came to represent postulates as to "the nature and origin of intrapsychic structures deriving from, fixating, modifying, and reactivating past internalized relations with others in the context of present interpersonal relations. Psychoanalytic object-relations theory focuses upon the internalization of interpersonal relations, their contributions to normal and pathological ego and superego developments, and the mutual influences of intrapsychic and interpersonal object relations" (Kernberg, 1976, p. 56). As such, it is naturally suited to a practice of psychotherapy that emphasizes the interpersonal dimension of psychic life, as group psychotherapy does, and one that uses interpersonal relations as the vehicle for both investigation and therapeutic change.

In its most restricted sense, psychoanalytic object relations theory refers to the "British psychoanalytic school" of Melanie Klein and her followers. She stressed the importance of very early internalized object relations in determining the nature of intrapsychic conflict and psychic structures. Her theories help to explain a gamut of normal and pathological ego states, particularly as these are revealed in relationships (such as those found in groups), by postulating that pregenital factors affect all relations as well as being important in determining the basic structure of both the ego and superego. The implication here is that primitive internal states not only affect all interpersonal behavior, but underlie even mature relationships. From an instinctual perspective, human relationships are prone to contamination by pregenital aggression, and from an ego perspective, they are affected by splitting and projective mechanisms (frequently projective identification). These mechanisms, in turn, reflect the (constant) resurrection of the "paranoid-schizoid position" within a range of human functioning and, as Bion (1959) discovered, particularly in groups.

Klein labeled the earliest developmental stage of the ego the paranoid-schizoid position. The term *position* was used to convey the notion of a relatively stable ego organization, with a defined array of defenses and a way of looking at the world. Specifically, this position is characterized by the use of splitting, projective identification, idealization, omnipotence and devaluation, and denial of internal and external reality. In this position, others are approached cautiously—often avoided and certainly distrusted—since the ego is flooded by fears of a persecutory nature. This paranoid-schizoid position is clinically descriptive of patients with schizophrenia and paranoid psychosis but can be applied to those social situations that are conflict-laden, such as the group setting.

Splitting and consequent part-object relations are central to the paranoid-schizoid position. Specifically, internal self and object representations are split, so that good and bad images are maintained separately. The view of self or other as totally loving or malevolent denies the reality of ambivalence, which is inherent in all human relationships. Splitting is linked with the mechanism of projection in that usually good objects are totally introjected while bad ones are projected. In projective identification, in contrast to simple projection, split-off and denied parts of the self or of an internal object are projected *into* another person. In this case, rather than simply dissociating itself from the projected part, the ego aims to enter, so to speak, the external object and to forcefully influence it (Kernberg, 1980). This process simultaneously serves as a defense against fantasized persecutors and unconsciously expresses primitive sadism in relation to the object.

These notions from object relations theory were applied to groups by Bion (1959), who, in fact, began the study of object relations in groups. His seminal contributions have been summarized time and again. Although limitations in the application of his metapsychology of groups to group psychotherapy have been reported (Kibel and Stein, 1981), many aspects of his theories are enduring and have penetrated group dynamic approaches to treatment.

According to Bion, "basic assumptions," which reflect primitive object relations, originate within the individual as powerful emotions associated with a specific cluster of ideas that compel the individual to react in particular ways in groups and also to be attracted to individuals imbued with similar or complementary attitudes (Sutherland, 1985). The forcefulness of intragroup bonds and their nonspecific nature struck Bion as more analogous to tropisms than to purposive behavior. For this reason, he said that they had "valency": That is, much like in a chemical reaction, individuals cannot *not* interact. Here we see the derivative of Fairbairn's object-seeking ego.

Because of valency, collective patterns of group relatedness invariably develop. Whether or not we choose to refer to them as basic assumptions, group mentality, or group culture is irrelevant. Bion insisted that behavior observed in groups was not merely a product of groups as such, but of the fact that "the human being is a group animal" (p. 132). Thus, it is human "groupishness" that produces group dynamics (p. 131). For this reason, the study of the (therapeutic) group and its holistic mentality "reveals the functioning of the individual member in his full complexity and should be the basis of therapeutic intervention" (Kibel and Stein, 1981, p. 410).

Bion, like Freud (1921) before him, described the curious development of regression as it occurs in all unstructured small groups, even those composed of normals. However, following a Kleinian tradition, he was able to see that the group as a unit activates primitive defense mechanisms in the members or, at least, we would now grant that the total emotional situation is remarkably similar to that of the early stages of ego development. More importantly, these regressive processes are present in the members while, simultaneously, most mature ego functions are preserved. Specifically, in Bion's terms, the basic assumption culture and work group function are contemporaneous. This means that, for purposes of psychotherapy, the dynamics of the group and its therapeutic interchanges will operate in ways analogous to both advanced and primitive levels of individual psychopathology (Kernberg, 1975).

Valency and the activation of primitive relatedness in groups are linked together in an object relations approach. The group is seen as a field for the interplay of part-object relations. Splitting and projective mechanisms operate in the group for each member, so that part-object relationships are reenacted and others are induced to play roles that complement one's inner needs. In short, each member of the group seeks others out and induces them to reenact his own internal object relations, but also is reciprocally induced by them for their own purposes. The result is a complex matrix of relationships based upon mutual projections.

Many workers (James, 1984; Ashbach and Schermer, 1987; Kosseff, 1990) have noted that the group itself serves as a container for projections. On the one hand, this allows the members to press certain individuals into specific roles that serve some group needs, such as is found in scapegoating. On the other hand, it permits members to experiment with latent tendencies or potentials and develop new ways of relating (Kosseff, 1990). At the same time, because of human groupishness, individual tendencies are combined so that collective phenomena emerge from the group interactions. These group-level processes contain a shared fantasy about relationships, one that functions as a preoccupation that engages the members and then, in turn, influences their behavior. This means that group roles, members' relations with one another, and group-level dynamics are all intertwined.

Leadership is central to Bion's metapsychology of groups, specifically to basic assumption mentality. However, it need not be embodied in the designated leader. It is projected in one of several ways. "This leader need not be identified with any individual in the group; it need not be a person at all but may be identified with an idea or an inanimate object" (Bion, 1959, p. 155). By members splitting internal objects into parts and projecting them, the basic assumption leader becomes the repository of their unwanted noxious internal states. This concept applies not only to the members' relationship to the therapist (Ezriel, 1950), but also to relationships with central individuals (Anzieu, 1984), as in scapegoating (Scheidlinger, 1982) and other group roles, to mythopoeic leaders, and even to the group matrix itself (James, 1984).

Bion's use of mythopoeic images has seemed obscure to many, yet it has heuristic value since it identifies the role of mental images in regression. Specifically, the imago[1] of the basic assumption leader is the container for fantasy. This shared image becomes the personification of a part-object relationship, that is, of a split-off introject which has been projected but is then related to. These split relationships operate within the group in a myriad of ways, involving the designated leader, specific members, dyads, or subgroups. Containment is important in treatment, since it permits the projective fantasy to be processed, toned-down, and ultimately corrected. In short, through regression the therapeutic group provides many opportunities for projective–reintrojective relatedness (Kibel, 1991). The latter will be defined later and, as we shall see, is an important vehicle for therapeutic change.

How the group becomes mutative was never specified by Bion; he never provided an outline for technique. Rather, he merely advised that "the psychiatrist should find interpretations that give the group insight as to what is going on; to bring the *ba* [basic assumption group] and *W* [work group] into contact" (p. 126). Once that happened, he reported, and the work group culture dominated, the individual would "learn by experience." (It was no accident that this phrase, slightly modified, became the title of a later work, having nothing to do with groups.) Later in his career, Bion returned briefly to groups in one volume where he elaborated the notion of "catastrophic change" (Bion, 1970). Herein lay the concept that experience, once contained, can then be transformed, given new meaning, and then integrated. In terms of the discussion in this chapter, this means that the group regressive process, by stimulating projective mechanisms within the paranoid-schizoid position, provides an opportunity for internal object relations to be modified by containment and its attendant functions. Since this occurs largely at a preverbal level, the mutative process in group psychotherapy can be said to be experiential, although solidified by insight. It will be described later in terms of internal structural change.

THE MISAPPLICATION OF THEORY AND NEWER CONCEPTS

Regrettably, object relations theory in groups initially became equated with a kind of treatment approach that emphasized the group at the

---

[1]The term *imago* is used throughout this chapter to refer to a complex, unconscious image that has the qualities of a person. It is a part-object, one that is often idealized, but may be devalued or perceived as malevolent.

expense of the individual (Malan, Balfour, Hood, and Shooter, 1976). American practitioners decried any such suggestion that there existed a "group mind" (Wolf and Schwartz, 1962) that should be treated. This view was bolstered by the application of group dynamic concepts to Bion's theories. These, in turn, were derived from the work of Lewin (1951), who believed that group and social systems have laws of their own which cannot be explained entirely as the summation of their components or, in other words, that the group is more than the product of its members.

More recent applications of object relations theory have clarified this misunderstanding. Many theorists have substantiated Bion's contention that group-as-a-whole experiences stir developmentally early layers of psychic functioning, even in relatively well-integrated patients and in normals. Regressive group forces propel members into acting and reenacting primitive object relationships. These unconscious strivings fuel the group interactions, which then consolidate to yield collaborative, sometimes holistic responses. Thus, collective group reactions can be explained as a product of individual contributions; however, because they emerge from the most primitive layers of each person's ego, they are characterless and malleable. That is why an individual's response in a group, at any point in time, can be nonspecific and appear to serve the group's need, as in the case of scapegoating (Scheidlinger, 1982).

An error that emerges from group dynamic theory has been the assumption that collective group reactions express a unitary theme or shared view that reflects homogeneity in the members. However, recently it has been shown that even group-level processes are often not homogeneous; that is, their creation was not equally contributed to, and they are not, therefore, merely the expression of a combination of the lowest common denominator of the members' individual conflicts (Hinshelwood, 1987).[2] It is true that when issues concerning the therapists are foremost, commonalities in each member's transference to the leader do combine to yield common group transference reactions (Sutherland, 1952). Yet group-level processes usually reflect something quite different; for example, the group configuration can be organized around the unconscious fantasy of one of its members who dominates its culture (Anzieu, 1984). According to this view, dominant members at times will determine the structure of the group and, to a large degree, influence the roles played by each member. Since, in psychotherapy groups, struggles for dominance are ubiquitous and hierarchies of organization inevitably follow, this occurrence

---

[2]They may resemble such when serving as resistances (Kibel, 1977).

is frequent. Group function here will be determined by the unconscious conflicts of its most influential member or subgroup. In other
words, the group configuration can become an isomorphic expression
of the fantasy of that member or those individuals who currently
occupy a central role (see Redl, 1942). The other members may complement this role, perhaps in a way that is specific to their psychopathology, but even in nonspecific ways.

Externalization of internal object relations are usual in groups. As
noted, part-object relations are played out. Often they have a generic
quality, in that they embody usual social modes of interaction. Certainly, relationships between group members may appear to reflect
characteristic social differences between them. However, simultaneously they function as "dramatizations" (Hinshelwood, 1987) of internal contradictions. In other words, conflicts and barriers between
subgroups are a consequence of mutual projections. These represent
internal splitting projected into the social system of the group. The
result is a culture that supports the psychological defenses of its members and thereby constitutes a "social defence system," as originally
postulated for organizations by Jaques (1955). It would follow that
healing these externalizations of splitting, as expressed by division
within the group, paves the way for the healing of internal conflicts
within the members.

TREATMENT OF GROUP-LEVEL FANTASIES

A group is of most benefit to its members when such group-level
fantasies are relatively inactive, as the attachment to the group entity
will then serve as a focal point, in a major way, for structuring regressive mechanisms. Ideally, the group entity should bind the libidinal
elements so that the therapist and, particularly, the other members
can become the objects of aggressive drive derivatives (as discussed
below). When this occurs, the group functions therapeutically in that
it is self-analytical. However, the ideal is frequently disrupted and
replaced by resistant patterns. This situation occurs for two basic
reasons. First, as will be discussed later, an insult to the integrity
of the group pits the members, or those most affected, against the
perceived source of insult. Second, rivalries that are inherent to group
life cause certain members' fantasies to be played out by the group as a
whole. This occurrence is the source of dominance and dramatization.
Often, in these instances, the fantasy of the few enjoys wide support
because it complements nonspecific resistance for the rest. The latter

is the source of "basic assumption configurations," as described by Bion (1959).

As Bion found (see below), interpretation of the participation by the majority in a group-level fantasy of the few has variable results. Sometimes it frees the majority from the web spun by the few and enables them to address elements of the fantasy directly. This occurs whenever the bonds between the fantasy protagonists and the rest are weak. However, when they are strong, the therapist's efforts to help members examine the fantasy can prove fruitless. In this case, the therapist needs to take a dual approach, addressing both the group and the principal players.

Unfortunately, it is difficult to discern which approach is needed at any point in time. The determination must be made by examination of the group's recent history and a knowledge of the forces that determined a particular group-level fantasy. The process of such analysis becomes the basis for intervention. Taken together—the analysis and the intervention—they constitute the art of treatment. This is precisely where group dynamicists have gone wrong. They have addressed only the group itself, that is, the common aspects of the resistance, rather than the protagonists of the fantasy. In the following example, both were necessary.

At the session to be described, the group members played out a complex fantasy that reflected a passive–aggressive position that was central to the psychopathology of two individuals, but nonspecific to the rest. The fantasy was comprised of images of "good" members who deserved attention by a nurturing group but who, in fact, were ignored by this maternal entity and were, therefore, justifiably resentful. Mrs. S. was an only child of overindulgent, doting parents. She had found adulthood, by comparison, to be an unhappy state. Mr. D. was the youngest in a large family in which he experienced insufficient nurturance and was teased relentlessly by his siblings. Both looked to the group as a potentially need-gratifying object, but found that it disappointed them. Their silent, stubborn resentment paralleled repressed rage in their lives outside.

The group itself had undergone changes in recent months. Two new members had entered. One had been integrated successfully. The second appeared to be, but the group atmosphere, by becoming inhospitable for all, had seemed uncongenial to her. Four weeks earlier than the session which will be described in detail, awareness of the group atmosphere had come to the fore. Members complained that their problems were ignored and that the group was unresponsive to their needs. Each member believed that he or she was contributing to treatment but was not receiving in kind. This view served to justify selective withholding, which resulted in decreased interaction and overall productivity. The therapist responded by vowing to structure the sessions so that members' dissatisfactions could be aired, which seemed to help a great deal in the next session. However, in the session to be described in detail below, the same fantasy was reenacted. By this time, it no longer enjoyed wide support. Thus, the resistance of the majority was easier to address and the fantasy of the two principals stood out. Nevertheless, at the end of the session it seemed clear that the passive–aggressive mode had residual support.

At the session previous to the one in question, attendance was reduced because of a minor snowstorm. Much of that session centered around one man who had been depressed. At the outset of the session to be described here, he was asked if he was still as depressed. He said he was feeling better, but was uncertain what had caused his improvement. Those members absent from the previous session asked what had transpired. This man shared some of the basic elements of his problems but remarked that he did not wish to be the center of concern as he had been last time. That session, he reported, had been painful, but helpful. Now he wanted to focus on the others, since (he correctly noted) several members had issues that required discussion. Despite his plea, he remained the focus of attention, as the previous session absentees took the leadership and explored his problems. In response (to the resistance), the therapist asked if it was the members' conscious decision to focus on this man despite his stated objection. They answered affirmatively, and one member added that exploring this man's problems made him seem more real to them, specifically, made him seem as vulnerable as they were.

There was one digression to focus on a woman who had been depressed that week. Possible precipitants were itemized, but none proved explanatory. Yet, the woman reported, it was a relief to share this information with the group. With this discussion, the area of inquiry had only expanded to include two of the eight members. The therapist again intervened and pointedly expressed doubt that this limited range was representative of the group's intent, particularly since this was the session before the holiday season.

Although the arena for exploration had expanded, Mr. D. (who had not been a focus for discussion) complained that the group seemed uncaring to him. When pressed for an explanation, he complained that he had been neglected this night as he had been in recent weeks when he had sought help to understand his feelings concerning his daughter's abortion. He now referred to obscure hints of soliciting attention, which he believed were overt yet were ignored by the members. This distortion in his perception was confronted by several people. The discussion elaborated a fantasy, which was held by him but was no longer accepted by the others, that the group ought to satisfy inner needs and ubiquitously serve as a source of comfort. This fantasy was deemed unrealistic and was noted to function as a source of unhappiness outside the group. Then the therapist noted that what members had observed about Mr. D. was also true for Mrs. S.

Following this discussion there was elaboration by the members of the fantasy shared by the two protagonists. Both were searching for a need-gratifying object in the group and in life in general. Both had pursued this quest in vain and inwardly blamed others for ostensibly failing them. Mrs. S. provided corroboration for this explanation. She had the fantasy of bringing to this session an essay written by her son. She had wished to read it to them, hoping to hear their praise. Yet she withheld the essay, believing that one particular member would disapprove of her behavior and that the others would support the critic. At this point in the session, it appeared as if the passive–aggressive mode of relating had been abandoned by most members and had been laid at the feet of its most ardent supporters, Mr. D. and Mrs. S., for whom it was clinically relevant (that is, it was specific to their psychopathology). However, at the end of the session, several members announced that they would be away for the holiday week to follow, which was an unexpected development. The therapist remarked that the lateness of their announcements reflected continued support for the abrogation of responsibility in treatment.

Previously, the therapist, by imposing structure, had reduced the effect of the dominant fantasy so that it could be exposed at the session described here. Yet because it had, over time, permeated the group's consciousness, its undoing was only partially accomplished. More work was to be required. Specifically, in subsequent weeks the therapist needed to repeatedly interpret its reemergence before it became inactive as a groupwide "assumption."

REGRESSION OF THE GROUP

It would seem from the preceding example that group-level processes are important in the treatment and require the attention of the therapist. In fact, they are *always* relevant. However, their origins are diverse. They may reflect any of the following: (1) collaborative resistance to mutual exploration, (2) an amalgamation of transferences toward the leader, (3) the emergence of dominant fantasies, or (4) dramatizations of various patterns of internal splitting within the members. In addition, when groups are conducted within a larger social setting, such as an inpatient unit or day hospital, (5) the group symbolically reflects the dynamics of the milieu within which it resides (Levine, 1980; Klein and Kugel, 1981; Kibel, 1981, 1987).

From an object relations perspective, group-level processes are said to be comprised of "primitive mechanisms" because the group's dynamics are derived from the early object relations of each of its members. However, when applied to the group as a whole, the word "primitive" is often misleading. This term from individual psychology becomes a misnomer when transposed to the group, losing its meaning in translation. A description of mental mechanisms at the level of the group-as-a-group should not be construed to mean that each member functions at that corresponding level of psychopathology. Put simply, but stated within the confines of current terminology with its acknowledged limitations, the group's level of functioning and the members' level of ego integration should not be equated. For example, in a Tavistock-styled experiential group, the impassive stance of the leader can produce group-level regressive reactions in members who remain well-integrated. Conversely, a supportive, cohesive group of patients with severe psychopathology can help members contain their fragmented egos and enhance their adaptive functioning while they are with the group, that is, while in session. Technique will influence the nature of the treatment, specifically, the regressive process, and can be adapted to suit the level of pathology for a variety of patients. The details are beyond the scope of this chapter (see Kibel, 1991).

In the following example, primitive mechanisms were evident early in one session. Specifically, scapegoating resulted from the use of projective identification by those with well-integrated egos. While the victim did have borderline personality organization and, therefore, used such mechanisms readily, the others did not. Once the group-level fantasy was dramatized, the group itself could be said to have functioned at a primitive level. Yet nearly all of its members had neurotic ego structure.

The fantasy contained a dyadic complement of persecutor–victim. It was played out between two members who alternated roles. The group had been experiencing problems, manifested by irregular attendance by two of its six members. Moreover, at the previous two sessions only two and three members were present, respectively. At the end of the last one, those present resolved to confront the attendance problem directly the very next time. However, as we shall see, their efforts were derailed by announcement by one of the problem attenders of a planned absence for seemingly unavoidable circumstances.

Mrs. X. and Mrs. Y. had the complementary relationship that served as the focus for the shared or group-level fantasy of the bond between a persecutor and a victim. The tension between them, as we shall see, had recently intensified. The former, the borderline patient, regularly incurred the group members' anger by being overly confrontational and critical of others. Playing a masochistic role in the group, and in her life, enabled her to avoid the tender feelings she feared would engulf her, yet helped to perpetuate her own (and sometimes the group's) fantasy that she served the needs of others through sacrifice, doing "the right thing," and having the courage to confront what others avoided. This stance enabled her to merge aggressively linked and libidinally linked self images, while projecting aggressively linked object-images into the group, or onto the world in general. Being an active group member, she was associated with Mrs. Y., another patient leader who was often the spokesperson for the members' protests of Mrs. X.'s style. Mrs. Y. was one amongst several who saw themselves to be the unfortunate victims of life circumstance and of its ironies.

Both Mrs. X. and Mrs. Y. suffered from maternal deprivation and had a well of unsatisfied longings for nurturance. These were partially gratified in the group through competition for dominance, that is, for an imagined favored position with respect to the group (which, as will be explained later, is often perceived as a maternal entity). Both women had had poor relationships with their own mothers and felt rejected by them, but had much better relationships with their mothers-in-law, to the consternation of their own mothers. Mrs. Y.'s mother had died a few weeks earlier. Mrs. X. responded quickly by confronting Mrs. Y. prematurely about her defensive denial of anger toward her mother and her superficial, insincere expression of grief. This confrontation occurred, literally, a few days after the funeral. The timing of this confrontation was inappropriate and its manner was highly abrasive. Despite the accuracy of its content, it was tasteless. The group condemned Mrs. X.'s actions. Realizing her error, she apologized and made amends the next week, at the session prior to the one to be described here.

This session began with the announcement by one of the problem attenders that he would be on jury duty the following two weeks and on a business trip the one after that. Then one woman remarked that she was concerned about her recent habit of overeating. It is noteworthy that this thin, underweight individual was sitting next to one who was markedly obese. Next, Mrs. X. diverted attention to herself by discussing recent family problems. Through this she revealed, once again, her caustic nature. The members became engrossed in this discussion, focused their attention on her irritating and masochistic behavior within her family, and confronted her harshly. In this way, the frustration members felt in face of the problem attendance, which had been inhibited by the announcement (but reflected by the thin woman's comment), was projected into Mrs. X., who was now seen as the source of aggression.

Interpretation of this process of scapegoating had two effects. It freed the members to forcefully confront the attendance problem, to identify the source of resistance in the worst offenders, and to reemphasize their commitment to one another. Then, it allowed them to collaborate with Mrs. X. in exploring her behavior in terms of its genetic origins. As a child, she occupied a similar role in her family of origin, where she saw herself serving their needs at her own expense. Once all this was revealed, members could discuss realistic aspects of her provocativeness in group, while being empathic with her. Thus, one woman, the thin one, shared that she, too, had fantasies about making caustic comments to others. In this postinterpretation phase of the session, as the members explored their ambivalent reactions to Mrs. X., they employed higher level mechanisms. Thus, the group's level of functioning had shifted.

This example demonstrates how a series of events in the life of a group caused it to decompensate, so to speak. Rather than functioning in its usual self-analytical way, a fantasy that emerged from the psychopathology of two women was grafted onto group-level processes. The result was a kind of primitivization of the group's "ego" by a process of collective projective identification, which required the therapist to come to the rescue.

THE IMPLICATIONS OF THEORY FOR PRACTICE

Bion's notion of valency is the foundation of an object relations theory of groups. It implies that members' attraction for each other sets in motion certain dynamic processes in groups that affect the nature of therapy. Specifically, intragroup bonding creates, on the one hand, a common matrix for the interplay of the members' affects and internal self- and object-images, and, on the other hand, ties each member to the group entity. The former provides a common pathway for the expression of both advanced and primitive object relations, each reflecting a different level of ego organization (Stein and Kibel, 1984). In other words, through the member-to-member interactions, individuals reenact transference patterns that are derivatives of a developmental stage in which object constancy reigned, and yet may avail themselves of primitive mechanisms, particularly projective identification, to express lower levels of internal organization or individual psychopathology (Kernberg, 1975).

The relationship to the group as an entity is fundamental to the dynamics of treatment. Self-involvement in the group, the "giving up" to others an aspect of personal identity, has its roots in valency. This object-seeking quality of each member's ego is expressed not only through attachment to other members but via attachment to the group imago. Scheidlinger (1964) postulated that a universal need to belong and to establish, in groups, a state of psychological unity with others, despite uncertainty and ambiguity, represents the effort to counteract a fundamental fear in all people of abandonment and aloneness. Others have noted how an individual's sense of self and boundary (Anzieu, 1984) are threatened in a group in a way that causes one to turn toward some image that is perceived as unifying and enveloping. Scheidlinger (1974) further postulated that bonding to the group as an entity, the transition from the state of *I* to that of *We*, and the state of oneness with the group represent a covert wish to restore an earlier state of unconflicted well-being that was once part of the infant's fantasy of exclusive union with mother. That stage of ego development, characterized by egocentricity and coupled with a symbiotic perception of the mother as a gratifier of needs, was one wherein splitting was pervasively operative. Accordingly, in terms of a therapy group, "in the face of individual and collective stresses and anxieties induced by group formation . . . while the group entity is . . . perceived in a positive and benign . . . [vein], the group leader and the other members become almost immediately the objects of a gamut of partially ambivalent but largely hostile and fearful attitudes" (Scheidlinger, 1974, pp. 424–425).

This formulation regarding the concept of the "mother group" has heuristic value. It explains the profound attachment to a group that individuals have and can sustain even in the face of rejection or poor treatment results. It accounts for the influence of group norms, group pressure, and persuasion on the members. It explains why termination from group psychotherapy is frequently erratic—too abrupt with some patients or interminable for others. It accounts for some of the effects of new members and other disruptions to the gestalt of the group, that is, the perception of its continuity over time. It explains how a cohesive group can manage intragroup conflict and even strife. It demonstrates how the very perception of the group as an entity "is progressively utilized by both members and by the therapist in the service of the 'therapeutic alliance' or of group maintenance and cohesiveness so that intragroup conflicts and personal problems can be subjected to analytic scrutiny in the context of an anxiety level which is not too threatening to the equilibrium of individual patients and of the group entity" (Scheidlinger, 1974, p. 425). In short, in groups the mechanism of splitting facilitates therapeutic tasks. Specifically, a libidinal attachment to the group entity permits aggressively determined internal object relations to be reenacted with a sense of safety.

This formulation of a bond to the group as a maternal image that permits selective regression explains how group psychotherapy can be simultaneously both supportive and expressive. Splitting operates to reveal early internalized object relations while more advanced aspects of the ego remain functional. Like Bion's basic assumption culture and work group function, primitive and mature levels operate contemporaneously. This accounts for the prevalence of projective identification in groups, even in those comprised of neurotic patients.

Group Cohesion and Technique

In order to optimize these facets of the group in treatment, the therapist must foster group bonding, that is, the development of substantive cohesion. This term does not refer merely to group acceptance, camaraderie, and a sense of belonging, but to the existence of profound ties among the members, which are based upon their mutual identifications with one another, their common attachment to the leader, and a shared identification with the group as an entity (Piper, Marrache, Lacroix, Richardsen, and Jones, 1983). A group-centered approach to treatment fosters these feelings (Stein and Kibel, 1984).

The style and attitude of the therapist are important here and methodologically crucial. He must maintain a group-centered orientation for purposes of comprehending all material; that is, he must consider how each group event, no matter how seemingly insignificant, relates to group-level processes. Often, he needs to bring these matters to everyone's attention to let them see how together they are affected by every element of group life. Through this technique, he maximizes the members' awareness that they are part of a collective, and he thereby strengthens latent elements of their group identity. Groupwide interventions do the same.

He must limit his interactions with individuals but make the kinds of interventions that maintain or foster cohesiveness. These may range from directing the members' attention to common concerns and shared resistances to engaging them in the exploration of individual issues and each other's conflicts, to clarifying and decoding collective processes. In groups comprised of individuals with severe psychopathology, the therapist needs to assume a fairly active role, helping patients interact with one another. At the same time, he must accentuate the cohesive aspects of each element of group life, such as universalization, a process of identification. In groups of well-integrated patients, the therapist only needs to foster group bonding before cohesion has developed, by directing virtually all of his comments—whether questions, observations, clarifications, confrontations, or interpretations—to the entire membership. When members' actions, words, or behavior are noteworthy, they should be called to the attention of everyone for scrutiny. Thus, comments by the therapist that draw attention to one or several members should include an invitation to all to further investigate the behavior and speculate on its meaning.

In more advanced, cohesive groups, the leader need not restrict himself so much; he can have greater latitude with his interventions. In this instance, because there already exists a common matrix of identifications in the group, an intervention with one member generally affects all of them. However, this is not to suggest that the therapist can do individual therapy in the group. Rather, individual interventions should be used only to alter the balance of dynamic forces in the group so as to correct any malfunctioning processes. Anticohesive tendencies, that is, the propensity for group dissolution, are always present. Too many individual interventions will augment their power. In order to maximize the potentials of group life, from an object relations perspective, the therapist should mostly attend to group-level processes and then to individual phenomena secondarily.

Cohesion operates therapeutically to bind the members to one another so that they view each other as primary objects for internal strivings. Then, through their interactions with one another, unconscious object relations are revealed. Peer relationships in groups reflect their several sources, including members' common conflicts with the leader, their need for relationships, and each one's character style and mutual defense complementation (Fried, 1965). In fact, to a large extent, group interactions function as a condenser, a final common pathway for the expression of a gamut of individual psychological processes that are activated by group life (Stein and Kibel, 1984). The constant unfolding of such transferential aspects of behavior make them available for therapeutic investigation by the members of the group. When a group is in a functional state, members can deal with each other's transferences, that is, clarify and decode them. The therapist's role, therefore, should be relegated to attending to malfunctioning group processes, since such malfunctions prevent group interactions from playing their therapeutic role.

Antitherapeutic Dependency

Therapeutic cohesion, that is, the functional state, is repeatedly opposed by the development of the phenomena akin to Bion's basic
assumptions (1959), which operate as group resistances (Kibel, 1977).
Their interpretation can serve to block their continued expression. In
this instance, the aim of interpretation is to alter the group's dynamic
balance so as to improve its functioning, not necessarily to promote
insight. At the level of the group, the therapist's interpretations have
an inhibitory effect, thereby converting a collective ego-syntonic assumption into an ego-dystonic state.

Of all types of groupwide resistances, the establishment of functional cohesion in groups is opposed primarily by the potential for
development of a leader-dependent group culture. Dependency is
inherently appealing, since it carries with it illusions of nurturance,
protection, and freedom from responsibility. The therapist, because
his influence is overriding, readily becomes the object of dependency.
His leverage derives, in part, from the realistic aspects of the treatment relationship. But, on a psychodynamic level, as Whitaker and
Lieberman (1964) noted, "The therapist's power to influence the
group derives from (1) the unique position from which he views the
group . . . and which permits him to intervene on the basis of information unavailable to the patient and (2) from the frequency from
which the patients impute to the therapist the power of gratification,
threat and magical solutions" (pp. 197–198). In short, information
yields power, social role solidifies it, and unconscious wishes give it
dynamic meaning. For this reason, the therapist, more than any other
individual and more than any idea or psychic image, can readily serve
as a focus for dependency wishes. Compared to individual treatment,
his influencing process is more subtle in group psychotherapy. Kelman (1963) has summarized the therapist's position well:

> The therapist often, in subtle ways, directs the patient; he approves
> of some things and disapproves of others. The patient picks this up and
> tailors his subsequent productions accordingly. . . . Also, he encourages
> certain kinds of contents, in contrast to other kinds, by responding to
> them, showing interest in them, and building interpretations around
> them. Patients learn to give the therapist what he seems to want. . . .
> Since the therapist's reactions are so much more important to the pa-
> tient and since the patient finds himself in a relatively ambiguous situa-
> tion in which he is searching for guidelines for his behavior, it seems
> more than reasonable to assume that he will be sensitive to subtle clues
> of approval or disapproval emanating from the therapist [p. 407].

The dependency position is common in groups composed of patients with severe psychopathology, but is frequently seen in groups with better integrated patients, particularly when there has been some insult to the members' perception of the group as an entity. This occurs whenever the group's integrity as a bounded system has been disrupted by events that affect its operation, such as absences, vacations, or the departure and entrance of members. Then members revert to former modes of relating in the group, namely, those found in the leader-dependent culture that was characteristic of an early phase of group development. Interpretation of this dependency position may not be sufficient to change it. As Bion (1959) noted, members usually experience basic assumption culture as real and reject any verbal penetration. Ironically, while the leader here is somewhat deified, his interpretation is experienced as tantamount to an attack on a religious belief: "an interpretation will often be followed by a silence that is far more a tribute of awe than a pause for thought . . . the psychiatrist may think that he is dealing with 'resistances' in the ordinary sense of the term, but I believe that it is more fruitful to consider the group as a community that felt that a hostile attack was being made upon its religious beliefs" (Bion, 1959, p. 85). Participation in the basic assumption group, with its primitive-like mechanisms, appears to be divorced from the intact ego functions of the participants, or, in other words, the group process (basic assumption mentality) is split off from each member's observing ego (work group mentality). When interpretation fails to convert an ego-syntonic assumption into a dystonic state, the malfunction needs to be worked through. Specifically, dependency must be worked out of the group through its interactional processes. The following clinical example demonstrates this process.

The session to be described occurred two weeks after a vacation break. One patient had been absent the previous week, being ill with the flu. Another was absent because of the flu this time. The breakdown of the group's integrity was reflected in the early phase of the session by its pace, which was slow and halting, as we shall see. The therapist became attuned to the dependency position through examination of his countertransference. As is typical in such situations, the therapist became anxious as omnipotent images were projected into him. The consequent fantasy of being persecuted by a powerful person was then displaced onto a group member who often assumed a prominent auxiliary therapist role. Working this out, first with him and then with the therapist, constituted the labor of the session that permitted the group to recover from the effects of the vacation and to restore its previous level of functioning.

The session began with the announcement that an absent member was ill. Another patient, who had been ill the previous week, asked the members what had happened at that session. She was met with a paucity of responses. No one even inquired as to whether she was fully recovered from her own illness. One young woman spoke of her persistent doubts about the appropriateness of group for her condition. Discussion of this concern was sparse and superficial in nature. The conversation up to this point had been meager, halting, and characterized by intermittent silence and quiet tones of voice. Thereupon, the therapist described the resistance and asked why the members were having difficulty responding to one another. He was met with defensiveness. For example, one patient said that she was preoccupied with the rain outside, and Mr. R., the one who often functioned as an auxiliary therapist, reported that he was deliberately trying to listen more and dominate less.

Next, one member talked about her reaction to a television program that depicted a mother's response to the successful suicide of her daughter. This show caused the patient to realize that her own attempts had greatly distressed her parents. Consequently, she decided to call them to make amends. Mr. R. expressed surprise that she had not realized previously how her suicide attempts had affected them. One member, Mrs. E., then took issue with him for having said this and claimed that he was being judgmental. A mild argument between these two ensued. The therapist tried to involve the others, who were silent, and get their reactions to these events. However, they ignored his efforts and proceeded to lend support to Mrs. E. against Mr. R., although there was no evidence that they agreed with her basic claim. Fueled by the others, the argument between the two escalated. She complained that he often made her look foolish and erroneously stated that he had criticized her recently for seeming to be unfeeling toward her children. She persisted with this complaint in the face of Mr. R.'s denial. Yet the others did nothing to correct her. Rather, they now blamed him for unduly upsetting her.

This interaction came to a halt when Mrs. E. whined that the session was "making me crazy." The therapist thereupon explained how her state was induced by the affects circulating in the group. In an attempt to rid themselves of inward distress, including angry feelings, the members had encouraged her to complain about Mr. R. By experiencing her anger toward him, they relieved themselves of their own angry feelings. All this was possible because they all shared the notions that other people were the cause of inner distress and, in various ways, affect one's inner being, that alleged criticism from others causes one to become upset and that, therefore, these others ought to be blamed.

This interpretation of group-level projective identification did nothing to alter the dependent position immediately. After a brief interlude, Mrs. E. resumed her complaints about Mr. R. and was again granted group support. The situation changed only after the therapist announced the upcoming entrance of two new members, several weeks hence. At that point, the patients' protestations turned against him. In doing so, the members took delight in criticizing various aspects of the therapist's technique. After this "manic"-styled review took its course, the members reviewed the events of the session. Now they were able to sympathize with Mr. R.'s position of isolation during this session and in the group in general. They even noted how Mrs. E. had distorted his comments earlier, as well as those of previous sessions. In other words, in this example, interpretation failed to correct the group's defensive stance. At most, it may have set the stage for working through. However, it was the minirebellion, the ridicule of the therapist's style, that proved palliative. Acting out transference anger with the therapist was needed before the members could become more observant of the group process. Then they could confront Mrs. E., no longer needed to scapegoat Mr. R., and could better appreciate reality.

Alternating attachment to the leader and the group entity constitutes a continuing dialectic in treatment. To some degree, transference to the leader is always operative, as are derivatives that are found in a variety of member-to-member interactions (Stein, 1970). In order to promote cathexis to the group itself, the therapist must gently deflect attention away from himself and enhance members' potential for group coherence. Cohesion is promoted when attention is focused on the common concerns of the members, both inside and outside the group. In this regard, comments should be made which encourage the sense of mutuality of experience, and attention should be paid to the group's boundaries and structure. Groupwide interventions—including questions, suggestions, clarifications, confrontations and interpretations—help a great deal.

The object relations dimension of the group is enhanced when members' communications are group-directed, so that complex interactional patterns occur. This is opposed to a dependent group culture, where interactional patterns are simple and focused predominantly on one individual. Recognition of this difference caused Foulkes (1948) to discard the term "leader" in favor of "conductor." His intention was to convey the notion that once the bond to the group entity became firm the therapist's task shifted. Then he was to steer the group, indirectly although deliberately, so that treatment occurred *by* the group itself. With resistant groups, noncohesive ones, and those comprised of patients with severe psychopathology, the therapist must work hard to move from the position of being the leader *of* the group to that of conductor *in* the group.

In summary, valency provides the glue that bonds the members together, thereby creating the group entity. Once dependency upon the therapist is diminished, the group itself assumes the attributes of leadership. This permits the emergence of defensive operations that derive from early phases of ego development. Then, projective and splitting mechanisms emerge to produce scapegoating, spokespersons, and the playing-out of a dominant fantasy, on the one hand, or externalization of split relationships, subgrouping, and dramatizations, on the other. At any point, basic assumptions may reemerge to operate as collective resistances to the therapeutic task; that is, the patients may act "as if" they are involved in productive work when, in fact, they are functioning in a way that is far removed from the reality for which they are there, namely, to learn about themselves through the group experience (Kibel, 1977).

The focus here, from an object relations perspective, is on group-level processes, specifically those that embody the reenactment of internalized object relations. However, these are not the only dynamic processes in a group. Groups are complex entities in which there are many classes of events: for example, those that pertain to the individual in the group, those that pertain only to dyads or subgroups, and those that reflect the transferences of individuals. Any of these may meld with group-level processes. The overall picture is exceedingly complex. Kernberg (1975) described, in a visual way, the dynamic components of the group as an amalgam of nonconcentric circles. In general systems terms, the separate systems of the group intersect with one another. Because of this, any action, including the therapist's interventions, at one level of the group will carom through its other systems. The therapist cannot attend to all these effects and their interrelationships. Therefore, selective attention to the sundry elements of the group is inevitable, and will arise from his treatment philosophy and view of the mutative forces in groups. The position here is that, from an object relations perspective, the attachment to the group entity and the resulting group-level processes are to be emphasized.

GROUPWIDE INTERPRETATION AND ITS PROBLEMS

Interventions in groups ought to be designed to keep the group functional, that is, in a state in which members are participating freely in the discussion, revealing themselves, equally sharing in the process, and trying to understand each other's behavior and problems. When this condition exists, members derive benefit from the treatment both experientially and cognitively. The former was alluded to previously in this chapter and will be described more fully later; the latter occurs when members provide meaning attribution statements (Scheidlinger, 1987) to one another. Because members are bound to the group and each other by primitive ties, these experiential and cognitive factors are especially penetrating. This is why it is reasonable to claim that members' "interpretations" to each other are therapeutically useful even though members lack the training and skill of the therapist. Such a view was articulated by Foulkes (1975), who repeatedly claimed that "in the group-analytic group interpretations are going on all the time, consciously and unconsciously" (p. 117).

The therapist's interpretive role in groups differs vastly from that in individual treatment. Basically, his role is to deal with group resistances (Kibel, 1977). Again, as Foulkes (1975) noted, "The guiding lines for interpreting on the part of the therapist may be stated as follows: Interpretation is called for when there is a blockage in communication. It will be particularly concerned with resistances, including transference" (p. 125). That is, to use the terminology previously introduced in this chapter, the therapist needs to attend to the group as an entity, including groupwide resistances, dramatizations, dominant fantasies, and other group-level processes. Then the group members will be free to attend to each other's conflicts or, in Bion's (1959) terms, the work group (*W*) will be operative. In practice, group-level and individual conflicts are reciprocally related. The therapist must address resistance wherever it occurs, either at the level of the group as a unit or with those individuals who are the locus of a resistant fantasy.

Attending to the group requires the therapist to intervene in whatever way is effective to manage the group's dysfunction. This does not necessarily mean that his meaning attribution statements to the group penetrate the individual in the way they were intended. In fact, groupwide interpretations are often relatively ineffective for the members. They affect the group's functioning sooner than that of its components because they are far removed from that which the individual can understand or accept. Kernberg (1975) noted that a group, in general systems terms, is composed of a series of subsystems. Its dynamic components interdigitate and overlap, and can be visualized diagrammatically, as an amalgam of nonconcentric circles that cannot be reduced to a unified whole. Therefore, the therapist's interventions at one dynamic level of the group will have uncertain and unpredictable effects on its other systems.

Traditional analytic interpretations are three-tiered (Ezriel, 1952) in that they aim to describe the behavior or the defense, the unconscious wish or impulse, and the attendant anxiety. Their effectiveness with patients in dyadic treatment is dependent upon the degree to which the therapist can describe the subtle aspects of each tier, that is, the nuances of preconscious and unconscious fantasies. This is impossible to do in a group; the therapist cannot be that well attuned to each member. Alternatively, it may be said that, for members of a group, as defensive patterns differ so does the relationship of each individual's conflicts to the collective defense. The degree of availability of those unconscious fantasies that contribute to holistic phenomena varies from one to the other (Kibel and Stein, 1981).

All this explains why group-level interpretations are often not effective in the way they are intended, as the following example demonstrates. This illustration occurred in a group that was undergoing a change in membership. One longstanding member had terminated the previous week, another member six weeks prior to the current session, and a third would be doing so in two months. One of two new members was to enter one month hence, but the other arrived at the session to be described. All of these comings and goings were planned.

Two of the seven group members were a few minutes late. There was silence at the outset and an apparent lack of introductions to the new member. Only after the therapist asked if this had transpired in the waiting room did the members introduce themselves. The silence and subsequent uneasiness were rationalized by the members as reflecting an intentional delay that was designed to avoid repetition for the latecomers. Yet after they arrived the paucity of interaction continued. There was more silence, sparse discussion, some joking, and generally resistive behavior. Humor arose and focused on the therapist, specifically, on his purchase of new furniture. This was done in an amiable, yet decidedly cutting way. The comments included the following: "I can see you are doing well in this business," "It's good to know that you're making money on us," and "If you really want to get up in the world, you might raise our fee."

Transference anger was unmistakable here, yet denied. Its relation to the change in membership was less apparent. Clarification by the therapist of the behavior and interpretation of its meaning only caused the members to turn their attention toward the new member. But the focus on her proved excessive, intractable, and nonsubstantive. Surprisingly, they praised her for allegedly seeming to be highly motivated for treatment. This was placed in contrast to others who were dubious about their progress in therapy and discouraged.

The therapist's efforts to help the patients examine the group's process was to no avail until a disgruntled member complained that the newcomer had monopolized the session. Only then did some of the ambivalence of the others about her entrance begin to emerge. Specifically, they expressed concern that the disgruntled one's attitude would scare the new member away. This attitude served as the segue for the exposure of unconscious anger attendant upon the disruption of the group imago, namely, the perception of its gestalt, caused by these comings and goings. In retrospect, it appeared that the therapist's intervention had some effect, but only on one member, the disgruntled one. The change in him unexpectedly served as the mediator for changes in the others who had resisted the therapist's efforts.

Penetration of groupwide defenses is possible when certain conditions are present. Sometimes the group resistance is full of internal contradictions and the members are at variance with each other, so the resistance is experienced as decidedly unpleasant. To extricate themselves from discomfort, the members seek the therapist's guidance or may even call upon their own resources of self-investigation. In most cases, resolution is mediated by the alliance of the members with the leader, which causes them to value his opinion. By identifying with his observing ego, they can "borrow" self-reflection, so to speak, and tentatively look at themselves. This process disrupts the collective resistance and helps the members move from a position of "acting in" to one of self-observation. In the absence of either of these two conditions—discomfort with the experience or retroflexive observation through identification with the therapist—the group is unable to examine itself. Then, members' immersion in the group matrix and its network of regressive processes, which accentuate early modes of object relatedness, impairs the function of each person's observing ego.

This situation is most evident when the state of group illusion, as described by Anzieu (1984), is in effect. Here the members psychically view the group as if it were a mini-Utopia. The group itself serves as a libidinal object and, through narcissistic identification, functions as an ideal ego. Aggression is thereupon primitively denied. The group illusion serves as a defense against exploration of the unconscious, since, in this instance, the (aggressively linked) ego function of investigation (work) is split off. Such a situation is illustrated in the following example, which again deals with the entrance of a new member, as well as a schedule change, both of which served to disrupt the integrity of the group as a bounded system.

The periodicity of sessions was disrupted by a change in schedule the week previous to the session to be described, due to a brief absence by the therapist. There was a make-up session which two patients failed to attend, one because of physical symptoms that may have had a psychological basis and the other because she forgot. Even though the therapist had been away and had been able to reschedule the group, he was not able to do so for this woman's individual session.

At the next regularly scheduled group session a new member joined, as planned. After her introduction, a fruitful discussion ensued concerning the difficulty some members had recently with participating fully in sessions. The focus soon centered on one woman who had been depressed all week. Whereas previously she had spoken about her parents in idealized terms, she now revealed her deep and abiding ambivalence toward them. She reported on the subtle ways in which, she believed, they made her feel worthless and guilty and how relieved she felt after her father died. Now, she feared, she might make the same mistake with her children that her parents had made with her.

The group's response was striking. They not only encouraged her to reveal more, but they clarified her feelings, shared their own reactions to her, and used her situation analogously to explore similar conflicts in their own lives. For example, one member told how his resentment toward his father caused him to secretly wish for the man's death. The members then related this discussion to the absences of the previous week and their psychological meaning.

This session seemed to be unusual, especially when compared to recent ones. Except for the newcomer, members had been participating fully and equally, and they were responsive to one another and mutually insightful. Previously this had not been the case. Rather, they had tended to focus on selected individuals at the expense of groupwide participation. On this occasion they appeared to be functioning as an ideal therapeutic group, yet their blatant disregard for the new member suggested otherwise: namely, that such apparent good work actually constituted resistant behavior.

The therapist then intervened to ask the members for their impression of the session thus far. They responded with unanimous praise for the way it was going and remarked that it was the best they had to date. The therapist next inquired if anything was missing. While saying this, he glanced at the new member. As if in response to his unspoken direction, the members promptly engaged the newcomer. However, this was short-lived; they resumed the former pattern, this time focusing their attention on members who previously had gotten less.

After a while, the therapist again intervened, described the character of this session at some length, and then invited the members to speculate as to why it seemed so productive, particularly in comparison to recent ones. He suggested several possibilities, including the introduction of a new member. The members rejected all explanations and chose to believe that their productivity this time reflected a natural progression in the life of the group. As evidence, they noted that previously the introduction of a new member had inhibited the process, particularly the sharing of personal material and the giving of feedback. Now, it seemed to them, the newcomer made no difference at all. In essence, they implied that the new member was unimportant, even that she was insignificant, and in this way they psychologically excluded her. The therapist confronted this view by asking them how they imagined she might feel hearing that her presence had no effect on them. Rather than answering the therapist's question for themselves, the members asked the newcomer if she felt excluded. Naturally, she said she did not. Next, the therapist gave them a more comprehensive interpretation that included a full description of their behavior and its motivation. This was met with a meager, mixed response. Most rejected it. Two members, who tended to be passively compliant, agreed with it. However, such acceptance probably reflected transference resistance on their part. One member, who was the most vocal, claimed that the therapist was imposing his own preconceptions onto the group. Ironically, his statements indirectly enriched the exclusionary hypothesis, by implying that disaffected ideas (and images) were worthless. Yet his negativism served to disown its applicability to them and project it back to the therapist.

Denial here was blatant. The members maintained the illusion that the group was "good," specifically, that this session was exceedingly productive and that they were exceptionally effective with one another. They reacted to the entrance of the new member as if it were an insignificant event and treated her as a nonentity. They devalued her, yet were blind to their hostile intent, which would have been quite evident to any observer. The therapist's efforts to penetrate the resistance were to no avail. In such instances, the group illusion needs to run its course; that is, the intensity of its motivation must wane before the group's self-investigative function can be restored.

This discussion is not intended to discourage the use of groupwide interpretations. Rather, it is merely intended to identify the limitations of such a procedure. Usually, group-level processes reflect basic themes of human strife, including conflicts over dependency, trust, love, envy, power, anger, fear, rivalry, and the like. There are many instances where interpretation at the level of the group will impact directly on the conflicts of some of its members, albeit each to a different degree. The variability will be a function of the place each patient is in the course of his treatment, as well as the severity of his psychopathology.

By the same token, technique within an object relations approach will vary in accordance with the nature of the members' psychopathology. Details are beyond the scope of this chapter. Suffice it to say that with the more psychologically disabled, technique will be directed toward building and rebuilding cohesion (Kibel, 1991), while with milder conditions it will be directed toward helping the members "own" split-off part-objects. In the latter instance, the therapist can allow regressive group dynamics to operate for a while before intervening. In the former, he must move in early. In any case, interventions by the therapist usually help the patients move from a mode of acting in to one of investigation and understanding. A major statement by the therapist about process serves to inhibit interaction. It gets the members to think about what is happening by halting the usual flow of discussion. The therapist's task is precisely to encourage the examination of events and the appreciation of each member's participation in them.

THERAPEUSIS

The mechanisms of change in group psychotherapy are uncertain. Yalom's (1975) now classic study on curative factors revealed only patients' perception of benefit in a particular kind of group, not what actually helped. Consequently, Bloch (1986) relabeled these as "putative" therapeutic factors. Nevertheless, Yalom's findings would support the clinical impression that group members are helped by a combination of interpersonal learning in the context of the here-and-now and the experience of being in the group itself. Change involves both cognitive and experiential learning. From an object relations perspective, the latter is of special interest. As we shall see, identification is the core for the mutative effects of experience.

Identification is a multilayered phenomenon. Members of a group have a fundamental sense of commonality with one another because they share the same relationship with the therapist and a common set of experiences in the group. By working together, they come to identify with the significant objects in each other's lives, so that they function as transference objects for each other. Freud's (1921) formulation that in groups members "identified themselves with one another in their ego" (p. 140), as well as with the therapist's, has been accepted by many psychoanalytic workers to explain the mutually enhancing effects of interpersonal, analytic investigation. Thus, on the one hand, relationships in the group help members reenact unconscious transference roles with each other while, on the other hand, they enable patients to develop an "identification with the self-investigative tendencies with the other members of the group and the therapeutic approach of the therapist" (Stein and Wiener, 1978, p. 239). This is the basis for cognitive interpersonal learning.

Members' transference patterns with one another are expressed in treatment, then explored and discussed. Patients comment on the unseen meaning behind each other's behavior and attitudes. This practice can produce a growing awareness of the unconscious significance of transference manifestations. However, given that the process in groups is fluid and unstable, insight may not always settle in (i.e., it may not be consolidated in the ego). Nevertheless, interpretations enhance members' ability to understand both self and others and, thereby, promote ego mastery. Thus, even cognitive learning has an experiential component.

Identification in the group also produces nonspecific benefits. On a surface level, members identify with one another because they are all dysphoric and sense similarities in each other's symptoms, attitudes, and conflicts. This condition has been termed universalization. Mutual acceptance enables patients to give each other sympathy, encouragement, advice, and guidance. Identification with the leader enables members to adopt his therapeutic attitude, one that encourages the expression of personal conflicts, is tolerant toward aggressive drive and superego derivatives, views interpersonal tensions as an opportunity for change, and contains the conviction that all these things will be worked out. It has long been recognized that, in many ways, faulty attitudes that produce character pathology are corrected "by a process of substitution, identification and ego and defense strengthening rather than by a basic alteration in dynamic structure" (Stein, 1956, p. 33). This is part of what constitutes the corrective emotional experience.

In group psychotherapy, the counterpart of the positive transference to the therapist and the working alliance in dyadic treatment is the identification with the group entity. This process enables patients to incorporate its standards and values and all the therapeutic attitudes previously noted that originated with the therapist. Horwitz (1974), in his review of the Psychotherapy Research Project of the Menninger Foundation, reported that a number of patients showed substantial improvement in a treatment which emphasized consolidation of the therapeutic alliance. These patients were able to achieve significant and stable structural change through a method that promoted the beneficial aspects of the dyadic transference relationship, including its gratifying aspects, rather than through its interpretation. Thus, the treatment alliance did not merely serve as a prerequisite for therapeutic work, it became the main vehicle for change. A similar process has been claimed for the group treatment of borderline and narcissistic conditions (Stone and Gustafson, 1982). To some degree the same may be true with all patients.

From an object relations perspective, structural change would be attendant upon the formation of new self representations through incorporation of elements of the group matrix. Over time, elements of each member's perception of the group becomes crystallized as a mental representation of self-in-the-group. Ultimately, this gets internalized and finally consolidated into new identifications. This occurrence, as we shall see, is the product of several processes in the group, amongst which is projective–reintrojective relatedness.

Internalization is used here in the manner defined by Shafer (1968): It "refers to all those processes by which the subject transforms real or imagined regulatory interactions with his environment, and real or imagined characteristics of his environment, into inner regulations and characteristics" (p. 9). In terms of group psychotherapy, structural change requires that the new, more gratifying and mature relationship that occurs between the self and the group, along with its members and leader, become assimilated into the individual's inner world of object relations. Regressive group processes make members impressionable, so that an internal representation of the self-in-the-group can be imprinted on the psyche. Over time, due to the force of the treatment experience, such an altered self concept gets translated into everyday relationships and, hence, the self is transmuted. In short, the group identity modifies personal identification.

As the treatment unfolds, new introjects of the self in relation to the group further influence each member's behavior. These introjects act in a reciprocally enhancing manner within the group so as to contribute to further growth of the therapeutic alliance. Stability of change occurs because improved attitudes and behavior induce positive reinforcement by others over a range of time and experiences. Augmentation of protherapeutic attitudes is prompted by the fantasy of winning the group's love and respect, not just the therapist's. Thus, both internal and external rewards serve as potent forces in the maintenance of change.

Reintrojection is the feedback loop of group interaction that has its origin in projective identification. The latter is a concept that is ideally suited to group psychology because, as Ogden (1981) observed, it "is one of the few psychoanalytic concepts that bridges the intrapsychic sphere of thoughts and feelings and the interpersonal sphere of real object relations occurring in the context of a given social system" (p. 331). Bion (1959) maintained that it is the cornerstone of mental life in groups and, hence, of group behavior (Horwitz, 1983). It is "so fundamental to group psychology that it, in a sense, *creates* the group as a distinctive, coherent experience" (Ashbach and Schermer, 1987, p. 42).

Through projective identification, patients attempt to manage aspects of themselves that they sense are noxious or even dangerous. In the group, they induce others to feel, think, and behave in a manner consonant with the ejected fantasy. Getting others to embody unwanted aspects of oneself serves denial and, ultimately, repression. Split-off or repressed aspects of the self are experienced as located in the group rather than in one's self. Feedback in groups has a dual function here. First, it helps the individual to "own" split-off aspects of himself. Second, it enables projected fantasies to be processed in the group matrix, that is, toned down or even corrected. This is the reintrojective part of the interactional loop.

When aggressively derived internal images are projected into the group matrix, they induce corresponding reactions in other members. The reintrojected object, when untreated, contains a kind of persecutory anxiety. Usual group interactions are influenced by this process, and this is why they are ordinarily so subject to distortion. The goal of treatment is ultimately to correct the reintrojective loop in terms of the way patients perceive themselves in the group. The resulting palliative experience becomes the foundation for new introjects. Therefore, feedback is a crucial element in treatment. It not only operates overtly, but in subtle ways influences the reintrojected object. When group interactions are subjected to analytic scrutiny and the therapeutic attitude is applied (an attitude of tolerance, understanding, and investigation), feedback functions in a constructive, corrective manner.

Projective–reintrojective relatedness in groups functions much like the "mirror reactions" described by Foulkes and Anthony (1965), which, they state, help developmentally in the differentiation of the self from the not-self. As they noted, "The reflections of the self from the outside world lead to greater self-consciousness, so that the infant . . . eventually learns to distinguish his own image from that of other images. . . . The mirror reactions in the group help . . . by externalizing what is inside and internalizing what is outside, the individual activates within himself the deep social responses that lead to his definition . . . as a social being" (pp. 150–151).

All this can be stated in another way, drawing upon the analogy of childhood growth and development. Group interactions function as a special kind of play (Kosseff, 1990) through which members develop ego functions and correct the sense of themselves in the world. Play is the opportunity to make trial relationships where there is relatively little fear of the consequences or of being held forever to what one has said or done or to the responses of others. Play allows one to project parts of one's self into the immediate world, place them into others, and yet recover them at will. It permits individuals both to confront and accept split-off parts of their egos on a trial basis or, more substantively, to experiment with new trial identifications. For this reason, Kosseff (1990) correctly noted that group psychotherapy is experienced in the area of transitional phenomena.

To review, the mutative process in group psychotherapy has both a cognitive and experiential component. The investigative attitude of the therapist and patients permeates the treatment atmosphere and becomes a template for the development of new internal representations and experiences of oneself. In this way, understanding stimulates ego mastery and functions in preparation for the experiential process. Projective–reintrojective relatedness lies at the heart of the experience and is the basis for the formation of healthier identifications. But, once again, even as internalization takes hold, understanding helps. Insight gives perspective to the experience, thereby shaping and solidifying internal object relationships while anchoring them to their external counterparts. During the course of treatment, insight can be found to follow the onset of change in group and secures it, so that the benefits endure.

CONCLUSIONS

Object relations theory turned psychoanalytic thinking away from its focus on instinctual development and toward study of the development of the ego in the context of reciprocal relationships with objects. It helped classical theory move from being an individualistic psychology to becoming an interpersonal one. As a supplement to traditional methodology, evolution in technique should be just that, namely, additions, modifications, shifts in emphases, and so forth, not radical deviations.

The theory maintains that the fundamental striving for all human beings is the drive toward object relations. Bion referred to this urge as valency. Drawing upon Kleinian notions, he called attention to the role of the paranoid-schizoid position in groups and described how projective identification functions as the cornerstone of mental life in groups and, hence, of members' behavior (Horwitz, 1983). Subsequently, others have shown that reenactment of part-object relations in groups and playing-out of defensive splits, particularly their generic aspects, constitutes dramatization or externalization of members' internal object relations at the level of the group.

When the group is constructed along therapeutic lines, it is often perceived as a sanctuary, a safe place, or cocoon, in which, for each member, a host of aggressively derived introjects can be revealed, played out, and then subjected to analytic scrutiny. The dichotomy between the perception of the group as nurturing and of the other members as sources of conflict is a basic condition for treatment. Here, splitting is put to therapeutic advantage. Members' valency bonds them together, creating this perception of the group. This illusionary aspect of the group as an entity serves as a variant of the narcissistic alliance of dyadic treatment (Alonso and Rutan, 1984).

Foulkes (1948) likened the therapeutic group to a hall of mirrors in which members serve as objects, both external and projected ones, that resonate with each one's inner reality. Transference distortions, emanating from the latter, sometimes meet with gratification, but usually with confrontation from the rest of the group, which tests reality (Alonso and Rutan, 1984). Because feedback comes from fellow sufferers, it is inherently empathic, even if sometimes delivered in an abrasive manner.

Cohesion in a group ensures a general atmosphere of tolerance, so that peer confrontations and interpretations can function supportively. Such a group "contains" members' projections—soothes them or tones them down—so that palliative reintrojective mechanisms can work. This process operates on an experiential level, which is to be expected since early object relations and early ego defenses harken to the preverbal years. No doubt, insight helps. But it has already been demonstrated that substantive change can occur in the absence of insight and its precursor, psychological-mindedness (Horwitz, 1974). No doubt insight is instrumental to change, but it has been overrated. It provides ego mastery, supplies links between experiences, and thereby consolidates change. It may be that what is mutative is not the substance of insight, but the process of gaining it (Appelbaum, 1975) in the context of an environment that permits projective–reintrojective cycles to operate in a salutary way. In the last analysis, the view of therapeusis presented here may prove to be the major contribution of object relations theory to the practice of group psychotherapy.

REFERENCES

Alonso, A., & Rutan, J. S. (1984), The impact of object relations theory on psychodynamic group therapy. *Amer. J. Psychiat.*, 141:1376–1380.

Anzieu, D. (1984), *The Group and the Unconscious.* London: Routledge & Kegan Paul.

Appelbaum, S. A. (1975), The idealization of insight. *Internat. J. Psychoanal. Psychother.*, 4:272–302.

Ashbach, C., & Schermer, V. L. (1987), *Object Relations, the Self and the Group.* London: Routledge & Kegan Paul.

Bion, W. R. (1959), *Experiences in Groups.* London: Tavistock Publications.

——— (1970), *Attention and Interpretation.* New York: Basic Books.

Bloch, S. (1986), Therapeutic factors in group psychotherapy. In: *Psychiatry Update: The American Psychiatric Association Annual Review*, Vol. 5, ed. A. J. Frances & R. E. Hales, pp. 678–698.

Ezriel, H. (1950), A psychoanalytic approach to group treatment. *Brit. J. Med. Psychol.*, 23:59–74.

——— (1952), Notes on psychoanalytic therapy: II, Interpretation and research. *Psychiat.*, 15:119–126.

Fairbairn, W. D. (1952), *An Object-Relations Theory of the Personality.* New York: Basic Books.

Fried, E. (1965), Some aspects of group dynamics and the analysis of transference and defenses. *Internat. J. Group Psychother.*, 15:44–56.

Foulkes, S. H. (1948), *Introduction to Group-Analytic Psychotherapy: Studies in the Social Integration of Individuals and Groups.* London: Heinemann.

——— (1975), *Group-Analytic Psychotherapy: Methods and Principles.* London: Gordon & Breach.

——— Anthony, E. J. (1965), *Group Psychotherapy: The Psychoanalytic Approach*, 2nd ed. Baltimore: Penguin Books.

Freud, S. (1921), Group psychology and the analysis of the ego. *Standard Edition*, 18:67–143. London: Hogarth Press, 1955.

——— (1923), The ego and the id. *Standard Edition*, 19:13–66. London: Hogarth Press, 1961.

Hinshelwood, R. D. (1987), *What Happens in Groups: Psychoanalysis, the Individual and the Community.* London: Free Association Books.

Horwitz, L. (1974), *Clinical Prediction in Psychotherapy.* New York: Jason Aronson.

——— (1983), Projective identification in dyads and group. *Internat. J. Group Psychother.*, 33:259–279.

James, C. (1984), Bion's "containing" and Winnicott's "holding" in the context of the group matrix. *Internat. J. Group Psychother.*, 34:201–214.

Jaques, E. (1955), Social systems as a defense against persecutory and depressive anxiety. In: *New Directions in Psychoanalysis*, ed. M. Klein, P. Heimann, & R. E. Money-Kyrle. London: Tavistock Publications, pp. 478–498. Rpt. in: *Analysis of Groups*, ed. G. Gibbard, J. J. Hartman, & R. D. Mann. San Francisco: Jossey-Bass, 1974, pp. 277–299.

Kelman, H. C. (1963), The role of the group in the induction of therapeutic change. *Internat. J. Group Psychother.*, 13:399–432.

Kernberg, O. F. (1975), A systems approach to priority setting of interventions in groups. *Internat. J. Group Psychother.*, 25:251–275.

——— (1976), *Object Relations Theory and Clinical Psychoanalysis.* New York: Jason Aronson.

——— (1980), *Internal World and External Reality.* New York: Jason Aronson.

Kibel, H. D. (1977), A schema for understanding resistances in groups. *Group Process,* 7:221–235.

——— (1981), A conceptual model for short-term inpatient group psychotherapy. *Amer. J. Psychiat.*, 138:74–80.

——— (1987), Inpatient group psychotherapy—Where treatment philosophies converge. In: *The Yearbook of Psychoanalysis and Psychotherapy,* Vol. 2, ed. R. Langs. New York: Gardner Press, pp. 94–116.

——— (1991), The therapeutic use of splitting: The role of the "mother-group" in therapeutic differentiation and practicing. In: *Psychoanalytic Group Theory and Therapy: Essays in Honor of Saul Scheidlinger,* ed. S. Tuttman. Madison, CT: International Universities Press, pp. 113–132.

——— Stein, A. (1981), The group-as-a-whole approach: An appraisal. *Internat. J. Group Psychother.*, 31:409–427.

Klein, R. H., & Kugel, B. (1981), Inpatient group psychotherapy: Reflections through a glass darkly. *Internat. J. Group Psychother.*, 31:311–328.

Kosseff, J. W. (1990), Anchoring the self through the group: Congruences, play, and the potential for change. In: *The Difficult Patient in Group: Group Psychotherapy with Borderline and Narcissistic Disorders,* Monogr. 6, ed. B. E. Roth, W. N. Stone, & H. D. Kibel. Madison, CT: International Universities Press, pp. 87–108.

Levine, H. B. (1980), Milieu biopsy: The place of the therapy group on the inpatient ward. *Internat. J. Group Psychother.*, 30:77–93.

Lewin, K. (1951), Constructs in field theory. In: *Field Theory in Social Science: Selected Theoretical Papers,* ed. D. Cartwright. Westport, CT: Greenwood Press, pp. 30–59.

Malan, D. H., Balfour, F. H. G., Hood, V. G., & Shooter, A. M. N. (1976), Group psychotherapy: A long-term follow-up study. *Arch. Gen. Psychiat.*, 33:1303–1315.

Ogden, T. H. (1981), Project identification in psychiatric hospital treatment. *Bull. Menninger Clin.*, 45:317–333.

Piper, W. E., Marrache, M., Lacroix, R., Richardsen, A. M., & Jones, B. D. (1983), Cohesion as a basic bond in groups. *Human Relations,* 36:93–108.

Redl, F. (1942), Group emotion and leadership. *Psychiat.*, 5:573–596.

Schafer, R. (1968), *Aspects of Internalization.* New York: International Universities Press.

Scheidlinger, S. (1964), Identification, the sense of belonging and of identity in small groups. *Internat. J. Group Psychother.*, 14:291–306.

——— (1974), On the concept of the "mother-group." *Internat. J. Group Psychother.*, 24:417–428.

——— (1982), Presidential address: On scapegoating in group psychotherapy. *Internat. J. Group Psychother.*, 32:131–143.

——— (1987), On interpretation in group psychotherapy: The need for refinement. *Internat. J. Group Psychother.*, 37:339–352.

Stein, A. (1956), The superego and group interaction in group psychotherapy. *J. Hillside Hosp.*, 5:495–504.

——— (1970), The nature and significance of interaction in group psychotherapy. *Internat. J. Group Psychother.*, 20:153–162.

—— Kibel, H. D. (1984), A group dynamic–peer interaction approach to group psychotherapy. *Internat. J. Group Psychother.*, 34:315–333.

—— Wiener, S. (1978), Group psychotherapy with medically ill patients. In: *Psychotherapeutics in Medicine*, ed. T. B. Karasu & R. I. Steinmuller. New York: Grune & Stratton, pp. 223–242.

Stone, W. N., & Gustafson, J. P. (1982), Technique in group psychotherapy of narcissistic and borderline patients. *Internat. J. Group Psychother.*, 32:29–47.

Sutherland, J. D. (1952), Notes on psychoanalytic group therapy: I, Therapy and training. *Psychiat.*, 15:111–117.

—— (1985), Bion revisited: Group dynamics and group psychotherapy. In: *Bion and Group Psychotherapy*, ed. M. Pines. London: Routledge & Kegan Paul, pp. 47–86.

Whitaker, D. S., & Lieberman, M. A. (1964), *Psychotherapy through the Group Process*. New York: Atherton Press.

Wolf, A., & Schwartz, E. K. (1962), *Psychoanalysis in Groups*. New York: Grune & Stratton.

Yalom, I. D. (1975), *The Theory and Practice of Group Psychotherapy*, 2nd ed. New York: Basic Books.

7

The Clinical Application of Self Psychology Theory

WALTER N. STONE, M.D.

Almost thirty years ago, Kohut (1959) commented on the central place of empathy in psychoanalytic psychotherapy: "The scope of understanding of normal and abnormal psychological phenomena have tended to obscure the fact that the first step was the introduction of the consistent use of introspection and empathy as the observational tool of the new science" (p. 405). Indeed for Kohut empathy is the *sine qua non* of our profession: "Only a phenomenon that we can attempt to observe by introspection or by empathy with another's introspection may be called psychological" (p. 462). These observations became the cornerstone of Kohut's explorations of narcissism, which resulted in a major reexamination of the theory of human development and led to the formulation of the psychology of the self. In this chapter I shall selectively review the evolution of the major concepts of self psychology and discuss their application to the theory and clinical practice of group psychotherapy.

In 1966 Kohut published *Forms and Transformations of Narcissism*, in which he outlined a developmental line for narcissism that would not be transformed into object love, but would lead to higher developmental forms of narcissism. In these formulations Kohut proposed that the child attempts to preserve the primary state of perfection by maintaining a grandiose and exhibitionistic image of the self, "the grandiose self," or, alternatively, by assigning it to another, "the idealized parent imago." Optimum development was thought to proceed as a result of nontraumatic disappointments. The infantile wishes and

177

needs would become integrated into an adult personality in the form of ambitions and goals in the first instance and ideals in the second.

From this beginning, Kohut (1971, 1977) gradually moved in his theorizing from conceptualizing narcissism as a separate line of development to the self as the central organizing structure of human experience. Kohut formulated the self as the overarching psychological structure, which he labeled the bipolar self. The concept of the bipolar self was presented in dynamic terms as a tension arc between the two poles, the grandiose self and the idealizing self. "With the term 'tension arc,' however, I am referring to the abiding flow of actual psychological activity that establishes itself between the two poles of the self, i.e., a person's basic pursuits towards which he is 'driven' by his ambitions and 'led' by his ideals" (p. 180). This view is in keeping with the traditional economic metapsychological perspective and focuses on the individual's successful and thwarted efforts to fully express the self. However, explicit in this formulation was a shift in Kohut's thinking. He no longer saw conflicts over the fulfillment of pleasure-seeking drives as the core of psychopathology. Instead he suggested that optimal human growth is a product of innate energy, a wish to learn and develop the self's basic skills and achieve its ideals. This formulation contrasts with the traditional drive psychology in which the developmental goal is to tame the instinctual drives and transform them into structures of the ego and superego.

The self has never been fully delineated, but Kohut (1984) stated, "it is a conceptualization of the structure whose establishment makes possible a creative-productive fulfilling life" (p. 5). The self is conceived of "as a unit, cohesive in space and enduring in time, which is a center of initiative and a recipient of impressions" (Kohut, 1977, p. 99). The coherent, stable, well-consolidated self enables one to utilize basic talents and skills, to fulfill ambitions and to achieve ideals. It is an experience of being whole and continuous, alive and vigorous, balanced and organized.

Kohut (1977) described the self both as a psychological structure (the organization of experience) and as an existential agent (an initiator of action). Stolorow, Brandchaft, and Atwood (1987) argue that the failure to distinguish between self as structure and person as agent creates a "theoretical conundrum." They illustrate their position by stating, "clearly, it is not the pieces of something (fragments of a self) that strive toward a goal (restoration). . . . This problem can be minimized if we restrict the concept of self to describe organizations of experience and use the term *person* . . . to refer to the existential agent who initiates actions" (pp. 18–19). E. S. Wolf (1988) addresses this problem as follows: "It is imprecise and, at worst, incorrect to speak about the self as if it were an existential agent. I should be speaking about a person whose self's strengths or weaknesses lead to experiences of agency" (p. 65). This use of self with both meanings is not infrequent in the literature.

The self cannot be defined in isolation. Rather, it is embedded in a matrix of selfobjects that are conceived of as essential nutriments for the consolidation, maintenance, and restoration of the self. The selfobject is an individual's subjective experience of an object that serves certain necessary functions. As such it does not refer to people but to functions. A certain confusion surrounds the use of the phrase self–selfobject relations, as if it describes a real relationship. As Kohut (1984) has suggested, the expression facilitates communication and is to be understood as an intrapsychic experience. In archaic self–selfobject relationships, the feeling of the person about the selfobject is that he does not exist separately from the self but is present to fulfill a particular set of functions or needs of the self. In more mature individuals, adult selfobject functions may be fulfilled by inanimate objects, for instance, by listening to music or observing art, where these activities may restore a sense of inner harmony to an imbalanced self (E. S. Wolf, 1988).

From his clinical work, Kohut (1966, 1971) formulated the presence of two archaic selfobjects that promoted maturation of the self. The mirroring selfobject (as seen in the mirror transference) was equivalent to the experience of the phase-appropriate maternal responses of reflecting, echoing, approving, and confirming the vigor, greatness, and the perfectionism of the child. The original (maternal) selfobject's responsivity was an essential step in transforming the individual's archaic grandiose and exhibitionistic self states toward an increasingly mature pursuit of goals and ambitions. The idealizable selfobject (as seen in the idealizing transference) was described by Kohut as the experience of merger with the calm, good, omnipotent, and omniscient selfobject. By merging with the idealized selfobject, the individual would experience a sense of calmness, intactness, and infallibility. Through a process of inevitable and nontraumatic experiences the growing individual gradually internalizes these functions, which lead to the capacity for empathy, creativeness, humor, and wisdom.

In 1984, Kohut added a third selfobject developmental line, that of the alter ego, which was intermediate between the two others. An alter-ego selfobject was understood as the self's need for sameness and was linked to an intermediate area of developing skill and talents. "I have in mind the early security that the baby must have in the mere presence of humans (voices, smell). I also think of the little guy just working next to daddy in the basement, or 'shaving' while daddy shaves (corresponding to the developing intermediate area of skills and talents)" (Kohut, quoted in Detrick, 1985). An additional selfobject experience is that of the adversary. These are the experiences of the person's healthy assertiveness in the context of a selfobject without fear of impairing that relationship. Examples are the two year old who says "no" without fear and can be admired for an independent self expression, and the teenager who defines the self in part by developing peer-related ideals, but needs the acceptance of the parental selfobject (E. S. Wolf, 1976). There appear to be multiple selfobject functions, but according to Socarides and Stolorow (1984/85), these "functions pertain fundamentally to the integration of *affect*, and the need for selfobjects pertains most centrally to the need for phase-appropriate responsiveness to affect states in all stages of the life cycle" (p. 105).

Psychopathology is conceptualized as an incompletely formed or skewed self structure. As a consequence of developmental failures, the self cannot withstand narcissistic injury and experiences fragmentation. The expression "fragmentation" is used as a metaphor to describe a disturbed sense of continuity and wholeness of the self experience. Fragmentation ranges from slight anxiety to a feeling of falling apart and disintegration. It is an internal experience and can be expressed, as well, by a sense of awkwardness and/or somatic symptoms. The narcissistically injured person may attempt to repair the fragmenting self experience by resorting to drugs or alcohol or by engaging in perverse or aggressive behavior.

The need for phase-appropriate selfobjects is a universal phenomenon. In the developmental process, everyone suffers disappointments, hurts, and failures of others to respond in the hoped-for manner or to be available upon command. As a consequence, each person has a store of sensitivities that he has learned to manage with varying degrees of success. The result is character formation with syntonic and dystonic solutions that protect the individual from being traumatized in the present as he *experienced* being traumatized in the past. For higher level functioning persons, this character structure generally does not create clinically significant interpersonal or intrapsychic distress. An intermediate functional level might include those patients who experienced particular recurrent injuries in limited areas, and as a consequence, might have circumscribed vulnerabilities that can be compensated for by strengthening other areas. A third level would be those individuals whose experience was that of more intense and/or prolonged failure of necessary selfobject responsivity. This might result in a developmental arrest and erection of defenses against further trauma, which potentially includes the adoption of a variety of methods of self-soothing behaviors (e.g., drugs, fetishes, compulsive rituals, etc.) that would—at least temporarily—restore the sense of self cohesion (Kohut and E. S. Wolf, 1978). It is this latter group of patients who are diagnosed in the narcissistic and borderline personality disorder spectrum.

The theory also addresses psychopathology associated with long-standing affective responses. Certain patients, who suffer from feelings described as loss of vitality, interest, generalized dullness, or anhedonia, may be best understood as a product of chronic selfobject failures. Their affective states are not easily distinguished from chronic depression. Their anger and rage are understood not as primary drives in need of taming but as responses to narcissistic injury.

The theoretical foundations of self psychology arise from the clinical encounter and an understanding of the patient–therapist relationship as it evolves over time. It is an "experience-near" psychology in contrast to more classical theories, which have become progressively removed from the clinical interaction. The self psychologically informed therapist utilizes his experiences with the patient in order to understand the patient's inner world. The therapist achieves this understanding via empathy, which encounters the inner experiences of the patient and differs from the position of the external observer, whose role is based upon maintaining a more detached, neutral stance from which interpretations can be made.

With this brief outline of the basic concepts of self psychology, I will now turn to the therapeutic process in dyadic and group psychotherapy.

THE THERAPEUTIC PROCESS

The application of self psychology to the conduct of psychotherapy has led many practitioners to reexamine their concepts of the therapeutic process. No longer is the primary task conceived of as examining defensive structures and exposing underlying vicissitudes in the expression and management of biological drives. Rather, the emphasis has shifted to an exploration of the self and the development of a coherent self that has the capacity to pursue goals and ambitions and to reach for ideals within the ordinary and sometimes extraordinary stresses of everyday living.

Central to the therapeutic task is the creation of an environment in which patients can expose their vulnerabilities. This would include both the surface and deeper manifestations of the distortions of the self. Some sensitivities emerge rapidly in the therapeutic encounter (or in everyday life) and others only after an extended period of therapy, when after numerous experiences of being understood in an empathic manner, patients can gradually expose the deeply embedded sensitive and vulnerable aspects of themselves. This takes place in the context of a reliable self–selfobject relationship that may develop silently, outside the awareness of the individual, but becomes quite apparent in the treatment transactions when there has been an empathic failure on the part of the selfobject-therapist. The therapist's activity in this process is an effort to empathically understand the patient and communicate that understanding. This role on the part of the therapist has many similarities to and overlaps with the concept of the holding environment (Winnicott, 1965) and has the effect of enhancing in the patient a sense of well-being and self coherence, which in itself can be growth promoting (Stolorow and Lachmann, 1984/85).

In the optimal therapeutic situation, the patient gradually establishes a stable selfobject transference that is an effort to repair the deficit to the self and restart growth (A. Ornstein, 1974). Resistances to the development of selfobject transferences have to be understood and interpreted before a consistent transference is achieved. These resistances might be viewed as the patient's efforts not to be traumatized in the present as presumably he had been in childhood. The therapist's inevitable empathic failures provide information about the patient's transference, self coherence, and restitutive responses to injury. For instance, in response to narcissistic hurt, patients might experience feelings of disorganization and fragmentation (e.g., feelings of falling apart or somatic preoccupation), or they might institute self-soothing and restorative responses (e.g., religiosity, perverse or addictive fantasies or behaviors, or emotional blunting). Through understanding and explaining (the interpretive process) the patient's experience of narcissistic injury and restitutive efforts, the analyst would reestablish the self–selfobject bond. These experiences, labeled "transmuting internalizations," enable the self to become more coherent and gradually assume some of the functions of the selfobject.

The empathic component of the therapeutic action of self psychology has been both misinterpreted and taken to represent the whole. Critics of the self psychological perspective have identified empathic understanding, which serves to strengthen the self–selfobject bond, both as if it were agreement with the injured person and as an expression of sympathy. Rather, the empathic stance is an effort to understand the inner experience of the individual from that person's perspective. It does not mean that the therapist agrees or disagrees with the position of the patient. The therapist, through empathic contact, creates an environment that strengthens the self and enables the patient to risk greater self exposure. The therapist is not detached; he is involved but value neutral.

E. S. Wolf (1988) has succinctly differentiated empathic understanding from gratifying the patient's archaic demands for mirroring: "if the therapist, instead of creating an ambience of acceptance, attempts to create an illusion of approbation and gratification, the patient will quickly discover the hollowness of the therapist's posture and feel betrayed" (p. 134). It is the patient's experience of the environment in which the therapist strives to understand and explain that leads to both a firming of the self and a willingness to take new risks.

Inevitably, there will be failures on the part of the selfobject that will be followed by a variety of efforts on the part of the individual to restore an inner equilibrium. The therapeutic task is to understand and explain the process of hurt and repair (Kohut, 1977). This is accomplished by the therapist's empathic immersion in the injured individual's experiences; the therapist thereby gains access to the patient's inner state. If the therapist can accurately understand the nature of the injury, then a second step of explaining the process to the individual follows. This process, which is equivalent to interpretation, arises most poignantly from the experience-near transactions and leads to psychic structure building, as evidenced by increased self coherence, an ability to generate additional anamnestic material, and greater courage in facing previously disruptive affects or interpersonal experiences.

This brief summary of the theory of the therapeutic process barely touches upon the subtleties of the treatment interaction, which emphasizes minute attention to the interaction between therapist and patient and a continued self exploration on the part of the therapist as he searches for areas of incomplete or inaccurate understanding of the therapeutic transactions as viewed from the perspective of the patient. The therapeutic focus, however, is not exclusively riveted on the consultation room since the therapist may apply these principles to understanding the patient's experiences of narcissistic injury and restitutive response in everyday life.

The Therapeutic Process in Group Psychotherapy

In the group therapy setting the processes are more complex than in dyadic treatment since the overlapping systems of group-as-a-whole, interpersonal, and intrapsychic all operate simultaneously. The therapist may shift his interpretive efforts among these levels with attendant advantages and disadvantages arising from each perspective.

Group-as-a-whole Aspects. At the broadest level, the patient may experience the group as a whole as a selfobject. The individual begins to experience belonging to a responsive, reliable group as if it were an idealized or mirroring selfobject. Expressions such as "my group is the greatest" or "the members are always in tune and understand me" are the surface manifestations of these transferences. With either of these transferences, failures by any member to fit into the expected or wished-for mold required by the narcissistic patient may represent a transference to the group as a whole. The injurious response may be ignored or denied in an effort to maintain the integrity of the group-as-a-whole selfobject transference. Only the warm glow of the positive transference (i.e., the group atmosphere) is experienced. Such responses seemed to have been commonplace during the height of the T-group movement in the 1960s. T-groups provided a temporary psychological glue, a bond, to counter the personal and societal alienation and fragmentation of that period.

The military experience provides illustrations of both positive and negative responses to a perceived formation and/or destruction of the group. Through the intense basic training experiences and development of common goals and ideals, soldiers subsequently entering combat as a unit experience a relatively increased sense of community and safety in dangerous situations. Acts of heroism may be understood not only as a product of the individual psychic development, but also as a response to the danger to the small group and a wish to protect its integrity. The opposite condition has been posited as one of the destructive aspects of the Vietnam experience. Units were fragmented as individuals were rotated back to the United States and/or casualties were replaced one by one. The resulting disruption in the solidarity of the small units led to more individualistic responses and may have contributed to the heavy drug experiences, which could be understood as attempts to soothe and restore a disrupted and fragmenting self.

In therapy groups the disorganization of a group-as-a-whole psychological matrix may lead to considerable acting-in or acting-out as a way of both signaling the disarray and as efforts to restore the group and the individual damaged self. Stone and Stevenson (1991) cite clinical examples wherein higher functioning individuals precipitously terminated their treatment when they experienced the group as becoming unstable following a series of terminations. In posttreatment interviews these patients cited the deterioration of the previous positively experienced group atmosphere and the loss of a sense of safety as a major reason for their departure. The therapist, retrospectively, indicated that he had overestimated the patients' "ego strength" and underestimated the negative impact of the disruptions in the group.

Exclusive interpretive focus by the therapist on the group as a whole often will result in narcissistic injury among individuals who feel inadequately understood or merely not responded to. Even the most accurate interpretations, focusing on groupwide processes and leading to positive therapeutic response, have this potential to evoke injury. Early in the therapeutic encounter, in particular, patients respond to this incomplete appreciation of them as hurtful. Only *after* a firmer bond between patients, therapist, and the group (selfobject transferences) has been achieved can the patient accept the inevitability of not being responded to or precisely understood in a group-as-a-whole interpretation. Patients achieving this level of response are capable of emotionally recognizing the therapist as a separate person with his own style and manner of relating. This sequence is similar to that suggested by Horwitz (1977), based on a more traditional object relations framework. He proposed that the therapist identify the central issue in the group and then work to facilitate each individual's understanding of their group interactions before making an integrative group-as-a-whole interpretation. Despite these caveats proscribing groupwide interpretations, these interventions may still stimulate members' self-reflection and mobilize therapeutic movement.

Members of successful psychotherapy groups begin to feel that belonging to the group will be useful on the basis of their expectation that they will be listened to and responded to, and that others will make efforts to understand them at deep emotional levels. The experience is that of the group serving as a valuable mirroring selfobject. Since narcissistic injury is inevitable, the therapist can utilize the disruption as an opportunity for understanding and explaining. The most frequent response to injury is withdrawal. A temporary retreat may not require attention, but prolonged or frequent brief withdrawal responses deserve therapeutic intervention. Other more dramatic reactions are easier to identify, but in either case, the therapist's (or eventually other group members') intervention bringing into focus the injury and subsequent restitutive and/or retaliatory responses serves to restore the inner equilibrium and to strengthen the bond among members with the therapist or with the image of the group.

The idealization of a group can have long-lasting benefits for some individuals without having to work through and completely resolve the transference. Fried (1973) quotes from a terminated patient's letter: "I'm helped when I recall how blessed it was to have the love and kindness of my friends in the group and of you [the therapist]. The memory of the intimacies we shared and the openness of our feelings helps keep me together" (p. 162). For some patients this may represent a satisfactory treatment outcome. Stone (1985) has suggested that similar treatment results may represent an enactment of the curative fantasy, in which the patient has entered into treatment with a conscious or unconscious wish to strengthen a depleted or fragmenting self. When that goal has been accomplished the patient may terminate. This formulation helps clarify treatments that have been previously classified as incomplete and helps explain the timing and meaning of some "premature" terminations. In the patients' experience, they have accomplished what they set out to do.

Conceptually, there is a difference between solidifying the self with a resultant diminution or disappearance of symptoms, and a transference cure. Freud (1915) formulated the notion of a transference cure as the disappearance of symptoms as a consequence of feelings of love or a wish to please the therapist, and not as a consequence of interpretation and working through. This formulation focuses on drives, whereas in self psychology the patient's empathic experience of the therapist, other members, or the group as a whole restores the equilibrium of the imbalanced self. This does not indicate a basic improvement, but the experience may provide a basis for strengthening the self structure. This process has been regularly observed in early sessions of psychotherapy groups, when a variety of the members' somatic symptoms or anxieties diminish or disappear as part of the experience of belonging to a group where the atmosphere is that of listening and attempting to understand. Stolorow, Brandchaft, and Atwood (1987) are more forceful in their belief that the selfobject transference cure plays a significant role at all levels of the therapeutic endeavor: "What we are stressing here . . . is the ubiquitous curative role played by the silent, at times, *unanalyzed* selfobject dimensions of the transference" (p. 44, italics added).

The variations in the patient's ability to maintain the "transference cure" can be reformulated in a selfobject frame. Some individuals whose self is mildly or moderately disrupted may utilize the experience of an empathic selfobject to consolidate the self, and spontaneously restart growth (A. Ornstein, 1974). Others, whose disturbances are more extreme may utilize the experience in a manner that enables them to seek other sustaining selfobjects, or they simply may be unable to maintain a sense of cohesion in the absence of the therapist.

Interpersonal Aspects. In the interpersonal experience an individual's need for a reliable and responsive selfobject can be met in a group in a different manner than in dyadic treatment by the very fact of the presence of a number of individuals. Patients have an opportunity to seek out, often outside conscious awareness, selfobjects that may fit their developmentally specific needs or serve as restitutive objects in response to a narcissistic injury (Bacal, 1983; Harwood, 1986). For instance, upon entering a group a patient often may look for some quality or characteristic in another member that will evoke a sense of familiarity. Apparently superficial questions such as "Where do you work?" "Are you married?" or "Do you have children?" may be the newcomer's efforts to search for similarities. This "strategy," which may be understood as a search for an alter-ego selfobject, helps contain the initial anxiety associated with joining a group. It does not necessarily imply psychopathology. Rather, it may represent a reasonable temporary response to a threatened or mildly anxious self. Upon further interaction such initial attractions may disappear or may fade only to be utilized again in periods of stress.

The presence of a number of individuals provides for a diversity of potential mirroring or idealized objects. Such interactions may represent safe displacements from the more threatening authority figure of the therapist, or they may represent particular developmental needs based on the meaning for the individual of certain interpersonal transactions or characteristics. Some of these attachments may be temporary responses to injury or may represent a greater need to overcome a developmental arrest.

A highly condensed example, from an ongoing outpatient group composed of patients with a variety of neurotic and personality diagnoses, will illustrate this process as it unfolded over a period of time. The members had achieved a group developmental level in which they examined their intragroup interactions. Adam, the last member to have joined the group, about eight months previous to the sessions described here, responded to a new member's entrance by assuming a host role and introducing all of the members by first name to the newcomer. Later, when this interaction was explored, Adam became angry when several members complained that he had usurped their prerogative to introduce themselves. He could not understand their complaints; he was only trying to help. Adam withdrew and contemplated terminating from the group because he felt that he didn't belong. Yet he was also intrigued by the intensity of his response to the critique. Adam told the group that he found himself preoccupied for several days after the meeting with how hurt he had been, and then reported that he continued to think about it intermittently for several weeks.

In a subsequent meeting, Burt complained that he had felt quite hurt when one of the women members had complimented another on a new and attractive hairdo but had not noticed or commented on his haircut, which he believed to have been quite noticeable. Affectively, members responded with surprise to Burt. Adam "teased" that others had not noticed how he (Adam) had trimmed his beard. The therapist wondered if underneath the teasing Adam had some additional feelings. Adam replied that he didn't know and then fell silent for an extended period. When the group conversation shifted to a discussion of nonverbal behavior, the therapist wondered if his earlier comment had startled and injured Adam, a feeling he signaled by his withdrawal. Initially, Adam stated only that he had been thinking about what had been said, but he followed this comment by revealing that indeed he was hurt. He then was able to recognize that he had wished to disavow Burt's sensitivity to being hurt by teasing about it. He had seen his own sensitivity in Burt. Following this, Adam wondered, for the first time, why he had introduced everyone to the new member. Before this time he had rather vehemently insisted that he was interested only in moving the group through the introductory phase, and he did not understand others' sensitivity. Adam subsequently acknowledged that the hurt he felt when he was criticized for introducing the others was a result of the disappointment he felt because he wished to be admired for his efforts.

From a self psychological perspective these sessions can be understood in the following manner. Adam's grandiosity (the meaning of the introductions) had not been mirrored (instead his action was criticized). He then experienced a narcissistic injury, withdrew, and contemplated terminating. A repeat of this process as experienced by Burt initially was met by humorous disavowal by Adam, but his humor was confronted, evoking another narcissistic injury. The therapist broke into the cycle by verbalizing his understanding of the process. Adam was then able to begin exploration of his feelings of injury, first in relation to Burt and then in relation to himself regarding his assuming the responsibility for the introductions, and to begin a tentative examination of the inner meaning of his behavior.

Adam's experience serves to differentiate between two theoretical usages of mirroring. The self psychological use was applied to the groupwide failure to mirror Adam's initial grandiosity. The other members, not unreasonably, responded to their inner affects and failed to mirror Adam's efforts. The second perspective on mirroring, that of group analysis, was evident in Adam's seeing himself in Burt. Observing oneself in another has been described by Foulkes (1961) as the experience of being in a "hall of mirrors," in which patients can see aspects of themselves they previously had been unable to see.

Intrapsychic Aspects. Group members' intrapsychic deficits and developmental arrests unfold in the interpersonal transactions, become manifest in the expressed and unconscious needs for particular kinds of selfobjects. In this process, however, considerable resistance to the development of the selfobject transferences has to be explored because patients do not wish to be disappointed and hurt in the group as presumably they had been in their past. As a result, patients protect themselves, generally by utilizing their prior adaptive characterological solutions.

These character configurations and resistances to transference development are observable in groups in the distinctive roles patients assume. In this discussion, the emphasis will be divided between the patient's unique character formation as it emerges as a role in the group (Benne and Sheats, 1948) and the role as used in the service of the group process. The adaptation or use of a variety of roles may be an expression of the inner experience and patterns of defensive behavior of the collective group (Ashbach and Schermer, 1987, p. 158). In this respect the role serves a bridge between individual and group dynamics (Agazarian, 1983).

Monopolizers crave attention and admiration but are overtly oblivious to the impact of their behavior (Stone and Whitman, 1977). The interpersonal alienation is outside the awareness of these patients, and they are conscious only of their need for attention or response. By assuming this role, monopolizers not only defend against the narcissistic injury of nonresponse but also simultaneously express the need for admiration. In a less pathological form, a patient will become demanding of reassurance even when it is obvious that the wish cannot be gratified and reassurance will be of minimal or temporary value. This is sometimes seen when a patient insists that others reassure him that he is likeable. Any statements indicating that the member indeed is liked are insufficient to calm the demanding member. The therapist, under these circumstances, may be successful in making contact and diminishing the patient's distress by understanding and explaining the patient's inner upset and his hope for someone to be able to calm him.

Similar dynamics are operative for the so-called help-rejecting complainer, who may wish for admiration or calming, only to reject any offers because of the fear that he will be disappointed in the future. The therapeutic challenge is to find a way to make genuine emotional contact with the patient so that he may feel understood.

Another role that has drawn attention in the literature but bears reexamination is that of the patient who idealizes the group or the therapist. Such an individual assumes a role that protects such a state and undermines any efforts to find fault or express disappointment or anger about the treatment. This kind of patient comes decked in a variety of labels, such as placater, soother, and so forth, but the important issue is to search for the meaning behind the role. Idealization is a developmental need and may be expressed through this role. Alternatively, it may be an elaborate defense against underlying anger (Stone and Gustafson, 1982). Self psychologically informed therapists have been primarily interested in the aspect of idealization that directly reflects a developmental arrest. The patient's need to merge with an idealized selfobject can appear very strange from the vantage of an external observer. Recognition of the member's inner merger need in order to experience a sense of wholeness and coherence enables the therapist to tolerate what may seem unreasonable. Premature debunking or attempts to inject "reality" into the transactions may meet with denial or narcissistic injury, followed by the patient employing whatever self-soothing measures are available. Following a hurt, the association to helpful powerful figures or introduction of reassuring religious themes signals the self restitutive nature of the process.

The angry role also may be self protective as well as a response to injury. It is not conceptualized as an expression of an aggressive drive or as primitive envy. The anger may serve to signal a hurt, to retaliate for being wronged, to overcome feelings of helplessness, or to gratify revenge fantasies (Krystal, 1975). A significant therapeutic task is to help the patient come fully face to face with the feeling of injury and vulnerability. Adam, in the example cited, initially did not stop to examine his narcissistic injury but bypassed these painful feelings and the associated shame of "a grown man having such childish responses." His wish to withdraw was a retaliation, a self protection, and a way of reestablishing a sense of control over a painful experience.

It is not uncommon in the context of boundary disruptions (e.g., vacations, change of therapist in a training center) for a therapist to be the recipient of one patient's particularly angry or provocative critique. The remaining patients seem uninterested or bland about the attacks. The therapist becomes sidetracked in wondering about their passivity and may not perceive that a member is in the angry role, expressing the groupwide response to the narcissistic injury (the loss of a reliable selfobject group).

Narcissistic rage and anger exist along a continuum. For some patients, the group interactions evoke chronic narcissistic rage. These patients are particularly difficult to work with in group psychotherapy because other members, even if they understand the self protective aspects of the rageful responses, wear down. Only through successful empathic contact with these vulnerable individuals can the group therapist begin to lessen the chronic rage. Sometimes, after a trial of therapy, these patients need to be removed from the group. For many constricted or inhibited patients, the fears associated with expressing anger may result in faint allusions to the anger. Progress is signaled when anger is expressed directly. This optimally occurs spontaneously in the context of the patient feeling safe, a situation different from the patient's childhood experiences, where presumably such expressions were inhibited or condemned. A further developmental achievement is signaled when anger is expressed in the face of obstacles and then subsides when the obstacle is removed (P. H. Ornstein, 1985).

The intrapsychic expression of self disturbance often is vividly portrayed in dreams. One patient dreamed of standing naked on a balcony in front of an orchestra nearly a hundred yards away. The dreamer expressed both exhibitionistic, grandiose wishes and at the same time fears of overstimulation and lack of response by putting distance between herself and the audience (Stone and Whitman, 1977). Another woman, in the context of wishing to remain in her group but terminate from concurrent individual therapy because she was ashamed of having to meet with the therapist weekly without making sufficient progress, reported the following dream: "I was on a trip with my husband. In the hotel room across the hall was Anne, a group member. I went to talk with her about our common interests, and I was feeling so comfortable and at ease I wondered if I could lie down. Anne said certainly. My husband came and said he wanted me to go to a movie with him. I went but felt angry and didn't enjoy the movie. I was very tired. I went looking for my room but got lost. When I asked some of the hotel guests to use their phone to call for help, they refused. Then I woke up." Among the many meanings of this dream the patient was able to sort out her feeling that the therapist wanted her to change in a way she had not been able to accomplish. Her wish to discontinue the individual sessions was an effort to diminish the exposure to narcissistic hurt. Anne represented an available group member, a selfobject, with whom she could merge and feel more whole. Clearly there is some differentiation among members since only Anne seemed to be able to fulfill her needs. Yet the therapist-husband continued to interfere with that effort. She also portrayed the remainder of the group members as unhelpful. The patient had accurately perceived the therapist's disappointment in her desire to stop the dyadic treatment. The dream brought this into focus and helped him recognize the impact of his countertransference reaction. A further discussion of dreams will be presented in the extended clinical example.

THE THERAPEUTIC FOCUS

The major implications of the theoretical position of the psychology of the self are the therapist's efforts to understand consistently the development of the self and the vicissitudes on forming a coherent self structure. E. S. Wolf (1988) explains that "strengthening the self takes precedence over all other possible aims, for example, making the unconscious conscious, remembering, reconstructing, resolving conflict, and the like. These latter aims are important also, but they usually become possible to the strengthened self without the need for specific measures" (p. 95). This perspective encompasses the members' inner experiences in relation to belonging to the group and interacting with the therapist and other members. The focus is on what is being experienced and expressed rather than what is being concealed. The therapist makes empathic contact with the patient rather than seeking primarily to interpret resistance and defense.

Moreover, the therapist attempts to keep in focus the members' narcissistic vulnerabilities, defenses against establishing selfobject transferences, and the nature of such transferences when they are firmly in place. Two major aspects of the theory of the self come to the foreground in the therapist's search for understanding. The first is attention to the patients' selfobject needs, including recognition of self deficits that are most likely to emerge at times of narcissistic injury. The focus is on the individual's inner state and not on the external responses—that is, the effect of the behavior on others. This is achieved through the therapist's spontaneous associations (counter-transferences, in the broad meaning of the word) or by an active effort to feel one's way into the emotional position of the patient, utilizing the historical and interactional data. The second is attention to patients who are unable or unwilling to respond to the needs of others. These patients may also be expressing narcissistic needs or vulnerabilities, and the therapist must make an effort to understand their inner experiences. In both of these situations the therapist tries to keep in mind that the responses may be products of the individuals' inner needs, their interactions, or group-as-a-whole dynamics. The choice of locus of the intervention is aimed at strengthening or restoring the disequilibrated self. The therapist's appreciation of group norms, values, and stages of development can serve as a guide to understanding the transactions that have narcissistically injured one or more members.

An example from an outpatient adult group will illustrate one aspect of the therapeutic focus and the therapist's interventions to a common group tension. In the session under consideration, members seemed to be responding with heightened anxiety to an angry interchange that occurred in the preceding meeting. In part the affects were conveyed nonverbally. One member sat rigidly with his arms crossed; another was dressed in an uncharacteristic rumpled fashion and stared blankly above the heads of the others. In the verbal interaction, members offered premature reassurances and understanding of feelings when the associations lacked both sufficient detail and the clearly delineated affect that would be necessary for meaningful emotional understanding. This atmosphere, which was a marked change from the previous lively and exploratory interchanges, was experienced by the therapist as a sense of dullness and disengagement. She assumed that the content of the discussion was a statement of the patients' need to be reassured and not merely a defensive posture. She silently wondered if the shift reflected the members' fears that they might be traumatized in some way by a repeat of the angry interchange.

The therapist suggested that the group seemed changed. She wondered if the members had experienced considerable tension during the angry interchange the previous week. She continued saying that she understood them to be making an effort not to reexperience those feelings by becoming cautious in talking to one another or by smoothing over possible conflicts. This intervention reflected the therapist's focus on the experiences of the prior week as they had impacted on the entire group.

This process is open to a number of interpretations that might include the members' fears of the destructiveness of their angry impulses, fears that their anger would feel disruptive, concerns that others would retaliate, or possibly a guilty reaction for either directly or vicariously participating in the angry interchange. The therapist's intervention was directed at the members' inner experiences, and, even though imprecise, it was formulated to make contact with their discomfort and to provide an understanding of why they might be responding as they were. In this empathic effort, the therapist hoped to restore the members' equilibrium from what she perceived to be a slightly traumatized state. The therapist was also inviting them to consider how they had managed the experience. They were free to disagree or alter her understanding. Empathic contact enables members to feel understood, in a manner similar to a holding environment, which at the level of the self experience results in firming up and consolidating the self. Thus, members become more capable of exploring hidden and/or previously "unacceptable" parts of themselves.

Any group-as-a-whole intervention will include some generaliza-
tions and, as such, has the potential for provoking narcissistic injury.
The injury will be signaled either verbally or through action. Most
therapists recognize this sequence but fail to utilize the experience in
the treatment process. Indeed, such transactions provide important
opportunities to help patients understand themselves. The therapist's
willingness to address these process issues is needed. A fictive example
following from the previous vignette might go as follows. The therapist wondered if A.'s and B.'s responses following her own previous
comment expressed their feelings that they had not been accurately
understood. She suggested that A.'s angry recall of how his mother
had told all the children to go to bed at the same time and not allowed
the older ones to stay up later, and B.'s description of his recurrent
headaches were their responses to her generalization about the group.
Perhaps they had felt hurt and their associations were a way of conveying their hurts to her and the others.

This intervention has the potential of impacting on the two members and the group at a number of levels. It signals that the therapist
is willing to examine and discuss her own impact on the here-and-
now transactions of the group. It serves as a model for identification.
It is not an apology but an effort to help the patients feel understood.
The patients may respond to any or all of these levels. All would serve
to deepen the therapeutic process.

The following example will illustrate a focus in maintaining an
empathic connection in a group of developmentally arrested individuals. In a relatively newly formed group, a borderline woman, Jane,
rather angrily attacked Ken, who had failed to attend the previous
meeting and had not notified the therapist. Ken said that he had to
stay home with his ill wife. However, it quickly became apparent that
he had chosen not to attend because he was angry with the female
cotherapist who had announced an extended vacation at the previous
session. Jane's anger was a response to her feelings of loss and to her
wish for men to be present and more active. This wish was essentially
meant for the male cotherapist, who, as the less experienced member
of the therapy pair, had been relatively inactive. Ken and Jane were
acting and speaking not only for themselves—they represented parts
of all of the members. The therapist's announced vacation had disrupted the tenuous selfobject functioning of the group as a whole as
well as evoking loss responses to the therapist. From the nature of
the interactions, the selfobject functions were more prominent than
those referring to the leader as an autonomous person. The nonspecific absence and the displaced request for responsiveness were the
best way available for the members to express themselves safely. In

addition, the members had not made sufficient "contact" with one another through examining likenesses (alter-ego transferences) so that they could sustain a satisfactory level of group cohesion. Jane's response, in part, was aimed at reenforcing rules as a substitute for understanding.

These responses are characteristic of groups composed of developmentally arrested members, and the therapist must be able to empathically tune in to both the members and the group as a whole. When a patient has acted out and violated the contract, the therapist is often hard pressed to maintain his balance. There is a tendency to "side" with the critique of the acting out member. The experiences of *all* the critical members are that of narcissistic injury. Yet it is easy to overlook the multiple levels of hurt, which in the illustration exist at the level of Ken's and Jane's behavior, the cotherapists' roles in the group, and the selfobject function of the group as a whole. The therapist's intervention can address any of these levels but must take into consideration the stage of group development, the tenor of the interaction, and the level of individual psychopathology. A stereotyped choice of picking the highest level of abstraction may act as a further source of misunderstanding. In general, the therapist does well to make empathic connection with one or several members around the central disturbing injury before making a broader, groupwide intervention (Horwitz, 1977).

AN ILLUSTRATION

The following is an example of a group conducted by a therapist experienced in integrating self psychology with traditional psychodynamic group processes. The comments in the brackets are the therapist's reflections upon the affects he was experiencing and the thoughts he had in processing the material during the session. The material for this session was reported in supervision.

The session was chosen because of a clear focus, the members' responses to an extended three-week interruption for Christmas. It also illustrates how the therapist integrates the individuals' and the group's developmental history into understanding the processes unfolding during the meeting. The therapist focuses on affective responses, both expressed and unexpressed, as they pertain to the members' experience of their selves.

The group is composed of seven adults ranging in age from late twenties to mid-forties. The newest member had been in the group for six months, the most senior members almost five years. The primary diagnoses were in the lower end of the personality disorder spectrum, with members experiencing major difficulties in initiating or sustaining satisfactory interpersonal relationships. The following is a brief description of the members in the order they are introduced in the vignette.

Norma is a married woman in her late thirties. She has periods of rage over her husband's perceived neglect but then is very ashamed. She has been in and out of treatment most of her adult life. She is often harshly judgmental and opinionated, and frequently asks questions to help anchor her own sense of self. *Diagnosis*: Personality disorder, not otherwise specified, with narcissistic and dependent features.

Doris is a single woman in her forties who has had more than a decade of treatment. She is sensitive to rejection and protects herself by avoidance. She feels that she has not made any significant linkages in the group, and this is displayed by a blank, aloof appearance. In her outside life she has held a steady job, but she becomes attached and then hurt in relationships that fail her. Doris cognitively appreciates that she wishes for unattainable responsivity, but this has not modified her self deficit. *Diagnosis*: Narcissistic personality disorder.

George is in his thirties, married with young children. He had two episodes of major depression requiring hospitalization, but he currently functions effectively as a college professor. He experiences marital turmoil, as well as sexual feelings toward students and group members. He is fearful of being abandoned. Sports are a source of satisfaction. *Diagnosis*: Major affective disorder, in remission; Dependent personality disorder.

Sally, a young executive, is single and in her thirties. She desperately wants to be accepted and to learn what she does to scare off suitors. She actually is quite passive and frightened, but tries to compensate with a bravado that alienates the others. In the group this behavior has diminished some. She has had a recent important promotion in the management of her firm. *Diagnosis*: Dependent personality disorder with narcissistic features.

Jane is single and in her forties. She has chaotic interpersonal relationships, characterized by rageful withdrawals when hurt, and idealization of other relationships. In the group she has complained bitterly about not being helped, but continues to attend regularly. At times she can be very insightful and empathic in commenting to others. *Diagnosis*: Borderline personality disorder.

Ross is a married accountant in his forties with four teenage children. He praises the group for its help but reveals little of himself.

He has chronic anxiety and has made little overt progress in the group or at work. He is the group pacifier. *Diagnosis*: Obsessive–compulsive personality disorder with anxiety features.

David, in his twenties, father of one child, suffered a major depression requiring hospitalization and ECT when his marriage collapsed. He lives with his parents and has been unable to return to full-time work. He talks of being angry about his divorce, but primarily he is silent and withdrawn in the group, yet is comfortable in chatting outside the meeting with the others. *Diagnosis*: Major affective disorder, in remission; dysthymia, Passive–aggressive personality disorder.

In the period before the Christmas holiday the members were exploring issues of intimacy and fears that they would not be heard or responded to. They were frightened by the anger they experienced when they felt frustrated and would silently withdraw. These two poles were represented by Norma, the opinionated confronter, and David, the silent member. The therapeutic efforts had been to utilize the group interaction to help members understand their fears about deeper involvement and the potential for narcissistic injury, as well as the experiences that they did have of injury with one another, the therapist, and the group as a whole. The meeting to be described followed the three-week interruption for the holidays.

All seven members arrived promptly. Norma began saying she was glad to be back, a feeling that surprised and pleased her. [These affects seemed to be a statement by Norma of her feelings about herself in the group. It was difficult for her to maintain a sense of continuity, and the comment may have reflected an unexpected feeling of renewed inner coherence upon returning to the group.] Doris said that she had been thinking of terminating because she had assumed increased responsibilities requiring longer hours. She felt she was getting very little from the group therapy but would continue her individual sessions with her private therapist. [Doris experienced the interruption as a loss of the selfobject matrix of the group and threatened quitting as an expression of her distress.] Norma questioned Doris, and it quickly became obvious that she had flexibility and control over her work schedule. The members became preoccupied with Doris's thoughts of leaving. The therapist commented that he felt it was important for the members to try to reunite after the interruption since they had been working to make the group a safe place in the past, and it seemed that the loss of one member would disrupt those efforts and leave them feeling incomplete. [This was an intervention aimed at recognizing the selfobject functions of the group as a whole. Other feelings about the interruption could be examined after the sense of cohesion had been reestablished. Since the comment did not directly address Doris's thoughts about quitting, she may have experienced it as neglecting her and as a further disruption of the transference.]

In response, George said that Sally looked different. She agreed, saying she had been both pleased and stressed about what had happened to her. She had received a promotion, but during the past two weeks, in the transition period, she had been doing both jobs. Her replacement had arrived that day, which was a relief. [The meaning of this pairing was unclear. One element was George's wish to reintegrate Sally into the group. The comment may also represent George's efforts to strengthen the self by being an effective group member. This would represent an experience of efficacy, that provides the self a sense of strength (E. S. Wolf, 1988, p. 60).]

Doris then commented to Jane that she had been pleased to see her at the bowling league. [This pairing may have expressed Doris's search for an alter-ego selfobject, as an intermediate way to test the safety of the group in the context of her thoughts about stopping treatment.] Jane went on to describe the stress she had been under. She had been trying to get on a new team after the Christmas break, but the captain was uncertain about her ability, and was rather negative about accepting her. They had an extra session, and Jane had bowled well, which had earned her a place on the team. Jane felt that her abilities should have been recognized in the first place. Members said it was reasonable to feel hurt. Doris continued by describing an ongoing problem she has in competing. When she bowls for fun she consistently scores better than during competition, where her scores are erratic. In the league she felt clumsy and feared hurting herself [an observation of her experience of fragmentation]. Jane said that outwardly she looked okay, but Doris reiterated how disorganized she felt inside. Jane suggested lessons, but Doris said that they wouldn't help and that the lessons actually seemed to confuse her and make it worse. [The therapist understood Jane's concern about being accepted in the group and her feeling that she constantly had to prove herself in order to be accepted. This was followed by a discussion of the presentation of a facade (the false self) which was recognized as such. External solutions (lessons) don't work, and Doris continued to try to explain her feelings of fragmentation. The therapist might have explored the covert anger. However, he felt that this would be better reserved until the equilibrium within the group had been restored.]

George continued saying that Doris's remarks represented the members' concerns about sharing feelings with one another—that is, you have to be careful and keep up a facade [an expression of his (the group's?) vulnerability]. Doris said that what upset her most was when someone said "nice ball," that is, she had bowled well. This was followed by a story from Norma describing how she pulled back when someone warmly reached out to her, and she told how she had refused an invitation to go to lunch with a girlfriend. She had felt inexplicably uncomfortable. [Norma seemed to signal that pairing discussion seemed too intimate for her.]

George and Ross, continuing the theme begun by Doris, then talked about their gamesmanship. They purposely upset competitors by praising them. Doris said that she could put up a facade of being OK, but it was difficult to let people know what was happening inside. [George and Ross found a compromise. They could pair and utilize the alter-ego "relationship" to protect themselves and simultaneously express the group's worst fears—if a weakness was exposed, it would be attacked. They were turning their passive experience of injury into an active stance, so they would not be hurt again when the group "failed" them.]

The therapist chose to address an observable change—Norma's in-group behavior. He said that there was a feeling that they might be hurt if someone was nice, and they were afraid. Yet there seemed to be one readily observable change, and that was Norma's sharing of her experiences rather than primarily asking questions. [The therapist recognized that he was mirroring Norma's achievement which had gone unnoticed. In supervision the therapist reflected that he had felt the hostility might further disrupt the group. The supervisor wondered if the therapist's mirroring of Norma's achievement was a countertransference response, deflecting anger by focusing on positives.] Norma agreed that she was different, and the therapist then continued by saying that good things seemed to lead to greater discomfort, and one solution was expressed in the group by David, who had remained silent. [Norma's response was confirmatory and enabled the therapist to take another risk in confronting David's silence and the group's tendency to ignore him. The therapist felt that the one remaining silent member needed to be brought into the interactions. This was both a systems intervention regulating closeness–distance and an object relations comment pointing out the possibility that the members' withdrawn state might be projected into David. It did not explore the inner experience of any member.] Norma said that she thought David was doing better since he had told the group about a job he recently had obtained. [This response addressed one part of the therapist's intervention by attempting to reach out to David. It could have been interpreted as defensive on Norma's part since she did not explore her own wishes to withdraw. Instead, the therapist recognized the positive aspect of her response.] David said

the job was temporary, but it was better than not working. Nevertheless, he still felt terrible inside and that coming back after a three-
week break felt like starting over. He added that his current girlfriend
was leaving town, which reminded him of how depressed he had been
when his wife had left him. Sally responded that she, too, felt like she
was starting over in the group. [Thus, the process effectively included
David, whose associations returned to the group focus of feelings
about the interruption and loss. Sally now spontaneously spoke up,
suggesting that she felt safer.]

George then said he had a dream that the therapist had died, and
he wasn't certain whether or not his own wife had also died in the
dream. Ross asked if George had settled back into work, since he
often had reported having difficulty after vacations. The therapist
then wondered what had just happened, but before Ross could respond, George added that actually he had strangled the therapist in
the dream. [George's mother was very abusive and had often punished him by crushing his fingers in dresser drawers. In addition,
several years earlier, following a vacation and just before returning
to work, George's wife had nearly died in a car accident that had been
a result of her drinking. He had been very ambivalent about this,
feeling rage and guilt about the incident.] George continued, saying
with some humor that he would like to have veto power over interrup-
tions in the future. His remark drew some laughter from the others.
[This sequence showed a deepening of the material, a sense of safety
that permitted the more direct expression of anger at the therapist.
In the group-as-a-whole transference, it also represents the sequence
of hurt, reactive rage, and a wish to control. The separation felt like
a narcissistic injury. The humor was an indicator of a more stable
self.]

Norma then reported a dream, after saying that she hadn't actually
planned to report it. In the dream another therapist, known to be a
close colleague of the group therapist, had died. There was no one
present to grieve, and Norma felt very alone. She quickly associated
to the dream, suggesting that the other therapist represented the
group therapist, and then added she was glad that everyone had come
back safely. [This dream was reported as if Norma wanted to assure
her membership in the group and not as an expression of loss of the
therapist. It was as if Norma had felt the loss more than she understood, expressed it in the dream, and then was primarily interested
in reestablishing her ties to the therapist and the group. Her hesitancy
in reporting the dream may have reflected her fear that the responses
would focus on hostile elements in the dream rather than her inner
feelings of loss.]

The therapist inquired if his prior intervention (he had wondered what had happened) may have hurt Ross, who seemed slightly withdrawn. He asked Ross what he had experienced when George had reported the dream. Ross said initially he was only aware of thoughts about George's return to work, but he had become uncomfortable because he had no feelings about the therapist's being away. He contrasted his response to that of David, who was so acutely aware of losses. Ross said that he also had been dreaming but could not remember the specifics. They were dreams of violence and abandonment. [The therapist felt he had made a connection with Ross by his question, which had implicitly communicated an understanding that he might have hurt him. Ross acknowledged his awareness of walling off feelings and suggested that he had become uncomfortable as a result. He felt disconnected from the group because he could not share the inner feelings of loss. Thus, his topic switch was his effort to manage these feelings. An empathic understanding of that sequence by the therapist might have been useful at that point. The dreams indicated that this understanding was not complete. Ross also seemed to be reporting that he dreamt in order to strengthen his bonds with the other dreamers and perhaps the entire group.]

Sally spoke up and said that she also had been dreaming, but she was afraid to speak about it because she might not report it accurately. Without further prompting she said that in the dream she had been a manager at a store and a customer had embarrassed her, sort of knew her weaknesses, and since she, as the manager, had made a mistake, the customer was also quite critical of her. Ross responded that Sally seemed to be asking what she should or shouldn't feel, and Sally replied affirmatively. The therapist then wondered if the dream, which had to do with a dissatisfied customer, was also a reference to the situation in the group, since there were feelings of dissatisfaction in the group, and the customer had made a pointed effort to upset the manager. He wondered if some of those feelings were also in Sally and might be directed to himself. Sally, in her rather characteristic fashion, said she would consider it. [Sally, when she entered the group, had needed to merge with the idealized therapist. The manifest content of the dream suggests that a developmental step had taken place. The therapist (manager) might have some defects, and the customer (patient) could be angry. These affects were in synchrony with the groupwide affect and were Sally's response to the experience of losing the selfobject group.]

The final segment of the session was a brief interaction between George and Sally in which George raised a question about his feeling that he often provoked her, although he hadn't meant to do it. Sally said that did happen but was uncertain about George's contribution because she was often quite irritable. The therapist commented that he thought this was important since it appeared that Sally and George were exposing how important they were to one another, and they seemed to want to repair their relationship. They agreed and then recalled a meeting several months before when both had expressed mutual warmth and affection. [These final transactions represented another effort on the members' part to make linkages with one another in the context of trying to cope with their experiences of loss and anger with the therapist. At the beginning of the session, the therapist thought these feelings were particularly disruptive for the members who might be fearful of either their own destructiveness or internal overstimulation if they were directly stated. Progress was signaled by the absence of guilt in the interaction between Sally and George.]

This session has been described in this chapter as one point in ongoing therapeutic work. It is an illustration of the processes and understandings that the therapist experienced and the theoretical perspectives that were stimulated as he listened and tried to organize the material. The primary position was that of trying to appreciate the members' responses to the interruption as a sense that the group and/or the therapist were at least temporarily unavailable as reliable selfobjects. The responses of pairing, withdrawal, and anger were conceptualized as a response to this interruption. The therapist also integrated object relations and systems perspectives with those of self psychology both in his conceptualizations and his interventions.

THERAPEUTIC GOALS

Within the scope of this chapter, I have not emphasized specific self-object transferences along the mirroring, idealizing, and alter-ego developmental lines. Rather, I have tried to illustrate how the group provides multiple opportunities for both successful and failed connection among these self–selfobject transferences. If the leader or one or more members fail to be available for a specific need, there are others present who may fulfill the needed response (Bacal, 1983; Harwood, 1986; Weinstein, 1987). The availability of multiple selfobjects may mitigate some of the more intense regressions. However, the opposite is also possible, in that an unempathic response from a particular member, or even worse, from the group as a whole may, for vulnerable patients, precipitate significant narcissistic injury that is not easily reversed. When such events take place, the therapist's efforts to empathically explain the process are usually not immediately effective in soothing the injured member. Nonetheless, the therapist's efforts to make the connection are observed by others, and they gain an understanding of the process. This, in turn, may encourage them to identify with the therapist and reach out in their own fashion to the injured patient, a process that may modify the narcissistic hurt.

Change is not the result of merely cognitive processes, since it is only through the patients' feeling genuinely understood from the perspective of their inner experiences that they are able to internalize the function of the therapist (or others) and build a more solid sense of self. This is the essence of structure building of the self and has been labeled "transmuting internalization." This incompletely understood concept refers to the processes that take place developmentally in childhood and in later life either in therapy or in extratherapeutic encounters. In the therapeutic milieu, the patient has the experience of being understood and having that understanding explained. There remains an element of frustration because the interpretive process does not gratify the self's needs. Yet it is thought that the repeated experiences of disruption followed by interpretation in the context of an empathic matrix lead to structure building. As with the definition of the self, the structure of the self is the theoretical correlate of these attributes and refers in general terms to cohesion, strength, harmony, and the feelings of being alive across time, and in balance and organized (Kohut, 1984, p. 98).

By keeping a focus on the members' experience of being in the group, the therapist uses his self as an object for identification for the members. His willingness to examine his own contributions to misunderstandings and empathic failures further serves this function. Moreover, the therapist comes to appreciate the sensitivity of the members as they work to make contact with one another. It is a common experience for the therapist to feel marked pleasure as he observes members making genuine emotional connections with one another. Often they accomplish this in ways that had not occurred to the therapist. This event serves as a frequent reminder of our limitations, but it also expands our horizons.

The goal of group psychotherapy is a consolidation of the self so that the individuals may meaningfully and consistently pursue their goals and ambitions. In this process patients become less vulnerable to utilizing maladaptive solutions following a narcissistic injury. The need for a selfobject changes, and no longer do members consistently require the presence of archaic selfobjects to provide soothing responses and bolster their sense of coherence. Many, but not all, of these functions have been internalized and assumed by the members. Within the group, members interact with each other much more openly and have increased capacity to take risks. When they are injured they are more capable of verbalizing the hurts and finding appropriate solutions. Withdrawal in the face of hurt is less intense or prolonged. If an obstacle is in the way, anger may be expressed until it is removed. Prolonged narcissistic rage is no longer evident. Other compensatory or self-soothing solutions are utilized in a less self-defeating or self-destructive fashion. As part of this outcome, members are recognized as separate individuals with their own wishes and needs. Differences are generally seen as such, and there is not a need to have others be identical.

The successful group will have served as a very real laboratory wherein patients can observe others interacting in ways that communicate empathic understanding and can also try out new ways themselves. One patient in the termination phase remarked how she had never felt she had the capacity to truly understand another person. The group, she said, had provided her proof that she could not only understand others, but through that understanding be helpful to them. These experiences served to further reinforce her feeling that she was ready to terminate (Stone and Whitman, 1980). This woman was able to achieve another of the goals of treatment—the individual's increased capacity to empathize and have the experience of efficacy (E. S. Wolf, 1988).

Many of these indicators of a positive treatment outcome overlap with the goals articulated in other theoretical models. In a very early paper, A. Wolf (1950), writing from a perspective of psychoanalysis in groups, described the increase in ego capacity associated with growth as the patients' capacity to process their emotional responses in the group and balance these responses between pursuit of their own goals and those of the group. In this formulation, patients are not under the sway of transferences as they had been in earlier phases of treatment. That is, they may experience the transferential feelings or responses but do not have to act upon them. These formulations are similar to those of self psychology that address a consolidated self that does not respond with fears of disruption or disorganization following narcissistic injury but can maintain its balance. Blanck and Blanck (1977) described additional objectives for patients with major developmental arrests. Their formulations include attainment of a stable identity, approaching object constancy, a more competent defensive capacity, and the ego exercising more and more of its function. In group therapy these gains may be demonstrated in the interaction within the group or reported in the patient's everyday life.

Self psychology expresses these outcomes in a different language, but again there is considerable overlap with traditional analytic ideas of expanding the ego. In a group conducted along the principles of self psychology, patients nearing termination report that they are clearer about their personal goals and ambitions. They pursue activities in a more goal-directed fashion and do not get sidetracked when the inevitable interferences arise. They no longer overidealize authority. Instead, they are able to more accurately describe strengths and weaknesses and tolerate shortcomings in others—this is similar to expansion of conscious ego controls. In addition, patients can more readily accept their own foibles and failures without becoming excessively anxious or experiencing a threat to the solidity of the self—this is similar to moderating a harsh and primitive superego. Indeed, patients may report some injurious events with a humorous tone. The self is more consolidated, and inner needs to achieve perfection, or even approximate it, are modified.

FUTURE DIRECTIONS

As with any major revision of theory, there is a great deal of exploration that is necessary to assess the boundaries of the new theoretical material. Self psychologically informed therapists have been primarily concerned with the group, leader, and the intermember functions as selfobjects and their therapeutic value in consolidation of the self.

The literature thus far has not informed us of an expanded ability to care for seriously self disturbed patients in groups. The usual recommendations of combined therapy have been useful in maintaining these patients in the group and providing opportunities to grow. However, there remain a substantial number of patients who appear to make little or no progress in group or individual therapy. Even with what appears to be the best efforts of the therapist or other members to understand their inner state, these individuals do not seem to change. In addition, if they are injured in the interaction, they are unable to step back from the experience despite efforts to understand their injury and consequent response. A variation of these themes is present for those patients who cannot tolerate tension and anger among other group members. They appear to anticipate that they will be the next one injured, and they either withdraw into a protective shell or they try to create restrictive group norms, which often seem very difficult to alter.

It sometimes seems circular to suggest that an intervention that was intended to be empathic was not experienced in that way by the patient. Therapists intervene the best they can, and try to listen to patients' responses, but with these difficult patients it is frequently difficult in the group setting to gain the depth understanding that may be necessary for therapeutic growth. Certainly, there is no dearth of patients with major deficits in self regulation, and only through further experience with both successes and failures will our knowledge base be expanded.

At the other end of the developmental continuum are those patients whose conflicts are primarily at the oedipal level. In patients who have attained a firmer consolidation of the self, the basic unfolding of goals leads to sexual interests. At this phase patients find themselves sexually attracted to one another. As in any human interaction, individual preferences may be expressed in choosing one person over another. For the "loser" the experience is that of narcissistic injury. The members' capacity to manage such injuries and the associated experiences of fragmentation, which may range from minimal to serious, can be observed and understood in the group setting. The literature has not focused on these processes in group psychotherapy, but self psychology, instead, has primarily examined earlier developmental stages.

From a group-as-a-whole perspective, the impact of an emphasis on the psychology of the self on group development has not been explored sufficiently. It is my general impression that a consistent emphasis on the members' vulnerabilities and responses to narcissistic injury has prolonged the initial dependency/joining phase of group development. A confirmation of this observation will be necessary, as well as a more general reexamination of group development within this theoretical framework.

Many other issues remain to be explored in order to enhance a positive therapeutic outcome of all group members utilizing self psychology. The theory is still evolving, and as advances emerge, their application to group psychotherapy will be explored.

REFERENCES

Agazarian, Y. M. (1983), Theory of the invisible group applied to individual and group-as-a-whole interpretations. *Group*, 7(2):27–37.

Ashbach, C., & Schermer, V. L. (1987), *Object Relations, the Self and the Group*. New York: Routledge & Kegan Paul.

Bacal, H. (1983), Object-relations in the group from the perspective of self psychology. *Internat. J. Group Psychother.*, 35:483–501.

Benne, K., & Sheats, P. (1948), Functional roles of group members. *J. Soc. Issues*, 4:41–49.

Blanck, G., & Blanck, R. (1977), *Ego Psychology: Theory and Practice*. New York: Columbia University Press.

Detrick, D. W. (1985), Alterego phenomena and the alterego transferences. In: *Progress in Self Psychology, Vol. 1*, ed. A. Goldberg. Hillsdale, NJ: Lawrence Erlbaum.

Foulkes, S. H. (1961), Group processes and the individual in the therapeutic group. *Brit. J. Med. Psychol.*, 31:23–31.

Freud, S. (1915), Observations on transference-love. *Standard Edition*, 2:157–173. London: Hogarth Press, 1958.

Fried, E. (1973), Group bonds. In: *Group Therapy 1973: An Overview*, ed. L. R. Wolberg & E. K. Schwartz. New York: Intercontinental Medical Book.

Harwood, I. (1986), The need for optimal, available selfobject caretakers: Moving toward extended selfobject experiences. *Group Analysis*, 19:291–302.

Horwitz, L. (1977), A group-centered approach to group psychotherapy. *Internat. J. Group Psychother.*, 27:423–439.

Kohut, H. (1959), Introspection, empathy, and psychoanalysis. *J. Amer. Psychoanal. Assn.*, 7:459–483.

——— (1966), Forms and transformations of narcissism. *J. Amer. Psychoanal. Assn.*, 14:243–272.

——— (1971), *The Analysis of the Self*. New York: International Universities Press.

——— (1977), *The Restoration of the Self*. New York: International Universities Press.

——— (1984), *How Does Analysis Cure?* Chicago: University of Chicago Press.

——— Wolf, E. S. (1978), The disorders of the self and their treatment: An outline. *Internat. J. Psycho-Anal.*, 59:413–425.

Krystal, H. (1975), Affect tolerance. In: *The Annual of Psychoanalysis*, Vol. 3, ed. Chicago Institute for Psychoanalysis. New York: International Universities Press, pp. 179–219.

Ornstein, A. (1974), The dread to repeat and the new beginning: A contribution to the psychoanalysis of narcissistic personality disorders. In: *The Annual of Psychoanalysis*, Vol. 2, ed. Chicago Institute for Psychoanalysis. New York: International Universities Press, pp. 231–248.

Ornstein, P. H. (1985), The thwarted need to grow: Clinical-theoretical issues in the selfobject transferences. In: *The Transference in Psychotherapy*, ed. E. A. Schwaber. New York: International Universities Press.

Socarides, D. D., & Stolorow, R. D. (1984/85), Affects and selfobjects. In: *The Annual of Psychoanalysis*, Vol. 12/13, ed. Chicago Institute for Psychoanalysis. New York: International Universities Press, pp. 105–119.

Stolorow, R. D., Brandchaft, B., & Atwood, G. E. (1987), *Psychoanalytic Treatment: An Intersubjective Approach*. Hillsdale, NJ: Analytic Press.

——— Lachmann, F. M. (1984/85), Transference: The future of an illusion. In: *The Annual of Psychoanalysis*, Vol. 12/13, ed. Chicago Institute for Psychoanalysis. New York: International Universities Press, pp. 19–37.

Stone, W. N. (1985), The curative fantasy in group psychotherapy. *Group*, 9:3–14.

——— Gustafson, J. P. (1982), Technique in group psychotherapy of narcissistic and borderline patients. *Internat. J. Group Psychother.*, 32:29–47.

——— Stevenson, F. B. (1991), Seeking perspective on patients' attendance in group psychotherapy. In: *Psychoanalytic Group Theory and Therapy: Essays in Honor of Saul Scheidlinger*, ed. S. Tuttman. Madison, CT: International Universities Press, pp. 339–356.

——— Whitman, R. M. (1977), Contributions of the psychology of the self to group process and group therapy. *Internat. J. Group Psychother.*, 27:343–359.

——— ——— (1980), Observations on empathy in group psychotherapy. In: *Group and Family Therapy: 1980*, ed. L. R. Wolberg & M. L. Aronson. New York: Brunner/ Mazel.

Weinstein, D. (1987), Self psychology and group therapy. *Group*, 11:144–154.

Winnicott, D. H. (1965), *The Maturational Processes and the Facilitating Environment*. London: Hogarth Press.

Wolf, A. (1950), The psychoanalysis of groups. *Amer. J. Psychother.*, 4:16–50.

Wolf, E. S. (1976), Ambience and abstinence. In: *The Annual of Psychoanalysis*, Vol. 4, ed. Chicago Institute for Psychoanalysis. New York: International Universities Press, pp. 101–115.

——— (1988), *Treating the Self*. New York: Guilford Press.

8

The Clinical Application of Social Systems Theory

JOHN F. BORRIELLO, Ph.D.

HISTORICAL OVERVIEW

This chapter focuses on the social systems approach to group psychotherapy, which is an open-systems model. This approach is not widely
used by group psychotherapists. In the literature, this mode of treatment is sometimes labeled as the group-as-a-whole or group-centered
approach. Essentially, all three labels describe a focus on the group
and the roles the group members take up in the group. The social
systems approach construes the group and the individuals within it
as open, evolving systems. Group psychotherapy is viewed as a
throughput process with input, conversion, and output phases. This
approach incorporates the group theory of Bion (1948a,b, 1949a,b,
1950a,b, 1951) and the open-systems concepts of Miller and Rice
(1967). Beginning this chapter with a historical overview of how this
model evolved will serve to put the clinical material in perspective.

In order not to confuse the reader, the approach described here is
not the one investigated by the Tavistock Clinic group psychotherapy
outcome research team headed by Malan, Balfour, Hood, and
Shooter (1976). This research team concerned itself with the psychoanalytic approach of Ezriel (1973). Ezriel's approach adapts psychoanalysis to the group situation. He joined the Tavistock Clinic in the
mid-1940s and stayed on after Bion left.

Bion and Group Dynamics

Wilfred R. Bion was the pioneer in the development of the social systems approach. During World War II, while he was a British army officer, he became fascinated by group dynamics, particularly the phenomena of leadership, followership, membership, and task accomplishment (Sutherland, 1985). In 1942, he was placed in charge of the training wing of a military psychiatric hospital. The administrative necessity of organizing 300 to 400 psychologically troubled soldiers into a manageable therapeutic enterprise led him to develop a sophisticated therapeutic community. The success of this enterprise brought an invitation from the Professional Committee of the Tavistock Clinic to continue his work there.

While at Tavistock, he established one of the first "study groups": a group explicitly established to examine its unfolding dynamics in the here-and-now. It was composed of staff and interested colleagues from other institutions. Bion defined his role as that of observer and interpreter of that which he saw occurring within the group. He believed in intervening only when what was happening was being left unsaid. He observed that the group had its own boundaries and that his function, to observe and comment on what was going on within its boundaries, facilitated its study. Defining his role as he did, he became the designated leader and focal point of interest. This role definition is consonant with that of the psychotherapeutic model. Bion's interventions in the group focused on the group's attitude toward him and the attitudes of individual members toward the group:

> There are times when I think that the group has an attitude to me, and I can state in words what the attitude is; there are times when another individual acts as if he also thought the group had an attitude to him, and I believe, I can deduce what his belief is; there are times when I think that the group has an attitude to an individual, and that I can say what it is . . . I judge the occasion to be ripe for an interpretation when the interpretation would seem to be both obvious and unobserved [Bion, 1952, p. 236].

Bion noted that all individuals have the propensity for joining with groups to become the active server and/or expresser of the different dynamics operative at any given moment. He calls this propensity "valency." According to this concept, the individual "chosen" to meet a particular need is the individual with the highest need to perform that particular function. For example, some groups will unconsciously select for the leadership function the individual with the highest valency to take care of others and to place others in a dependent position vis à vis himself.

Miller and Rice

Another important influence in the development of the social systems approach to group psychotherapy is Eric Miller and A. K. Rice's (1967) application of Bion's group theory to complex organizations. They focused on primary task, role, authority, and boundary management. Miller and Rice view the individual as an "open system." According to this view, human beings need to interact with the environment to maintain themselves. Without these interactions individuals would die. At birth the infant is dependent upon the mother and is in daily interaction with her. Later these interactions extend to include such other significant figures as father, brothers, sisters, grandparents, teachers, and peers. These interactions, coupled with the infant's biological inheritance, shape his personality: They form the internal and external worlds of the person. The mature ego differentiates between what is real in the outside world and what is projected onto the outside world from the inside. When a member of a group is able to do this consistently, he is ready to terminate.

GROUP PROCESSES

Basic Assumption and Work Groups

From his experience with both study groups and therapy groups, Bion (1948a,b, 1949a,b, 1950a,b, 1951) postulated the existence of a variety of phenomena. Among them were "basic assumptions," which he believed are operative in all types of groups, whether they be psychotherapy groups, study groups, political groups, or even such large and diverse groups as the army or the church. The three "basic assumptions" he described are (1) fight–flight, (2) pairing, and (3) dependency.

Fight–flight is evident when members behave as if they have convened for the purpose of fighting or fleeing from someone or something. Pairing is evident when members behave as if they have convened for the purpose of waiting for and receiving salvation from some single pair of persons, ideas, equipment, or the pairing of the present with the future. Dependency is evident when members behave as if they have convened for the purpose of receiving nurturance from someone through a special relationship (Merrill, 1981).

According to Bion (1948a,b, 1949a,b, 1950a,b, 1951), a group is defined by a task or function. Without a task or function, there is not a group; rather, there is a collection of individuals. With a task or function, this collection of individuals becomes a group. Bion observed that a group is "working" when it demonstrates consciously motivated behavior directed toward task implementation on the basis of reality. He observed further that basic assumption mentality is forever impeding work group functioning. According to him, basic assumption mentality stems from an unconscious assumption on the part of members that the group has met for some purpose other than the accomplishment of its task. However, he observed that in specialized groups, such as the army or church, basic assumption mentality and the task of the specialized group coincide. The army, for instance, must mobilize the basic assumption of fight–flight in order to accomplish its work: fighting or fleeing. Likewise, the church must utilize the basic assumption of dependency to accomplish its work: meeting the spiritual needs of its members.

The psychotherapy group is a special kind of work group in which basic assumption mentality must be recognized and interpreted. This is crucial since basic assumption mentality often functions as resistance to doing the work of psychotherapy, which is to provide opportunities for the group's psychologically troubled members to cognitively and affectively learn about themselves through their membership in the group. The member's role/task is to come, sit, and be curious about what is happening in the group, and be curious about his reactions to the therapist, other member(s), and the group. The therapist's role/task is to facilitate the group psychotherapy process through the management of the boundaries around the group, its members, and its therapist, and to comment on that which gets left unsaid (Borriello, 1976a).

Projective Identification

Projective identification assumes an interpersonal/interactional/relational process for its operation. It is a term used by, among others, Bion (1952) and coined by Melanie Klein (Segal, 1964). Klein was Bion's analyst. She influenced him in his work with individuals in psychoanalysis (Trist, 1985). Two years after he stopped working with groups, Bion (1952) reviewed his *Human Relations* group papers and made an attempt to relate Klein's theories to his group theories, but he was not interested in applying psychoanalysis to groups (Sutherland, 1985).

In a group, members fit each other and the therapist into unconsciously created roles. Between and among themselves and the therapist, they form relationships that are ongoing and that are possible avenues for the expression and gratification of repressed needs. In projective identification, members project their repressed needs (parts of themselves) onto each other and onto the therapist. For this projection to be taken on (the "identification" aspect of projective identification), a member must be prone to play the reciprocal role in the process (Borriello, 1975, 1976b). For example, an extremely aggressive member unwittingly may be prompted or coerced to express to the therapist the hostility that many, or all, feel. Another example is when a very dependent patient may be unconsciously established by the group as the "sick" one, the identified patient to be taken care of by the therapist as a means of vicariously satisfying the dependency needs of all. Sometimes, the expression of the need arouses too much anxiety or guilt, and then the patient being used for its expression is scapegoated and either attacked (fight) or rejected (flight). Obviously, projective identification can be destructive unless interpreted by the therapist.

When one individual becomes the repository for the collective dependency of the group, he can easily become crippled under the staggering weight of the others' projections of dependency, with their accompanying unconscious identifications. When the therapist frustrates this dependency need by refusing to meet the combined needs of the other members, the group may behave aggressively toward him (the therapist) through another member.

Similarly, the patient with the greatest propensity to act on and express the aggression of the group may become locked in this role. The result is that he usually becomes the recipient of the aggressive projections of others as well as of their accompanying unconscious identifications. Eventually such patients may find themselves experiencing an unmanageable burden of such feelings.

Likewise, an air of hopeful expectation may permeate the group. During this period the group may pair with ideas such as that group therapy for world leaders would eliminate war, or that divorce would disappear if couples experienced group therapy. The pair need not be human and need not be a discrete pair. The pair could be the addition of something new to the status quo. What is crucial is that the group is charged with hopeful expectation that something magical will occur. The hope must never be realized, since only by remaining a hope does hope exist.

If the therapist is ignorant of the projective identification phenomenon, such behavior may prompt him to consider hospitalizing the member who is carrying the group's projections, or the member may terminate, to the relief of both the therapist and the other group members. Either of these eventualities will likely result in the projective identification of the dependency or the aggression in the group onto the next most appropriate member, or the hope and expectation onto the next most appropriate pair. This can only be avoided by interpretation of the phenomenon to the group (Borriello, 1976b, 1979).

Countertransference versus Projective Identification

The group psychotherapist needs to be in touch with his own emotional reactions in the group if his interventions are to be useful (Bion, 1952). He has to distinguish between feelings due to countertransference, which are not to be interpreted to the group, and feelings due to projective identification, which are to be interpreted to the group. While this distinction is difficult to make, it is the obligation of group therapists to do the best they can to do so. Therefore it is crucial to have sufficient data from what is occurring in the group to support the interpretation before it is given. If there is not sufficient data, it is reasonable to assume that countertransference is operative, and the interpretation should not be given. A rule of thumb to follow is to always check the data within the group to see if it supports the therapist feeling pressure to take on the role of gratifying the group, rather than addressing the basic assumption currently operative in the group.

CASE ILLUSTRATIONS OF BION'S GROUP THEORY

Basic Assumption Dependency

Basic assumption dependency operates when a group behaves as if it has met in order to be sustained by a leader on whom it depends for nurturance, protection, and safety. It demonstrates the human being's strong need to want to be taken care of, to have someone else do for you even if you can do it yourself. It relates to the struggle to gain autonomy. Dependency is often a very powerful emotional state within a group. Psychotherapy groups can be permeated with this basic assumption, which is often a major impediment to work group activity.

Dependency is evident when group members behave as if the therapist is the repository of all knowledge, adequacy, and maturity, and as if all they need to do is worship the therapist and their problems will go away. They seem to feel the therapist is the only one who can make sense out of the information that is available to all, and the only one who can work out solutions for their problems.

An illustration from the first session of a long-term psychotherapy group clearly demonstrates this basic assumption. This group was composed of four women and three men. Basic assumption dependency prevailed, which is typical in the first session of a group. All members had been interviewed and educated about the group before entry. At the appointed hour for the first group session, five of the seven patients were present. Almost immediately there was silence, and all members stared at the therapist. The therapist simply looked at each member but said nothing. One patient asked the therapist if the two empty chairs meant there were two more members. Again the therapist did not answer the question. When the two latecomers arrived, one volunteered that she had been in group psychotherapy before and that that group started when all members had arrived. The therapist responded by looking at his watch, at the clock on the wall, and then at each of the members in turn.

Shortly thereafter a patient asked what they were supposed to do. The therapist did not respond. Another patient said she had heard that the therapist rarely talked and that they would have to work on their problems themselves. Another patient said that if this was so, he was going to join another group. He didn't think a group of neurotic people could help themselves. A number of others agreed they did not have what it takes to solve their own problems. Despite some patients recalling that the patient and therapist roles/tasks had been explicitly defined during their initial sessions with the therapist, most continued to insist they could not help themselves or each other. The therapist was the only one who believed the patients had something to offer, and said so. The session ended on this note.

The therapist's interventions were an attempt to establish and reinforce a group culture in which work was the focus. The emphasis on time, the communication of concern by the therapist, and the belief that the patients have the resources to work productively were all efforts in this direction.

The following example also highlights basic assumption dependency as well as the efficacy of interpreting projective identification in the interest of accomplishing work. The group consisted of four women and three men, and all members suffered from affective disorders and had had multiple admissions to psychiatric hospitals. Sessions lasted for forty-five minutes and were held five times a week. This session frequency is atypical, but the setting within which this group was formed provided the opportunity to meet this often.

By the thirtieth session, Ms. L. had become the repository of the group's collective dependency through the process of projective identification. As such, she expressed the dependency belonging to all in a dramatic manner. From the social systems perspective, a member of a group assumes a role for as long as the role serves a purpose for other members. When this situation was interpreted by the therapist, it was vigorously denied by all.

At one particular point, Ms. L. got up from her chair, laid on the floor, and began to hyperventilate. When the therapist did not jump in to attempt to rescue her, many complaints were expressed toward him. However, shortly thereafter another group member went over to Ms. L. and told her to get up and return to her chair, and to talk about what she was feeling. Ms. L. followed these instructions and reported that she felt less helpless and less pressured as a result of what had occurred. A number of patients then described looking to the therapist to manage the situation and being surprised and enraged when he did not. What followed was a very productive period of work in the group. Patients began talking more about their feelings of helplessness and hopelessness, thus "owning" their projections, and this resulted in Ms. L. feeling less pressure to behave so incompetently. Why was Ms. L. chosen to bear this sentiment for the group? The reason is that she had the highest "valency" for this role: She was the most dependent group member, she had made the most suicide attempts, and she was the most withdrawn and lethargic member of the group.

Basic Assumption Fight–Flight

Basic assumption fight–flight operates when the group behaves as if it has met to fight somebody or something, or to flee from somebody or something. Action and panic are essential ingredients of this basic assumption.

Fight is evident when group members attack, either verbally and/ or physically, the therapist for things that have no basis in reality or focus on an external enemy in a way that is inflated or otherwise distorted. The most paranoid member is usually the one who emerges as the leader when *"ba fight"* (Bion's term for basic assumption fight–flight) is operative. This member is most adept at identifying enemies, either real or imagined, and at finding ways to dismiss whatever data there might be that are not consistent with his personal view, and the group's view, of the way things are. Such patients frequently join groups at the behest of someone else (e.g., judges or disgruntled spouses), so they are not really there voluntarily. Such a member is often used as the spokesperson for the resistance to work that belongs to all. Once again, persistent interpretation is the only way to undermine the projective identification process. This work has succeeded when other members begin talking about their resistance and the spokesperson begins manifesting less resistance.

The following is an example of this process. A forensic group consisting of four women and four men met three times a week for ninety minutes. After a year in which there were no additions to or terminations from the group, Mr. W. told the group that he had observed the therapist talking to a probation officer. Mr. X. expressed intense anger and distrust toward the therapist, and immediately became the *ba fight* leader of the group. After persistently interpreting the projective identification process over the course of a number of sessions by pointing out the ways in which others were instigating Mr. X., some group members began expressing their rage directly. Concomitantly, Mr. X.'s expressions of anger and distrust became less strident. He came to realize that he was expressing not only his own distrust and anger, but also the distrust and anger of the other members. Sometimes change starts with the other members owning their projections, and sometimes it begins with the spokesperson abandoning his role.

While it is the most paranoid person who usually becomes the spokesperson when the group is in its *ba fight* mode, it is the most schizoid person who represents the group when it is in its *ba flight* mode. Flight is evident when the group tries to organize a party during its work time, focuses on problems or people outside the group, or otherwise seems to be fleeing from work.

Basic Assumption Pairing

Basic assumption pairing operates when a group behaves as if it has convened for the purpose of reproduction: to bring forth a savior through a particular pair in the group. An essential ingredient of this basic assumption is an air of hopeful expectation not related to reality considerations. It is as if by a pair "getting together" for the group, all will be well. In the meantime, there is no need to work; there is only a need to wait for the messiah to fix everything. In this way, *ba pairing*, like other basic assumptions, is used by the group to avoid work. However, in this basic assumption, the messianic hope must never be realized, since hope only exists when something remains to be hoped for.

Pairing is evident when the power of the group for its members, or for society more generally, is talked about in grandiose terms. For instance, in a group conducted during the 1960s, there was a good deal of talk about group therapy being the answer not only for the problems of members and their friends, but also for the Vietnam war. It took a great deal of interpretation to get the group into a genuine work mode.

SOCIAL SYSTEMS APPROACH TO GROUP PSYCHOTHERAPY

Central Concepts

Some of the key concepts of the social systems approach to group psychotherapy are defined below. The way they are used is illustrated in the case examples throughout this chapter.

1. Open system: An enterprise whose boundaries are permeable enough that an input–throughput–output process can occur that is responsive to the environment's needs.

2. Closed system: An enterprise whose boundaries prevent an input–throughout–output process that is responsive to the environment's needs from occurring.

3. Activities: Operating activities define an enterprise, differentiate it from other entities in the environment, and are necessary for the input–throughput–output process. Maintenance activities provide that which is needed for operating activities (supplies, space, etc.). Regulatory activities relate different activities to each other and to the external environment.

4. Boundary: The line or space which separates that which is in from that which is out. Transactions occur across boundaries both within the individual and between the individual or entity and its surrounding environment. Boundaries define such things as task, time, space, membership, thoughts, feelings, and so forth.

5. *Role*: A position one adopts within a group, determined by a group's culture, norms, and mores as well as its agreed-upon task. Some roles are prescribed by an organization, such as chief executive officer, teacher, fireman, or group psychotherapist. One can call these structured, designated, or formal roles. Roles are also prescribed by the dominant basic assumption operative in a group at any particular time in the life of the group. Members take these roles depending upon their valence for the prevailing basic assumption. One can call these unstructured, informal, or nondesignated roles.

6. *Primary task*: The reason for the existence of an entity, or that which is necessary for an entity to survive.

7. *Projective identification*: The process by which individual members of a group collectively disown and project certain aspects, emotions, or parts of themselves into/onto one member, and by which that member "accepts" the projections and becomes the repository or spokesperson for that which has been disowned.

8. *Valency*: An individual's predisposition to assume a particular role within a group, which is a function of one's skills as well as conflict areas.

9. *Work group*: A group that works cooperatively and on the basis of data rather than myths and assumptions toward the accomplishment of its agreed-upon task(s). Such groups are characterized by a functional organizational structure.

10. *Basic assumption group*: A group that gets sidetracked from productive work by the intrusion of irrational beliefs or assumptions which come to govern its behavior.

Open-System Application

Social systems theory views group psychotherapy as a conversion process with input–throughput–output phases. Its primary task is to treat persons with psychological dysfunction. The input is the people who present themselves for group psychotherapy. The conversion is the change or transformation of their psychological dysfunctions. The output is the people who leave the process, more functional psychologically than when they entered, or so it is hoped.

What distinguishes the social systems approach from others is the attention paid to the group and its members as evolving systems. It assumes that there are no innocent bystanders in the here-and-now of the group. That is, whatever occurs happens because all members and the therapist sanction it and contribute to it in their own unique ways. As such, the group provides each member the opportunity to study his own behavior, especially the role he assumes, his contribution to interpersonal dynamics, and his relationship to authority. The task of the therapist is to try to elucidate the nature of the group process and the contributions different members make to it.

Social systems theory is not defined by any particular theory of personality. It can be thought of as a metatheory that can be coupled with any theory that attempts to account for motivation.

Theory of Therapeusis

The social systems approach to group psychotherapy views the group and its individuals as open, evolving systems. It postulates that conversion/transformation/change for each individual member occurs through an examination of the roles that each takes on in the group. These roles can be either enhancers or impeders of the work of the group. The examination occurs through the analysis of the projective identifications within the group. The goal for each member is to achieve consonance between what he experiences (feelings, thoughts) internally with what is happening externally.

CASE EXAMPLES

Ongoing Group

The session to be described here was the fiftieth session of a group that was conducted with the same membership for three years. It was composed of eight members: four men and four women. All were employed and college educated. Two were lawyers, and the others were, respectively, a personnel specialist, a research scientist, a psychiatric resident, a social worker, a college instructor, and a budget analyst.

The group met in the evening for two hours once a week. In this session, the group convened at the appointed hour and Sue, the budget analyst, began to talk. She was the most vocal about "Dr. B. not doing enough to help us." Through projective identification, each member colluded to maintain her role as the dependency leader. In doing so, others were able to avoid directly confronting and acknowledging their dependency.

At the beginning of the group, members affirmed Sue's statements that the therapist was not doing enough. The therapist intervened with the following statement: "There is a myth in the head of each member that if I told them the cause of their disorder, they would get better." With this interpretation, the situation changed in the group. Members no longer overtly affirmed Sue's pleas to the therapist to tell them what to do. Instead, they would let her talk but then would behave as if they were bored. The therapist commented, "I observe that although you are bored with what Sue is saying, none of you are doing anything about it."

Other similar interventions eventually sparked the members' curiosity, and they began a painful dialogue among themselves about how scary it was to feel dependent. Lisa, the social worker, stated that there was a part of her that supported Sue's wanting the therapist to tell them what to do. Phil, the psychiatric resident, stated that he was studying group therapy but when he came to group his mind was a blank. He was not able to think of anything to say. He fantasied how nice it would be if the therapist just waved a magic wand and their problems would go away. Sam, Donna, and Mary nodded in agreement. Jim and Carl, the two lawyers, inquired if the therapist had something like a brief that the members could read to help them. They said that they had been thinking about this but did not have the courage to talk about it until that session.

At the next session, Sam said, "I am getting sick and tired of wanting you to solve my problems, but I must admit I felt good about your pleas, Sue, to Dr. B. to help us more." Phil, Mary, Lisa, and Donna talked about their difficulty admitting that they have strong dependency needs. Phil stated that he read in his psychiatric texts about how tenacious denial is, but he really never knew what it meant until he experienced in the group how he and all the members were using Sue to avoid experiencing their dependency. Jim and Carl said that for them to admit they were dependent would have blown their images of themselves as tough, independent law associates who were struggling to become partners in their law firms.

As the group continued, the group's need to contain its dependency in Sue lessened. Jim, Carl, Mary, Phil, Lisa, Sam, and Donna became curious about and acknowledged dependency feelings in the here-and-now of the group and also in their everyday living.

Sue described realizing that she loved to feed others, and she suddenly realized that, figuratively, she had been doing this in the group. She said that she was not aware of this need until recently, when she felt less pressure to take care of others. Dr. B.'s comments helped her, she commented, even though she would make fun of them and the other group members talking about their dependency feelings in the group. She said she had felt that Dr. B. did not know what he was talking about when he would question what was in it for each and every member of the group to have her behave as she did. She had daydreamed that the group did not appreciate her care and concern, and she felt sorry for herself. She had felt that Dr. B. was the cause of all this because "he made these ridiculous group statements." Similarly, she stated that now she didn't find herself wanting to get up early to stop by the bakery to buy pastry and make coffee for the office.

She spoke of her thoughts of feeling good when the group members ranted and raved about the therapist not doing what he should to help the members, but she never felt that she was with the group during these times. Now she was beginning to experience anger, and it was scary. Others described the alleviation of dependency longings as well, and described the particular ways this change was manifesting itself in their lives.

This group was able to get to the point of confronting the fact that they joined not to work but instead to be taken care of. They were also able to see how they colluded in projecting their neediness into/ onto Sue, who naturally "accepted" these projections. Through the experience of being in the group and adhering to the task, the members educated themselves about their dependency needs and the futility of not acknowledging them.

Initial Group Session

This group was composed of seven members. Six were employed and one was a full-time student. This group was scheduled to meet for ninety minutes once a week.

The group convened at the appointed hour for the initial session. At first there was silence. Kathy broke the ice and introduced herself, and the others followed suit. Questions were asked about what they did, after which silence ensued. Next Valentina volunteered why she was in the group. Members asked each other questions and offered advice to each other. Then all looked at the therapist, and Frank asked what they were supposed to do. The therapist commented that through Frank the members of the group were behaving as if they had not been prepared for what to do in the group. This comment resulted in members comparing what preparation for the group each had had, sharing their commonly felt anxiety, and periodically demanding to be told how to behave. The therapist continued to not respond to this demand.

Next, Frank spoke of an encounter he had had the previous week with his boss. He had to go to court to represent a client. He was shocked when his boss told him that he would be in court by himself. He told his boss that he did not think he would be able to do it. His boss told him that he had faith in him. He went to court and, much to his surprise, did a good job.

Following this, the therapist commented that he wondered if Frank was speaking on behalf of others and talking in camouflage about what was happening in the group. Silence came over the group. Then Frank explained that for him it meant that "each of us has to take responsibility for working on our problems in the group, that the therapist is not going to do it for us." Others responded with their understandings of what the therapist meant, and soon the appointed time to end had arrived. The therapist got up, opened the door, and left the room.

In the hall one patient approached him and said that she had a dinner engagement the following week so she would not be able to attend the group. The therapist responded that she should talk about it in the group next week. She did attend the following session, and she said she really did not have a dinner engagement but she was thinking then of not coming back because of her anger at the therapist and felt that the fiction would make a good excuse. She asserted that she believed some of the others were just as irritated with the therapist as she was but that they pretended they weren't. In this session she also continued in her role of not understanding how the group was going to help her or any of the other patients. This role lessened as the other group members began to own up to their doubts about whether the group was going to help.

This vignette illustrates how a therapist can begin to inculcate the notion that all members are involved in, and contribute to, everything that occurs in the group. Also, it highlights the way a therapist can avoid colluding in basic assumption dependency: namely, by not answering any questions if the information is available to group members. The postgroup colloquy that was described illustrates how a therapist can funnel material into the group in the face of an attempt to deal with something outside the group's boundaries.

SUMMARY

This chapter has described the application of social systems theory to group psychotherapy. This approach views group psychotherapy as a throughput process with input, conversion, and output phases. Social systems theory is a metatheory that views the group and the individuals within it as open, evolving systems. It can be coupled with any of a number of theories that address individual motivation.

Social systems theory contains within it important limitations. For one thing, it relies heavily on the concept of projective identification, and this construct is hypothetical rather than directly observable. This makes it difficult for both patients and therapists to grasp and work with at times. Second, of course, is that there has been no empirical data as yet reported that demonstrates the efficacy of the theory. As such, it is crucial for those who subscribe to it to construe it as an open and evolving perspective that remains receptive to new thinking. It needs to move in the direction of concretizing its operating principles and demonstrating its efficacy in the years ahead.

REFERENCES

Bion, W. R. (1948a), Experiences in groups, I. *Human Relations*, I:314–320.
——— (1948b), Experiences in groups, II. *Human Relations*, I:487–496.
——— (1949a), Experiences in groups, III. *Human Relations*, II:13–22.
——— (1949b), Experiences in groups, IV. *Human Relations*, II:295–304.
——— (1950a), Experiences in groups, V. *Human Relations*, III:3–14.
——— (1950b), Experiences in groups, VI. *Human Relations*, III:395–402.
——— (1951), Experiences in groups, VII. *Human Relations*, IV:221–228.
——— (1952), Group dynamics: A re-view. *Internat. J. Psycho-Anal.*, 33:235–247.
Borriello, J. F. (1975), W. R. Bion's "Experiences in groups" and other papers. [Book review.] *Internat. J. Group Psychother.*, 25(5):348–356.
——— (1976a), Group psychotherapy in hospital systems. In: *Group Therapy 1976: An Overview*, ed. W. R. Wolberg, M. L. Aronson, & A. R. Wolberg. New York: Stratton Intercontinental Medical Book Corp., pp. 99–108.
——— (1976b), Leadership in the therapist-centered group-as-a-whole psychotherapy approach. *Internat. J. Group Psychother.*, 26(2):149–162.
——— (1979), Intervention foci in group psychotherapy. In: *Group Therapy 1979: An Overview*, ed. L. R. Wolberg & M. L. Aronson. New York: Stratton Intercontinental Medical Book Corp., pp. 52–60.
Ezriel, H. (1973), Psychoanalytic group therapy. In: *Group Therapy: 1973*, ed. L. R. Wolberg & E. K. Schwartz. New York: Intercontinental Medical Book Corp., pp. 183–210.
Malan, D. H., Balfour, F. H. G., Hood, V. G., & Shooter, A. M. N. (1976), Group psychotherapy: A long-term follow-up study. *Arch. Gen. Psychiat.*, 33:1303–1315.
Merrill, W. P. (1981), *Group Phenomena Concepts*. Unpublished Manuscript. Group Training Section, Saint Elizabeth's Hospital, NIMH, Washington, DC. (Now the Group, Family and Organizational Consultation Branch, D.C. Commission on Mental Health Services.)

Miller, E. J., & Rice, A. K. (1967), *Systems of Organization*. London: Tavistock Publications.

Segal, H. (1964), *Introduction to the Work of Melanie Klein*. New York: Basic Books.

Sutherland, J. D. (1985), Bion revisited: Group dynamics and group psychotherapy. In: *Bion and Group Psychotherapy*, ed. M. Pines. London: Routledge & Kegan Paul, pp. 47–86.

Trist, E. (1985), Working with Bion in the 1940s: The group decade. In: *Bion and Group Psychotherapy*, ed. M. Pines. London: Routledge & Kegan Paul, pp. 1–46.

9

Summary: Clinical Applications to Patient Care

HAROLD S. BERNARD, Ph.D., DAVID L. SINGER, Ph.D., and
ROBERT H. KLEIN, Ph.D.

The authors of the chapters on clinical applications to patient care were asked not to explicate in depth the theoretical underpinnings of the perspectives they represent, but rather to identify the key concepts which inform their clinical work. Therefore, the first section of this summary chapter will compare and contrast the constructs our authors highlighted in their chapters. We will then go on to discuss the role of the therapist, the view of how therapy works, the level at which work is conducted, and the range of applicability of each of the theories being considered in this volume.

KEY CONCEPTS

In his chapter on the object relations approach to group psychotherapy, Dr. Kibel begins with the basic premise that the individual is from the beginning primarily object-seeking rather than satisfaction-seeking. Thus, instead of seeking the discharge of biological drives, a process in which "objects" (other people) play an incidental role, the object relations notion is that the pursuit of a particular kind of connection with the "object" constitutes the basis of human motivation.

Experiences with key "objects" are internalized and then reenacted, both in the treatment situation and in one's everyday life (Greenberg and Mitchell, 1983). The group is the optimal modality in which to observe and work on object relations because the group setting

227

constitutes an interpersonal field that evokes the unconscious paradigms that underlie each individual's internalized object relations. As Dr. Kibel puts it, the group becomes a field for the interplay of each member's part-object relationships. By this he means that group members induce both the therapist and other group members to play roles that complement, and reciprocally reflect, aspects of their inner needs and conflicts. The group, including the therapist, becomes a container for the collective projections of its members. The interaction between each individual's tendencies, or valences, determines the processes and developmental sequences that come to characterize a particular group.

All groups can be described in terms of the individual and collective defenses that predominate at any given stage in their evolution. The object relations perspective emphasizes splitting, projection, and projective identification and tends to view the use of these mechanisms as typically resulting in restricting and disabling "solutions" (compromises) to the dilemmas with which the group is grappling. The therapeutic goal is to help members recover disowned and split-off parts of the group members, move from splitting to ambivalence, and thereby broaden the range of individual and collective solutions available. When clear differentiation between integrated self and other is achieved, the individual can initiate conflict-free paradigms necessary for successful interpersonal relations.

In a critical departure from traditional theory, Kohut asserted that there is a separate line of narcissistic development (Kohut, 1966). As Dr. Stone points out, Kohut's view was that development does not lead eventually to the transformation of narcissism into object-love (the traditional view), but rather to higher forms of narcissism. He construed optimum development as occurring when life's disappointments lead to infantile wishes and needs becoming transformed into adult ambitions and ideals.

Kohut moved from his original emphasis on narcissism as a separate line of development to the concept of the self as the central organizing structure in human functioning (Kohut, 1971). As Dr. Stone elucidates, the concept of the self must be understood in two ways. In one sense it is a psychological structure that organizes the individual's experience. In another sense, it is an existential agent that initiates action. For self psychologists, the relationships between the self and its various selfobjects are the cornerstone of the human experience. Hence, in this regard as well, groups are an excellent setting for learning about and working with people, since an array of available selfobjects inevitably stimulates the reenactment and examination of deficient self–selfobject relationships.

A variety of self–selfobject relationships need to emerge during normal development. Kohut particularly emphasizes the seeking out of mirroring, idealizing, and alter-ego selfobjects. As Dr. Stone describes them, the mirroring selfobject reflects and confirms the goodness and value of the self; the idealizable selfobject provides the opportunity to merge with an omnipotent and omniscient other, thereby enhancing the value of the self; and the alter-ego selfobject fulfills the self's need for sameness, which also contributes to the self's development and flowering. When the required self–selfobject relationships are unavailable, the development of the self is either retarded or completely arrested.

Treatment is construed as an effort by the self to seek out the mirroring, idealizing, alter-ego, and other selfobjects necessary to get development back on track. The primary requirement of the group therapist is to provide "empathic attunement": to understand the nature of what the individual is missing, and therefore seeking, in the treatment context. When the individual is able to find the needed self–selfobject relationships, he thereby acquires the nutriments for the consolidation, maintenance, and restoration of the self. Self psychologists refer to this process as "transmuting internalization."

Whereas object relations and self psychology practitioners work in various treatment modalities, including both individual and group therapy, clinicians who work out of a social systems model almost always work in a group setting. While some of the constructs that define social systems theory can be used to elucidate any treatment experience, they are most useful in elucidating group processes, undoubtedly because they were developed in group settings (Bion, 1961; Miller and Rice, 1969). Social systems practitioners tend to focus most of their attention on group-level processes, and to explore the roles individuals take up in the group setting and how these relate to their presenting concerns.

As noted by Dr. Borriello, the notion of "valency" refers to the fact that the member with the highest propensity or predisposition for a particular role is the one who will assume it within the group. He will not necessarily be the only person who holds the sentiment or disposition he is expressing; rather, he will assume the role and thereby represent that sentiment or disposition on behalf of others as well as himself. A good deal of the effort in treatment is to work toward others "owning" their part of what a particular individual represents on their behalf; this is known as "reowning," or recovering, projections. The process of representing feelings on behalf of others who unconsciously identify with these sentiments but endeavor to induce others to contain or enact them is what has come to be known as projective identification.

As Dr. Borriello illustrates, another central construct used by social systems practitioners is that of boundaries. In the treatment situation there are critical boundaries that differentiate what is in from what is out with regard to tasks, roles, time, place, the boundary between self and others as well as that between different parts of the self, and so on. Social systems practitioners pay careful attention to defining such boundaries precisely so that each individual's adherence to them, or violation of them, can be accurately understood and interpreted. Such interpretation, offered at the group level but available to each individual to consider, constitutes a key element at the heart of the social systems treatment process, together with work on projective identification within the group matrix.

In social systems–based practice, considerable attention is paid to the way the group in question relates to the therapist; hence, social systems work is often described as focusing on "authority relations." When the therapist is engaged in a way that facilitates task accomplishment, the group is operating as a "work group." But more often the therapist is responded to in a way that thwarts the accomplishment of its agreed-upon task; at such times the group is operating as a "basic assumption group" (Bion, 1961). Sometimes the therapist is responded to as a benign, powerful caretaker entrusted to nurture helpless, needy members ("basic assumption dependence"), sometimes he is asked to fight with or flee from a real or imagined enemy ("basic assumption fight–flight"), and sometimes he is urged to collude in a fantasy that the group can be saved by a productive pair ("basic assumption pairing"). Clarifying and interpreting how the group is relating to the therapist serves as a means for elucidating unconscious wishes and fears in relation to people in authority, but also as a means for examining how the group is using its members to deal with these concerns.

Dr. Borriello focuses a good deal of attention on the distinction between projective identification and countertransference. In order to understand accurately and to correctly interpret the projective and projective identification processes that unfold in all groups, therapists must be relatively free from countertransference dynamics that can distort their experience of what is occurring. This requires a constant monitoring of one's internal responses. In a sense, the task for the therapist is to monitor the boundary between that which originates from his own internal processes and that which originates from external processes (that is, what he is experiencing because of what he is being induced to contain or enact on behalf of others in the group setting). Because the social systems therapist makes such prominent use of his internal experience to understand what is occurring in the group as a whole, this is particularly important when one is working within the social systems model.

Thus, the three approaches focused upon in this volume all emphasize what group members do in relation to each other and to the therapist that can ultimately illuminate the unconscious dynamics of the individuals who comprise the group. They all focus on splitting, projection, and projective identification to understand what is occurring in the milieu of the group. The group setting is particularly valuable for uncovering different facets of the individual psychologies of its members because of the opportunities it provides for the interpersonal stimulation and reenactment of internal dramatizations.

THERAPIST ROLE

The issue of therapist role is the explicit focus of Part 3 of this book. Nevertheless, we asked the authors of the chapters on clinical applications to patient care to address the implications of their theoretical perspectives for the way therapists take up their roles in the treatment situation. What follows is a review of what each author says about this issue.

Dr. Kibel makes it clear that in his view the object relations approach to group therapy falls within the rubric of psychoanalytic approaches in that the main task of the therapist is to interpret resistance and transference. Of course, where analytic therapists differ is in precisely what, when, and how they interpret. In Dr. Kibel's approach, most interventions are made at the group level in an attempt to identify members' common concerns. His notion is that such interventions foster a sense of cohesion among members and help the group develop the capacity to be the primary therapeutic agent (therapy *by* the group). A good deal of time is spent examining the various group-level resistances that emerge over the course of treatment; the efforts made to resolve these resistances, followed by interpretation of various transferences among members, and between members and therapist, constitute the bulk of the work in group treatment.

In the self psychology model, therapists attempt to work in an "experience-near" way: That is, they attempt to understand the patient's experience from the patient's perspective. Empathic contact, not interpretation of unconscious conflict, is critical in this approach. In a way, self psychologists try to get under the skin, or inside the psyche, of the individual in question and genuinely understand and empathize with the individual's experience. The therapist focuses primarily on the ways in which different individuals attempt to get their selfobject needs met. This follows from self psychology as a deficit model, wherein the therapist adopts the view that development has been arrested not because of unconscious conflict but because of a lack of adequately responsive selfobjects.

Dr. Stone makes a number of interesting points about the self psychologist's therapeutic stance. For one thing, he asserts that the self psychologist is involved rather than detached, but neutral with respect to values. Another way he puts this is that the self psychologist offers acceptance, but not approval, of what the patient discusses in treatment. The hoped-for therapeutic action involves psychic structure building as evidenced by increased self coherence via "transmuting internalizations" (see below).

It is somewhat more difficult to comment on the role assumed by a group therapist working from a social systems model because this approach to conceptualizing what occurs in groups did not begin as an approach to treatment per se. However, as represented by Dr. Borriello, it can be said that, in contrast to self psychology, it is an "experience-distant" approach to treatment. What this means is that instead of trying to get *near* the patients' experience via empathy, the social systems practitioner uses as his primary data base *his own experience,* not his empathic understanding of the patients' experience, on the basis of which he makes interpretations of unconscious conflicts that exist at the level of the group as a whole. Thus, the social systems group therapist takes note of what he is being asked to "contain" and infers what is occurring in the group from what he finds stirred up within himself. He formulates his interpretations on this basis.

There are some important ways in which the social systems group perspective overlaps with the object relations approach. For one thing, the basic task of the therapist is to interpret resistance and transference. The social systems emphasis on what is being avoided through the development of various basic assumption cultures is analogous to the object relations emphasis on resistance. Finally, the exclusive use of groupwide interventions is meant to emphasize the role of the group as a "container" and to help the group become the primary therapeutic agent (again, therapy *by* the group).

One more aspect of the role of the social systems therapist needs to be emphasized: namely, the attention that is paid to boundary establishment, boundary management, and boundary transactions. The social systems perspective is that there is no better way to learn about groups, and the individuals who comprise them, than to establish clear boundaries (of task, role, time, place, and so on), and then to explore how those boundaries are managed as the treatment unfolds. Examining transactions at the boundaries not only provides a useful means for identifying resistances, but it also reveals important clues as to unresolved transference phenomena.

THEORY OF THERAPEUSIS

The issue of what brings about change in psychotherapy is age-old. Each of the authors in this section offers a point of view about what is therapeutic when working from his particular theoretical perspective. The three approaches we are considering in this volume have very different notions about, or at least use very different language to describe, what is transforming for patients who are successfully treated in accordance with their perspective.

Dr. Kibel is explicit about what he sees as therapeutic when working from an object relations perspective. As we have already indicated, object relations practitioners focus heavily on projective processes. When therapy goes well, what occurs is that material that has been projected out or enacted in relation to others is reintrojected in a neutralized or corrected form. The interpretation of unconscious conflict, as well as the giving and receiving of interpersonal feedback, is central in this process.

In order for structural change to occur, the processes of identification and incorporation need to be mobilized. The patient's positive attachment to the group and the therapist allows him to reown previously projected aspects of the self in less toxic form. In order for this to occur in a benign and therapeutic way, the group must serve as a suitable container, and the individual must form a positive attachment to the therapist and to the group as an entity, so that the interpretations and feedback received can be taken in and utilized. When this occurs in a thorough fashion, the individual emerges with new self and other representations. This is tantamount to structural change, that is, growth of the ego. Such change incorporates both cognitive and experiential components, though Dr. Kibel very much emphasizes the latter. Meaningful structural change cannot occur in the absence of an experiential process; insight is seen primarily as a means for understanding and consolidating whatever change has been achieved.

Dr. Stone's comments concerning what is therapeutic about the self psychology approach to treatment have a very different thrust. He indicates that the therapist's most important tool is his capacity to empathize. To be sure, this aspect of the treatment process is acknowledged both by object relations theorists such as Winnicott, who emphasized the importance of the "holding environment" (Winnicott, 1965), and social systems theorists such as Bion (1961), who construed the group as a "container." However, the role of empathy is highlighted to a much greater extent by self psychologists than by adherents of the other theories explored here. It is through accurate empathic attunement that a safe group environment is created in which patients can expose their vulnerabilities. When such exposure is responded to with continued acceptance and empathy, thereby permitting the development of necessary self–selfobject relationships, change occurs.

Dr. Stone also comments on structural change in particular, what others call either personality change or character change. The building of a more resilient self structure occurs in response to a "transmuting internalization": The individual achieves additional capacity to carry out for himself selfobject functions, and the self is thereby strengthened. As Dr. Stone observes, empathic failures are inevitable in the ongoing ebb and flow of the treatment process. Patients respond to such failures in a variety of ways, and these responses are examined, often in considerable detail. When the process goes well, the self–selfobject bond is eventually reestablished and strengthened. As an outgrowth of this process, the patient internalizes additional capacities. This is not unlike the building of increased ego capacities within the framework of classical theory, although it is discussed here in terms of growth of the self, consistent with Kohut's notion of a separate and independent line of narcissistic development that continues throughout the life cycle (Kohut, 1966).

The social systems theory perspective concerning what is therapeutic about the treatment experience is the most consonant with the traditional psychoanalytic view. Dr. Borriello emphasizes that the therapist must comment on what is *not* being said by group participants, that is, what is being defended against. The goal is for group members to be able to acknowledge, and accept, more and more of themselves, thereby effectively expanding the realm of the ego. Since the social systems therapist's main tool is interpretation, the therapeutic aim is to help members achieve increasing degrees of insight into themselves and the complex forces which motivate them. The particular slant of social systems theory is to emphasize the roles individuals assume in multiperson settings, as well as the individual's relationship to authority. This is why social systems work is best undertaken in multiperson settings.

LEVEL AT WHICH WORK IS CONDUCTED

Different group practitioners tend to give greater or lesser emphasis to what is occurring at particular points within the group matrix at any given moment. Some practitioners focus on the individual or intrapsychic level, some on the interpersonal level (dyads, triads, subgroups, etc.), and some on the group-as-a-whole level. Although the levels exist simultaneously, thereby permitting examination of phenomena on all of them, most practitioners pay differential attention to the levels at various points in time. More importantly, there are significant differences in emphasis among the three theoretical perspectives we are exploring here.

The basic proposition of the object relations approach is that the group is an arena for the expression of the internal worlds of object relations of its members. While these internal worlds are idiosyncratic, there are group-level processes that are always operative when a number of people meet over an extended period of time to work (or play). While object relations practitioners differ from each other in how they do work, Dr. Kibel describes an approach in which group-as-a-whole phenomena are highlighted. This allows individual group members to reown that which they have projected into or onto the group and to confront the ways they have contributed to the dynamics that prevail in the group at any given time. Some object relations practitioners explicitly point out individuals' contributions to prevailing group dynamics, while others leave this for individual group members to do for themselves. In most cases, object relations practitioners work primarily with group-as-a-whole and interpersonal phenomena.

Self psychology practitioners appear to have a different attitude toward group-as-a-whole phenomena. While at least some of them do attend to this level of what is occurring in the group, they remain fundamentally concerned about the impact of this level on individual group members. Specifically, Dr. Stone expresses the concern that if the group as a whole is the only level attended to, some individuals may feel narcissistically injured, which can have the effect of shutting them down and preventing meaningful work from occurring. Thus, self psychologists tend to focus more explicitly on individual members and the nature of their subjective experiences of being in the group. Others in the group serve as potential mirroring or idealizing objects; individuals are helped to understand themselves by exploring the nature of the relationships they establish in the group, and what these relationships represent. Thus the focus is primarily intrapsychic and interpersonal; the emphasis is on what is being experienced and expressed at these levels.

In contrast, the emphasis in the social systems approach is on what is being concealed by the group. As mentioned above, the social systems practitioner comments on what is *not* being said, that is, on what unconscious conflict is being defended against. The social systems approach is the one that appears to adhere most strictly to working at the group-as-a-whole level. The contributions of individuals, dyads, and subgroups are all construed as reflective of groupwide dynamics. The therapist's comments are pitched at this level, and individuals are invited to consider their roles in what is occurring. Most social systems practitioners are unlikely, however, to do the intrapsychic- and interpersonal-level work for participants. As a result, group members tend to learn most about the roles they assume in group settings, with particular emphasis on how they manage themselves in relation to designated authority (the therapist) and their own personal authority. How and whether this translates into or leads to growth and change at the intrapsychic and interpersonal levels is seen primarily as a responsibility for members to assume.

RANGE OF APPLICABILITY

It is difficult to assess the range, and the limits, of applicability of different theoretical perspectives, largely because there is so little empirical evidence to support or refute them. Dr. Kibel does not address this issue directly. Since object relations theory emanated out of the work of Melanie Klein (1964), it tends to be associated with the exploration of relatively primitive, preoedipal difficulties. However, there is no reason to believe it cannot be useful in working with people with less severe pathology. Its premise that people are motivated by the need for connection with others, rather than by the need to discharge basic intrapsychic drives, and its focus upon internal and external self and object representations and schemata, can be useful in working with individuals at all points along the psychological continuum. Thus, at the level of theory, it is a way of thinking with very wide applicability. The frame of reference it provides can be used in conjunction with a broad range of therapeutic techniques that can be tailored to fit the individuals in question. Finally, it lends itself particularly well to treating people in groups because of its emphasis on the need to connect with others and the difficulties people have in doing so.

There are conflicting notions about the range of applicability of self psychology. On the one hand, it has focused primarily on patients with early developmental deficits, and its emphasis on empathy might make the treatment setting feel safer and therefore more viable for patients whose self structures are fundamentally shaky; that is, those whose presenting problems are primarily preoedipal. Also, its focus on issues of self cohesion, self maintenance, and self-esteem regulation suits it for work with more severely disturbed patients. On the other hand, as Dr. Stone asserts, self psychology has not yet been shown at an empirical level to be effective with patients suffering the most serious self disturbances. Self psychology emphasizes the inevitability of narcissistic injury and the therapeutic value of exploring how people respond to it and recover from it. It remains to be seen whether it is applicable for more fragile individuals who cannot tolerate, or easily recover from, such injuries (this encompasses some neurotics as well as characterologically impaired and psychotic individuals).

Social systems theory must be thought about in different terms. In contrast to object relations theory and self psychology, which are both theories about human motivation, social systems theory, with its emphasis on boundary issues, roles, tasks, authority relations and the various sociotechnical characteristics and properties of groups as systems, is really a metatheory. As such, it can be used in conjunction with any theory of motivation, including classical theory, object relations theory, self psychology, or ego psychology. Hence, it would seem to have potentially wide applicability.

However, as Dr. Borriello makes clear in terms of technique, the typical therapeutic stance of a social systems theory adherent, such as himself, focuses on the group as a whole and relies almost exclusively upon interpretation. This approach is likely to be experienced as highly depriving and unnourishing for individual members. Such a posture may well provoke a great deal of regression, which most clinicians would regard as highly undesirable for people with relatively severe ego deficits. Thus, from the perspective of therapeutic technique, the social systems approach seems applicable to that segment of the clinical population that is relatively intact and stable. Patients with more severe deficits are more likely to require a therapeutic approach that is more structured, individually nourishing, and supportive.

Thus, there are differences among the three theories in this area as well. The breadth of approaches subsumed under the "object relations" umbrella makes this conceptual framework, in one form or other, very widely applicable. In contrast, the range of applicability of self psychology, the newest model examined in this volume, is not yet clear. Finally, because of the techniques favored by social systems adherents, this broad-based metatheory appears to have a relatively narrow range of applicability for clinical populations in which there is some significant impairment of ego functioning.

REFERENCES

Bion, W. R. (1961), *Experiences in Groups*. London: Tavistock Publications.

Greenberg, J. R., & Mitchell, S. A. (1983), *Object Relations in Psychoanalytic Theory*. Cambridge, MA: Harvard University Press.

Klein, M. (1964), *Contributions to Psychoanalysis, 1921–1945*. New York: McGraw-Hill.

Kohut, H. (1966), Forms and transformations of narcissism. *J. Amer. Psychoanal. Assn.*, 14:243–272.

———— (1971), *The Analysis of the Self*. New York: International Universities Press.

Miller, E. J., & Rice, A. K. (1969), *Systems of Organization*. London: Tavistock Publications.

Winnicott, D. W. (1965), *The Maturational Processes and the Facilitating Environment*. New York: International Universities Press.

Part III

The Role of the Therapist

10

The Role of the Therapist from an Object Relations Perspective

SAUL TUTTMAN, M.D., Ph.D.

In this chapter I will explore the role of the group therapist who works from an object relations perspective. After reviewing the major object relations concepts and the most relevant group-dynamic considerations dealing with the therapist's role, I will also present some clinical examples. I wish to begin by stressing that *object relations* is not a single theory but a broad and complex area within the psychoanalytic framework. It is therefore more accurate to speak of *object relations theories*.[1]

Freud's (1895) determination to formulate an "objective" scientific psychology led to his concern with biological drives and their objects. Throughout his writings, his general theory focuses on the management of intrapsychic tensions. In the course of developing structural formulations, he dealt with object relations: "from 1923 [Freud, 1923] on, objects were understood as providing sources for identifications, which came to constitute ego and superego qualities" (Tuttman, 1981, p. 7).

In my view, object relations theories provide perhaps the richest overall framework currently available for dealing with depth psychodynamics, developmental psychology, psychopathology, and treatment. Object relations formulations encompass drives, metapsychological considerations, the role of reality and fantasy, social and

---

[1]Since the history of theory is not the primary task of this chapter, I refer readers interested in that issue to *A Historical Survey of the Development of Object Relations Concepts in Psychoanalytic Theory* (Tuttman, 1981), and to the work of Ganzarain (1989) and Greenberg and Mitchell (1983), as well as to the primary sources referred to in the text and noted in the references.

biological forces, and self and developmental psychology. Some object relations theorists conceive of objects (or their internal representations) primarily as targets of drive discharge, whereas others conceive of a fundamental drive toward relationships and bonding with others as primary. I consider both of these aspects of object relations to be important and applicable to varying degrees in particular instances.

Object relations theories make a natural "marriage" with group therapy since a group is a collection of interacting and relating individuals. The group itself is composed of a multiplicity of "objects"[2] and their internal representations. In addition, the group becomes an "object" itself. Object relations theories are concerned with the important role of object representations in the formation and possible modification of personality (especially regarding the identificatory processes in the development of the "self" and the capacity to relate to and interact with others). An important function of the object relations–oriented group therapist is to facilitate an atmosphere in the group which encourages in members an increased openness to sharing and exploring feelings and fantasies. Ideally, group members gradually learn to describe and identify projections (related to earlier life internalizations). Object relations theorists consider these projections, which can interfere with reality-oriented and adaptive capacities, to be ubiquitous in group and dyadic interactions.

SOME RELEVANT BASIC CONCEPTS OF OBJECT RELATIONS THEORIES

From an object relations perspective, healthy emotional development hinges upon a sincere and intimate relatedness and "good fit" in the caretaker–infant interaction in early life. A similar bond between therapist and patient (in both dyadic and group treatment) is seen as essential for effective therapy.

It may seem paradoxical to suggest that an effective therapeutic stance requires spontaneity and the natural flow of feelings, while, at the same time, offering therapists a "handbook of guidelines" for treatment, which might appear to encourage contrived or calculated

---

[2]"In psychoanalytic literature, the word 'object' . . . is understood . . . in a sense comparable to the 'object of my passion, of my hatred' " (Laplanche and Pontalis, 1973, p. 273); that is, as those persons and things toward which impulses and affects are directed. The complex nature of objects and their mental representations is explored in Ganzarain (1989), Sandler and Rosenblatt (1962), and Tuttman (1981).

therapist behavior. However, the subtleties and complexities of providing meaningful treatment mitigate against either a totally "free" and simple stance or an inflexibly rigid role. Although authentic relatedness is important to therapists of different persuasions, the issue is central for the object relations group therapist since, from this perspective, critical factors in treatment involve (1) the internalization of the therapist's qualities (via identification), and (2) the creation of a safe and open atmosphere in the group, conducive to the exploration of the unconscious repertoire of object representations subtly influencing each group member, which need to be acknowledged and explored.

It is my conviction that the therapist's successful personal therapy experience as patient in psychodynamic individual and group treatment is very important in this context. When successful, such experiences enhance the therapist's capacity to respond openly and therapeutically; that is, without the encumbrances of unresolved, unconsciously based problems and ambivalences which can lead to "mixed messages" and "acting out."

Perhaps an expeditious means of surveying the applicable concepts which guide object relations group leaders would be to provide a *summary* of concepts and *glossary* of some critical terms (which will later be illustrated by specific group case examples). One central concept deals with the task of providing a *facilitating object for internalization* in the form of the group therapist; an object unlike the often pathogenic[3] caretaker of the vulnerable child's early development. *Authenticity* is defined as "being what it professes, as being genuine" (*The Compact Edition of the Oxford English Dictionary*, Vol. 1, 1971, p. 143). It is difficult to measure this quality objectively in clinical situations (Singer, Astrachan, Gould, and Klein, 1975). Theoretically, *the lack of a sustaining and supportive relationship during vulnerable developmental dependency stages* plays a major role in the etiology of pathological self and object relationships. There are many important subtle issues related to this point, and I shall briefly highlight the relevant positions of major theorists and refer to their main terms and concepts.

DEVELOPMENTAL PERSPECTIVES

Melanie Klein (1932) proposed that the press of strong libidinal and aggressive forces distorted the naive and anxious infant's subjective

---

[3]"Pathogenic" is not meant to imply a value judgment about a caretaker. For example, a baby with coeliac disease may not be able to digest mother's milk normally. Although the milk is fine, the infant experiences feeding as "pathogenic."

experience of important objects (Segal, 1973). Ferenczi (1932) reported the developmental problems that result when caretakers impose, often unconsciously and insidiously, their personal needs on youngsters rather than providing the nurturance their charges need. (He had parallel concerns about the adequacy of psychoanalysts to respond therapeutically, and advocated that therapists undergo intensive training in which attention would be devoted to transference–countertransference issues [Dupont, 1988]). Balint (1968) described the "basic fault," the pathological consequences to the child's personality when caretakers have been unable to provide the crucially needed "harmonious inter-penetrating mix-up" (that is, the infant–caretaker state that results from experiencing security and blending with one another) in the course of the youngster's vulnerable dependency period in earliest life. The reports of mother–child interaction by Winnicott (1960b, 1975) are consistent with these formulations.

Winnicott (1963) described the importance of a supportive, helpful caretaker who supplies what is needed and thereby provides a "facilitating environment," offering needed psychological and physical "holding." Winnicott also noted the need for "good-enough" mothering and observed that when the parent is sufficiently caring and understanding, but not intrusive, the dependent child dares to express the developing self spontaneously. This cannot occur when a needy, anxious parent imposes conditional acceptance by requiring that the child alleviate the parental anxieties. Since the youngster senses a need for the primary caretaker's continued presence and caring, the child automatically (and nonverbally) censors and represses the developing "true self" and complies with parental requirements by developing a "false self" organization. This occurs because the dependent youngster's priority is to have the needed caretaker maintain interest and presence.

Winnicott's (1951) paper on "transitional objects" has importance for object relations theories generally and for group treatment specifically. Winnicott described the transitional object as a symbol of the available object (in this case, usually the caretaker) upon which the dependent child relies. The purpose is to "bring back" in some form the presence of a representation of that object when the child experiences anxiety at the prospect of loss. When observing his toddler grandchild during a visit, Freud (1920) observed the child's symbolic play as a striving to master separation. The spool of thread plaything was used as a substitute object for the mother who disappeared and re-appeared. Thus, Freud (1920) anticipated Winnicott's (1951) "transitional object" concept.

Winnicott noticed that, in general, youngsters utilize objects (e.g., their thumbs, soft toys, or blankets) as soothing substitutes for the caretaker—"transitional objects." Psychoanalytic group therapists have posited that the group may become such an object for a patient who needs both connectedness and distance from a transference figure such as the group therapist. Mahler's (Mahler, Pine, and Bergman, 1975) study of the symbiosis–separation phases in development relates to these concepts. Her emphasis was on "phase specificity"—how the youngster needs particular support and reactions from the caretaker as determined by which developmental phase the child is experiencing at a particular time. This relates to Spitz's (1965) notion of "critical periods" and Jacobson's (1964) and A. Freud's (1965) view of the "lines of development."

All of these theorists, though approaching the issues from different psychoanalytic frameworks, have contributed to object relations theories. Their overall message is clear: The healthy delineation of boundaries, a sense of security, realistic self concepts, and the capacity for empathic understanding of others (objects) is determined by the early life developmental drama centering around the vicissitudes of the primary caretaker–child dyad. These factors have impact on the ability to trust others and engage in realistic relationships, both intrapsychically and interpersonally.

Object relations theorists hypothesize that a parallel situation exists in both group and individual treatment. True, the patient is not a child and the therapist is not a caretaker. Nonetheless, in the course of therapy there are regressive inclinations and repetition compulsions that represent a recapitulation of unresolved "old" issues and provide patients with a "second chance" to work through problems and engage in constructive internalization processes. The crucial issues of a capacity for separateness and autonomy, on the one hand, and the capacity to share and be together, on the other, are related to these developmental object relations theories and are critical in determining the role of the object relations group therapist at any given time.

To recapitulate, the basic concepts of object relations theories elaborated above influence and determine the object relations group therapist's role. This framework emanates from the idea that the patient's sense of self and his attitudes about and representations of objects develop primarily in the context of early life engagements with significant figures.[4]

---

[4]It is important to emphasize that patients' archaic perceptions contribute to what was *experienced* as the qualities of "significant figures." These perceptions may have been even more important than the actual attitudes and behavior of the caretakers. Patients in group therapy have a powerful opportunity to learn that perceptions and

The object relations leader thus has a specific developmental framework and an appreciation of unconscious processes and historical factors in the etiology of psychopathology, which underlie object relations theory and its treatment approach. One benefit of recognizing the variety of mental representations "embanked" in each person's psyche as a result of past experience is that individuals are able to learn (through the observing ego) to sense and recognize when manifestations of primitive, "leftover" mental images of early life influence their perceptions and behavior. Such understanding can permit more reality-oriented, contemporary perspectives. In the course of a therapist's empathic, monitoring approach, group members come to see in one another (and, ideally, in themselves) the contaminating effects of unconscious fantasies, which tend to interfere with present-day reality interactions.

Object relations–based concepts and theories that guide group leaders include the archaic "basic assumptions" at work in groups (Bion, 1959); the regressive tendencies that occur in groups (Freud, 1921); various group cohesion factors, the potential use of the group and group members as transitional objects (Kosseff, 1975; Tuttman, 1980; James, 1982); and the monitoring of splitting and projective identifications within the group (Ganzarain, 1990; Horwitz, 1990). Such group-dynamic factors are central to object relations group treatment and influence how the group leader takes on his role.

The group provides an opportunity to explore and elucidate infantile introjections and identifications that make up mental representations. These usually underlie acting out by patients who have been encumbered by the "ghosts of the past" and the primitive unconscious assumptions that have contributed to maladaptation. The role of the object relations leader is to encourage and facilitate a group atmosphere in which it is safe for members to experience and communicate underlying fantasies, impulses, wishes, and fears. An *observing stance* of self and others (Tuttman, 1987) can help toward insight and understanding, more objective awareness, and better reality testing.

In the course of carrying out the role of leader, it is often enough to generate a conducive group atmosphere and to provide identificatory qualities which will encourage group members to do the necessary

---

"experiences" of others in the group are probably colored by "embanked" mental representations that have remained in memory since the early developmental period of that self (Guntrip, 1969; Tuttman, 1988). It is important that the therapist and the group appreciate each patient's history in that context. Particularly important are impressions and experiences with caretakers, parents, teachers, siblings, and peers as the qualities of "significant figures."

work. When the group resistances are too strong, empathic and direct interpretations may be needed.

Key Intrapsychic Mechanisms or Dynamics Observed in Individuals in Group

The following terms are among the most useful applicable to the object relations group.

Identification is the unconscious process of incorporating within oneself a mental picture of an object, and thinking, feeling, and acting as one conceives the object to think, feel, and act. This process may apply to part-objects (for example, parts of the body such as the "good" breast). The sense of the object may be colored by primitive affects and drives when construed at a time of naive, limited reality testing. This form of incorporation is important from early life on for internalizing qualities one notes subjectively in the behavior of objects and part-objects and which become models for one's own ego and superego processes. This is an important step in the process of acquiring a sense of selfhood and an understanding about the nature of objects.

Sometimes these archaic object qualities that we internalize also get projected out and are externalized. We then experience and perceive others as manifesting the qualities of such objects. This process involves the mechanism of *projection*. (Kleinian object relations theorists tend to see these mechanisms of identification and projection as occurring from the beginning of life and therefore as often influenced by the most archaic distortions. Ego-psychological-developmental object relations theorists conceive of these processes as occurring somewhat later and therefore as being less primitive.)

Transference refers to a patient's displacing of positive or negative repressed unconscious feelings, attitudes, or impulses onto the therapist or group. Transference may involve the projection of feelings, thoughts, or wishes onto an object representative of the patient's past.

When the patient's transferences elicit from the therapist an unconscious response related to the therapist's own issues, we speak of *countertransference*. Sometimes, sensing and analyzing one's countertransference helps the therapist appreciate and understand the patient's unconscious productions, but this only takes place when the therapist can respond to the situation realistically and gain insight about and understanding of both his and the patient's unconscious behavior. Thus, transference and countertransference may lead to further distortions, but they also provide an opportunity to productively confront our acting out and unresolved traumas, pains, longings and needs.

Projective identification is a mechanism, first described by Melanie Klein, which relates to "a splitting process of the early ego whereby either good or bad parts of the self are split off from the ego and as a further step projected in love or hatred onto external objects which leads to fusion and identification of the projected parts of the self with the external objects" (Grosskurth, 1986, p. 374). This mechanism may serve to defend against separation, to rid oneself of conflict-laden noxious impulses and feelings, or to get control of an object. Often the recipient may become identified with that which has been projected and somehow takes on the role assigned by the projecting person.

Acting out refers to unconscious behavior motivated by unconscious conflicts and needs. It is contrasted to *working-through,* which involves behavior the motivation for which the individual is aware. Such awareness is often achieved by deciphering the underlying motives and history.

Splitting is a defensive mechanism, described initially by S. Freud (1940). The concept is frequently utilized by Kleinian analysts dealing with the division of objects (or part-objects) psychologically into "good" and "bad," or the experiencing of them as such.

Although most of these terms are part of the general psychoanalytic vocabulary and not confined to object relations theories, these concepts are all particularly important in object relations theory and especially applicable to understanding group interaction. They will be illustrated later in the group case examples.

The following terms are also important to object relations theories and were developed by a Kleinian group therapist and psychoanalyst, Wilfred Bion (1963).

When Bion visited New York, he wanted to see *Guernica,* the anti-war Picasso mural. After studying it, he mentioned that when he served as a young tank officer in battle in World War I, he noticed that the infantrymen, exposed to cannon fire in the field, suffered shell shock, while he survived relatively comfortably within his tank. At that moment, he thought of the concept of the *container* as that which can protect and insulate, absorb and take in the chaos and panic of early life anxiety and confusion. He concluded that every child needs a parent who can "contain" the tensions (as every patient needs a therapist who can understand and cope with psychotic-like, overwhelming primitive anxieties).

Objects Relations Notions about Group Dynamics

Basic assumptions is a term of Bion's (1959) that is applicable to group dynamics. He proposed that all groups operate unconsciously in terms of specific primitive basic assumptions that serve as collective defenses against anxiety and which frequently underlie and energize group-as-a-whole functioning. These he described as the *dependency* assumption, *fight–flight* assumption, and the *pairing* assumption.

The *work group,* according to Bion, is reality oriented and dedicated to the solution of problems. It is mainly conscious, rational, and goal directed. This orientation functions when the group and leader overcome the resistances and acting out ordinarily operating when the basic assumption group modes prevail.

The *group-as-a-whole* approach to group therapy focuses on the group themes and underlying focal conflicts of primary importance in the conducting of group business. Usually, leaders interpret the general group reactions rather than singling out the responses of specific members. It contrasts with an approach that focuses upon the motives and reactions of the individual group members. Object relations theories can be applied either to the group as a whole or to the individuals who comprise the group. Horwitz's (1990) paper on this issue explores the complex factors involved and the merits of either or a combined approach.

Several psychoanalytic group therapists (including Kibel, Kauff, Kosseff, Scheidlinger, and myself) believe that the group milieu can provide a matrix: a "holding environment" (Winnicott, 1960b), or what Scheidlinger (1974) called a "mother group." This offers the most useful atmosphere for working-through unconscious primitive fantasies and mental representations for disturbed patients. Part IV of *Psychoanalytic Group Theory and Treatment* (Tuttman, 1990) is devoted to this area. A group-centered holding environment based on an object relations approach is particularly applicable to preoedipal and borderline patients whose relationships, both with others and self, are handicapped by archaic impulses, affects, and fantasies.

ROLE OF THE OBJECT RELATIONS LEADER DURING INITIAL GROUP STAGES

The role of the object relations group therapist during early phases of treatment is essentially twofold: first, to generate a therapeutic environment conducive to a cohesive "working group" (Bion, 1959), and, second, to recognize and monitor the manifestations of the archaic unconscious basic assumptions expressed in group behavior, as well as the projective identifications, introjections, and splitting mechanisms of group members.

From the beginning, it is the role of the group therapist to listen empathically and to record internally (without necessarily overtly verbalizing) what is taking place in the group. To accept and process unconscious data need not mean to interpret initially or attempt to make such phenomena immediately conscious for group members. In time, the working group will develop the observing skills to acknowledge, to monitor, and to work through these vital factors, with the skillful facilitation of the therapist.

Although group assumptions and individual dynamics in part shape the group therapist's role from the very beginning of treatment, such issues are not usually openly explored by the object relations group therapist until later. At the start of treatment, it is important for the leader to listen carefully to the speech and behavior of the group as a whole and the individual group members, appreciating feelings and other communications with the aim of discerning manifestations of unconscious internalized archaic mental representations that had probably been embanked in the course of early development. At this time the primary role of the object relations leader is to generate a conducive atmosphere within the group. Giving consideration to resistances and "phase specificity" factors, the therapist does not generally openly acknowledge the monitoring of unconscious processes until a later stage of interaction. The leader's objective is to provide a holding environment (Winnicott, 1960b) and "contain" (Bion, 1959) the patients' projections.

SPECIFIC DETAILS OF THE OBJECT RELATIONS GROUP THERAPIST'S ROLE

How do I function, as leader, in creating a conducive, therapeutic atmosphere in which open exploration, play, and experimentation will develop in the group so that "true self" (Winnicott, 1960a) authenticity can dare manifest itself? How can I help to generate a situation in which a "group matrix" and a "holding environment" (Winnicott, 1963) can develop? Achieving this is a critical component of the object relations therapist's role. What concrete factors are important in structuring the group treatment situation and in enhancing a therapeutic experience?

One key element in helping to create an atmosphere in which group members feel safe involves the therapist's genuinely valuing whatever is expressed whenever a member shares with the group personal feelings, memories, fantasies, hopes, and expectations as well as fears and complaints. This is not a simple matter for most patients, since they frequently have histories in which it did not feel safe or even possible to express openly anything that might have generated disapproval or aroused anxiety in the caretakers upon whom they were dependent earlier in life.

I appreciate that efforts to establish such an atmosphere in the group do not always provide the kinds of structure that some group therapists would consider desirable (cf., Singer et al., 1975). While I believe that consistent, clearly delineated structure is often needed, to my mind there is also a question as to whether an authority figure such as a group leader focusing on such matters too early and in too great detail may not put at risk the task of generating a quality of relatedness, which is so important to establish in the group. I recognize that there are various views on this issue. The skill of the therapist and the needs of a particular group (R. H. Klein, Hunter, and Brown, 1990) should determine policy in a particular case.

Although some therapists always negotiate formal, clearly spelled-out arrangements early in the life of the group, most object relations group therapists tend to allow them to evolve gradually over time. An informal poll of my object relations leader colleagues reflects reasonable consensus among them that an open-ended group situation in which patients feel free to explore and express is more productive in helping patients work through deep inner issues and in developing ego strength than a tightly structured group. Nevertheless, in the course of a nonverbal initial stance[5] there are usually consistent indications of an implicit frame and contract. I attempt to convey "an appreciation and acknowledgment of the patient's experiences . . . [which ideally provides the group and members with] . . . the feeling of being understood or validated. . . . In the course of treatment, there is a shared vivid experiencing of the patient's subjective world" (Tuttman, 1987, p. 32). Although most group therapists will generally strive to create an open, comfortable atmosphere, the object relations leader's concept of treatment and therapeutic objectives makes this style essential. The more comfortably open-ended the situation, and the more that group members' subjectivity and spontaneity are valued, the more likely it is that archaic fantasies, internalized object representations, and projections will emerge. With skillful leadership, there will then be a clear opportunity for the group as a whole and for the individual members of the group to experience, identify, and

---

[5]For further discussion applicable to group as well as individual therapy, see Tuttman, 1987.

more realistically channel and harness these archaic fantasies and assumptions that have been unconsciously at work.

The style that I have advocated can lead to ambiguities and problems. The case example that follows is an example of such confusion. It should be noted, however, that the dilemmas were clearly soluble; their being worked through added an important sense of mutual regard, so vital to the facilitating atmosphere in which to achieve the object relations group's goals.

Last year an attorney, a relatively new patient in group therapy, missed a group session, for which he was billed. He objected to being charged, especially since the matter had not occurred previously and he had not been informed that this was my policy. I acknowledged that a group member might feel that way but noted that I intentionally leave such issues open because it seems more conducive to a therapeutic milieu when relationship issues are unencumbered by many rules and regulations. I also said that I understood that some individuals might be distressed about an arrangement that had not been spelled out in advance and that in such cases, if necessary, I would accept responsibility the first time this happened, and I would be willing to remove the charge for that session. Now that arrangements are understood, I noted, we have a policy for the future.

Sometimes, for reasons of their own (e.g., being compliant, ingratiating, or valuing my motivation), some patients will accept my explanation and pay for the session in question. Some may benefit from further exploration, depending on the situation and the patient. Personally, as therapist, I prefer to lose an occasional session fee rather than encumber the relationship with detailed regulations.

Generally, I consider it inadvisable for the therapist to theorize, rationalize, and justify behavior to patients. In some instances, the issues or the patient's needs necessitate a negotiation. I recognize that there are individual personality factors among therapists that would make my particular policy possible and comfortable for one leader and uncomfortable for another. In this instance the situation permitted the therapist to communicate an earnest desire to provide space, to accept assertion and disagreement, to flexibly modify a position when the patient communicated need while maintaining a self-protective conviction respectfully, flexibly, and yet firmly.

In this case, the incident aroused memories of the patient's interaction with parents he experienced as self-righteous, demanding, and controlling. The leader's policy, combining firmness with flexibility and a wish to communicate and resolve the situation, proved therapeutic. I maintained, guided by the object relations notion of a safe holding environment, a commitment to patients and group while maintaining my own boundaries and "self" needs. I hope that this offered a balanced, reality-oriented model. This interaction between patient and therapist contrasts with the often pathogenic transactions that took place during formative years when the patient had been a vulnerable child interacting with insecure or rigid caretakers.

One area where problems may arise from time to time, though rarely, involves structure and ambiguity in the "therapeutic frame" (Langs, 1977) regarding the issue of private socializing among group members away from the formal group sessions. Here again, I make no advance rules and different groups develop different styles. For example, some groups go out together for coffee after sessions. In my experience, this rarely leads to problems. However, what may lead to difficulties is when two members secretly develop a private relationship.

Eventually, one or both members share the details with the group. These disclosures provide an excellent opportunity for every member to react and fantasize. Group members sometimes vent envy, indignation, longing, anger, love, and so forth. More often than not, the group is interested in the motives and the elements of acting out involved. The "data" get worked through in the group and the situation is resolved without the leader having been in the unfortunate position of becoming an autocratic controller who needlessly restricts group members. Thus far, in over twenty-five years of conducting group practice, this matter has resolved itself within the group whenever it has occurred.

As an object relations therapist, I hope that group members perceive my functioning as manifesting a deeply felt, calm optimism. I enjoy my involvement with the group and members and I find the interaction, the process, and the inevitable problems interesting as well as meaningful. It seems to happen rather quickly that new group members appreciate the open-endedness of the situation. This is an inherent part of the therapeutic engagement, which leaves "space" for each member's exploration. Since newcomers enter ongoing groups, it is not unusual for a new patient to ask the others: "Why are you here? What are you seeking and are you getting it here?" Usually it becomes clear in the course of the responses to such inquiries, that those who have been participating for some time value the process and are pleased with their accomplishments. This interaction, comparing hopes and experiences, can be facilitated by the attitu 'es manifested by the leader.

On occasion the group, or individual members, will test out situations, sometimes consciously, at other times without awareness. I consider it desirable for the therapist to recognize when this occurs, and I believe that the capacity of the group therapist to "pass" such tests is vital. Frequently patients test leaders by making challenging, unrelenting demands and attacking the leader's values or security. The leader's acceptance and understanding *must* be real and not a matter of lip service. Patients know the difference intuitively.

These tests often reflect the concern of group members that the therapist be genuine and meaningfully responsive. Many patients, in the course of early development, did not feel entitled to their feelings and needs. Such a member might suspect that the group therapist is not sufficiently caring or able to tolerate his "true self" (Winnicott, 1960a). Until this individual can differentiate the therapist's reactions from the anticipated mistreatments, the "testing" will continue.

Although a group leader may believe in a flexible and benevolent therapeutic stance, his own unresolved personal issues may result in a subtle but strong controlling leader attitude. An emotional clash may then ensue between patient and therapist, which may subtly encourage the patient's acting out while the therapist unconsciously deals with his anxiety by a greater rigidity in behavior (which will be rationalized and disguised, since the therapist idealizes a flexible stance that he cannot maintain). One can only hope that whenever such a distressing scenario occurs, it becomes apparent to the therapist soon enough so that he can constructively address it by obtaining supervision or treatment, or finding some other way to work it through. In any event, a testing-out period is probably inevitable in the life of any group, and the successful working through of such tests will facilitate the establishment of a cohesive and therapeutic group situation (the working group).

The object relations group therapist listens carefully and is attentive and accepting of whatever the patient has to offer (be it critical, realistic, seductive, assuaging, complimentary, etc.). When patients clearly understand that the sessions are to serve *their* needs and that the therapist in no way needs to impose values or extract gratification, a constructive frame has been created. This concept can be related to Bion's (1963) "container" and Winnicott's (1960b, 1963) "holding" and "facilitating" environment. In such an atmosphere, usually, after trial and error, patients come to recognize and appreciate the safety and the potentially productive nature of the setting. Under such conducive conditions, group members increasingly feel free to acknowledge and explore their impulses, wishes, fantasies, and needs, and to disclose their embarrassments, shameful details of history, and so forth.

The object relations therapist can be of help by appreciating and "mirroring" the patient's courage and determination to change what is difficult to confront and work through. The works of Ferenczi

(1932), Balint (1968), and Winnicott (1951, 1960b) make clear the importance of empathic reflections in caretakers in the child's early period as an undergirding and base for cohesive self feelings and self-esteem. Kohut's (1977) formulations are very similar and are mainly based on their work. Ego psychologist object relations theorists also contribute to this area: for example, see the work of Mahler et al. (1975), Anna Freud (1965), and Jacobson (1964). All of these writers agree that the therapeutic task is achieved through empathy, mirroring, and interpretation.

When a group member's expectations are filled with tyrannical and lofty self demands, other group members often sense this and confront him. In such circumstances it is sometimes helpful for the group therapist to become allied with the patient who is challenged as a way of maintaining group safety and a secure holding environment.

A key role of the therapist is to handle the entry of new members. In my own therapy groups, a new member may join a group that is already in operation. I only admit one new member at a time, informing the group in advance that a new person is considering joining and would like to attend the next session. Although the admission of a new patient to group can require some adjustment for both the individual and the group, the result can be positive when the leader deals thoughtfully and empathically with the situation from an object relations vantage point. For example, a new member often generates feelings and reactions dealing with the birth of siblings during childhood, issues of cohesiveness and bonding, or concerns about isolation, rejection, and not belonging.

I utilize my clinical judgment in attempting to ascertain whether or not the potential member can mobilize adequate ego functioning[6] (which includes a realistic sense of boundaries and frustration tolerance), so necessary for ongoing interaction given the inevitable ambiguities and occasional clashes of needs and conflicts that are likely to occur in groups. Although strains are inevitable, the group generally offers a great deal of support and nurturance to members. However, it is important for the leader to recognize that this may not always be apparent to newcomers.

Strict confidentiality is essential and mutually advantageous in group therapy, and this is one area in which I believe it is important for the therapist to provide definitive structure. I am as firm and clear about this as possible. Since the group therapy situation involves at

---

[6]See A. Freud's (1965) Diagnostic Profile (which is often applied to adults) and the extensive literature on criteria for membership in therapy groups (e.g., Bach, 1954; Rutan and Stone, 1984).

least one therapist and many individuals sharing intimate details, potential problems concerning confidentiality are inevitable. It is vital that everyone involved accepts responsibility for confidentiality so that no one need hesitate to discuss personal and delicate matters, the disclosure of which to "outsiders" might have unfortunate ramifications and could generate an atmosphere of potential betrayal within the group.

Most object relations leaders encourage their groups to proceed by means of spontaneous exploration, free-as-possible communication without prearranged agendas or restrictions regarding subject matter. I recognize that the relative absence of structure and the ambiguities in arrangements sometimes lead to problems, but I find that these issues are usually resolved without much difficulty and that therapeutic benefits can be derived from the very process of resolution. I hope that the examples offered thus far convey the therapeutic climate encouraged by the object relations group leader's role, which can lead to open communication and potential growth.

The question of disclosure of the therapist's personal experiences and relations is a complex issue deserving of consideration. We have already explored the importance of therapist integrity and authenticity, but this does not necessarily mean the therapist should disclose personal *details* (although there are times at which this approach can be very beneficial to group members). While I believe it is invaluable for group therapists to *utilize* their experiences and relationships with patients and the group, I distinguish (for myself) my needs and inclinations as *apart and distinct from those of the group members.* I attempt to assist growth for group members by conducting myself in a manner conducive to the needs of participants. I concern myself with the experiences of each member and of the overall group. Thus, while I am not elusive, evasive, or withholding, I simply devote myself to my role. For me, the object relations leader's role involves responding realistically and therapeutically to what the patient needs, which is dependent upon where the patient is developmentally and what the balance is within the patient's personality in terms of transferences, fixations, defenses, resistances, developmental stages, and real-life considerations.

By considering the issue of "phase specificity" (Blanck and Blanck, 1974) the leader may obtain clues as to what response may be productive at any particular moment. The object relations group therapist who applies the developmental perspectives of Mahler (Mahler et al., 1975) and Spitz (1965) is usually sensitive to phase specificity. Just as it is important for caretakers to respond empathically and appropriately to the developing child's concerns about issues or tasks with which that youngster is preoccupied at a particular time, so should the object relations therapist's interpretations "fit in" wherever the patient and group are psychologically at that moment, as in the following example.

> A novice male group leader was describing in supervision his interpreting to a group member the psychological fusion state with group and leader. Although the supervisee seemed accurate in his perception, I raised the question: Is it truly therapeutic to interpret this need at a time when the patient seemed to be "finding" and experiencing symbiotic fulfillment, which had been craved for since early childhood and which needed to be experienced, in terms of "phase specificity," before the task of separation and individuation could be negotiated profitably?

This example illustrates the object relations concept that psychoanalytically oriented group and individual psychotherapy relationships may, in ways, parallel child development and that the parent–child dyad may have some important similarities to that of the therapist–patient (or to therapist–group relationships). This hypothesis is central to the object relations notion of the curative factor—especially for those object relations therapists who utilize developmental ego psychology. At the same time, it is important also to recognize that the patient is *not* a child relating to a "knowing adult"—the therapist and/or the group. The theory purports that there are percepts and assumptions that are unconscious and unresolved from earlier life and that are interfering with patients' effective functioning which become activated and expressed, without awareness, in the course of treatment, and that as these are experienced and worked through in the more benign environment of the group, healing occurs.

More specifically, the parent–child aspect of the therapy group provides an opportunity for further exploration and possible resolution of what has been repressed.[7] I attend in particular to each patient's (and the group as a whole's) position along the symbiosis–individuation developmental line. Such ego-psychological object relations considerations have been utilized meaningfully in individual psychodynamic treatment (e.g., Winnicott, 1951, 1960b; Jacobson, 1964; A. Freud, 1965; Balint, 1968; Mahler et al., 1975). Such concepts have also been applied to object relations group therapy (e.g., Scheidlinger, 1974; Kosseff, 1975; Tuttman, 1980; Kauff, 1990; Kibel, 1990). Many

---

[7]What some object relations therapists consider to be manifestations of true regression in treatment, others consider to be the expression of latent content which has always been present in some unconscious forms but which becomes overt under conducive conditions (Gill, 1982; Tuttman, 1982).

object relations theorists believe that early life experiences mold subtle, unconscious lifelong patterns related to the struggle to individuate
and mature emotionally. There are also those (Eagle and Wolitsky,
1982; Gill, 1982; Stern, 1985; Eagle, 1987) who encourage therapists
to avoid a role that can stimulate adultomorphic, infantomorphic, or
pathomorphic confused thinking about such matters. I believe it is
possible to appreciate the connections between early life influences
and adult concerns without becoming condescending. This is most
readily accomplished by the practitioner who is not rigidly bound by
theory, but who applies concepts respectfully when there is evidence
to support the relevant hypotheses.

I have mentioned that I do not disclose my own experiences readily
and automatically in the group situation, unless it is specifically indicated by an appreciation of the patient's psychodynamic state. That
is, I remain neutral unless the need for direct interaction is great and
the patient will experience me as duplicating the missing or "empty"
parent if I remain neutral; I would be more inclined, in such instances, to relate somewhat more personally. Thus, for example, when
a person has been very isolated by a schizoid parent (or no parent),
there is sometimes such a hunger for human connection that neutral
interpretations about these matters are of no avail and may even
further traumatize. Applied indiscriminately, the classical concept of
the "blank screen" neutral therapist can be a caricature. This does
not mean, however, that there is no merit in leaving "space" and
maintaining some ambiguity, under appropriate circumstances.

In one sense, however, I always make use of my own life experiences and my relationships with both the individual patients and the
group as a whole. As a careful and concerned listener, over a period
of time, I "collect" many memories. It is sometimes poignant and
therapeutic, in my object relations group therapist's role, to make a
connection between what is taking place in the group at present and
something explored in the past. For example, something from the
life of the patient speaking may be connected with another patient's
history discussed in a group session months before or may stimulate
a particular feeling in the therapist that is familiar. Such juxtaposi-
tions may arouse meaningful perspectives and insight. The understanding thus derived may be of benefit or have application to everyone, to the group as an entity, or to one or more group members.

Because every individual leader responds in terms of personal considerations as well as theoretical orientation, it is difficult to give specific examples of how to carry out the object relations group therapist's role. Furthermore, certain therapist attitudes and policies may
result, in part, from general treatment concepts. Although I have

tried in this chapter to specify how the leader's role emanates from object relations theory, some of these concepts are not unique to one specific theory. What I have endeavored to convey is that the rationale of the object relations therapist is *always* influenced by certain key concepts that I have stated earlier in this chapter but reiterate here.

1. Patients' psychic situations result from earlier identifications that affect behavior.
2. The projection of these unconscious mental representations leads to acting out, which can be modified in the course of treatment when the therapist's attitude offers a "containing," "holding," and facilitating milieu.
3. Through identifying with an accepting, "observing," and empathic therapist stance, patients begin to gain perspective and control.

The following detailed clinical examples illustrate this process. Although non–object relations therapists may have similar general goals, object relations theories provide the overarching rationale, sensitivity, and *modus operandi* described in these examples.

EXAMPLE OF THE LEADER'S ROLE IN AN ONGOING OBJECT RELATIONS GROUP

Frequently, patients express their feelings or perceptions about the leader or about one another. From an object relations viewpoint, this is potentially invaluable because, in so doing, members may be expressing in the present feelings and memories of important figures from their past, as in the following example.

> Jim, who always accuses me and other members in the group of condemning his homosexuality, is clearly projecting his personal disdain for his own feelings and behavior. The group and I have come to appreciate the factors in Jim's background that have probably been instrumental in forming some aspects of his sexual orientation and his self-critical feelings.
> I, as leader, acknowledge the fact that he has developed to the point of wanting a deeper involvement with others, now that he has better control over his self-destructive pattern of choosing dangerous and unworkable pseudoconnections with unsavory characters. The group members and I express admiration for Jim's recent "new" relationship. It seems that Jim has become more aware of having a "self" and is

becoming interested in having better choices and exerting better control over his actions. Add to this the memories (or, in object relations terminology, the *mental representations*) of his strict, moralistic, conventional, religious mother and stepfamily, and it becomes likely that, via projection, Jim is living out an internal conflict about his guilt and defensiveness for violating the demands of those who originally were important in his personality formation.

But that is only one side of his conflict. The second issue deals with his desire to be loved by a man. Jim longed for his father, who had rejected him and disappeared shortly after his birth. (Perhaps the men Jim chose were unrewarding because they were selected on the basis of their tendency to reject him, which made them appear more like his father.) The group and the leader have pointed out these "connections" and also offered some perspective when Jim mercilessly attacked a woman group member (of his mother's age) as if she were his hypocritical, rejecting mother.

A self-defeating object choice is an old pattern of his; however, we observe his changed behavior in choosing this time an available person who treats him well. It is the first time he has chosen a partner where there is a chance for a relationship. It is also his first conscious awareness of his displaced rage toward women.

Here is an example of how the group leader focuses on clarifying and encouraging group members to decipher and examine internal mental representations—"ghosts of the past"—that influence present behavior both in the group and in outside life. Two opposing representations can be discerned here: one expressing an inner libidinal yearning for the missing and longed-for person, and the other, projecting onto the leader and group a disapproving, moralistic constraining critic. This material is valuable for the working-through of such intrapsychic and interpersonal history. The tenacious nature of the power of internalized, part-object, unconscious mental representations and their projections (and the need to carefully monitor and experience them) usually requires many repeated exposures to these manifestations. The group members, *encouraged by the leader's attitude,* are gradually sensitized to a deeper appreciation of each others' life stories and personality characteristics.

This example reflects the object relations leader's role in first recognizing archaic mental representations and "old" internalizations and their impact on behavior, and then monitoring the past and providing, in the context of the present relationships with group and leader, reality-directed constructive new sources for internalization. A skillful object relations leader encourages group members to do this important task as a working group (Bion, 1959). Utilizing empathy and insight into the power of unconscious introjects, the object relations leader encourages the detection of what is taking place from new perspectives.

Group members, gradually influenced by identification with the leader, provide for each member and the group entity the benefit of two valuable approaches: (1) to *observe* and become aware of what is going on and perhaps, sometimes, to acquire possible insights into "why" it is happening, and (2) to *express* and *experience* feelings and reactions. From a theoretical vantage point, it is the reality-oriented, organizing, administrating part of the personality (often referred to as the *ego*) that has been encouraged to enhance, via identification, the important potential capacities of *observing* and *experiencing*. These functions are essential if the members and the group as a whole are to work toward greater freedom from a repetition of and often painful, automatic acting out of old patterns and prejudices.

Object relations therapists understand these repetition compulsions as manifestations of the inner reservoir of archaic mental representations, everpresent and unconscious, leading to endlessly maladaptive responses continually at work until monitored, understood, harnessed, and modified. Ideally, through insight and the gradual internalization of more benign and constructive objects, healthier options and more reality-based experiences with others become possible. These changes often result from new and useful identifications with a viable, dynamic group leader.

Sometimes, the group situation is more complicated. The following vignette offers an example of *projective identification* in the course of a group session led by an object relations leader.

> Jim may project his sexual impulses (which he finds unacceptable in himself) onto another group member, let us say, Michael. Jim then assumes the antisexual, critical attitude of his early-life mother, who attacked him. He viciously tears into Michael for the "unacceptable" impulses (which are really Jim's disowned impulses). Thus, Jim unconsciously projects his own longings onto Michael while consciously manifesting in himself the internalized mental representation of his moralistic mother as if this were his own reaction to that which is now attributed to Michael.
>
> As a consequence of the leader and group monitoring and clarifying what is happening between Jim and Michael, both men begin to appreciate the dynamics operating in their interaction. This situation also provides a therapeutic opportunity for another group member, Beverly, who has recently become an effective and helpful participant, increasingly capable of "deciphering" the interactions in the group. This is a new position for her, especially since her highly critical, accomplished father had expressed contempt for her ineptitude throughout her

growing years. Both Michael and Jim benefit from Beverly's effectiveness and understanding and express appreciation and admiration for
her concern and astuteness. Michael refers to Beverly's father and how
he probably never sensed this wonderful and constructive sensitivity in
her. The group tries to understand why her father had not been more
constructive.

Jim also wants to "confess" to the group that he is aware of liking
Michael very much but is uncomfortable feeling it and talking about it.
Michael wants to explore the parallels in his interaction with Jim and
the way he felt as a seven year old about his bullying older brother.
And so it goes. What was formerly a fight–flight pattern operant in the
group as a whole has been converted into a work group session, mainly
by identification with the therapist, who in his object relations role
provides structure and adequate *holding, observing,* and *empathizing.* In
the group, at this time, we can find the beginning of insightful relationships as group members learn to work through projective identifications.

One benefit of being aware of the variety of mental representations
that get embanked in each person's psyche as a result of past history
and experiences is that we are all able to learn how, through the
observing ego, to sense and to try to recognize when manifestations
of primitive, "leftover," early-life, mental representations are at work.
These have interfered with a reality-oriented, reasonable, contemporary perspective. In the course of time, with the therapist's empathic,
monitoring approach, patients increasingly come to see in one another, and, ideally, eventually in themselves, the contaminating effects
of unconscious fantasies and mental representations that tend to interfere with present-day reality interactions.

FURTHER EXPLORATION OF THE OBJECT RELATIONS
GROUP LEADER'S ROLE

The ancient poet Lao Tzu (Scheidlinger, 1982; Henricks, 1989; Anthony, 1990; Tuttman, 1990) described the good leader as one who
is *not* experienced by the group as responsible for the good work of
that group. In that spirit, I do not offer much active leadership except
when necessary. For example, it was not needed at the stage of the
particular group just described. That example reflects a particular
object relations leader understanding group members in a nonintrusive but catalytic manner. The role I assume is rather characteristic
of most psychoanalytically oriented object relations therapists. One

possible exception may be those who follow the style of Melanie Klein's (1932) early work, when she made ongoing, active interpretations of unconscious impulses as a matter of policy. Nevertheless, the most prominent, contemporary Kleinian therapists I have worked with (among them Bion, 1959; Rosenfeld, 1966; Segal, 1973; Ganzarain, 1989) function in a less active manner.

Only during instances where there is incredible resistance on the part of one individual or when there is an alignment among patients to resist reality developments do I consider it useful or necessary to directly intervene by focusing interpretations on resistances of the group as a whole or of individual members. Often group members actively interpret resistances of other members. This is ideal since the work group operations often effectively help individuals overcome and work-through resistances. This process not only helps the beneficiary of useful insights but can also be very useful to the other group members, who often benefit from enhanced self-esteem and a greater sense of confidence and autonomy. One can conceive of the leader's role in terms of facilitating a work group atmosphere rather than as a zealous pursuer of "resistances."

I agree with Saul Scheidlinger (1980) that group behavior is manifested on at least two depth levels: the *contemporaneous dynamic* and the *genetic-regressive*. I believe that leaders' responses to the group and members contain both conscious and unconscious reactions and that these responses are often activated by the patients' conscious and unconscious conflicts, styles, patterns of interaction, and projections. In the group example offered above, Jim and Michael were caught in regressive projective identificatory patterns which eventually were worked-through on contemporary dynamic levels.

Sometimes the therapist experiences strong feelings or impulses that are not characteristic of himself. This may be an indication that some group member has induced such reactions in the leader by means of *projective identification*. Ideally, the therapist recognizes and monitors this dynamic and, instead of acting out, arrives at a perspective about the patient's conflicts and the patient's internalized representations, part of which have been projected onto the therapist. Sometimes, however, such projections evoke countertransference responses within the leader. In such instances, having had successful personal treatment often helps the therapist regain equilibrium and perspective. At such times, sharing this experience with the group can be quite productive, providing useful modeling.

It takes effort and discipline for the leader to resist the "suction" of some unconscious association to something in the group or a group member and to avoid acting out countertransference reactions.

Clearly, the leader's first step is to discern the sources of the responses both in the group and in himself. This is work worthy of undertaking. The leader's personality is an important instrument in the effective and realistic functioning of any group. There is a wealth of meaningful unconscious data about the patients and the group that can be discerned from monitoring consciously what were unconscious mental representations manifested in the projections and projective identifications taking place in the group, which may, in turn, give rise to countertransference reactions in the therapist. These developments offer opportunities for resolution and insight when a leader's countertransference reactions may be aroused in response to a patient's transference. Consider the following example.

> A group patient may suggest, in the course of a group session, that the leader is greedy, is primarily interested in fees, and has little regard for the problems of the group members. This may be a projection of the patient's feelings. Undoubtedly this is a form of attack. Some group leaders may feel distressed. In the fortuitous event that the group leader is comfortable enough to consciously face such reactions, the work of the group can continue with focus on the relevant issues. If the leader cannot accept the accusation, is not able to tolerate feeling hostility from or toward the patient, or is unable to face the possibility of some merit to the accusation, then it is quite possible that the therapist will repress his reactions and countertransferential behavior may result.

We must also consider that countertransference may, at times, be the result of the therapist's distortions and pathology rather than a reaction to the patient's transference. Although this is an unfortunate state of affairs, it indeed happens. In some instances, a group that has been helped by a leader may, in turn, help the therapist.

A COMPLEX OBJECT RELATIONS GROUP TREATMENT EXAMPLE

We have thus far examined major theoretical concepts that guide the role of a group therapist dedicated to an object relations psychodynamic approach to treatment. Relevant group dynamic factors have also been summarized. Some simple group examples were offered to demonstrate the theoretical underpinnings and the role of the therapist in action. In this final section I shall present an example of a difficult object relations group involving a complex interplay of histories, pathology, and confrontations. Bracketed material provides commentary.

Melvin listened very carefully as another group member, Jim, reported the story of his life and his ongoing struggle since his father abandoned him shortly after birth.

Mel recalled how sometimes he wished his father also had disappeared, because throughout Mel's childhood the presence of his belligerent, hyperactive, probably psychotic father tormented him. His dad owned a vegetable store in an Italian tenement area of New York City where the family lived. He insisted that the youngster help in the store after school. Mel was pressed to carry heavy crates of vegetables. Since he was a rather sickly child he did not always have the strength to follow Father's orders. At such times, Father would get very provoked, would stop his own work, and would tell Melvin to take Father's belt and to hit him as hard as Mel could.

Mel was quite familiar with these peculiar, sadistic tricks. He knew he was trapped. No way could he win. Compliance would be dangerous and opposition would be equally hazardous. Mel had learned to act silly and seductive, sometimes to tease and, in that way, attempt to distract Father from his frightening games. This time Mel did not succeed and so, hesitatingly, he struck his father with the belt. Father mocked the son's weakness and proceeded to show his own strength by grabbing the belt and striking the lad with full fury.

This demoralizing kind of experience recurred frequently. Mel was not terribly successful in coping with his father, but he somehow learned the tactics of being a neighborhood clown when dealing with the street bullies. He amused these tough older kids, but sometimes he would needlessly provoke them through his jesting grins. Although he was trying to ward off attacks, his own frustration and anger may have also sent provocative signals in the form of his jesting.

During one group session Melvin recalled a childhood memory of a "real-life" group event. When he was a young student at a public school in a tenement area, there was a public shower room where the boys were to shower after gym class. In typical roughhouse manner (and in accord with the tradition of teasing and taunting Melvin the clown), several boys made a circle around Melvin and urinated on him. He told this story with great embarrassment.

[The leader's role in the early stages of this group had contributed to an atmosphere wherein it had become safe to look back, to open up, and to release painful memories and express disturbing emotions. This shows how a conducive alliance in a facilitating group can permit the recall and working through of traumatic group experiences left over in a painful memory bank from earlier torments. Perhaps many group patients are inclined to remember traumatic group events in a constructive group situation. Patients who have had individual sessions do not always recall group traumas of earlier life, but these memories sometimes return to consciousness in the course of group treatment. This event is more likely to occur when the leader's role facilitates an open, exploratory approach in accord with the object relations concepts described in the theory sections of this chapter.]

It became clear to myself, the group members, and Melvin himself that he had developed a masochistic style in identifying with and responding to his father and the neighborhood bullies. As a teenager, Melvin had been referred by a social worker for individual therapy. Following this, he moved away from his family, went through public college, working in his spare time to provide the money for treatment as well as for living expenses. His self-negating and provocative manner dramatically diminished, and he continued working in both group and individual therapy.

At that time, young men had the choice of being drafted for military service or joining the state National Guard and spending a few weeks each summer on maneuvers at a military camp. During one such period, I received an anonymous letter that contained the words: "You no good son-of-a-bitch." I looked at the envelope and, indeed, the only clue as to who had sent it was the postal mark of some unfamiliar northern New York state rural area. A bit of detective work led me to recognize that the area from which this letter came was in the vicinity of Melvin's military camp. Clearly, this required a therapeutic response unencumbered by countertransference. I decided that if approached cautiously in group, Mel could probably benefit from an exploration of this matter.

[A group therapist often is required to evaluate ego functioning, resistances, the strength of the therapeutic alliance, and the capacity of the individual and the group to tolerate stress, anxiety, rage, and so forth.]

Upon Melvin's return to the next group session, it was important that I, as group leader, ascertain his capacity to tolerate exploration of a potentially embarrassing or humiliating matter. I mentioned rather quietly and somewhat parenthetically that his letter had arrived! He looked quite flustered and then explained to the group that it was he who had sent the letter and he somewhat reluctantly described its content. After a bit of laughter, members of the group inquired, rather sensitively, as to what were the conditions and what were his thoughts and feelings at the moment he impulsively wrote.

Melvin contemplated, and he then said, "This time, going to camp, I was tense and scared. I knew the guys would tease me in the old way and I didn't want to be the butt of the barracks anymore. I no longer have to use this painful way of adjusting. I have learned to avoid teasing.

Not having been with these soldiers for a year, he clearly was worried and frightened at the thought that they would certainly go into the old routine they enjoyed as an annual ritual. How angry they would be if he wouldn't play the old games! Indeed, he was correct. The fellows began the usual teasing routine. At a moment of frightening confrontation, Melvin glanced at his watch. He knew the mail was about to go out. He claimed he had to write a letter quite urgently. He ran off, scribbled the message, hastily addressed the envelope and sealed in his rage, while thinking about me and the group. He appreciated how he had found enhanced self-esteem and a sense of poise, but he bitterly resented the newfound danger (which ironically resulted from his "growth") as he dropped the letter in the mail sack.

When describing all of this to the group, everyone in the room shared the sense of irony and meaningfulness Melvin had just recounted. We all understood how awesome, frightening, and dangerous groups of people can be. We also felt the healing power and the changes in each of us which the group can catalyze.

[This incident reminded us all how reassuring and yet confusing change can be. It reflects the tenacity and pressure of past mental representations and the impact of the leader's role and the group's attitudes upon object relations.]

Another member of the same psychotherapy group was a rather attractive, energetic, middle-aged woman, Abigail, who saw herself as hungry for affection, having been much tormented in a marriage that had ended in a bitter divorce. Twenty years had passed since her husband ran off unexpectedly with the sixteen-year-old daughter of a neighbor. At that time, Abigail was pregnant with her third child. Despite the humiliation and pain, she maintained herself valiantly and went through the birth and cared for all three children with little or no support. She saw herself as having admired and supported her husband's artistic abilities. She sacrificed a lot on behalf of his career. She also felt betrayed by the teenage girl who, as a neighbor, unhappy with her own family life, had been a constant visitor. Abigail considered herself very decent to have concerned herself with this girl, who frequently took meals with the family. Understandably, Abigail felt betrayed by both her husband and the teenager.

Now, years later, Abigail, sixty-two years of age, continues to see herself as an altruistic, liberal, caring person who has not been treated very kindly by those whom she indulged and valued. Although group members appreciated how unkindly she had been treated, it gradually became clear that Abigail could only see herself as noble and suffering and that she was completely unwilling or unable to recognize her own rage, or any possible responsibility that she might have for the difficulties in her life. These tenacious self-concepts have limited her insights and adaptability. Although everyone disapproved of her husband's behavior, after a while her endless expressions of anguish and her inability to consider that she might have played a role in her situation aroused frustration and hostility in group members.

[The leader's role was to express the following positions: (1) Abigail's protective self-representations were understandable in terms of her history, and (2) the group, critical of her and impatient with her self-destructive behavior, was unable to help her see their perspective. Both attitudes need support from the therapist while he encourages gradual "work group" approaches to these problems.]

Michael was an attractive male in his early fifties who also attended group. He had a history of both individual and group psychotherapy in the past and had been married and divorced twice. His manner was gracious and intellectual. He held an impressive university position in the department of philosophy.

Michael openly expressed feelings of insecurity and inadequacy and, although many responded with admiration, in time, group members began to question something about Michael's frankness and "confessions." It became apparent that, despite these insights, Michael did not change within himself.

Gradually the group came to learn his history: When he was about five, his mother committed suicide. He had been assaulted sexually by an older sister during early childhood. In addition to her sexual interest in him, his sister frequently acted sadistically when Michael tried to reinforce a bond with their father. Father was somehow unsuccessful, despite his efforts as a writer who valued literature and the intellect.

Although Father could not afford the expense of tutors, private schools, and music lessons, nevertheless, Michael was given all of these opportunities. It was clear he had to be brilliant and accomplished. He *had* to attend Ivy League schools. He *had* to erase his raw Eastern European accent and become a proper Anglicized scholar. Gradually, with pressure from the group, Michael recognized that he had become quite pretentious and that his reactions to Father's pressures had robbed him of his true self and of the opportunity to be authentic. Group members confronted him with their feelings that he was posing and was not genuine. They told him he appeared to be superior and condescending.

Abigail seemed deeply interested in Michael. Although he was considerably younger, she appreciated his intelligence and his cultured manner. Despite her enthusiasm, she was very cautious and hesitant.

At one group session, Michael vented distress about the bohemian waitress he had been wooing (without having told the group about this before). He had encouraged her to write poetry and he had hoped they could get closer, but the other night she informed him that she cared about a man much younger than he. His fantasy was shattered. He felt betrayed. Abigail was deeply distressed when she heard this and spontaneously launched an attack. She suggested Michael was probably exploiting this young waitress. She expressed doubt that he had informed the girl of how much older he was than she and furthermore, she said, "I bet you didn't even tell her about your herpes! Why do you exploit this vulnerable, sweet, naive girl?" Michael recoiled in indignation and shock. "How could you accuse me so unfairly at the moment I confess such pain? Aren't you confusing me with your lecherous ex-husband? Who could blame that pathetic guy of yours if he desperately needed respite from you? You . . . are a righteous, controlling, constricting, boring, and endlessly suffering nag!" [Tuttman, 1985].

[In a moment of introspection during these emotional fireworks, the therapist recognized group-dynamic forces at work that were leading to the great irritability and the lack of empathic resonance among group members, especially Bion's (1959) fight–flight basic assumption. As a result, an interpretation was offered that encouraged group members to shift attention from an attack upon one another to a focus on awareness of each member's own feelings and thoughts as an alternative to assaulting other persons in the group. The purpose was to attempt to shift from a defensive unconscious basic assumption mode to a "work group" mode, so that the group could generate and explore more effective, reality-oriented resolutions. Furthermore, the leader was familiar with Michael's and Abigail's backgrounds. Both had been raised by demanding, critical parents. The internalized mental representations of these intrusive, angry figures readily came to the foreground and supplied each of them with righteous assaultiveness, which they directed at one another. The leader said, "Wait a minute. Aren't you just attacking one another now? What about how each of you feels, and why at this moment do you feel the way you do?"]

As a consequence, each member of the group began to focus on and share inner feelings and perceptions. For example, Jim acknowledged that Abigail acted in a way that reminded him of his mother. Only once had she seen him after sending him to the orphanage. At that time, Jim was a graduate student. He had suffered a psychotic episode and needed to be hospitalized. Mother visited and attested her deep love for him in a manner he found to be hypocritical. Jim saw Abigail's constantly demeaning her husband (the father of her children) in front of the kids as acting in a manner that reflected no appreciation of her son's need to find something within his father with which he could identify. Jim certainly could identify with someone who is suffering when that person's father is devalued and taken away from him.

Jim then also recalled Abigail's earlier expression of distress in the course of a former incident. She had told him how worried she was that he might contract AIDS. He now turned to Abigail and said, "Your concern doesn't help me. I cannot trust your sensitivity or your sincerity. At that time I was facing deep disappointment and anxiety and I struggled to control my anxiety and to build a personal relationship with someone I liked. Exactly when I was trying so hard to find an alternative to my promiscuous life history, you tuned in with the AIDS scare" (Tuttman, 1985). He accused her of hypocrisy, and then realized that this reminded him of his mother.

Jim also told Michael that the group has been the only family he has known. He was hurt and angry that Michael, though a newcomer, tried to "seduce" all group members into valuing him as the favorite. Jim acknowledged that Michael had serious problems to work on, but nonetheless, Jim confessed, he was envious of the care and privileges Michael had received. "I can't let you take this family [the group] away from me." He also expressed distress at Michael's inauthentic manner. Abigail turned to Jim and stated, "Jim, you reject all women and, in the way, you deny my value. You only see my contradictions and failings without expressing any compassion or real caring. It genuinely troubles me how you mistreat and sabotage yourself. I guess I haven't faced how much that reminds me of myself. I fear that perhaps I do to myself the things you do to yourself!"

Abigail then turned to Michael. She accused him of often behaving in ways like her insecure father and her self-indulgent husband. She also acknowledged being hurt that Michael was rejecting her by choosing someone else. Once again, she finds herself frustrated by a man whom she feels she could relate to and treat well, but he prefers a nonavailable, immature, younger female.

In response, Michael told the group how Abigail reminded him of his dead mother, who had always appeared unavailable and noncaring. He was tormented by her lofty standards and values (as he also was by his father and, indeed, by himself). Michael turned to Jim and expressed how intolerable Jim's negating Michael's worth felt. He acknowledged he could understand how Jim would find him threatening in the group, but he added that even when he struggled toward more genuine warmth and intimacy, he was distressed at how Jim pushed him away by means of dripping sarcasm and bitterness.

[It is difficult to report the full complexity of interactions in any group situation. For one thing, as in life, there are endless details and subleties. In this example, I have referred to the lives and interplay of many personalities, focusing on the situation of one patient at a time. Group-as-a-whole factors also need to be responded to and understood. As noted in the preceding examples, emotions and insights can be expressed in group suddenly and spontaneously and often erupt in the course of interaction. Each detail reflects multidimensional complexities. The object relations leader's role requires sensitivity, conceptual clarity, good clinical judgment, and spontaneity, offered in a facilitating, holding environment (Winnicott, 1960b, 1963) that also provides continuing selfobject differentiation (Jacobson, 1964; Mahler et al., 1975) and good observing and experiencing ego functions for identification (Tuttman, 1987)].

CONCLUSIONS

Having pointed out the natural connection between group therapy practice and the concepts of object relations theory, I will now discuss the strengths and weaknesses of an object relations approach to the group therapist's role. One of the strengths (which can also be construed as a weakness) is that the group therapist's style and personality is an important (if not crucial) factor in this type of treatment. It is valuable when the therapist has been well analyzed to the extent of being able to effectively avoid acting out, resisting the transference "pulls" and the projections that, according to object relations theory, are inevitably present in the transactions between group leader, members, and the group as a whole. There is little else to ensure that a therapist does not act out. The object relations leader plays a vital role in facilitating the patients' growth and development by the working-through process described earlier. Of course, some therapists do not understand or value an object relations perspective. That does not mean the problems described disappear! On the contrary, if our theory relates to reality, we must conclude that, in such instances, the therapist is more likely to be unaware of important dimensions operant in the group. Unfortunately, such a therapist may act out more in response to the group's evocative or projective pull and may get sucked into problems to a greater degree.

In applying a simpler theory, where the frame and the therapeutic task as well as the contract can be more clearly spelled out, with greater specificity and more undimensional role definition, the burden on the therapist may appear to be less, although there is also the possibility that the likelihood of achieving therapeutic objectives is lessened as well. For example, Rogerian (Rogers, 1951) therapy can be learned more readily since the therapist's role is concrete and clearly defined. Work from a Kohutian vantage point, although requiring sensitivity and maturity on the therapist's part, is also less complex. The variables are limited to a single developmental line (namely, that of narcissism). To stress empathy, primarily, and to focus on mirroring, the value of selfobjects, and accepting idealization does not require as much subtlety as dealing with the multidimensional factors in the broader object relations theories, where the interaction of drives (libido and aggression), affects, several lines of development, metapsychological considerations, and so forth are all involved. (Of course, this is not to imply that providing empathy is easy or that it is not of great value.) Further, since Kohut (1977) rejects the notion that aggression is a drive,[9] he eliminates from consideration many problems in treatment dealing with aggression.

One may conclude, then, that the intricacies of object relations theories are both an advantage and a disadvantage as a theoretical framework. Though complex, intimate knowledge of object relations frameworks offers a rich base for working with groups and individual patients toward meaningful change and achievement of therapeutic goals.

A related problem with object relations viewpoints is that we are dealing with multidimensional conceptualizations. For example, when we discuss the "internalization of objects from the past," are we talking about the *experiential component* (the *subjective*) way in which the impressionable child internalizes objects, where perceptions are colored by drive impact (such as the derivatives of aggression and libido), or are we dealing with the internalization of *real* objects? Or both? The question of distinguishing reality from its complex intermix with fantasy is one of the intricacies related to this theory. I do not consider this a weakness of object relations theory, since I believe that life is complicated, and the relationships between external and internal reality are dynamic and involve ever-shifting mirroring and fantasy possibilities.

As a bit of a footnote, I should add that I consider object relations theory particularly useful in dealing with certain populations: borderline patients, patients with character disorders, and some patients suffering psychotic conditions. Borderline patients often make good candidates for group therapy because of their inclination to split and project part-objects onto other members of the group and the leader. Such material can be explored, monitored and contained in a group context—usually to everyone's advantage. This provides important data for working-through. Object relations therapists are generally familiar with and accustomed to working with such data. In addition, the degree of hostile projections onto the therapist is so great in dyadic treatment of some borderline patients that group treatment may be particularly advantageous. The group permits a diffusion of the intensity of the hostile projections among the various members and the leader. The leader's interpretations (or merely his being) and the patient's projections often arouse profound transference rage in some borderlines when confronted in individual treatment. The fact that in group other members often take on a monitoring, observing ego function and offer interpretations can aid the group leader in

---

[9]Kohut (1977) sees aggression as secondary to frustration; it is what he calls a "disintegration product" (pp. 120–121; p. 262).

that the therapist need not always be the source of injury or the object of retaliation. Sometimes, the leader primarily functions as a support. This permits the borderline group member to function more effectively. Furthermore, the group as a whole may become a "matrix" which can be helpful in providing the structure and stability that is important for successful treatment of preoedipal conditions (Kauff, 1990; Kibel, 1990; Kosseff, 1990; Tuttman, 1990). For psychotic patients, the development of cognitive skills and social learning (Yalom, 1985; Liberman, DeRisis, and Meuser, 1989) can offer another object relations application that can prove dramatically effective. The "mother group" function, the "group matrix," and the "holding environment" can help patients who are frustrated, frightened, and reluctant to expose their disturbances to dyadic treatment.

I do not believe that object relations psychodynamic group therapy is *always* useful in the treatment of narcissistic conditions. Such patients may first need to have established a therapeutic alliance with an individual therapist before being able and willing to tolerate the inevitable narcissistic injuries that individuals in group must be prepared to sustain (Tuttman, 1990).

Since everyone needs attention, the press of emotions of several different, "competing" group members can make the group experience quite frustrating for most members. Nevertheless, the "good family" feeling of sharing and understanding one another can be a vital bond which, in time, group members use to great benefit. At a certain stage in the treatment of narcissistic patients, when a therapeutic alliance is clearly established (usually in dyadic treatment), I believe that it can be profitable and catalytic for certain narcissistic patients to enter group—preferably with the same therapist. Such patients should be well prepared in advance for anticipating the inevitable narcissistic injuries and mortification in group. Where there is enough of a therapist–group member alliance and a sense of underlying support, the narcissistic patient can benefit from the group matrix, the feedback, and the opportunity to experiment in relationships afforded by the group milieu.

In this chapter I have described my role as a group therapist influenced by object relations theories. From my vantage point, it seems likely that, despite the therapist's efforts to "frame" the relationship in group treatment, there will be distortions and fantasies in the form of projections and displacements, which result inevitably from each group member's internalized unconscious mental representations and from the automatic patterns of interaction developed in earlier living. Although this complicates the situation, these distortions are exactly what enriches the therapeutic possibilities in group treatment, from an object relations viewpoint.

The presence of unconscious fantasies and mental representations is potentially valuable in providing an opportunity for the observing therapist and group members together to experience and monitor the powerful unconscious influences operating at all times. Under conditions where the therapist provides less structure, there will be, along with greater ambiguity, the likelihood of more parapraxes and distortions. The sophisticated group therapist can strive to facilitate a therapeutic opportunity appropriate to the needs of a particular group. A more or less structured therapeutic atmosphere may prove to be conducive to achieving treatment goals under particular circumstances (Klein and Brown, 1987).

In this chapter I have attempted to clarify certain aspects of the role of the object relations group therapist. In particular, object relations leaders encourage group members to experience and work-through unresolved developmental problems. Certain object relations concepts prove to be most helpful in such endeavors. Among these are Winnicott's notions of transitional phenomena and experimental play; Mahler's ideas about fusion, symbiosis, and separation–individuation phases; Klein's notions about splitting and projective identification; Kohut's conceptualization of adequate mirroring and idealization experiences; and the notions of constructive identifications, good ego observation, accurate cognition, and clear perception. Transference and countertransference, regression and reintegration, and group dynamics all play a part in the process as well.

Most of the foregoing factors are automatically involved when the therapist encourages the group in the ways that have been discussed throughout this chapter. Although it is not always necessary for the therapist to offer interpretations, to impose specific strategies, or to engage in artificial techniques, it is important that therapists proceed flexibly so that creative and effective applications are available to better serve group treatment in an object relations context.

REFERENCES

Anthony, E. J. (1990), The dilemma of therapeutic leadership: The leader who does not lead. In: *Psychoanalytic Group Theory and Therapy*, ed. S. Tuttman. Madison, CT: International Universities Press.

Bach, G. R. (1954), *Intensive Group Psychotherapy*. New York: Ronald Press.

Balint, M. (1968), *The Basic Fault*. New York: International Universities Press.

Bion, W. R. (1959), *Experiences in Groups*. London: Tavistock Publications.

——— (1963), Elements of psychoanalysis. In: *Seven Servants*. New York: Jason Aronson, 1977.

Blanck, G., & Blanck, R. (1974), *Ego Psychology: Theory and Practice*. New York: Columbia University Press.

Compact Edition of the Oxford English Dictionary, The, Vol. 1 (1971), New York: Oxford University Press.

Dupont, J., ed. (1988), *The Clinical Diary of Sandor Ferenczi*. Cambridge, MA: Harvard University Press.

Eagle, M. N. (1987), *Recent Developments in Psychoanalysis: A Critical Evaluation*. Cambridge, MA: Harvard University Press.

———— Wolitsky, D. L. (1982), Therapeutic influences in dynamic psychotherapy. In: *Curative Factors in Dynamic Psychotherapy*, ed. S. Slipp. New York: McGraw-Hill.

Ferenczi, S. (1932), *Final Contributions to the Problems and Methods of Psychoanalysis*. New York: Basic Books, 1955.

Freud, A. (1965), Normality and pathology in childhood. In: *The Writings of Anna Freud*, Vol. 6. New York: International Universities Press, pp. 140–147.

Freud, S. (1895), Project for a scientific psychology. *Standard Edition*, 1:283–397. London: Hogarth Press, 1966.

———— (1920), Beyond the pleasure principle. *Standard Edition*, 18:3–64. London: Hogarth Press.

———— (1921), Group psychology and the analysis of the ego. *Standard Edition*, 18:69–143. London: Hogarth Press.

———— (1923), The ego and the id. *Standard Edition*, 19:12–66. London: Hogarth Press.

———— (1940), Splitting of the ego in the process of defense. *Standard Edition*, 23:273–278. London: Hogarth Press.

Ganzarain, R. (1989), *Object Relations Group Psychotherapy*. Madison, CT: International Universities Press.

———— (1990), The "bad" mother-group: An entension of Scheidlinger's "mother-group concept." In: *Psychoanalytic Group Theory and Therapy: Essays in Honor of Saul Scheidlinger*, ed. S. Tuttman. Madison, CT: International Universities Press, pp. 157–173.

Gill, M. M. (1982), *Analysis of Transference, Vol. 1*. New York: International Universities Press.

Greenberg, J. R., & Mitchell, S. A. (1983), *Object Relations in Psychoanalytic Theory*. Cambridge, MA: Harvard University Press.

Grosskurth, P. (1986), *Melanie Klein: Her World and Her Work*. New York: Alfred A. Knopf.

Guntrip, H. (1969), *Schizoid Phenomena, Object-Relations and the Self*. New York: International Universities Press.

Henricks, R. G. (1989), *Lao-Tzu Te Tao Ching*. New York: Ballantine Books.

Horwitz, L. (1990), The evolution of a group centered approach. In: *Psychoanalytic Group Theory and Therapy*, ed. S. Tuttman. Madison, CT: International Universities Press.

Jacobson, E. (1964), *The Self and the Object World*. New York: International Universities Press.

James, D. C. (1982), Transitional phenomena in the matrix in group psychotherapy. In: *The Individual and the Group: Boundaries and Interrelations*, Vol. 1, ed. M. Pines & L. Rafaelsen. New York: Plenum Press, pp. 645–661.

Kauff, P. (1990), The unique contributions of analytic group therapy to the treatment of pre-oedipal character pathology. In: *Psychoanalytic Group Theory and Therapy*, ed. S. Tuttman. Madison, CT: International Universities Press.

Kibel, H. (1990), The therapeutic use of splitting: The role of the "mother-group" in therapeutic differentiation and practicing. In: *Psychoanalytic Group Theory and Therapy*, ed. S. Tuttman. Madison, CT: International Universities Press.

Klein, M. (1932), *The Psychoanalysis of Children*. New York: Delacorte Press, 1975.

Klein, R. H., & Brown, S. L. (1987), Size and structure as variables in patient–staff community meetings. *Internat. J. Group Psychother.*, 8:85–98.

——— Hunter, D. E., & Brown, S. L. (1990), Long-term inpatient group psychotherapy. In: *The Difficult Patient in Group*, ed. B. E. Roth, W. H. Stone, & H. D. Kibel. Madison, CT: International Universities Press.

Kohut, H. (1977), *The Restoration of the Self*. New York: International Universities Press.

Kosseff, J. W. (1975), The leader using object-relations theory. In: *The Leader and the Group*, ed. Z. A. Liff. New York: Jason Aronson, pp. 212–242.

——— (1990), The infant and mother and the mother group. In: *Psychoanalytic Group Theory and Therapy*, ed. S. Tuttman. Madison, CT: International Universities Press.

Langs, R. (1977), *The Therapeutic Interaction: A Synthesis*. New York: Jason Aronson.

Laplanche, J., & Pontalis, J. B. (1973), *The Language of Psychoanalysis*. London: Hogarth Press.

Liberman, R. T., DeRisis, W. J., & Meuser, K. T. (1989), *Social Skills Training for Psychiatric Patients*. Champaign, IL: Research Press.

Mahler, M. S., Pine, F., & Bergman, A. (1975), *The Psychological Birth of the Human Infant*. New York: Basic Books.

Rogers, C. R. (1951), *Client Centered Therapy*. Boston: Houghton Mifflin.

Rosenfeld, H. (1966), *Psychotic States*. New York: International Universities Press.

Rutan, J. S., & Stone, W. N. (1984), *Psychodynamic Group Psychotherapy*. Lexington, MA: D. C. Heath.

Sandler, J., & Rosenblatt, B. (1962), The concept of the representational world. *The Psychoanalytic Study of the Child*, 17:128–145.

Scheidlinger, S. (1974), On the concept of the "mother-group." *Internat. J. Group Psychother.*, 24:417–428.

——— ed. (1980), *Psychoanalytic Group Dynamics: Basic Readings*. New York: International Universities Press.

——— (1982), *Focus on Group Psychotherapy*. New York: International Universities Press.

Segal, H. (1973), *Introduction to the Work of Melanie Klein*. New York: Basic Books.

Singer, D., Astrachan, B., Gould, L., & Klein, E. (1975), Boundary management in psychological work with groups. *J. Appl. Behav. Sci.*, 11:137–176.

Spitz, R. A. (1965), *The First Year of Life*. New York: International Universities Press.

Stern, D. N. (1985), *The Interpersonal World of the Infant*. New York: Basic Books.

Tuttman, S. (1978), Kohut symposium. *Psychoanal. Rev.*, 65:624–629.

——— (1980), The question of group therapy—from a psychoanalytic viewpoint. *J. Amer. Acad. Psychoanal.*, 8(2):217–234.

——— (1981), A historical survey of the development of object relations concepts in psychoanalytic theory. In: *Object and Self: A Developmental Approach*, ed. S. Tuttman, C. Kaye, & M. Zimmerman. New York: International Universities Press.

——— (1982), Regression: Curative factor or impediment in dynamic psychotherapy? In: *Curative Factors in Dynamic Psychotherapy*, ed. S. Slipp. New York: McGraw-Hill.

—— (1984), Applications of object relations theory and self-psychology in current group therapy. *Group*, 8(4):41–48.

—— (1985), The unique opportunities offered by group psychotherapy. *Washington Square Institute*, Monogr. 12. New York: Washington Square Institute.

—— (1987), Exploring the analyst's treatment stance in current psychoanalytic practice. *J. Amer. Acad. Psychoanal.*, 15(1):29–37.

—— (1988), Psychoanalytic concepts of "the self." *J. Amer. Acad. Psychoanal.*, 16:209–219.

—— (1990), Principles of psychoanalytic group therapy applied to the treatment of borderline and narcissistic disorders. In: *The Difficult Patient in Group*, ed. B. Roth, W. Stone, & H. Kibel. Madison, CT: International Universities Press.

Winnicott, D. W. (1951), Transitional objects and transitional phenomena. In: *Collected Papers.* New York: Basic Books, 1957, pp. 97–100.

—— (1960a), Ego distortion in terms of true and false self. In: *The Maturational Processes and the Facilitating Environment.* New York: International Universities Press, 1965, pp. 140–152.

—— (1960b), The theory of the parent–infant relationship. In: *The Maturational Processes and the Facilitating Environment.* New York: International Universities Press, 1965, pp. 37–55.

—— (1963), Psychiatric disorder in terms of infantile maturational processes. In: *The Maturational Processes and the Facilitating Environment.* New York: International Universities Press, 1965, pp. 230–241.

—— (1975), *Collected Papers: Through Paediatrics to Psychoanalysis.* New York: Basic Books.

Yalom, I. (1985), *The Theory and Practice of Group Psychotherapy.* New York: Basic Books.

11

The Role of the Therapist from a Self Psychology Perspective

CHARLES ASHBACH, Ph.D., and VICTOR L. SCHERMER, M.A.

The following statement by Heinz Kohut, made early in the development of self psychology, provides a framework and rationale for the
therapist's role in the treatment process:

> The analyst is not the screen for the projection of internal structure
> (transference) but the direct continuation of an early reality that was
> too distant, too rejecting, or too unreliable to be transformed into solid
> psychological structures. . . . He *is* the old object with which the patient
> tries to maintain contact, from which he tries to separate his own iden-
> tity, or from which he attempts to derive a modicum of internal struc-
> ture [Kohut, 1978, pp. 218–219].

In self psychology, the therapist is thus a functional extension of the
patient's and the group's collective self who will fulfill or frustrate
archaic but ongoing needs for empathy, mirroring, and idealization
in addition to, or at times in place of, objective commentary and
interpretation of conflicts, resistances, and unconscious phantasies.[1]
In self psychology, the stance of the therapist is therefore guided
primarily by "empathy" rather than the experience-distant "neutrality" of classical Freudian analysis. In what follows, guidelines and

---

[1]The authors wish to acknowledge that in this chapter, in keeping with the usage of
the Kleinian school, *phantasy* is used to refer to the deep, unconscious component of a
thought or wish, while *fantasy* is used to refer to conscious images, stories, and images
of individuals and groups. Conscious group *fantasies* are often barometric indicators
of deeper dynamics which reflect unconscious group *phantasies*.

issues regarding the role of the group psychotherapist will be seen to derive from this fundamental shift in the role of the therapist vis-à-vis the patient, a change that is metapsychological, technical, deeply personal, and ever-present in the here-and-now interactive therapy process.

Self psychology is a relatively recent development in psychoanalysis, one which holds great promise and has added significantly to the repertoire of psychotherapists who work with a range of severe character disturbances, particularly the narcissistic personality disorder. At the same time, it needs to be integrated with other perspectives: ego psychology and object relations theory, in particular. Therefore, while we provide in this chapter an exposition of the group therapist's role from a self psychology standpoint, we advocate that the therapist strive for a working synthesis of self psychology with other aspects of psychoanalysis and group dynamics that have proved useful and curative. The therapist should also note where his own working principles and strategy coincide with and anticipate self psychology, since there is considerable overlap between the latter and what has been traditionally held to constitute a good foundation for therapy interventions: empathic listening, a nonjudgmental approach, avoiding premature or traumatic interpretations, and careful monitoring of the therapist's own internal processes and countertransference.

The basic therapy frame to which Kohut and his students have subscribed, and which will be followed here, is that of psychoanalytic psychotherapy. From this perspective, therapy proceeds by putting feelings and thoughts into words; there is a clear contract regarding fees and attendance; other practical aspects of the treatment are established from the beginning; and the individual patient and the group are allowed maximal freedom of verbal expression. In addition, group psychotherapy will require special considerations about contact outside of sessions and special norms, such as whether the therapist will address individual members or the group as a whole, and so on. The rationale for the conduct of groups comes from group dynamics, an area to which self psychology has made important contributions, but which incorporates a large corpus of data and insights from a variety of disciplines.

This chapter will begin with a conceptual overview of the role of the group psychotherapist within a self psychology perspective. It will then proceed to consider the finer details and practical aspects of such a perspective, looking first at the frame and contract for treatment, the screening process, and the patient populations that may benefit from this approach. Some guidelines for group start-up, cotherapy, and supervision will be discussed. Next, issues of strategy and technique—management of transference, the "middle game," and termination of therapy—will be considered, followed by matters of therapist countertransference and self-disclosure. Finally, an evaluation and critique of self psychology vis-à-vis therapist role behavior will be offered.

OVERVIEW OF SELF PSYCHOLOGY, THE GROUP, AND THE LISTENING PROCESS

Psychoanalytic group dynamics has been profoundly shaped by two seminal essays: Freud's (1921) *Group Psychology and the Analysis of the Ego* and Bion's (1959) *Experiences in Groups*. Freud viewed group dynamics as comprised of individual oedipal transferences onto the leader. Parenthetically, he addressed the role of narcissism in group formation in terms of the idealization of the leader and the competition for mirroring among the "sibling" members, as well as in his emphasis on the ego ideal in leadership function. But narcissism as a group motive was regarded by Freud as secondary to the themes of incest and revolt depicted in *Totem and Taboo* (1913).

From this perspective, any leader, especially the leader of a therapy group, is a highly differentiated figure, essentially above or outside the group and perceived by the members in what ultimately prove to be distorted ways. In training groups and group therapy, the leader's role is to help each member achieve a realistic picture of himself by correcting transference distortions and to achieve for the group more mature object relatedness with appropriate levels of libido and aggression (see Bennis and Shepard, 1956). This is the oedipal perspective that for decades has guided the majority of psychoanalytically oriented group therapists.

Bion in 1959, utilizing the insights of Melanie Klein (Segal, 1974) regarding primitive defenses and phantasies, emphasized group-as-a-whole transference rather than individual transference manifestations. The role of the leader, according to Bion, is to remain objective and differentiated in the sea of psychotic-like group-as-a-whole processes and to address group concerns exclusively. He believed that if the group is not functioning as a "work group," that is, rationally, guided by its task, the individual members cannot benefit therapeutically from it. Bion held that internal objects and phantasies are projected by the members into the group matrix, and the analysis of these "projective identifications" provides a consistent formula for group analysis, especially as they constitute what Bion called "basic assumptions," or implicit groupwide belief systems of a primitive, regressed nature.

The self psychology formulation of group dynamics and the leader's role overlaps with, but clearly diverges from, either Freud's or Bion's. For Kohut (1978), "[G]roup processes are largely activated by narcissistic motives" (p. 843). This is in accordance with Freud's emphasis on the ego ideal, which today can be called a "narcissistic structure." Kohut (1972) adds a further dimension to Freud's ego-ideal hypothesis. He states, "Group cohesion is brought about and maintained not only by an ego ideal held in common by members of the group, but also by their subject-bound grandiosity, i.e, by a shared grandiose self. . . . [T]he psychic life of groups, like that of individuals, shows regressive transformations in the narcissistic realm" (p. 397).

In the Kohutian scheme of things, the members come into the group with needs for empathy, mirroring, and idealization. They are incomplete or, in some cases, fragmented and in need of an external "selfobject" to fulfill these functions. These needs are *real*, not merely wishful fantasy or transference repetition. The members use the group and especially the leader to meet these selfobject needs as revived in the group regression. According to Kohut, society or the group, as an extension of the self, too often fails in these mirroring and idealizing functions, resulting in narcissistic injury, fragmentation, and rage. This is one reason for the increasing incidence of narcissistic personality disorders in modern culture.

Kohut maintains that archaic selfobject transferences will be revived in the group, thus giving the therapist two roles: (1) to accurately empathize with the selves of individual members, especially when they experience narcissistic injury, and (2) to facilitate a group climate that allows the group itself and the interactions between the members to provide the appropriate selfobject functions in the context of optimal frustration which promotes the development of psychic structure.

Considered carefully from the vantage point of the therapy frame and technique, a subtle but crucial shift is thus indicated in the therapist role. The overt behaviors and norms of the psychoanalytic group therapist do not change in any way: He is mostly silent, calm in his actions, nonintrusive, nonjudgmental, sharing relatively little about himself and his history. But now, in Kohut's frame, he is no longer the neutral observer who focuses and comments upon the impulse–defense configurations that surface in the group transference. Rather, he is *in* the group, a part of it and a part, indeed, of the patients' selves. This is neither an illusion nor distortion: It is a reality of psychic (and group) life. According to Chessick (1985, p. 302), Kohut saw empathy as more than a mode of observation; it became a bond between therapist and patient, a means of emotional nutriment, and a buffer against rage and acting out.

Independently of Kohut, two important formulations of group dynamics traditionally used in group therapy have similarly stressed how the leader is an integral part of the group system and the members' selves. Foulkes' (Foulkes and Anthony, 1973) theory of the group matrix focuses on the leader as a nodal point in a communications network and the self as receiving its definition from this network. Lewin's (1951) field theory depicts the individual member as negotiating a perceptual field or gestalt in which the leadership is both a goal and an obstacle. Conversely, the leader, like the membership, is immersed in a field (as Kohut's self is immersed in a selfobject matrix) and his effectiveness depends on where he is located in this field, the norms he brings to it, and the impact he has in it.

To be sure, the way in which the therapist enters the group field and becomes an extension of the members' selves (in Kohut's terms, a "selfobject") is highly specific to the technique of self psychology. It is through empathy and introspection, which Kohut (1977) regards as defining the psychological field (p. xxi), that this aim is accomplished, and *not*, in sharp contrast, through control, suggestion, or other nonanalytic means. Empathic introspection is a mode of listening central to Kohutian therapy and essential to the therapist's role. In order to understand what it means to listen effectively in the empathic mode, it is helpful first to reconsider the traditional analytic listening posture.

In classical analysis as well as in psychoanalytic group psychotherapy, the therapist strives to maintain a nonjudgmental stance, evenly suspending his attention among the tripartite structures of id, ego, and superego, thereby achieving what Kernberg (1975) terms "technical neutrality." From the data that the therapist receives from the patient's or group's verbal associations, combined with nonverbal behavior and the internal processes of the therapist himself, a "trial identification" is formed. The latter is a cognitive and intuitive grasp of what it is like to be the patient, to experience his inner and outer world, to use his particular means of defending and coping. From a series of such partial identifications, the therapist may gain a mental picture of the patient's personality, dynamics, and transference—what Greenson (1967) has called a "working model," which the therapist utilizes to anticipate developments in the treatment process and to formulate interpretations of intrapsychic conflict for the patient. By extrapolation, one can extend this process to observations of the therapy group itself and its "focal conflicts" (Whitaker and Lieberman, 1964).

Kohut concluded "that the continuous participation of the depth of the analyst's psyche is a *sine qua non* for the maintenance of the analytic process" (1977, p. 251). For Kohut, the so-called "neutral" mode of listening is too removed from the subject's experience of himself to reach the narcissistic patient at the level of his structural deficit. By adopting a "neutral" position, the therapist places himself "outside the psychic apparatus." He becomes a detached observer, experiencing himself as an *object* of transference rather than a participant who is strongly identified with the patient as *subject* in the here-and-now interaction (but not swayed by his psychopathology!). Further, the classical working model and its consequent interpretations distance the therapist even more by establishing a highly abstract level of inference regarding inner conflict. The patient may have to do considerable mental work to internalize these abstractions in a meaningful way, something which the narcissistic patient is unprepared for and unable to do and which he may experience as an attack on the self.

In contrast with technical neutrality, the central feature of Kohut's listening process, empathic introspection, is a variation, expansion, and deepening of the trial identification. This imposes special rigors on the therapist, who now must immerse himself fully in the subjective experience of the group members in order to grasp their "experience-near" sense of self and self-esteem as these fluctuate in the context of the ongoing group processes, archaic transferences, the therapist's countertransference, and the "empathic failures" that inevitably occur in and out of session.

The consistent, nonintrusive application of empathic introspection can produce the following yield:

1. The therapist can assess and allow the emergence of narcissistic or selfobject transferences (mirroring, idealizing, twinship, and merger), which represent revivals of developmentally phase-appropriate and legitimate needs of the self. These transference manifestations are the working material of Kohutian technique and need to be facilitated by the listening process.

2. The therapist can identify normal empathic failures in the patient's life and in the therapeutic interactions. These failures produce a reemergence of symptoms and states of narcissistic injury, fragmentation, and rage. By acknowledging these occurrences to the patient (or group) the process of maturing and integration ("transmuting internalization") of the self and its structures can be facilitated and potential psychic trauma and disruptions of the therapy process can be circumvented.

3. The therapist can become alert to subtle fluctuations in self cohesion that would otherwise escape notice. Therefore, he can address anxieties centered around fragmentation of the self, which might otherwise be misunderstood as a higher level intrapsychic conflict.

4. The therapist can detect small countertransference perturbations and prevent their escalation into counterresistances. A common form of counterresistance is to "attack" the mirror and idealizing transferences through premature interpretations, as they emerge, judging them to be both a failure of, and defense against, object-relatedness rather than a normal, phase-specific development. The empathic stance is sensitive to disruption and can serve as a subtle barometer of the treatment process.

Thus, the fundamental role of the group psychotherapist from a self psychological perspective is to maintain the listening process of empathic introspection in the face of individual, group-as-a-whole, and countertransferential pressures to do otherwise. The therapist thereby becomes an integral part of the (incomplete, deficient) self system of the members: a selfobject. He then interprets, primarily in the here-and-now, the state of the selves (individual and collective) of the members in terms of the experienced affects, emotions, states of fragmentation, cohesion, and self-esteem fluctuations. In this way, self cohesion is restored and strengthened.

If this process is maintained consistently—and it is especially difficult to do so in a group context where there are so many events going on simultaneously—the archaic selfobject transferences will emerge both individually and in the group process itself. The gradual resolution of these transferences, described so well by Kohut (1971) in *The Analysis of the Self*, results in an improvement in self cohesion and self-esteem of the membership through the "transmuting internalization" of narcissistic structures (both those of the therapist and other group members) and the establishment of ambitions and ideals that provide age-appropriate satisfactions for the narcissistic sector of the personality.

Carrying out this agenda in group therapy is indeed a complex task. To fulfill that requirement, it is helpful now to proceed to a step-by-step account of the therapist's role from the initial screening process to the session-by-session experience of a self psychological approach as the group struggles to form a cohesive unit and moves through its various stages of development. It has been frequently observed that "a therapist gets the kind of group he deserves," and one can expect that if a therapist changes his role definition, the group processes themselves will change as well.

SCREENING AND INITIATING THE SELF PSYCHOLOGICAL THERAPY GROUP

The powerful leadership role of the group therapist is exercised, albeit implicitly, from the very beginning in making the initial arrangements, choosing the type of group, selecting a cotherapist (if applicable), and then screening the patient population to assure proper group composition. Yalom (1975) and Rutan and Stone (1984) have provided excellent guidelines for these tasks, and the following is intended only as an addendum to their suggestions. The best criterion of all is clinical experience.

It is important to point out from the self psychology perspective how much actual power is initially invested in the therapists, no matter how much they may facilitate a democratic process subsequently. This power contributes to an initial idealizing transference in the membership that often is undetected and even exploited. The awareness and management of the therapists' own narcissistic strivings for power, control, praise, and self aggrandizement is critical at all times, but especially in the formation of a new group. For example, there is a tendency of some therapists to choose what have aptly been called "ego enhancers" for group members. Such individuals flatter and improve the self-esteem of the therapist by virtue of their achievements, attractiveness, capacity for insight, and so forth. Narcissistic personalities, with their tendency toward gradiosity and idealization, and their very real brilliance and accomplishment in some areas, initially come across as such ego enhancers. In short order, however, their tendency to treat the therapists and the group members as extensions of themselves can create a powerful sense of deflation and depletion in the therapist. It is impossible to imagine what an entire group of true narcissistic personalities would be like! Fortunately, the self psychological approach is suitable for a range of disturbances in the sense of self. A somewhat heterogeneous grouping, but one that excludes certain individuals who will not easily benefit from the empathic stance, is recommended.

Let us backtrack for a moment. The first two individuals to be selected for any group will often be a supervisor and a cotherapist. Supervisors of self psychology group therapy are still hard to find. However, many excellent group supervisors today are familiar with the work of Kohut and have treated narcissistic personality disorders with some success. Because of the qualitative differences between groups of neurotics and groups of borderline or narcissistic personalities, the supervisor must be comfortable in moving back and forth between oedipal and preoedipal levels and addressing the differences between such groups that occur in affect, ideation, transference, and group management. Whether a group event is primarily a manifestation of power and sexuality, or whether it is an example of a need for a selfobject which contains, holds, and mirrors is a subtle question, yet one of grave import.

Cotherapy (see Agazarian and Peters, 1981, pp. 257–264, for a discussion) can be very helpful in working with patients' narcissistic issues. The cotherapist arrangement assists in maintaining the boundaries of both therapist and group and in helping to tolerate the profoundly disturbing affects associated with narcissistic disturbances. The cotherapist relationship provides the opportunity for feedback, reality-testing, and for validation in the grueling and demanding work that is so often required in working with narcissistic patients, or with the narcissistic sectors of the personality.

The cotherapists should be able to stay differentiated from one another and yet possess a high degree of mutual empathy for each other. Thus, they will be both object and selfobject to one another. They also will need to become comfortable with the slow, painstaking work and limited goals that so often characterize the therapeutic efforts with these patients and with these types of groups.

One of the authors of this chapter had the fortunate experience of working with a cotherapist who was a nurse supervisor with extensive experience on trauma and critical care units. It is difficult to describe how valuable her compassion and sensitivity were in working with the fluctuations of self-esteem, fragmentation, and loss in the group. The feelings induced in working with loss of self cohesion are not unlike those of treating severe physical illness, which also tests self cohesion. The importance of the personal qualities of the cotherapists, and, in particular, their tolerance and their ability to care for their own and each other's narcissism cannot be underestimated. This should be openly discussed before convening the group, and the ability to help each other through countertransference vicissitudes carefully assessed.

Screening

Screening patients for group therapy based on self psychology needs to be done flexibly and with an emphasis on the interaction and early transference manifestations in the evaluation interview. The self psychology approach has been gradually extended from the narcissistic personality disorder per se, to the narcissistic character disorder (acting out, addictive, and impulsive types who show brief fragmentation of self and develop selfobject transferences), and, more recently, to some neurotics with narcissistic features, clinical depression, where the predominant cause of low self-esteem is not guilt, but a narcissistic deficiency and feelings of shame, as well as to certain higher functioning borderlines. Severe borderlines and patients with a psychotic core should be screened out of such groups, since the empathic stance can blur their already fragile ego boundaries. Highly manipulative and overaggressive character structures pose logistical problems for the group as a whole, and some assessment should be made regarding their potential ability to cooperate in the group. Sometimes, as they find tolerance for their grandiosity, such individuals will soften up and become less controlling. This is a good prognostic indicator.

The diagnostic *sine qua non* for membership in such a group is the presence of a disorder of the sense of self with fluctuations in self-esteem of a preoedipal origin but with simultaneous resilience—the capacity to reintegrate under benign and empathic conditions. Kohut cites hypochondriasis, brief fragmentation experiences, and the compensatory use of the environment for soothing and to restore self cohesion as symptoms and behavior pathonomic of narcissistic states.

One possible technique for assessing capacity to benefit from self psychology–based group therapy is to make a trial empathic interpretation during the screening interview. One can say something to the patient like "You must feel upset and at sea meeting a new person like myself and possibly a whole new group of people." A patient who reacts positively to such an intervention and feels understood probably will benefit from a self psychology group. Someone who is defensive or withdraws in response to such an intervention may not be able to benefit from an empathically based approach and may need greater differentiation and structure than the self psychology group would provide.

Patients who require more structure may later drop out of the group if this feature is not detected in the initial interview:

> A female patient who had previously benefited from a highly structured group quickly screened herself out of a self psychology–oriented group. Severely abused sexually and physically as a child, she relied on overly rigid boundaries to maintain self cohesion. She insisted that the group have a written set of rules with no flexibility. For example, she asked that members be prohibited from talking with each other after group. She showed intense anxiety throughout group sessions and left the group after two meetings, continuing in individual psychotherapy.

Another important guide to screening is the early presence of narcissistic transference manifestations, such as grandiosity. One patient, for example, who turned out to have a narcissistic personality disorder, sat in a rotating chair and swung it around, conversing animatedly as if he were on a television talk show! In addition, therapist countertransference may provide an early clue to a disorder of the sense of self in patients. A male patient with a long and unsuccessful treatment history led the therapist to feel completely disregarded while he (the patient) egocentrically, persistently, and grandiosely espoused an elaborate view of mental well-being which he obtained from a popular self help book. This view to which he clung with almost fanatical religiosity served him as a last ditch defense against overstimulation and negative intrusiveness of a mother (in the transference) who for the patient lacked any sense of appropriate social boundaries. This patient later disclosed fragmentation experiences too severe for him to benefit from an unstructured therapy group. An empathic stance in individual therapy did, however, help this patient.

In any event, groups are ultimately self-selecting. Nevertheless, it is important to realize that unresolved countertransference on the therapist's part can screen or extrude some individuals from group who might otherwise benefit. A therapist's inner pressures may create subtle biases against certain patients that render them unable to function effectively in the group when they might otherwise profit from the self psychological approach. For example, we learned of a case of a borderline alcoholic woman who was successfully treated over a period of ten years (!) using Kohut's method. Many therapists would not have sustained faith in her for that long a time period. Because of their ability to generate strong countertransferences, narcissistic individuals are very vulnerable both to being inappropriately elevated to high positions and also unfairly excluded from both social and therapy groups.

Selections for group should not be based too much on outward personality traits, but, rather, upon a careful assessment of structural development. Practically speaking, structure formation should have proceeded to the point where periods of loss of self cohesion are brief and reality testing is maintained, and the candidate should have a network of social relationships (which, however, will very likely lack depth and intimacy and may be tumultuous) and have sublimation resources (areas of potential fulfillment and creativity) to sustain him through the more difficult periods of the therapy. A major factor in deriving benefit from a self psychological group is the potential to form mirror and idealizing transferences. Sometimes, a trial period in the group or in individual therapy may be required to assess this factor.

Start-up

The start-up of the group follows the traditional guidelines for psychoanalytic group psychotherapy, but there may be subtle differences in the way that interventions are phrased and the way they are carried out. We instruct patients individually about the fee, the long-term commitment that is necessary, and the time and place of the group. In the first group session itself, the basic group rules are stated: no physical contact, putting feelings into words, minimal contact outside of group, and the rule of free association. How this rule is phrased seems quite important. Exhorting the members to "say everything that comes to mind" appears to invite a regressive and isolationistic set of norms for many patients today. It is perhaps better to ask the members to "share with the others about yourself, your feelings, and your difficulties, as freely as you can." The goal is to establish a non-threatening atmosphere that encourages interrelatedness rather than withdrawal. It does no harm for the therapists to be active, available, and provide simple, basic explanations of the therapy process at the outset. This availability and receptivity of the therapists will promote group interaction.

The narcissistic injuries implicit on entry into the group should be responded to with great attention and empathy. The shame and embarrassment of being an identified patient, the loss of specialness attendant upon being one among many, and feelings of exposure and vulnerability all contribute to an initial diminution of self-esteem. For example, two members of another therapy group that had terminated entered an ongoing therapy group. They formed a subgroup that distanced from and challenged the others, and vice versa. When the hurt involved in having an old and familiar group terminate and the difficulty of sharing their vulnerability with strangers were explored, the members integrated very well and the group was able to proceed. The therapist should be alert to nonverbal and verbal expressions of hurt related to being an "identified patient" and to entering a new group. One of the predominant affects in stranger groups is shame (Alonso and Rutan, 1988). This emotion needs to be explored from the outset to facilitate the proper group climate.

A much-discussed question these days is whether the therapist should address his remarks primarily to the individual members, to their interactions, or to the group as a whole (see Kibel and Stein, 1981). Systems-theoretical issues are involved here, but the following example will make the point more simply:

Convening an outpatient group of young adult substance abusers, the therapist decided to use Bion's group-as-a-whole approach. The rationale for this decision was to explore the intense collusive resistances of such patients before proceeding to address individual pathology. The members came to the first session, and the therapist was silent. The group as a whole began to introduce themselves to each other and explore what the therapy task was, although in a somewhat "as if" manner. The therapist commented that the group seemed to be struggling with its task but underneath were anxious and needy. This process of long periods of observation followed by group-level interpretations went on for three sessions. Someone finally volunteered, "Who is this 'group' he is talking about anyway?" The members said they felt they weren't getting anywhere and asked the therapist to address themselves and their problems directly.

The reason that such a group-as-a-whole approach was premature was not because there weren't collusive resistances—there indeed were. Rather, the interventions were too "experience-distant," failed to provide adequate mirroring, and induced excessive amounts of anxiety. The members felt ignored and abandoned.

An excellent guide for the self psychological group is to address that group system which is most "experience-near," which is phenomenologically and affectively predominant at the time. If an individual member is preoccupying the group, he should be spoken to and about: It is likely that he is expressing something for the entire group. If a particular interpersonal relationship in the group is disturbing everyone, work with that relationship. If the group has a "we" feeling and is discussing group norms and procedures, speak to the group qua group. For this population, one needs to be less a detached consultant and more a participant-observer. In any event, as Kissen (1980) has suggested, interventions made in one system will carry over into the others by virtue of the principle of systems isomorphisms.

If these basic principles are followed, the therapist should be well on the way to establishing a group climate suited for the emergence of the selfobject transferences and the resolution of self pathology in the group context.

THE MANAGEMENT OF SELFOBJECT TRANSFERENCE, NARCISSISTIC INJURY, AND RAGE

The basic treatment strategy of Kohutian individual psychotherapy is to allow the emergence of narcissistic selfobject transference (mirroring, idealization, twinship, and merger) in an atmosphere of empathy, being attuned to the members' developmental needs, and with

special attention to narcissistic hurts and vulnerabilities. These transferences, often full blown, are then gradually resolved through deep
interpretation *at the level of the actual self deficit.* This process facilitates
the development of the self through transmuting internalizations,
that is, the introjection of the empathic and soothing qualities of the
therapist. As a result, narcissism moves "upwards" from primitive
grandiosity and idealization into their sublimated forms—ambitions
and ideals.

The two narcissistic structures identified by Kohut are (1) the grandiose self and (2) the idealized parent imago. These structures are
called "archaic, transitional selfobjects" and emerge as a consequence
of the vicissitudes of early parental response, empathy, and mirroring.
They are required for maintenance of narcissistic homeostasis. Kohut
(1971, p. 27) characterized these configurations quite simply: In the
grandiose self the central meaning is "I am perfect"; for the idealized
parent imago, it is "You are perfect, but I am part of you." Out of
these two structures arise the basic transference configurations and
dynamics.

The transference that emerges from the grandiose self is the *mirror
transference,* so named because the therapist and group members serve
the patient as a mirror that confirms the existence of the self. As
Kohut (1971) phrases it, "the analyst is experienced as an extension
of the grandiose self and he is referred to only insofar as he has
become the carrier of the grandiosity and exhibitionism of the analysand's grandiose self and of the conflicts, tensions, and defense which
are elicited by these manifestations of the activated narcissistic structure" (p. 114).

Two subtle variations of the mirror transference which may appear
in some patients and group formations are the so-called "merger," a
most primitive transference in which the therapist and group members are treated as non-separate aspects of the self. Typical countertransference reactions in response to the merger transference are
feelings of being non-separate or fused, or conversely a feeling of
rebellion against what may seem like domination and control over the
therapist's own self.

A second variation of mirror transference is what has been termed
variously the "alter ego" or "twinship" transference. In this mode, the
patient overly regards others as similar to him (denies differences) or
feels that specific features are the same, as if the other were his or
her identical twin. The therapists and members may react to such
comparisons with great surprise and confusion or even a feeling that
their individuality and identity are being threatened.

The full mirror transference emerges from the grandiose self which
in turn is (or ought to have been) based on the child's experience of

being the "gleam in the mother's eye," i.e., her loving, attuned, empathic ministrations, reverie, and play. The other's purpose is to "confirm the child's self-esteem" (Kohut, 1971, p. 116). The goal of the treatment, in regards to the transferences associated with the grandiose self, is the transformation of structure so that narcissism will be tamed and energies formerly bound to "archaic goals are freed and become available to the mature personality" (Kohut, 1971, p. 116).

The "idealized parent imago" is a structure that produces the *idealizing transference*. In this situation the patient attempts to preserve the infantile experience by "giving it over to a narcissistically experienced omnipotent and perfect self-object" (Kohut, 1971, p. 105). The goal of this transference is to keep the other (therapist or group member) in the condition of perfection. The countertransference reaction is frequently a rejection of the glowing praise, love, and attention that one receives in such a state. The taming of this transference leads to the establishment of healthy ideals.

In both of these basic forms of the transference the therapeutic stance remains the same: consistent empathy, the exploration of the sense of self (fragmented or cohesive), and attunement to prevailing affects, especially the hurt, deflation, and rage characteristic of these patients. This stance leads to transmuting internalizations (the establishment of "accessible introjects") and the transformation of the self.

In the group therapy context, it is unlikely that the full expression of the narcissistic transferences is either desirable or resolvable. Instead, somewhat more limited goals are appropriate. As Foulkes and Anthony (1973, pp. 150–151) have argued, the group is a mirror of the self to begin with, so aspects of mirroring and idealization will appear everywhere in the group matrix. Consistent work with these multiple manifestations can achieve considerable gains, although it is unlikely that a full structural cure can be accomplished. Kohut proposed that acceptable limited reconstructive therapy aims are to enable the patient to have a sustaining selfobject matrix in his social life and to achieve realistic ambitions and ideals, and these goals do seem achievable in the group context.

Group regression (Ashbach and Schermer, 1987, pp. 172–173) is a natural facilitator of selfobject transference. Narcissistic impulses inevitably surface in groups. A simple example is the desire to entertain and be applauded. Group roles will reflect and focus this impulse toward grandiosity and idealization: The group clown, the maternal and protective patient, the resident intellectual, the power-driver roles are all cathected with narcissistic libido. The scapegoat is an interesting role vis-à-vis narcissism. Although largely the result of "all bad" projective identifications into a particularly vulnerable member, it can also derive some of its impetus from a masochistic narcissism in that person. For example, one patient became scapegoated because he made excessive demands for attention and also voiced enormous needs for nurturing and feeding, which the others had suppressed. In addition, he recently had a series of successes in life after a long history of failures; preening his success provocatively stimulated destructive envy in other members as well. Wong (1979) points out how important it is to prevent such a member from being extruded from the group.

It is important to realize (see Agazarian and Peters, 1981, pp. 104–108) that the evolution of roles in the therapy group has as much to do with group-as-a-whole dynamics and the functions these roles serve for the group as they do with individual needs, behaviors, and valences. The object relations explanation of role induction would focus on mutual projective identifications that become "contained" by particularly vulnerable individuals. Such an explanation is by no means incompatible with the self psychology viewpoint. However, the latter would emphasize as a key factor in role development the achievement of narcissistic homeostasis or self cohesion as the group forces press toward increasing vulnerability of the self. This could occur, as mentioned earlier, as a result of the loss of specialness and entitlement in the "one among many" group situation. It might also be triggered by situations such as a change in the therapist's expectations of the members or the departure of a group member, which would alter the "mirror" effect of the group matrix. One can, for example, observe that as the members' self-esteem is empathized on a more realistic basis, the role requirements become more appropriate and less reflective of splitting and other narcissistic defenses.

As the therapy group regresses, the collective ego ideal of the members is projected into the therapist and the group as a whole. The members thus increasingly form mirror and merger transferences to each other: They see themselves as similar and bonded in magical and merged ways. This partial fusion of selves forms what might be termed a narcissistic or "selfobject matrix" in which the group as a whole has become a selfobject, which can be addressed as a group development with individual ramifications. The group therapist must attend to the self of each of the members, but likewise must maintain an empathic sensitivity to the "self" that the group has become.

Therapy work within the selfobject transference matrix can be explained best by examples. First, an instance will be given from a training group. In the actual group, the event was initially regarded didactically from the standpoint of primitive object relations, to suggest how the same process may be viewed from a Kohutian standpoint:

In a staff training group in a teaching hospital, the group developed a mild delusion that the video technician was giving the tapes of the group to the head of the Psychiatry Department, who would use it as a basis for grades and residency appointments. The group considered what it could do to prevent this feared eventuality, but when reality testing was encouraged by the trainer, the members recalled their confidentiality agreement and recognized the emotional source of their distorted belief.

The free associations of the members suggested that the persecutory phantasy was a regressive attempt to fend off the awareness that the group was to terminate shortly. As a defense, the trainer became overly idealized ("all good") and the badness was projected into the video technician and the institutional context. That is, to avoid feelings of loss and separation, the members projected an attack by significant authority figures whom they regarded as plotting against them. Working through the separation feelings related to termination of the group facilitated the integration of the "good" and "bad" part-objects. A mourning process ensued, leading to a restoration of accurate perceptions of the situation and the persons involved. The brief paranoid delusion is an instance of Bion's fight/flight assumption and of the psychotic-like anxieties which constitute an aspect of primitive group culture [Ashbach and Schermer, 1987, pp. 39–40].

In this object relations depiction, undoubtedly valid, the members were coping with an issue of separation and loss through a temporary group regression. The narcissistic component, which one would want to look for if one were treating a group of patients with self disorders, would postulate that the leader had "failed" as an idealized and empathizing figure. The resultant narcissistic injury defended against in the group by a fantastic attribution of power to the video technician and department chairperson. The paranoia was a reflection of temporary fragmentation of the selves of at least some members. In a self psychological approach, the leader could manage this fragmentation by empathizing with the members regarding their feelings of insignificance and shame as they approached a point of change in their lives. He would interpret that they also felt disappointed in him and the way he conducted the group. He would explore how they were struggling with and building self-esteem in the group and how that process may have become sidetracked or damaged. That is, he would address his interpretations to their core problem of the security and cohesion of the self. Gradually, the idealizations would become less defensive and more realistic.

This example illustrates how narcissism and object relations are not mutually exclusive categories. Rather, they are two separate but interrelated tracks which are copresent at all times (Grotstein, 1982).

The decision to address the narcissism derives from the clinical judgment that key deficits in the members in that sector of the personality have been activated and are available to be worked with.

The following example illustrates some of the session-by-session work that will come up as selfobject transference and narcissistic injury emerge in group psychotherapy.

> A male therapist replaced a female one in a long-term therapy group that had met for ten months in an outpatient clinic setting. The group had developed a strong attachment to and idealization of the woman therapist, as well as a sense of group cohesion and identity. Continuity was maintained by the outgoing and the new therapists conjointly being present for several sessions and also by retaining a student intern cotherapist who had been with the group for several months.
>
> When the female therapist departed, the group experienced a painful deflation and demoralization. She was irreplaceable, they felt. Indeed, she was exceptionally nurturing and supportive, and this needed to be acknowledged as a group reality. Further, the members' feeling that they could not survive without her meant that she had become a selfobject. Two of the female members then began to act out in relationships: One was masochistically abused, and the other struggled ambivalently with sexual attraction versus a need for security and warmth. A homosexual member whose father was cold and overdisciplining became angry with the new therapist and said in a joking way, "You're probably a Freudian and think that I'm reacting as if you're my father!" The sarcastic humor perhaps indicated that this was not the central issue, but, rather, that the patient felt misunderstood by the new therapist and also felt the loss of a protective maternal figure.
>
> For several weeks, *the narcissistic injury attendant on the loss of the female therapist was explored almost exclusively.* The group at first masked most of their feelings and did therapy in a "play pretend" fashion. Gradually they began to share how they felt rejected when she left, how they acted out in overstimulating ways outside the group, and how deficient they were in self-esteem, so that whatever modicum of self love they felt always seemed to derive from an outside source: a parent, therapist, lover, and so on. Too often this contemporary source failed them, as had happened in childhood. Only after weeks of consistent exploration of these reactions to narcissistic wounds (and a continual testing of the new therapist) did the group affect stabilize and the acting out decline. For a period of time subsequent to that, the members discussed and worked through pathological interpersonal relations in their daily lives, with considerable gains in insight and autonomy.

THE THERAPIST'S ROLE IN GROUP DEVELOPMENT

Therapy groups do not remain constant, but undergo progressive development that bring about and reflect changes in group structures, communication systems, experiences of intimacy, and roles. Characteristic patterns of group behavior and ideation–affect are termed group phases. The phasic movements of groups has received extensive attention in the literature (see, for example, Ashbach and Schermer, 1987, Chapter 9, for an overview). Theories of group phases and development exist within classical, object relations, and group-dynamic perspectives. We are not aware that any have been proposed following Kohut's theory. However, it is evident that narcissism has an enormous impact on group identifications, role development, power struggles, boundary phenomena, and leadership issues.

At each point in the growth and consolidation of the therapy group, the therapist's task changes, and he needs to be alert to individual and group events particular to a given phase. In actual practice, these phases are not precisely sequential but shift back and forth according to particular group conditions. For example, when a new member enters, the group may revert to patterns characteristic of early group formation.

In what follows, a process of group phase development is hypothesized, viewed in a selective way from the point of view of narcissism and selfobject transference, and presented as a heuristic device for the group therapist. Each phase is described by predominant narcissistic features, and the therapist's role and task are resolving these features.

The dynamic process, key issues, and therapist role in each of the group phases that we have identified are summarized in Table 1 (see pp. 305–307).

Phase I: Orientation

In Phase I, the group begins and the basic rules are stated and discussed. Personal therapy goals may be articulated by the membership. Initial observations can be made about each member's entry into group, intimations of special difficulties that may arise later, and how the therapists themselves are responding to the members and the group as a whole.

Each person comes into a group with a particular "valence" for a group culture or mentality, i.e., his or her special role and behavior pattern in each group formation. Entry into group or the commencement of a group are opportune times to note such valence patterns. For example, a narcissistically grandiose individual would flourish in a group culture which acknowledged his "extraordinary qualities" but feel highly anxious in a culture which failed to acknowledge his narcissism. A narcissistically "wounded" person would seek a climate, such as basic assumption dependency, in which hurts and vulnerabilities could be acknowledged.

Self psychology would view member valences from the standpoint of each member seeking roles which restore his or her self cohesion and self-esteem. Initially, those roles are adopted which defensively mask narcissistic injury and vulnerability, or those which overinflate the grandiose self, or those which provide immediate relief. The therapist can note how each member adopts a group role as a defensive cover for slights and injuries to the self.

"Narcissistic injury" is experienced subjectively in its corresponding affect of *shame,* which pervades the lives of narcissistic personalities. Therefore, the observation of shame responses in the group provides a good early indicator of narcissistic vulnerability in the "here and now" of the group interaction. Initially, the therapist must articulate the underlying narcissistic concerns of the individuals, for part of their pathology is that they lack the means to do so themselves. "You must fear that the group will reject or abandon you"; "You must have felt that Joe's criticism took away something from you" are interpretations which strive to address the members' inarticulate fears and soft spots.

Shame and other intense group experiences are contained largely by virtue of what Winnicott (1960) called "holding," the therapist's and group's management and modulation of feeling states, akin to the way the mother "holds" the baby in a stable setting. The holding environment of empathy and containment generates a group atmosphere that contributes to a strong therapeutic alliance early in group development.

It is useful in this phase to reframe member concerns and goals from a self psychology perspective as it relates to patient goals and the intent of the treatment. For instance, it could be pointed out that a member's desire to succeed in a business venture represents an effort to fulfill a long-standing ambition that may have been frustrated and that other members may similarly have felt thwarted or perhaps empty and depleted in their work life. The aim of such interventions is to bring the narcissistic component into focus for the membership. Members should be given a "feeling vocabulary" (words for expressing emotions) and should be encouraged to make "I statements," or else they will want to externalize and avoid psychic pain. They need to begin to develop affect tolerance.

Phase II: Group Regression

Over time, in Phase II, the members will, ideally, regress safely to points of narcissistic fixation or derivatives thereof. The therapist must help manage and contain the level and intensity of the regression.

> One member, G., of a therapy group signaled that she and the group had arrived at an early plateau of narcissistic deficit by sharing a fantasy that she was a newborn baby and her parents were watching her through an observation window. Her associations suggested that she was feeling distanced from the therapists in much the same way as her parents were not empathically in tune with her. The sterility of the maternity ward and the separation of the observation window symbolized this empathic failure. The members resonated with this fantasy by sharing experiences in their current lives where they were misunderstood or ignored by people they were attracted to or idealized. They also recognized their collective wish for rebirth with idealized parent surrogates—the therapists.

Group regression is a critical way station. Symptoms may be exacerbated or occur in new forms. Resistances to "regression in service of ego" may prevent the group from developing a mutual transference and from reexperiencing early trauma in the reparative context of the group. The role of the therapist is to manage and guide the regression and to establish a climate in which the members can experience, observe, and reflect upon narcissistic concerns. It is most important to monitor countertransference at this time, since the difficulties the therapist experiences with narcissism may limit the degree to which the members can permit such experiences to be revived in themselves. *The therapist strives to be in a position to allow narcissistic expressions and to minimize his intrusion into the group.* It is important to monitor how both individual resistances and group demands (which in some ways imply a sacrifice of personal narcissism to the aims of the group) inadvertently serve as resistances and obstacles to the development of grandiose and idealizing manifestations, which in effect say, "I'm important, the group isn't." Helping the group to establish a healthy balance between contributing to group life (object relations) and basking in mirroring (narcissism) is in itself a desirable therapeutic aim and objective. The struggle between narcissistic mirroring and true investment in others is but another dimension of what is known as the "fusion-individuation dilemma" (Gibbard, 1974) in group life, the dialectic between individual needs and those of the group, between oneness and separateness.

Phase III: Establishment of Selfobject Transference

To treat narcissistic pathology at a deep level, it is important in Phase III to establish stable narcissistic transference. The instrument that facilitates such transference is therapist empathy, so the role of the therapist during this phase, which constitutes the longest, most pervasive stage of the group, is to immerse himself empathically in the selves of the members through the key process of vicarious introspection (see pp. 283–285).

The basic forms of selfobject transference, namely mirror, merger, twinship, and idealizing transference, have been discussed and described earlier (Kohut, 1971). Here, it is important to note that if phases I and II have been properly negotiated, the members will have sufficient sense of trust and safety to risk expressions of the selfobject transference. Such expressions may range from an individual member who is typically shy becoming very verbose and demonstrative, to the entire group becoming somewhat enamored of itself, e.g., an upsurge of enthusiasm for its curative powers or ability to provide support. Or, in what has sometimes been called a "utopian group" formation (Hartman and Gibbard, 1974), the group seeks its own perfection and to rid itself of negative influences. Or, group members may show unusual amounts of "voyeuristic" and "exhibitionistic" expressions, "exposing" their hurts, seeking to know more and more about the therapists.

As such narcissistic selfobject transferences begin to develop in their various forms and manifestations, the most difficult part of the therapist's role begins, and will continue throughout the treatment process: *sustained empathy.* This means that to properly nurture and modulate the selfobject transferences, the therapist must stay in an empathic stance on a consistent basis, and immediately return to it when it has been ruptured. This process of continually experiencing the phenomenological field of the group members through vicarious introspection is what, for Kohut, is the chief curative factor in the treatment of the narcissistic personality disorder. It is most important not to judge nor to impose a more "objective" understanding on that of the subjective self of each member. This process will lead to the full unfolding of the emotional states related to the pathological splitting characteristic of narcissistic personality.

Phase IV: Intensification of Narcissistic Affects

Through the development of selfobject (mirror, idealizing, twinship, and merger) transferences in the group, the patients' proneness to narcissistic injury is intensified in Phase IV. The affects in response to such "slights" are shame, vulnerability, and rage. Alonso and Rutan (1988) have dealt extensively with the management of these affects, especially shame, in therapy groups. The therapist must understand and contain yet remain sharply differentiated from these emotional states. *He must work consistently to alleviate their pathological consequences and also provide a role model of someone who can experience narcissistic needs and vulnerability without feeling unduly ashamed, angry, or fragmented.* (The therapist does this through his supervision process; maintaining good, solid personal boundaries; and gratifying his own *healthy* narcissism. It cannot be overestimated how much the *group* benefits from the healthy narcissistic balance of the therapist!) The resolution of these affects by mitigating the narcissistic injury that underlies them is a major gain of the therapeutic process and initiates the resolution of the selfobject transference.

Phase IV is a critical period, filled as it is with subgroup splits, hostility, and negative projective identifications. With the surfacing of aggression in the group, the need to minimize acting out is imperative. Appropriate limit setting in this context will increase rather than decrease the group's self-esteem as they experience their aggression as safely contained. Scapegoating is common during this phase, as is subgrouping into opposing camps and excessive contact outside of group. Bennis and Shepard (1956) pointed out the roles of the dependent and counterdependent members in this phase of group development. Dependents are often the members with narcissistic deficits manifested in such traits as shyness, overidealization, shame propensity, and inhibition of spontaneity and aspirations. Counterdependents are frequently members who are grandiose, extroverted, controlling, and dominating. *It is helpful in resolving the "vertical split" of narcissism (the split between the grandiose self and the depleted, empty self) to show the dependents and counterdependents how each possesses a part of the personality which the other lacks or defends, and that if they can integrate these elements, they will achieve a state of greater wholeness.*

Phase V: Reemergence of "Horizontal" Split-off States of Neediness

One of Kohut's great clinical contributions has been to show that underneath the narcissist's alternation between grandiosity and depletion are states of intense neediness that had been profoundly blocked by an "empathic wall" (Nathanson, 1987, p. 43). Tolerance of these need states and learning to meet these needs through interpersonal relations and intimacy are the great struggles of the narcissistic personality. The goal may not always be fully achieved, and Kohut cautions therapists against unrealistic expectations in that regard. However, it is a well-known therapeutic function of groups to facilitate the working through of issues of deeper internal needs in a social context (Foulkes and Anthony, 1973).

The "horizontally split off" and repressed underbelly of narcissistic disorders is characterized by its initial greediness and insatiability (until it is integrated with the main body of the personality). It is as if the child had learned to function (obtain nurturing and mirroring) in an "as if" manner, with no real meeting of needs. Grotstein (1991) has compared this portion of the personality to a "black hole," a void which sucks up everything in its path. Clearly, the initial reexperience of the "horizontally" split off part of the self can be quite intimidating! Its impact must be modulated by the therapist and the group so that it can be gradually assimilated as a human experience. A good beginning is made when the experience is given form and put into words and images. Some common ones from therapy groups include: "I feel a big, gaping hole, an emptiness inside"; "I feel as if I want everything all at once"; "I desperately need something from the group right now, but I don't know what it is."

The tolerance for narcissistic selfishness and greed is important in resolving these dilemmas.

> R. had all her life cared for others in a way that made her appear like Cinderella. First and forever it was her mother, whom she said always put her down and made her feel inferior, whom she took care of. Then it was her husband, who was totally unresponsive to her, and then her children. In group, she immediately became the rescuer, denying that she had any needs and, indeed, serving the others very well.
>
> The group gradually brought to her attention how her self-sacrificing role got in the way of her self-fulfillment. They were surprised that their attempt to help her met with anger and refusal rather than acceptance. It proved painful and difficult for her to acknowledge the profound state of deprivation that had caused her to overeat, stay overdependent on her mother, and exist in a state of chronic denial regarding the extent to which her life was impaired by her need to rescue others.

The emotional pain of coming into contact with intense need states that have been split-off and repressed is extremely difficult for patients to deal with. The support of group members and the ability of the therapists to manage these needs are in themselves of great importance in successfully working through this phase of group therapy.

Phase VI: Transmuting Internalization and Integration

As the membership becomes aware of the split-off elements of their personality, and with the healing and supportive context of the empathic selfobject matrix, the development of higher level narcissistic structures comes about through a gradual incorporation of these split-off features into the main body of the personality. Kohut's (1977) term "transmuting internalization" (p. 4) emphasizes the use of the therapist's empathy to build inner "microstructures" that allow for narcissistic satisfactions at a mature level of adult functioning (such as ambitions and ideals) and with lessened propensity toward acting-out and fragmentation.

An important role of the therapist during this Phase VI is to "make connections"—to bring together individual and collective memories and experiences into an interwoven fabric that shows members the totality of their group experience and their individual life trajectories. The therapist will find out how alert he has been to the group process and dialogue by how much he can bring together, sort out, and connect for purposes of integration.

The process of transmuting internalization is akin to what is traditionally called working-through. It is a learning process in which new awareness of connections and new responses are "practiced" in numerous situations as if to strengthen the new neural and mental/emotional connections so that they may form a reliable pattern of living. Daily life experiences form an "adaptive context" (Langs, 1976a) that is especially useful in consolidating the gains that heretofore have been internal to the group. This ongoing application of therapy to daily life is often surprisingly neglected in treatment. This omission constitutes a form of overprotection from the vicissitudes of life. Many patients, for example, who have had extraordinary "peak" experiences in a therapeutic community where they find supportive and caring therapy sometimes may suffer upon discharge from feelings of frustration and anger that the "real world" does not always afford such love and support.

Phase VII: Termination, Oedipal Manifestations, and Fulfillment of Ambitions and Ideals

Kohut emphasized two criteria for a successful outcome of treatment of the narcissistic sector. In Phase VII, these may become evident for some patients in the group therapy context, and are suitable indicators that the therapy task has been completed and the patient is now able to continue to grow without therapy.

First of all, Kohut (1977) saw in his patients the emergence of a new and "joyful Oedipal," one which is relatively uncontaminated by either neurotic conflict or self pathology. It is as though the patient finds contemporary parent surrogates, especially the therapist, with whom to live out healthy exhibitionistic and voyeuristic impulses of the oedipal phase in the context of empathy, admiration, and delight, which had previously been unavailable to them, as the following case illustrates.

> H., a female in outpatient group and individual therapy, after years of unsuccessful treatment (and during which she had become dependent on drugs, been ineffectual in her work life, and had heterosexual and homosexual relationships of a superficial nature) was finally able to establish an idealizing selfobject transference to a therapist who most particularly replaced her beloved father, whom she lost to a progressive and deteriorative disease when she was in her mid-teens.
> Therapeutic success was signaled when she became engaged to an adequate and caring man who gave her a profound sense of belonging and security. The therapist in turn became a maternal figure to whom she reconciled herself as she formed this new relationship. She formed a benign triangular relationship in which she could finally "bask" in admiration and pleasure.

A concomitant of a "joyful Oedipal" is the consolidation of ambitions and ideals, which reflect the development of higher level self structures.

> The same patient, H., at around the same time, showed a resurgence of healthy narcissism in which she sang, took ballet lessons, and performed in theater, delighting in her own spontaneity, creativity, and personality. At the same time she started in a new career in which she was successful, and she became devoted to spiritual values that had been imparted to her by her parents but which she had previously found unfulfilling.

Narcissistic personalities typically show a difficulty incorporating and including a third party (symbolically, the father) in their object relations, preferring or demanding exclusivity in their relationships with others. An indication that the group process has had a transformative effect on these types is their increased ability to allow and even benefit from triangular object relations such as the mother/father/infant triad, what Sonne (1991) has termed "triadic transference." Sonne points out that the ability to establish such triadic transferences leads to the development of what he calls a "triadic self," a self which is able to internalize complex object relations.

It is very important that patients establish outside of group a satisfactory interpersonal world in which they can fulfill their ambitions, ideals, and creativity. An often neglected aspect of the therapist's role is to appraise this factor in conjunction with patients and to help them work out a successful transition to life without therapy. It is also true that some patients will not achieve a level of integration in which they can fully negotiate this transition, and it is no shame if such individuals continue to use psychotherapy as a support system and selfobject matrix over an extended time frame.

As some members depart the group, their respective missions accomplished in varying ways and degrees the sense of separation and loss is naturally heightened. Members who have only recently begun therapy may experience such losses as traumatic and have a real need for extra support from therapist and group (without such support, there is a danger they will revert to pathological acting out). More advanced members may be able to work out their grief reactions at deeper levels and grow in their capacity to accept both intimacy and aloneness. In a certain sense, the narcissist has never known in-depth attachment, always having denied its existence or experienced loss as total abandonment, and these experiences of loss, familiar to most people, may be entirely new and hard to manage for them.

TABLE 1
Group Phases and the Therapist's Role from a Self Psychology Perspective

Phase	Dynamic Process	Key Issues	Therapist Role
I	Orientation	Entry into group Shame, vulnerability Verbalizing feelings Treatment alliance	Observe entry into group and member "valences" Establish ground rules and "holding" environment Encourage "I" statements Articulate narcissistic concerns
II	Group Regression	Building individual and group tolerance for regression Fusion–individuation dilemma Narcissism emerges at group level	Provide a safe context for regression Monitor countertransference Minimize intrusiveness Maximize group cohesion

TABLE 1 (continued)

Phase	Dynamic Process	Key Issues	Therapist Role
III	Establishment of Selfobject Transference	Early manifestations of selfobject transference Denial of differences, limitations "Utopian" group phase "Exhibitionistic" and "voyeuristic" expressions	Maintain sustained empathy Explore narcissistic "slights" as they occur in the group context
IV	Intensification of Narcissistic Affects	Narcissistic injury Shame, vulnerability Narcissistic rage, hostility Scapegoating, polarization, negative intermember projective identifications Dependent/counterdependent role formation	Continue empathy Maintain own boundaries and healthy narcissism Full working through of intense affect states Minimize acting-out
V	Reemergence of "Horizontal" Split-off States of Neediness	Fall of the empathic wall Articulation of needs for closeness, nurturance, "filling the void" Primitive greed, envy The "black hole" phenomena Facilitate self-regulation of need states	Build affect tolerance in the group Reinforce intimacy and awareness of deeper needs
VI	Transmuting Internalization and Integration	Resolution of splitting through structure building "New beginning" Awareness of ambitions and ideals	Make connections among memories and experiences Encourage practicing new behaviors

TABLE 1 (continued)

Phase	Dynamic Process	Key Issues	Therapist Role
VII	Termination, Oedipal Manifestations, and Fulfillment of Ambitions and Ideals	Triangular familial object relations Coping with separation and loss Life planning of ambitions and ideals	Enjoy and accept the members' joyful, intimate, and creative expressions Work-through separation and establish member goals and plans

COUNTERTRANSFERENCE, SELF-DISCLOSURE, AND COTHERAPY ISSUES

The therapist (and cotherapist, when present) is a member of any number of groups (e.g., family, friendships, professional organizations, institutions), and he forms an interface between them and his therapy group. He also has a world of inner objects that affect his conscious and unconscious reactions to the group members. Therefore, his behavior in group is influenced by his selfobjects, his current interpersonal and group relations, and the therapy group itself. How these object and selfobject relations affect his unconscious responses to the group constitutes his countertransference and, in the broadened "totalistic" definition of that term today (Kernberg, 1975), includes a range of reactions that would be regarded not just as conflictual, but highly informative, about patients and group.

Since more is known now about how profoundly the therapist's countertransference affects the therapy process (cf. Langs, 1976a,b), the question of when and how he should openly acknowledge his inner thoughts and feelings, his clinical errors (once recognized), and his reactions to patients becomes increasingly important. There was a time when the psychoanalytic group therapist was opaque, a "pure" transference screen, disclosing as little about himself as possible. That is a stance that is being challenged in psychoanalysis today. In addition, if there is more than one therapist, they form a subgroup, and their relationship plays a crucial part in therapy outcomes.

In the "great debate" of the seventies between Kohut and Kernberg regarding narcissism, the two were in agreement on at least one matter: that the concept of countertransference should be expanded to include the sum total of the therapist's reactions to the patient (and group). The important point is that if the therapist can sort out his own inner conflicts from the component of his reactions evoked by the patient, countertransference becomes an instrument through which he can learn much about the patient. A further consideration is that, with borderline and narcissistic disorders, the countertransference can be a more subtle indicator of dynamics, and especially of transference, than the patient's verbal productions as such.

Regarding the conflictual aspect of countertransference, Chessick (1985) concisely summarizes the way in which unresolved narcissism in the therapist disrupts empathy:

> On a clinical basis, it is the anxiety of the individual therapist, so often disguised and unrecognized which interferes with empathy most of all. . . . As Kohut (1971) pointed out, an especially great barrier to empathy is formed by unanalyzed narcissism in the therapist, since the tendency to experience others as selfobjects precludes the recognition of their individual personalities and points of view [p. 300].

Some basic guidelines for the group therapist's self-examination of issues of narcissism include the following:

1. his management of his own shame and vulnerability in the group situations;
2. his ability to take pleasure in his own and the members' selves and accomplishments;
3. his tolerance for periods of nongratification of his narcissism by the group;
4. his ability to work appropriately at the level of the members' pathology rather than to treat them at a higher or lower level; and
5. his tolerance for a wide range of affect expression in the group.

In group therapy work with self disorders, considerable "role strain" is produced by countertransferential pressures that stem from the patient's narcissism and that are an integral part of the therapy process. The following case is an example of an overt situation of this kind.

> A counselor trainee interned as cotherapist in a group of substance abusers. One of the patients, a grandiose, manipulative, and seductive male, made some remarks about how attractive and expensive her jewelry looked. The counselor experienced and properly contained her anxiety until after the group, when she approached her supervisor to

discuss the matter. Her initial reaction was a fear of robbery and sexual assault. Pursuing the problem further, however, showed that the group had reacted to the nurturing "selfobject" qualities of the counselor, her empathy. The counselor was then able to return to group next session and continue her empathic stance, while at the same time attending to the sexual and aggressive component of the group's behavior. A potential polarization of therapist and group was thus obviated [Adapted from Ashbach and Schermer, 1987, p. 251].

Feelings of being manipulated and controlled are more likely to be evoked by character-disordered patients who act out than by the narcissistic transference as such. The most common (and sometimes chronic) therapist response to the latter is a sense of being treated as if one doesn't exist or exists only for the patient's sake. The group members may share this feeling with the therapist, as in the following case.

> J., a female member of an outpatient group of young adults which met once weekly, always seemed to shut people out. She ignored the therapists and treated them as if they weren't there, not responding to their interpretations, avoiding eye contact, and consistently appearing annoyed with them. She tried to make the group leaderless, and at times succeeded in doing so. At those moments the whole group would work in disregard of the therapists, whose subjective reaction went from initial bemusement to exasperation.
>
> As the group developed, J., who had been stifled in her development by a mother whom she perceived as cold and paradoxically overintrusive, became more and more grandiose, acting like a prima donna, as if she were the therapist. (This is a prime example of a primitive mirror transference.) The group confronted her about her dominance, producing a stalemate that induced manifest anxiety bordering on panic in the group. Around this time, a new female group member, P., was brought in. P. was an intensely feeling and vulnerable type with hysterical character structure. A dyadic relationship soon developed between P. and J. with mutual projective identifications and replays of their relationships with their respective mothers. The level of anxiety was raised to a fever pitch and P. had to leave the room at one point to compose herself.
>
> It was only at this point of intense anxiety that the therapists were allowed to intervene and participate again. They worked as a team to bring out the lack of empathy and the feelings of abandonment that both patients had experienced from their mothers, the narcissistic rage evoked in J., and the fragmentation or "feeling of falling apart" experienced by P. The group was then able to continue satisfactorily, and the therapists felt great relief that they were no longer excluded from the group. If they had not carefully monitored and discussed their feeling

of being ignored, they might have acted out by obtruding themselves insistently into the group, thus perpetuating the stalemate and preventing J.'s grandiosity from evolving (admittedly at great risk to P.!). It proved important to point out the scapegoating element to the group, in which first the therapists and then P. were excluded and attacked. It was also valuable to show how everyone in the group shared in J.'s grandiosity and underlying suffering and lack of maternal empathy.

A variety of intense affects inevitably will be evoked in therapists working with the narcissistic sector of the personality and the full range of selfobject transferences. Importantly, as above, these feelings in both patients and therapists are sexually and aggressively tinged, and it is important to distinguish between the oedipal component, the preoedipal splitting of good and bad objects, the narcissistic deficit and injury in the transference, and the resultant countertransference. With narcissistic personality disorders, the narcissistic core is often masked by oedipal erotic and hostile overtones, which may actually serve the secondary function of stimulation to compensate for the feeling of emptiness and depletion. This may be as true for the therapists as it is for patients, and a personal analysis of one's own narcissism is thus very important in the therapeutic work.

Some feelings which not infrequently surface in therapists in the treatment of narcissism include boredom, emptiness, vanity, pride, shame, chronic anger and annoyance, intense neediness and dependence, and depression or sadness. The tone of these affects is a sense of being a mirror and extension of someone who is struggling profoundly with self image and esteem and having diffuse self–other boundaries. The therapist may develop grandiose fantasies and daydreams, such as being on a tropical island with a lover, owning a Rolls Royce, engaging in perverse activity, and so forth. There can be subtle pressures to act out these fantasies. In the motion picture *The House of Games,* a female psychiatrist is increasingly attracted to the dangerous and narcissistic world in which her patients, who are compulsive gamblers, live. The authors have from time to time worked with narcissistic patients who have consummated phenomenal business deals, had unusually exciting sexual relations, had power over large numbers of people, or had some other kind of spectacular success. The unconscious attraction of these lived-out fantasies must be carefully monitored and reflected to the patients as useful interventions and interpretations. This process offers a means whereby the empathic stance of the therapist is restored.

A common countertransference pitfall in work with narcissistic personalities is the tendency to suppress expressions of narcissism and thus establish a therapeutic impasse. The authors observed through a one-way mirror a therapy group in which an especially clear instance of such an impasse occurred.

An outpatient therapy group for mixed character disorders, ranging from neurotic to low-functioning borderlines, met weekly in a large institutional setting. It was led by a senior male therapist and a female psychiatric resident and included in its membership a female patient with anxiety hysteria, a young and attractive woman who suffered from work inhibitions and interpersonal difficulties, a sociopathic, substance abusing and overweight male, a homosexual graduate student with severe depression, and a gay male with alcoholism in remission and narcissistic and borderline features.

A chronic problem in this group was that the sociopath and the gay alcoholic male dominated the group interaction so that the other patients could hardly get a word in. The observers reflected that there may have been a problem in the screening process, since the composition of the group was somewhat skewed, a possible warning sign of a countertransference problem.

The gay alcoholic male would frequently take control of the group by dominating the conversation, provoking fights, acting sulky and withdrawing, and the like. His behavior frequently rendered the group helpless and bound with frustration and substantial rage. His communications, actually harangues, were expressions both of intense need for mirroring and validation and simultaneously a defensive process whereby distance and protection against intimacy were maintained. His anger and need were especially focused on the senior, male therapist. One observer commented that this patient seemed to be on the verge of fragmentation during some of these agitated, provocative periods.

The other members, especially the work-disordered female, attempted to relate to his problems. Genuine empathy was systematically rebuffed and countered with ever more aggressive and disputatious barbs, complaints, and cynicisms. The members, blocked and stymied, turned to the therapist for help.

The senior therapist took the lead, with the female resident assuming a more passive and supportive role, especially toward the other members. The senior therapist would at times mirror back the gay male's distress, but quickly this mirroring was transformed into confrontation. An aggressive tug-of-war would then ensue, where the member and the therapist were paired in this enmeshed dyad, characterized by mutual bitterness, frustration, and helplessness. Mired in this interaction, the group was stuck, and generally would collapse into a hopeless state. Other members would, at such times, question what they were getting out of the group, express pessimism, and, in general, express their needs for deliverance from the condition of impasse.

Observers commented on the need for the senior therapist to more fully interpret the panic and fragmentation of the member. The bickering, counteraggression, and distancing only served to facilitate a group context that was precisely a reenactment of this patient's child-hood experience of his family: aggressive, judgmental, and without an empathic capacity.

The preceding example vividly reveals the loss of the empathic stance in the presence of aggressive grandiosity, fragmentation, and the emergence of selfobject transference. Empathy in such cases must be accompanied by limits to the acting-out in group. Not even Kohut would object to the appropriate setting of limits for this patient. (Kohut might have said that curtailing the monologue would be meeting a phase-legitimate and accurately empathized need for regulating overstimulation and drive intensity.) However, the senior therapist overreacted, overemphasizing the aggression and devaluation at the expense of empathizing with the underlying panic and loss of self cohesion. He was responding countertransferentially by attacking the patient rather than empathically interpreting what the patient was feeling.

The resident cotherapist, on the other hand, responded with emotional withdrawal and overprotectiveness, some of which was a response to the anxiety and vulnerability of the group as a whole. Her withdrawal prevented her from functioning as a team with her cotherapist. Thus, both therapists, who otherwise were highly competent, reacted without insight or empathy to the patient's narcissism, as did the group members. It is likely that everyone present unconsciously resonated to the deeply thwarted need for mirroring that this patient expressed. The defense against this awareness appeared to be preventing the therapists and group from working effectively in that context.

The self psychology model emphasizes the real need of the members for empathic responses from each other and the leadership, providing an ongoing empathic matrix that facilitates and sustains self cohesion and transmuting internalization. At all times, and especially in the early stages of group formation, the therapist is the key figure in meeting this need. In this framework, not all perceptions of the therapist by the patients are projections or distortions, nor do they always represent transference as such. Langs (1976a), from a classical analytic perspective, has emphasized the realistic basis of unconscious perceptions and communications that had hitherto been labeled "transference." He stated the importance of *openly acknowledging* therapist errors and the validity of patients' symbolic communications. Searles (1979) makes a practice of frequently disclosing his deepest feelings and reactions to the patient. Thus, the principle that the therapist should not disclose or discuss his countertransference (since that would be an imposition on the patient and endanger the "safeguarding of the transference") has been seriously challenged in recent work.

Our impression is that Kohut himself adopted the more traditional position of nondisclosure of countertransference, with the exception that the analyst acknowledge specific empathic failures that induced narcissistic injury in the analysand. In his writings, he does not mention sharing his feelings with the patient. However, he and his students continually emphasize, almost to the point of establishing a new principle of technique, the necessity to detect, articulate, and explore the inevitable moments when the analyst is out of tune with the patient and the patient reacts with a narcissistic injury or a feeling of being slighted. Often, this reaction is not disclosed by the patient, who may act out or become resistive in sessions.

> R., a member of an outpatient therapy group, entered the group to deal with a problem of shyness. In the screening process, he spoke about how his father's inaccessibility and unrealistic expectations had caused lasting emotional wounds and a fear of human interaction. In the early sessions of entry into group, he was accepted by the others but played a distancing role of observing, protecting, and occasionally giving feedback to the others. However, after group, he would come up to the male therapist and privately ask whether the group or therapists were angry or upset with him.
>
> The therapists were aware that R. was especially sensitive to hurts, but the male therapist initially reacted to this trait with detachment and lack of interest rather than empathy. R. withdrew emotionally and then missed a group session for an ostensibly practical "reason."
>
> The therapists correctly understood this to be a signal of a failure of mirroring. They reflected to him that they might have misunderstood or neglected his need for responsiveness from them and praised him for his commitment to group and his support of the others. R. was very pleased, judging from the smile that broke out broadly on his face, and he became considerably more involved in the group interaction.

Clinically, this approach of acknowledging and exploring empathic failures and narcissistic slights is often effective and has the great virtue of being "user friendly" and benign to the patient's defenses and self-esteem. It could perhaps be correctly criticized for covering over certain transference distortions and sexual and aggressive derivatives.

The more radical sharing of countertransference dilemmas and feelings advocated, for example, by Langs (1976a), and even more by Searles (1979), has attendant risks to both patient and therapist. For one thing, the balance of authority and responsibility may shift from therapy of the members to treatment of the therapists! For another, the therapists may be overexposed and vulnerable personally and professionally. The group members may feel attacked or insecure on learning that their therapist is flawed or conflicted. This disillusionment may at the level of archaic narcissism injure their vanity (injury to the grandiose self), and on an adult level, it may correctly signal to them that the therapist is abandoning his professional role.

Yet in psychotherapy, and particularly group therapy, there is sometimes great virtue in a careful and well-thought-out sharing on the part of the therapist of personal experiences and inner feelings in the here-and-now. Done judiciously, and with careful follow-up attention to the members' reactions, sharing of countertransference is a very powerful intervention that can "reach" patients at a deeper level than otherwise, as the following example suggests.

> In a group of substance abusers within an inpatient addictions treatment setting, one of the members kept interrupting the group and engaging in long harangues that prevented the therapy work from continuing, while the members sat by, helpless. The therapist tried several strategies that had virtually no impact. He interpreted the behavior as a repetitive pattern that helped the patient protect against his inner feelings; he asked him gently but persistently to limit the length of time he spoke; he pointed out how the behavior prevented the group from working effectively. These and other appeals to the patient's observing ego had no influence whatever, and the pattern became more and more distressing. (These tirades are a "smokescreen" defense mechanism frequently used by substance abusers to avoid more disturbing affects of hurt and vulnerability.)
>
> The therapist realized that his attempt to remain "rational" with the offending patient was ignoring his own countertransference reactions of anger and annoyance. He decided to share this directly with the patient and the group and finally said, "You know, I'm really beginning to feel furious with you. If you weren't a patient, I think I would be a good deal less controlled about this than I am now. I'm very angry with you." The patient relaxed, and said, "That's the first time I felt like you understood me—you're talking my language." The disruptive verbiage lessened considerably, and the patient's affect improved.

The reason such disclosure was constructive and not experienced as an attack was because the therapist phrased it in such a way as to indicate that he was aware of the context and his role. In addition, he came across to the patient in a language that was familiar to him and concrete enough to be perceived as "emotionally real." The danger of sharing countertransference with narcissistic personalities and self disordered individuals is both the premature spoiling of the mirror and idealizing transference, a part of which is an illusion of mutual perfection, and the attacking of newly developing narcissistic structures by an implicit criticism of the patient or an inappropriate demand on him.

In our view it is thus strategically important that sharing of countertransference be done judiciously and selectively, with careful attention to the state of the self (cohesive versus fragmented) and tact and timing. This position differs from experiential and existential treatment approaches, which utilize sharing of therapist self experience as an everyday part of the treatment process. The difference points up further the fact that self psychology stays well within the traditional psychoanalytic framework for the conduct of psychotherapy and is not, as appears to some, an "existential therapy of the self."

SELF PSYCHOLOGY AND THE ROLE OF THE THERAPIST: AN EVALUATION AND CRITIQUE

Having surveyed the group therapist's role and the various pressures that impinge on him in the course of his work, pressures which can be turned to therapeutic advantage if they are properly monitored, it is important now to assess the pros and cons of the unique perspective that Kohut and his students have given us. We believe that self psychology is an extremely valuable clinical tool, and yet that, at the same time, if it is not corrected for in certain ways by other viewpoints, it can lead either to a type of "sector analysis," which treats only one component of the many complex dimensions of the personality, or to profound errors in the treatment of certain patients within the narcissistic spectrum. While some clinicians hold that self psychology is a comprehensive view of the personality, we disagree, believing instead that it is but one significant contribution to the mainstream of psychoanalytic thought.

One of the great values of self psychology vis-à-vis the therapist's stance is that it gives empathy a central place in the listening and interpretive process. Although traditionally assumed to be a background element in properly conducted therapy, self psychology brings it into focus as one of the most potent ingredients of cure. Psychoanalytic therapists have been properly chastised for sometimes being too distant and too "above" the patient (cf. the term "hovering" attention). Empathy restores a balance to therapy and enables early narcissistic affects and transferences to be elicited more strongly in the patient and perceived more sensitively by the therapist.

It is possible, however, for the therapist, like a parent, to be *too* empathic, which would be experienced by the patient as an intrusion, an impingement on those very structures that Kohut wants to strengthen. Winnicott (1958) recognized the importance of the capacity of the infant to be "alone in the presence of the other." Aloneness and privacy in the therapy context are as important to the maturing of the self as mirroring. Indeed, a truly empathic therapist will perceive this need and respond to it by offering some distance. Too much empathy, which of course is paradoxically unempathic, especially early in treatment, can actually exacerbate shameful feelings, undue feelings of exposure, and a deficiency in the very empathy that the therapist offers so liberally.

The group therapist's empathy with an individual member must also take into account the group's need for attention and the multiple needs and tasks of the group matrix:

> In one group a narcissistic member continually preoccupied the group and demanded its attention. He would compete for attention whenever another member "held the floor" for any length of time. In a particular session this demandingness caused fighting and bickering to erupt in the group. The therapist attempted to make a mirroring interpretation, highlighting the difficulty that the narcissistic member had in maintaining himself in the face of focus on others and their problems. As he did this the group members spoke up: "Look here, you can't treat this man with tact and understanding because he will eat this group alive. We must have time for us, and you need to help us with that."

The membership understood the therapist's attempt but insisted that their object-related needs could not be subordinated to that member's demands and manipulations. The group leads, the therapist responds.

Kohut was attempting to correct for a defect that he perceived to be almost universally present in parenting in the modern era: a lack of empathy and responsiveness to feelings in the growing child. Here is an observation of enormous therapeutic and social consequence. At the same time, it is possible in observing these same families to see the loss of objectivity and matter of factness that exists when boundaries begin to blur in the midst of emotional turmoil. These stormy emotional "moments" (Pine, 1981) are seen by some as significant contributors to later pathology.

Schermer (1988) has presented a view of psychotherapy that advocates alternating between an empathic stance and an objective view, the therapist being both a "mirror" and a "window" on the patient's (or group's) unconscious. Such an ability to flexibly shift listening modes can provide a binocular perspective which gives the richest possible picture of individual and group dynamics. It allows the therapist to perceive the defenses and phantasies of the object relations spectrum as well as to be attuned to the needs and vulnerability of the self.

A special corrective to self psychology is necessary in working with narcissistic rage. In our view, Kohut's position that narcissistic rage is resolved when the underlying hurt is alleviated is only partly true. Kernberg (1975) was also correct in pointing to the intensity of the aggressive drive in many narcissistic personalities, exacerbated by harsh superego introjects and extreme feelings of deprivation and envy. In group therapy, it is thus necessary to set clear limits to angry acting-out. Boundaries are crucial in containing and resolving rage. In addition, interpretation of pathological projections and introjections as revived in the therapeutic interaction is essential for achieving long-term relief from chronic envy and hostility.

The group therapist also needs to keep in mind that oedipal dynamics will coexist with narcissistic ones, and a central therapeutic task is the appraisal of whether the oedipal is a defense against the narcissistic or vice versa. It needs to be constantly remembered that sex and aggression are powerful forces in the human personality.

In addition, not all group members are narcissists, and not all narcissists have only narcissistic selfobject transferences. One must be aware that in group treatment one is always experiencing admixtures of both object-directed and selfobject transference. Any attempt to treat all phenomena in a group as reflecting narcissistic dynamics or emanating from the narcissistic sector can well be understood as a defense by the therapist against the multilevel nature of the self and reveals a tendency toward a foreclosure of the true therapeutic situation, with all of the attendant negative consequences.

Self psychology is especially important in providing a psychoanalytic vantage point that coincides with the group dynamicist's notion that the therapist is an integral part of the group, not an outside observer. Self psychology, like object relations theory, has the great potential of speaking directly to the experience and practice of group psychotherapists, who work primarily with relationships and interrelationships. A model of group therapy interventions that combines object relations theory and self psychology into a unified perspective offers the greatest hope for group treatment of the profound deficits that many patients nowadays bring into the consulting room.

REFERENCES

Agazarian, Y., & Peters, R. (1981), *The Visible and Invisible Group.* London: Routledge & Kegan Paul.

Alonso, A., & Rutan, S. (1988), The experience of shame and the restoration of self-respect in group psychotherapy. *Internat. J. Group Psychother.*, 38(1):3–27.

Ashbach, C., & Schermer, V. (1987), *Object Relations, the Self, and the Group.* London: Routledge & Kegan Paul.

Bennis, W., & Shepard, H. (1956), A theory of group development. *Human Relations,* 9:415–417.

Bion, W. (1959), *Experiences in Groups.* New York: Basic Books.

Chessick, R. (1985), *Psychology of the Self and the Treatment of Narcissism.* Northvale, NJ: Jason Aronson.

Foulkes, S., & Anthony, E. (1973), *Group Psychotherapy: The Psychoanalytic Approach,* 2nd ed. Harmondsworth, UK: Penguin.

Freud, S. (1913), Totem and taboo. *Standard Edition,* 13:1–164. London: Hogarth Press, 1955.

——— (1921), Group psychology and the analysis of the ego. *Standard Edition,* 18:67–135. London: Hogarth Press, 1955.

Gibbard, G. S. (1974), Individuation, fusion, and role specialization. In: *Analysis of Groups,* ed. G. S. Gibbard, J. J. Hartmann, & R. D. Mann. San Francisco: Jossey Bass, pp. 247–276.

——— Hartman, J. J. (1974), A note on fantasy themes in the evolution of group culture. In: *Analysis of Groups,* ed. G. S. Gibbard, J. J. Hartmann, & R. D. Mann. San Francisco: Jossey Bass, pp. 315–335.

Greenson, R. R. (1967), *The Theory and Technique of Psychoanalysis,* Vol. 1. New York: International Universities Press.

Grotstein, J. (1982), *The Dual Track Theorem: Part I.* Manuscript submitted for publication.

——— (1991), Nothingness, meaninglessness, chaos, and the "black hole" III: Self- and interactional regulation and the background presence of primary identification. *Contemp. Psychoanal.*, 27:1–33.

Kernberg, O. (1975), *Borderline Conditions and Pathological Narcissism.* New York: Jason Aronson.

Kibel, L., & Stein, A. (1981), The group-as-a-whole approach: An appraisal. *Internat. J. Group Psychother.*, 31(4):409–427.

Kissen, M. (1980), General systems theory: Practical and theoretical implications for group intervention. *Group,* 4(1):29–39.

Kohut, H. (1971), *The Analysis of the Self.* New York: International Universities Press.

——— (1972), Narcissism and narcissistic rage. *The Psychoanalytic Study of the Child,* 27:360–400. New York: Quadrangle Books.

——— (1977), *The Restoration of the Self.* New York: International Universities Press.

——— (1978), *The Search for the Self,* ed. P. Ornstein. New York: International Universities Press.

Langs, R. (1976a), *The Bipersonal Field.* New York: Jason Aronson.

——— (1976b), *The Therapeutic Interaction.* 2 vols. New York: Jason Aronson.

Lewin, K. (1951), *Field Theory and Social Science.* New York: Harper & Row.

Nathanson, D., ed. (1987), *The Many Faces of Shame*. New York: Guilford Press, pp. 1–63.

Pine, F. (1981), In the beginning: Contributions to a psychoanalytic developmental psychology. *Internat. Rev. Psychoanal.*, 8:15–33.

Rutan, J., & Stone, W. (1984), *Psychodynamic Group Psychotherapy*. New York: Macmillan.

Schermer, V. (1988), The mirror and the window: A self psychology and object relations paradigm for psychotherapy. Paper presented to Jefferson Medical College, Department of Psychiatry, May 4.

Searles, H. (1979), *Countertransference and Related Subjects*. New York: International Universities Press.

Segal, H. (1974), *An Introduction to the Work of Melanie Klein*. New York: Basic Books.

Sonne, J. C. (1991), Triadic transference of pathological family images. *Contemp. Family Ther.*, 13:219–229.

Whitaker, D., & Lieberman, M. (1964), *Psychotherapy through the Group Process*. Chicago: Aldine.

Winnicott, D. W. (1958), The capacity to be alone. In: *The Maturational Processes and the Facilitating Environment*. New York: International Universities Press, 1965, pp. 29–36.

——— (1960), The theory of the parent-infant relationship. In: *The Maturational Processes and the Facilitating Environment*. New York: International Universities Press, 1965, pp. 37–55.

Wong, N. (1979), Clinical considerations in group treatment of narcissistic disorders. *Internat. J. Group Psychother.*, 33(2):171–191.

Yalom, I. (1975), *The Theory and Practice of Group Psychotherapy*. New York: Basic Books.

12

The Role of the Therapist from a Social Systems Perspective

MARVIN R. SKOLNICK, M.D.

Being "in role" has connotations of playing at something or performing a set of functions that are divorced from one's person. From a social systems perspective, however, a *work role* is understood as an authorized constellation of functions within a task system (Miller and Rice, 1967). A role is further delineated by its relationship with other roles within the same task system. Within this conceptual framework, any role is distinguished from the *occupant* of the role. At the same time, however, a complex dynamic link between role and person is a vital aspect of the work process. A committed stance of "taking on the role" requires mobilization of skills, experiences, feelings, and attitudes within the self and a suppression of other parts of the self that are not relevant to the task. It entails a subordination of the self to the task and the limits and values inherent in the task. The individual becomes accountable, vulnerable to failure, anxiety, and guilt, but on the other hand may achieve some of the deepest satisfactions possible (Hirschhorn, 1988).

Our understanding of what it means to take on the role of group therapist can be greatly enriched by analysis from this perspective. Being a group therapist can be likened to embarking on an odyssey with its potential for excitement, satisfaction, and development, but also with its powerful undercurrents and temptations. The well-delineated role can be thought of as providing a binding structure that enables the group therapist to experience the siren songs of both the group and his own longings without flinging himself overboard, wrecking the enterprise. However dangerous, experiencing these songs is critical to a deeper understanding of the group experience. If one can stay in role (or learn to recognize falling out of role and to right oneself) the rewards of such a journey can be profound. This chapter is an attempt to explore in depth the complexities, underlying assumptions, and dilemmas of the role of the group therapist with the hope that it might serve as a useful guide for those who embark on this exciting adventure.

THEORETICAL CONSIDERATIONS

My view of the psychotherapy group as a social system has been derived from several sources. The work of Wilfred Bion (1959) uncovers powerful, irrational, mostly unconscious forces inherent in the group as a whole from a psychoanalytic perspective. Ludwig von Bertalanffy (1968), Miller and Rice (1967), and other social scientists have utilized an open-systems perspective to illuminate group life. The blending of these seemingly disparate conceptual frameworks in the study of group relations at the Tavistock Institute stimulated insights and hypotheses that have intrigued and provoked group psychotherapists and researchers and have had an important impact on the conduct of group psychotherapy.

Bion's Psychoanalytic View of the Group

Bion's (1959) study of the group revealed a vital aspect of social psychology not accessible in the analytic dyad. His work contains profound implications for the emotional and work capacities of individuals. He saw man as a group animal who was also partly at war with his "groupishness" because it posed a threat to his individuality. In this he was influenced by Melanie Klein's (1959) portrayal of the infant's complex struggle to reconcile his need for his mother's breast with dread of destructive attack by this same breast. Klein believed that the infant, particularly when frustrated, experienced the mother's breast as filled with projected rage, envy, and greed. Bion (1959) stated, "The adult must establish contact with the emotional life of the group in which he lives. This task appears as formidable to the adult as the relationship with the breast is to the infant and the demands of this task are revealed in his regression" (p. 141).

As evidence for this regression, Bion cited the group members' shared perception that the group exists as an entity separate from and greater than the aggregate of the individuals comprising it. He believed that the individual unconsciously experiences other individuals as "members" or parts of the mother's body into which split-off unacceptable, unintegrated parts of the self are projected. This process triggers psychotic-like fears of annihilation, disintegration of the self, and powerful greed, envy, and rage. Group members defend against these threats through an unconscious regression to the defensive constellation of the paranoid-schizoid position.

Melanie Klein formulated the *paranoid-schizoid position* as a set of primitive defensive operations in which the infant protects himself against persecutory anxiety and maintains some sense of inner goodness by projecting hate, envy, and greed into the mother and then unconsciously identifying with her as the repository for these projections. She formulated the *depressive position* as a developmentally advanced alternative in which the child experiences depressive anxiety related to responsibility and guilt for destructive emotions. Klein further maintained that from the depressive position the child is motivated to make attempts at reparation and is able to appreciate the existence of goodness and badness in both the self and in the other. Klein posited that the paranoid and schizoid positions were not only relevant to infancy and childhood but also oscillate in the adult throughout life, a concept that Bion incorporated into his formulations about oscillating phenomena in groups.

An examination of these theoretical considerations and his own experience in groups led Bion to the discovery of the bifocal perspective of groups. He conceived of all groups as containing simultaneously two levels of organization, though in different admixtures at any given time. Under the conscious and overtly observable level of the group, he inferred the existence of another group level—a pool of irrational mental processes containing the unacknowledged regressive aspects of individuals. He termed this level, with its unconscious contributions of individual members, the *basic assumption group*. This *basic assumption group*, organized around irrational, primitive, and defensive mental processes of its members, coexists and interacts with the more obvious *work group*, organized around the task and the rational, scientific, problem-solving capacities of its members.

Bion identified three distinctly different irrational belief systems or *basic assumptions*, only one of which is active in a group at a given time: *basic assumption dependency, basic assumption fight–flight, and basic assumption pairing*. Bion hypothesized that all members contain unconscious mental representations that correspond to the inferred basic assumption of the group. Group members who play leading roles in the prevailing basic assumption are often experienced as powerful or larger than life because in unconscious fantasy they are filled with split-off parts of other members.

In *basic assumption dependency,* a shared illusion is created that the leader can satisfy all the needs of the group. The members behave passively, as if they have no competence, judgment, or power, implicitly pressuring the leader to take care of them and the task. In a psychotherapy group, for example, the patients may maneuver one of their own into the role of the helpless person in crisis in order to engage the therapist's tendencies to rescue. The group experiences the rescue vicariously, temporarily reassured that greed will be kept in check.

In *basic assumption fight–flight,* the group members collectively behave as if the task of the group is to fight or flee from an enemy either inside or outside the group. In a psychotherapy group the enemy may be a patient who is revealing feelings that are threatening to others, the therapist who is confronting the group with painful realities, mental illness, or other parts of a treatment facility. The fight or flight is undertaken by members to avoid owning and integrating what is threatening or unacceptable in themselves.

In *basic assumption pairing,* the group behaves as if a sexualized pair will produce a messiah or an ideal that will enable the group to circumvent the necessity of working through the pains of development. In a psychotherapy group, for example, members of the group may covertly promote the courtship of a male and female member. The other members then may vicariously enjoy erotic and hopeful fantasies about the couple and their relationship as an alternative to confronting oedipal fears that are inhibiting them from grappling with their own sexual and procreative development.

The *work group* strives to make sophisticated use of the basic assumption group as a source of energy, hope, and protection from incapacitating anxieties. However, like the maladaptive aspects of defenses used by individuals, the basic assumption group can also exert an undermining effect on work efforts. For example, a surgical service can utilize basic assumption dependency to engender in patients awaiting surgery a passive, trusting, optimistic state of mind, which is likely to facilitate the surgical process. However, during the rehabilitative phase, this same dependency is likely to discourage a patient from the active role essential in restoring bodily functions and promoting recovery.

In the early phases of a psychotherapy group, dependent assumptions about the omnipotence of the therapist may facilitate group formation and cohesiveness. In later phases of the psychotherapeutic process, however, these assumptions may foster nonproductive passivity on the part of patients and forestall pursuit of the therapeutic task. From this perspective, the dynamic interaction between the work group, its task, and the basic assumption group exerts significant influence on the success or failure of the enterprise at any given time.

Bion believed that an individual cannot exist without the group, even if it is a group to which he insists that he does not belong. If he is physically alone there continues to be a group in his mind (derivatives of groups of the past or the present) that shapes his identity and expectations of others. Contemporary object relations theorists have elaborated on this notion in terms of developmental psychology, in which the group in the mind is built from self–other experiences (Kernberg, 1980). Bion believed that since an individual lives in a symbiotic relationship with his group, he cannot be fully understood or understand himself without an appreciation of the complexities of his interaction with a group.

For Bion, the task of group psychotherapy was to illuminate the covert and unconscious shared group processes that were interfering with real work on psychological and developmental problems, particularly those that pertained to the conflicts and dilemmas of group membership. He believed that his role was to grapple with the here-and-now realities of the group experience rather than conduct what he considered a debased form of psychoanalysis, as though members were lying on couches arranged in a circle, waiting for their turn with the analyst (Lyth, 1989). In Bion's view, if the group therapist responds directly to individuals rather than to what the collection of individuals are playing out in the group, it is evidence that he has been seduced out of role and into basic assumption.

As a therapist, Bion addressed the group by articulating his view of the group's attitude toward him which was "obvious but unobserved" and its implication for the basic assumption prevailing at the moment. Bion relied heavily on his own subjective experience and his capacity to shake himself free from the "numbing reality" of the basic assumption. He first allowed himself to join the group emotionally, experience his countertransference and what the group had projected into him, then interpret (Bion, 1959). By resolving to begin each session without "memory or desire," Bion emphasized the importance of working with the here-and-now experience, rather than using preconceived notions (Bion, 1970). Ezriel (1952) and Sutherland (1965) further developed Bion's insights into frameworks for group psychotherapy that retain emphasis on therapist-centered interventions that address the group as a whole. Horwitz (1977) identified a unifying factor in holistic group approaches, which he termed the "group-centered hypothesis." Holistic group therapists believe that a common group theme influences all group behavior at any given moment.

Kibel and Stein (1981) reviewed the strengths and liabilities of this perspective.

Foulkes (1975), influenced by Lewin (1950), and perhaps Bion, underscored the significance of the group by asserting that while the basic biological unit is the individual as an organism, the basic psychological unit is the group. A person in this conception is considered a nodal point in a group nexus, corresponding to the position of the neuron in the matrix of the brain. Foulkes believed that if the individual is dysfunctional in his original group, the family, and currently disturbed in his relations with others, he can resolve these disturbances by becoming a functioning member of a group conducted according to therapeutic principles.

Foulkes and his followers, Pines (1978) and James (1984), describe a role for the group therapist that is more pragmatic and less austere than that delineated by Bion. Therapists influenced by Foulkes play a more active role in facilitating communication at all levels of the group and are more responsive to the individual as well as the group. They do not limit themselves to interpretation of the group's defensive relationship to the therapist, but they nevertheless incorporate many of Bion's insights.

General Systems and Social Systems Theory

Bion's initial Northfield Hospital experiment in 1945 was the first modern intentional therapeutic community. In just six weeks, this treatment program for World War II psychiatric casualties showed significant superiority over traditional individual medical model approaches. However, despite his success, Bion was transferred to another assignment because his innovative methods stirred up opposition among professionals in other parts of the hospital (Bridger, 1985). "Violation of protocol" was cited by authorities as the reason for the transfer, but according to Bridger, the real reason was Bion's failure to attend to the relationships at the boundary between his program and the larger system, where repercussions of Bion's innovations were not adequately managed.

The group therapy enterprise, like any other system of work activities, is a part of a larger system with a boundary region between it and the larger system, across which transactions occur that require management. This concept is a crucial derivative of social systems theory, expanding and enhancing the group-as-a-whole approach by adding the concept of the group as a system subject to the dynamics of all open systems. The group is thus understood as a *part* of a system as well as a *whole* unto itself. The individual, the group, and the environmental context in which the group is embedded can be treated as an interactive, open, living system, hierarchically arranged. The individual is a subsystem of the group, and from the individual vantage point, the group is its suprasystem. The group is a subsystem of a larger environmental system, which in turn represents the group's suprasystem.

A system is understood in terms of the dynamic interaction with its environment across a boundary. A boundary holds together interdependent components of the system that it delineates. The boundary of a living system is permeable. It is not a line, but a region where discriminating work and decision making occurs in regard to input and output of matter, energy, and information. Outside the boundary of the system, there is discontinuity with what is inside. A system imports matter, energy, and information across its boundary, subjects these imports to a conversion process, and then exports products and waste across its boundary to the external world (Baker, 1968).

Social systems theorists at the Tavistock Institute asserted that every enterprise involves both technical and social subsystems. They argued that appreciation of the technical system dynamics dealing with the material realm and appreciation of the social dynamics dealing primarily with the social and psychological realm and their interaction are both essential to the understanding and management of the enterprise as a total system. By applying systems concepts to both the technical and social dimensions of work, they showed that productivity and the quality of the experience for workers could be improved in such diverse work settings as a coal mine (Trist and Bamforth, 1951), weaving factory (A. K. Rice, 1953), and home for incurables (Miller and Gwynne, 1972).

How does this apply to group therapy? A manufacturing enterprise imports raw material, machinery, and employees. The employees are converted into trained workers and arranged in complex social subsystems. Employees, machines, and technologies are arranged in bounded subsystems to convert raw material into new forms that are exported back to the environment. In a psychotherapy group, patients are brought across the boundary into the group and subjected to interactive processes, guided by psychological theories, a framework with ground rules and a therapist. If all goes well enough, the patients leave the group transformed psychologically. In both cases, the receptivity of the larger environmental system to the quality of what or who is produced exerts a feedback effect on the system by influencing future inputs—availability of new orders for the factory or new applicants for the psychotherapy group. The management of the external boundary, both in regard to inputs and outputs and their interrelationship, can be as crucial to the survival of the enterprise as what transpires inside.

Input and output of matter, energy, and information are required for the development and viability of all living systems from the micro level of the cell to the macro level of the nation/state. On the other hand, excessive flow across the environmental boundary that overwhelms the system's integrating capacities can lead to loss of the distinction between the system and its surrounding environment and ultimately to the destruction of the system. The psychotherapy group is often faced with critical choices between conservative management of its external boundary, in order to facilitate the development of sufficient stability and cohesion for therapy to proceed, and more open management of the boundary, to allow for needed resources and creative disruptions.

Both the factory and the therapy group have social and technical aspects that must be related to each other in ways that enable the task to be accomplished. In accord with contemporary science, a social systems perspective is oriented toward multivariate, recursive relationships between interactive components—all influencing and constrained by each other—rather than toward bivariate, linear, cause-and-effect relationships that apply only to closed systems. Applied to a psychotherapy group, this principle suggests that changing the way members behave in relation to each other, the group, and the environment is as critical to therapeutic change as insight into the historical causes of their difficulties. The system principle of equicausality asserts that the beginnings alone do not determine the final outcome. Decisions or changes of permeability at various boundaries and at varying times can change the course of a system and its fate—whether an organization or a human being. At every region in the system where there is discontinuity and interchange, a boundary is defined requiring human judgment and decisions. It is at boundaries that management, the exercise of human judgment, and decision making are required in group psychotherapy as well as any other enterprise (Singer, Astrachan, Gould, and Klein, 1975, 1979).

Inherent in all living systems are resistances to change which often need to be managed if therapeutic or developmental processes are to prevail. In the psychotherapy group, in addition to the resistances of the patients to psychological change, more subtle, recursively interacting resistances from other sectors of the system play a significant role. These include such resistances as a therapist's reluctance to face and process painful countertransference, a clinic's reluctance to lose patients or revenue to improved mental health, or other family members' intolerance of painful feelings provoked by changes in the member undergoing group psychotherapy.

A crucial aspect of a social systems perspective is that successful living systems are open and do not conform to the second law of thermodynamics, that of entropy. A living system, through continuous import of matter, energy, and information, moves toward increasing levels of complexity and differentiation. In "systems language," this is termed morphogenesis, and is in contrast to closed systems, which manifest morphostasis—fixed structures that move toward disorganization and eventual decay (Baker, 1968).

One of the remarkable characteristics of living systems is that they are capable of maintaining a relatively steady state while they are engaging in the throughput (input, conversion, and output) process. Steady state differs from the equilibrium of closed systems in that developmental change can occur in one part of the system witout requiring regression in another part of the system to balance the change, yet the identity and integrity of the system and its structures are maintained. An important implication for a psychotherapy group is that if the group and its boundaries are managed properly, the group can continue to evolve in complexity, thereby also enabling its members to evolve in complexity, even while individual members enter and leave the group after having undergone change.

The terminology of systems theory may seem at first to have a cold, mechanical ring. It is primarily a skeletal and metatheory that in itself does not provide enough psychological content to guide work with human beings in the empathic or feeling way required in psychotherapy. However, it does provide an invaluable road map for integration of different levels of phenomena, such as the intrapsychic system, the interpersonal system, the group system, and their interaction (Astrachan, 1970). It can also serve as a bridge between different psychoanalytic frameworks such as object relations, self psychology, and drive defense theory, and between different disciplines, such as psychology, biology, and sociology. It is compatible with existential and humanistic values such as the interdependence of people, responsibility, opportunity for development, and respect for the autonomy of individuals (Durkin, 1972). Some of the recent work involving the concept of the "transference/countertransference matrix" (Marshall and Marshall, 1988), which recognizes the interconnectedness of patients and therapists and the reciprocal nature of transference and countertransference, is an illustration of open-systems thinking within a psychoanalytic frame. Perhaps most importantly, its elucidation of the management of boundaries, structure, and role can provide the therapist with invaluable assistance in developing a framework that allows the psychotherapy group to plumb the depths of its emotional life and regress in the service of the ego without chaos prevailing.

A SOCIAL SYSTEMS APPROACH TO GROUP PSYCHOTHERAPY

The Patient and the Group

Disturbances in relationships with significant others often motivate individuals to enter group psychotherapy. While Bion focused on group phenomena, he did not forget that the group was composed of individuals, each of whom had an inner world or group in the mind that interacted with the inner worlds of other members to produce basic assumption group phenomena. Bion (1959) used the term *valence,* borrowed from physics, to describe "the individual's capacity for the instantaneous involuntary combination with other individuals for sharing and acting on a basic assumption" (p. 116). Valence also refers to the individual's predilection, determined by inner-world configurations and character, for playing a leadership role in a particular basic assumption. For example, an individual whose defensive style relies heavily on projection is more likely to play a prominent role in basic assumption fight–flight; an individual who utilizes denial and naive hopefulness is more likely to be a leader in basic assumption pairing; one who has a dependent character style is often a central figure in basic assumption dependency.

The inner world of the individual derived from internalized experience with significant others can also be thought of as a system with a boundary that is regulated by the ego (A. K. Rice, 1969). A well-functioning ego regulates this boundary between the inner world and external world of others by discriminately allowing input of new experience vital in reality testing and learning and output that enables the individual to influence others and the environment, and by offering resistance to intrusions that could have a destructive or disorganizing impact on the inner world. The ego utilizes the senses, thinking, feeling, and memory as guides in managing the boundary subsystem. To the extent that early formative experiences were discouraging, hostile, painful or frightening, this boundary is often managed so defensively that interactive experience with others is severely restricted or defensively distorted. As a result, the inner world fails to develop toward integration and a good fit with contemporaneous self and others. Ganzarain (1977) has labeled a boundary subsystem or ego that operates in this fashion as "archaic" (p. 444).

An encapsulated inner world is likely to consist of self–other models that are predominantly primitive, split, and heavily associated with negative and painful affects. These anachronistic inner systems, no matter how hidden by defensive facades, result in disturbances within the personality and serve as a faulty guide to work and relationships with others. While no individual is totally closed, the more the boundary of the self–other world is impermeable to modifying experience, the greater the reality of the self and the other will be obscured by rigid transferences, splitting, and projective distortions.

Gould (1989) and Singer and Shapiro (1988) described how the family authorizes the child to develop and utilize capacities to work in various roles. Presence or absence of empathy as well as positive or punitive response to individuation are some of the subtle ways that this authorization occurs or does not occur. Like the continuum of authorization that one can receive from one's adult work group, the family can authorize the developing child to observer status (to merely observe), to delegate status (to act, but only according to prescriptions of others), or to plenipotentiary status (to utilize capacities to observe, think, feel, and take action based on the current circumstances but in accordance with objectives and values of one's family or work group). If the individual has not received sufficient authorization from family, roles in life are likely to be shaped by dictates of others and perseverative emotional reactivity, rather than thought, imagination, and sound reality testing.

From the systems perspective, the psychotherapy group offers the patient an opportunity to transform the relatively closed, archaic aspects of the inner self–other world into a more open system that can serve as a springboard for development of the self. Typically, as individuals join the nondirective psychotherapy group and wrestle with the anxieties and dilemmas of group life, boundaries between members become more permeable. The boundaries of the individual's intrapsychic system tend to "redissolve" into self–object subsystems attached to intense affects (Kernberg, 1980). Members, unconsciously trying to protect themselves, split off and project unacceptable parts of the self (including undigested introjects) into each other. These *projective identifications* are not simply intrapsychic acts of the individual but have an interpersonal and group reality (Horwitz, 1983). Group members subtly treat each other in ways that provoke feelings and behavior consistent with projections, thereby avoiding the painful ambivalence and emotion associated with their respective self–object internal worlds. Strong affects are generated in the recipients of projections, who then feel invaded. The projectors fear retaliation and feel depleted. Through these mechanisms, group members maneuver each other and the therapist into emotional roles that externalize their inner worlds and create an unfolding series of unconscious group configurations, which Ezriel (1952) termed *common group tensions*. The power of the group to suck members into roles was described early on by Redl (1942). Scheidlinger (1982) called attention to the role of scapegoat as critical in destructive group processes in which unacceptable or frightening impulses and feelings are put into a vulnerable member who becomes at risk of sacrifice in order to preserve group-defensive equanimity. Despite its hazards, this regression and externalization are crucial steps in the therapeutic process of crossing the bridges between the intrapsychic and the interpersonal in the group and making accessible for group work the core problems in the individuals' intrapsychic systems.

Simultaneously, there are also strong pulls for group members to collusively avoid and/or deny what has happened in order to preserve defensive internal images of self and others. It is here that the group may congeal around defensive collusions (like the basic assumptions described by Bion, in which members gravitate to defensive roles determined by their valence) as an alternative to confrontation and a working-through process. To the extent that therapeutic processes prevail over resistance, the individual has the opportunity to identify empathically with what he has previously hated, feared, and then projected into the group (Lofgren, 1976). This in turn can lead to reinternalization with greater integration and self acceptance and the conversion of the more archaic aspects of the inner self–other world into an open system. From a Kleinian perspective, the individual is able to move more readily from a paranoid-schizoid position to a depressive position in which he can assume ownership of destructive impulses instead of projecting them. Through experiencing guilt and responsibility for his actions and feelings, and allowing for the experience of both goodness and badness residing in both self and others, a more realistic map of self and others develops. Partially freed from his investment in defensive delineation of self and others, and authorized to think and face reality, he can now participate more constructively and creatively in interpersonal and group life.

The Therapeutic Group

Although Bion was a brilliant pioneer in discovering the subcontinents of group life, his theory made little provision for the evolution or development of groups to more differentiated states, but rather envisaged groups shifting from one basic assumption to another in an endless dialectic between irrational assumptions and rational work. Insight into the irrational group collusion was thought by Bion to benefit the individual without the group necessarily changing its essential character. This therapeutic perspective can be considered "therapy through analysis of the group."

Utilizing the group-as-a-whole construct, but shifting perspective to view the group as a *therapeutic agent* in itself, brings other dimensions of the group into focus. Boundary management, conflict management, values, cohesion, and member-to-member relations are all significant dimensions that determine a group's therapeutic effectiveness. Slater (1966), utilizing many of Bion's insights but moving beyond the notion of oscillation between primitive defense and work, described how groups (and by implication, group-focused psychotherapy groups) can evolve and mature toward increasing sophistication and complexity. Slater conceptualized self study groups as social microcosms that can recapitulate the development of social history as well as that of the individual. The group begins in a state that is primarily dependent and paranoid, in which bonds between members are unconscious, roles of members are rigid, and irrational forces are projected into the group as a whole, the leader, or the environment. With sufficient leadership and structure, the group has the potential to evolve to a state in which bonds between members are more conscious, roles less rigid, process more democratic, and scientific and irrational forces are more harnessed and owned.

Newton and Levinson (1973) described small work groups as having "cultures"—particular belief systems and values beyond basic assumptions that determine task effectiveness. Whitaker and Lieberman (1964) described therapy groups as developing cultures that enable rather than restrict by building a repertoire of conflict-resolution capacities through facing conflict directly and living through it. Many authors (Frank, 1957; Yalom, 1970) believe that cohesiveness is an essential factor in forging a group culture that is therapeutically effective. However, from the point of view of group process, cohesiveness can be a two-edged sword. If it is based on primitive and defensive postures such as basic assumption, it can impede therapeutic work, although group members may experience and report a sense of oneness (Turquet, 1974).

The therapeutic effectiveness of a group culture might also be judged by the group's ability to provide a "good-enough mother" for its members. The "good-enough mother," according to Winnicott (1965), establishes and maintains a "holding environment" for the infant by providing gratification of biological needs, structure, capacity to endure hatred and rage, and empathic soothing. Winnicott labeled this part of the mother's role as the "environmental mother," which he distinguished from the function of the mother involved with person-to-person relatedness. Grotstein (1989) described dynamic psychotherapy as proceeding simultaneously on two tracks. One track involves the development and maintenance of a "holding environment" and the other track the analysis of personal relations.

In psychotherapy groups that aspire to be a place where early object relations pathology can be worked-through, the group must be ready and able to function as a nurturing environment. James (1984) links Bion's (1970) "containing," Winnicott's (1965) "holding," and Foulkes's (1975) "group matrix" to enhance understanding of what characteristics enable psychotherapy groups to promote the psychological development of individual members. To qualify as a "holding environment," "container," or "matrix" the group must be able to contain and process hatred without sacrificing members, to contain the polarities and paradoxes of group life without splitting off individuals or subgroups that have come to represent the problematic pole (Smith and Berg, 1987), and to be able to offer soothing empathy for members who are experiencing intense pain, anxiety, or need. From a self psychology point of view, the group needs to be ready and able at crucial moments to function as an empathic selfobject for members (Bacal, 1985).

From a developmental perspective, the therapeutic group must also, at times, function as a "transitional object" or "container" for parts of individuals that are not yet experienced as fully themselves or fully others. It needs to have a "transitional space" in which feelings, thoughts, and object relations heretofore experienced as too noxious or threatening to be acceptable within the self can be played with creatively and humorously as a crucial step toward integration and differentiation of self and other.

Bion commented that there can be no understanding without love (Sutherland, 1985). Bion made this remark after he had discontinued his work with groups. It is intriguing to speculate that if Bion had continued to work with groups, he may well have incorporated aspects of holding and facilitating as an important contextual ingredient in group psychotherapy. On the other hand, because of the intensity of the anxieties aroused and the power of regression, it is often not obvious how members, including the therapist, offer themselves or are offered up by the group for defensive purposes (Eisold, 1985). Thus, even the psychotherapy group that is evolving toward more differentiated and mature functioning is capable of a precipitous metamorphosis from a *good-enough nurturing mother* to a *terrible mother* (Neumann, 1955) who exploits or swallows up its members. Any group therapist who assumes that his leadership or the group process will necessarily be nurturing for its members and not destructive ignores Bion's insights, to everyone's peril.

Therapist

How is the role or behavior of a group therapist with a social systems orientation different from that of therapists who are adherents of other schools of psychoanalytic group psychotherapy, such as psychoanalysis of individuals in a group setting, interpersonal group therapy, or analysis of the group as a whole? Interventions at any one moment may be indistinguishable. The psychological content of interventions, in most cases, is informed by the same psychological theories, such as classical psychoanalysis, object relations theory, and self psychology. However, many of the objects of attention, as well as many of the decisions and activities that are an integral and inevitable part of the group therapist's role, fall outside the boundaries of traditional theories, and it is here that social systems theory makes a most significant contribution.

Many group therapists tend to minimize or ignore the managerial aspects of their role in favor of focusing almost exclusively on psychodynamics and interpretation (Singer et al., 1975). However, if management of time, space, task, role, and environmental boundaries integral to the development and maintenance of a therapeutic "holding environment" is neglected, patients are not likely to be available to utilize even the most profound or eloquent interpretations.

In a complex human system like a psychotherapy group, pertinent boundaries are not only territorial, spatial, and temporal, but are also psychological and functional. A boundary is that which separates what is inside from what is outside of an individual, group, or institution. Any transaction that involves exchange of matter, energy, or information that is accessible to examination and decision making implies the existence of a boundary where exchange and relationship can be managed or influenced. Breakdown of internal boundary management in the individual results in mental illness; breakdown in boundary management in a group results in chaos and/or group dissolution (E. Klein and Gould, 1973). The group psychotherapist manages or influences an array of complex boundaries. These include the group's boundary with its relevant environment, group membership and role boundaries, task boundaries, communication and information boundaries, boundaries between members and subgroups of members, boundaries between different levels of psychological phenomena (such as conscious/unconscious), and boundaries between intrapsychic, interpersonal, and group process (C. A. Rice and Rutan, 1981).

In the nascent group, the therapist can be thought of as the "decider subsystem" for the group, making most of the decisions about the group in accordance with its task and hierarchy of values (Ganzarain, 1977). The therapist experiences, analyzes, and acts to enhance the task. From a systems boundary-management point of view, the therapist (1) defines and monitors the task, (2) selects and takes in members, (3) delineates intragroup boundaries (roles, ground rules, culture, and contract), (4) delineates and manages his own role/person boundary, (5) delineates and manages the group/environmental boundary, (6) serves as catalyst and protector, and (7) processes information and interprets. It will be useful to examine each of these subtasks.

Defining and Monitoring the Task. Whereas Freud (1921) emphasized the libidinal attachment to the leader in group formation, Bion introduced the concept that a collection of individuals becomes a group when it has a *task* (Rioch, 1970). Miller and Rice (1967) defined the primary task of the group as that which it must accomplish in order to survive. The formulation of the primary task is the seminal criterion against which every subsequent decision is measured. In general, the primary task of group psychotherapy is to produce psychological change and reduce emotional disorder. A variation or increased specificity in this task is often indicated when working with specific categories of patients in certain contexts. For example, the task of a psychotherapy group within a psychiatric ward of a general hospital should be formulated so that it is compatible with the mission, value system, and social structure of the larger system (R. H. Klein, 1977; R. H. Klein and Kugel, 1981; C. A. Rice and Rutan, 1981). If the mission of the larger psychiatric system is to promote rapid reconstitution of patients and return them to the community within weeks, the task of the psychotherapy group should emphasize reality testing, support, and a here-and-now, practical, problem-solving orientation. If the therapist ignores these practical realities and focuses instead on personality restructuring with its attendant regression, serious conflict with other ward staff as well as resulting confusion and fragmentation in the patients is likely to occur.

Complex social systems–like psychotherapy groups often have more than one task and/or covert tasks that are in competition with each other. For example, a psychotherapy group in a clinic may have the stated primary task of providing psychotherapy for a group of patients, a vaguely acknowledged secondary task of providing training opportunities for residents and interns, and the unstated task of holding overflow patients or patients who are considered poor candidates for psychotherapy. These other tasks, often not stated, may or may not be compatible with the primary stated task.

Lawrence and Robinson (1975) have described the primary task from three different perspectives: the existential task, the phenomenal task, and the normative task. By existential task he refers to what people *believe* about what they are doing. The phenomenal task is what people are *actually doing*. The normative task is what people *should be doing*. It is an important part of the therapist's role to monitor what is really being worked at in the group and to attempt to lead the group toward a congruence between the normative, the existential, and the phenomenal tasks. The therapist, on the boundary, often faces pressure from patients within the group and pressure from vested interests outside the group (such as families or institutions) to adopt other tasks than the one that the group has undertaken. A clear commitment to the primary task is essential to maintain one's direction in the face of covert pressures to stray.

Selecting and Taking in Members. The boundary region that separates the psychotherapy group from the environment is a place where critical work needs to be done by the therapist. This involves making assessments of the suitability of prospective members for the group and converting them from non–group members into group members. The therapist needs to bring together members who are heterogeneous enough in characterological style to generate emotional tension (Kellerman, 1979) and who are homogeneous enough in ego strength and tolerance of anxiety to form a cohesive unit.

In psychotherapy groups with the task of producing meaningful personality change, the group therapist needs to select members who through exchange of projections will enable each other to re-create in the group the most important parts of their respective inner worlds, particularly the parts that are shadowy. It is through the working through and understanding of these interactions that transformations in the members occur that produce greater integration and differentiation.

Groups with more focused behavioral goals, such as abstinence from alcohol or drugs, expedite the development of cohesion and peer pressure by selecting members who are more alike than different. The art and science of composing groups is crucial in building treatment group systems, but there yet remains much to discover about it. There seems to be no substitute for knowing the patients well and matching the tasks to the special needs of the patients. In hospital settings in which the group therapist often has limited authority to select patients, the group task and the structure should be designed to fit the particular patients and their needs.

In the intake process, the therapist must assess the patient's appropriateness for the group and establish the beginning of a therapeutic relationship through empathic listening. However, it is also a vital part of the therapist's role in the process of converting nonmembers into working psychotherapy members to impart to the prospective patient the task of the group, the nature of the activities that take place (including possible risks and benefits), and the role and responsibilities of members.

It is through this process that a contract is negotiated between the prospective patient and the therapist acting on behalf of the group. This shared understanding between therapist and group members becomes the foundation of the therapeutic frame in which participants authorize each other to work and boundaries are defined while autonomy is respected. Most patients are not able to fully comprehend the implications of the contract or fully accept their own authority and responsibility until they have benefited from the therapeutic process. However, unless they are given an opportunity to make informed judgments about what they are agreeing to by becoming group members, the integrity of the therapeutic process will be compromised from the beginning (R. H. Klein, 1983).

After the assessment and contracting phases have been completed, the therapist plays an important part in enabling patients to join the group: to move from the import boundary region into the group. Any member of a psychotherapy group belongs to many other groups simultaneously (e.g., family groups, work groups, churches, or AA), and these sometimes compete for his loyalty and involvement with the psychotherapy group. Also, anxiety and fear of loss of identity stir considerable resistance to joining the group emotionally. One key question for each patient is "How much of myself will I bring into the group?" One group queried a new member, "Will you be here with just your brain or will you bring your gut and your heart?" It is the therapist's job to encourage the patient to join with as much of himself as is necessary for therapeutic transformations to take place. (Groups in which members join with only limited parts of themselves can be conceptualized as being considerably less than the sum of their parts.) Interpretation of neurotic and psychotic anxieties and defenses involved in joining as well as an empathic understanding of the real risks of group life are ways the therapist can encourage greater joining.

Delineating and Managing Intragroup Group Boundaries. What most group psychotherapists term "group ground rules" are conceptualized by the social systems therapist as the delineation and management of boundaries and roles and the establishment of a social contract. To many people, "following the rules" connotes submission to someone else's authority at the cost of one's own autonomy. The novice group therapist is particularly vulnerable to being heavily influenced by a dependent group mentality in which boundaries are revered as though they were the equivalents of biblical commandments and boundary crossings (for example, lateness) are treated as though they were sins. When such a climate prevails, offenders are often reprimanded without collaborative efforts to understand the meaning of behavior and its implications for the group.

From the social systems perspective, boundaries provide a frame of reference that enables members to recognize and process behavior that reveals unconscious affects, conflicts, and memories. It is a challenge for the therapist to collaboratively develop work roles, structures, and boundaries that will facilitate the process of psychotherapy without interfering with the spontaneous, nondirected expression of thoughts and feelings and without undermining the authority and responsibility of patients.

Without "laying down the law," how can the therapist play an appropriate leadership role in establishing a structure that is "holding" and therapeutic? In the assessment and contract phase of intake, the therapist must communicate what he considers to be the essentials of the group in order to enable the patient to make a realistic assessment of whether the therapist and group are appropriate for him. The therapist's willingness to clarify and explain his positions on role and boundary, in addition to interpreting or responding with a question to a question, make the collaborative nature of the development of a social contract more credible.

If the therapist has adequately internalized what he conveys to patients, he will also lead in the development of therapeutic practices and norms by example. If the therapist comes on time, works from his feelings as well as his thoughts, and avoids missing or canceling sessions, his words on these matters will carry more weight. The way in which the therapist furnishes and cares for the group room is another powerful nonverbal vehicle to influence group norms and culture. The establishment of the therapeutic group from a systems perspective is also an unfolding evolutionary process in which the therapist's response to live situations in the group defines and refines boundaries and culture. Paradoxically, when the patient can fully understand and accept his work role and work completely in accord with the boundaries of the group, he is often ready for termination.

The following are role, boundary, and value considerations that are crucial dimensions of the treatment contract and the development of a therapeutic group from a social systems perspective.

The experience of responsibility and the exercise of authority are integral parts of the group patient's role and are crucial to the growth of the individual and the group. An effective therapeutic group process enables its members to experience self authorization and the utilization of more of one's person in role. The therapist plays a critical role in this process when he conveys by his words and actions that it is not only his interpretations that are relevant to treatment, but that the thoughts and feelings of each member contribute to the enlightenment and development of the group. The acceptance of dependent feelings is a critical requirement of the patient role, particularly during early stages of group formation, which can be in itself threatening and problematic for some patients. However, too often therapeutic processes become mired in a spurious dichotomy between patients and therapists, in which "sick dependent patients" are conceived of as the passive, nonresponsible objects to be treated, while "healthy therapists" are assumed to be responsible for the healing. A stultification can occur if patients are unwittingly discouraged from becoming responsible members of the work group as well as recipients of treatment.

Consistent and punctual attendance at group meetings maintains continuity, strengthens the holding power of the group, and underscores the interdependent nature of the process. As part of the intake process, it is important that the therapist introduce to prospective members the relationship between regular and punctual attendance at group meetings and the reliability of the group as a therapeutic instrument. However, the therapist can most effectively influence the adoption of this standard by helping the group appreciate the significance and meaning of lateness and absences when they occur, without being parental or punitive in making this point.

Some means of charging for every session regardless of whether the member attends can help underscore this principle. Though many group therapists give each patient a certain number of "free misses" each year, or negotiate whether a particular miss is "legitimate" or not, in my view such an agreement is misleading and may unwittingly reinforce a counterproductive group fantasy that it is the therapist who is the only valuable member of the group with knowledge and meaning for the group task. In Bion's terms, this could be described as a combined fight–flight and dependency basic assumption, in which members projectively identify all the work aspects of the group into the therapist and then fight with or flee from him. Groups will inevitably gravitate to such basic assumptions in the course of the work, but when the therapist institutionalizes an avoidance of the work by financially reinforcing absence, his interpretations are less credible. Collecting even a partial fee for missed sessions underscores the importance of each members' presence.

Confidentiality and the principle that whatever transpires between members of the group outside scheduled sessions should be brought back into the group stresses the importance of the group as a container. The conventional wisdom that the therapist strongly recommend that patients avoid socializing outside the boundaries of scheduled group meetings in order not to dilute the transference generally makes good sense. However, in work with schizophrenics or patients with severe character disorders who have not developed sustaining relationships, social involvement of patients outside the boundaries of scheduled meetings can at times enrich the therapy by allowing a more secure holding environment to develop. In small communities extragroup contacts are sometimes unavoidable.

When there is involvement of patients outside the boundaries of the group, the importance of bringing these experiences back into the group sessions should be emphasized. This ground rule may be framed in terms of the group's need not to lose vital information and experience. Unreported outside contacts can result in a predicament that is like trying to put a puzzle together with important pieces missing and can easily lead to counterproductive group secrets and triangulation of either the therapist or members.

This principle also pertains to whatever might transpire between therapist and patient in concurrent individual meetings (Rutan and Alonso, 1982). The therapist and patient have the same responsibility as any two patient members to carry back to the group what they might be holding and experiencing that is relevant to the group. If one believes at all in the power of unconscious communication in group process, promising confidentiality to a group member with whom one is meeting individually also reveals an exaggerated belief in the power of one's conscious will. At best this will encumber the therapist in his functioning in the group; at worst it will be deceitful and lead to the fantasy that the therapist and the group are corrupt.

As a result of these considerations the external group boundary is thus drawn around not just what transpires in the group but what occurs between any two or more participants anywhere; this is an example of a boundary that is functional rather than territorial, extends through time, and is essential for the group's reliability as a container.

Resisting the impulse to leave the group precipitously is often a critical aspect of the developmental process. The strength of the group as a container can also be enhanced by discussing with patients in the intake process that anxiety and confusion are often inherent in the change and growth process, and that from time to time the temptation to act on the belief that one can leave painful issues behind by leaving the group can be very compelling, and misleading. Some understanding by group members that the impulse to leave could signal imminent growth might help encourage the fleeing patient to stay long enough to determine if leaving is in his interest or is a defense against change. Bion (1959) has reflected on the hatred of learning through experience and the wish to avoid the pain involved in containing and processing as-yet-undigested experience. A precipitous departure leaves other group members with the experience of losing a part of themselves without adequate opportunity to discover what important pieces of the group feeling and experience this patient has been carrying. Another aspect of this principle is the possibility that the group may "load up" an individual with threatening traits, feelings, or impulses which are about to emerge more overtly in the group but can be eliminated in fantasy by driving him out of the group. An agreed-upon moratorium of several weeks before termination provides everyone the opportunity to sort through projections and introjections, allowing for more clarity in the separation process.

Physical violence or intimidation is incompatible with psychotherapeutic work. This aspect of the group contract is often very relevant in groups with borderline or psychotic patients, or patients with poor impulse control. It helps reassure every group member that the group is a safe-enough place to engage in the delicate work of psychotherapy when an explicit provision is included in the group contract that any member who engages in physically threatening behavior will leave the group until he is ready to assure the others that he is back in control and is able to communicate his distress in more workable ways. The therapist should keep in mind that the group may unconsciously conspire to provoke violence in one of its members as a defense against accepting their own rage against the therapist or others. The group should be committed to resuming work with a suspended member not only for the sake of the suspended member, but also for the sake of the group. To lose a member prematurely is everyone's loss.

Most patients, no matter how disturbed or psychotic, can understand and incorporate ground rules and boundaries with adequate time and effort. In the course of therapy, despite having explicitly agreed to a treatment contract in the intake process, patients often act as if such an agreement never existed. One can conceive of group psychotherapy as a process in which the therapist and group members work toward the development of a therapeutic alliance that cannot be fully realized until the therapeutic process takes effect. The interpersonal disturbances that bring people to treatment usually interfere with the trust and commitment necessary for a fully realized alliance. Nevertheless, if carefully cultivated from the beginning by the therapist, the important ground rules and boundaries can be internalized enough to provide a frame that enables the group to survive the inevitable periods of chaos and acting out that are an integral part of the rich but risky business of group psychotherapy.

Delineating and Managing Therapist's Own Role/Person Boundary. Notions about the role/person interface and the use of self in role provide the most powerful contribution of social systems theory to an understanding of the role of the group therapist. The therapist functions as a boundary manager, a communication expert, and an interpreter, but he is also involved as a person, a member of the group—a subsystem among other subsystems. A. K. Rice (1969) defines "work-in-role" as utilizing sectors of one's person in delineated activities toward achievement of a task, while containing those parts of one's person that are not pertinent to the task.

Like other members, if the therapist meaningfully joins the group, his boundaries will become permeable to the group experience. In the interaction between his person and the group, the therapist's emotions are stirred. This experience can add depth to whatever he sees and hears or considers objectively and theoretically about the group, or it can lead him astray into nontherapeutic behavior. From a social systems perspective, the therapist cannot be immune to the powerful unconscious forces that suck other members into defensive roles. Thus, not only will he be perceived in transference or mythic fantasy roles such as the good and bad mother and father, lover, hero, and devil, but at times he will feel and behave as though to some extent he has been transformed into these figures.

At times when group members are denying and splitting off emotions that they are unable to process or verbally express, the therapist may well find himself filled with intense emotion. In Bion's terms, these circumstances are indicative that the therapist has been called upon to fill a role in the basic assumption group and/or to act as a "container" for what is too threatening for the group to experience in itself. The therapist as "container" receives projections and holds them within, where they become material for thought and digestion instead of for evacuation through projection. Just as the "good-enough mother" contains noxious projections of her enraged, frustrated infant, converts them into thought, and then can better respond to the infant's needs, the group therapist recovers from what Bion (1959) terms the "numbing feeling of reality" (p. 149) of the group experience to put this experience first into thought and then into an intervention that is responsive to both the group situation and the patients' therapeutic needs. In these crucial "containment" and "digestive" processes, the therapist uses his own feelings, fantasies, and behaviors that deviate from role as invaluable information about how the group is penetrating and using him in unconscious and covert ways.

This capacity to use one's personal experience in the role of therapist to facilitate work comes in part from one's ability to differentiate between role and person and in part from the ability to manage this internal boundary with the therapeutic task clearly in mind. Consider the following hypothetical example:

> Members in a therapy group are behaving as if they are all in desperate predicaments in their lives and totally unable to help themselves or each other. They relate to the therapist with admiring deference as they wait for rescue, while their guilt about dependence and greed is denied, split off, and projected. The therapist begins to feel himself as wise and powerful and becomes filled with guilty feelings about allowing group members to suffer needlessly. This in turn resonates with guilt he felt as a child who was unable to cure his mother's depression.

If the therapist recovers by examining his feelings and fantasies and testing them with the current reality, he is then in a position to interpret the situation. An interpretation that is empathic with the anxieties of the members, yet also recognizes the group members' collective projection of competence into him can enable the group to reclaim its competence and get on to work on problems. If the therapist fails to contain and process his experience adequately, he may find himself giving a protracted lecture on how to solve members' problems of living. Group members might then continue to admire the therapist but remain befuddled. This reciprocal intertwining of the patients' and therapist's transference and projections illustrates the transference–countertransference matrix.

In the preceding example, if the therapist lectures the group, he is utilizing a part of his person (the lecturer) that is probably not relevant to the task. Ideally, the therapist utilizes only the relevant parts of his person; however, there will inevitably be occasions when he will be captivated by irrational forces in himself and/or the group and stray from his role as therapist. Such lapses may also be commented on and worked with for therapeutic benefit. The therapist who remains so detached that he does not participate to some degree in the irrational processes of the group maintains the illusion that he is only functioning as an interpreter of others and a projection screen and is most likely to function sooner or later as a roadblock to the necessary unfolding process of the group.

Whatever the group may project onto the therapist, it is also inevitable that aspects of the archaic, nonintegrated inner world of the involved therapist will be activated and projected into the group. A vital aspect of the therapist's management of his person in role involves recognizing and recovering the inappropriate parts of his person that are slipping into the group. Langs (1977), for example, has asserted that a transference interpretation cannot be constructive unless the therapist has recognized and rectified the countertransference component. The therapist can more effectively monitor his own role/person boundary by:

1. considering what he hears about himself as possibly valid and not necessarily transference;
2. examining any deviations in his management of group boundaries like time or task for indications of countertransference;
3. monitoring feelings, fantasies, slips, and dreams for indications of countertransference;
4. questioning the timing of his interventions, as this can illuminate ways in which he uses interpretations unconsciously to protect or enhance his status in the group;
5. being alert to temptations to disclose details of personal life or feelings that are not linked to an understanding of what is occurring in the group—indications that he is abandoning his role;
6. examining premature terminations of group members as possible evidence of countertransference rejection of patients.

While the task of the group is to promote the growth and development of the patients, it follows from a systems perspective that the therapist must also be able to change and grow to allow the system to develop fully. Protracted countertransference suggests resistance in the therapist to his own development and may require in some cases further supervision or psychotherapy.

There is also a developmental dimension to the therapist's management of his role/person boundary. In the early stages of psychotherapy groups, the therapist is usually the central figure. It is often the positive transference and trust engendered by the therapist that enable members to join the group emotionally despite their deep anxieties about revealing themselves to a group of strangers. The therapist's capacity to receive, contain, and process noxious projections from the group often makes him essential for the management of anxiety and aggression, particularly before the group has matured into an effective holding environment. In later phases, as the group can assume some of these functions, the therapist becomes less central.

As the group matures, group members identify with the therapist's containing and processing of experience and develop their own capacity to think rather than evacuate or act impulsively. The therapist then needs to accept that the group members can assume many of his functions. To do so he needs to be in touch with and manage his own narcissistic needs, for if he clings inappropriately to his special status the development of the group can be seriously impaired.

Delineating and Managing Group/Environmental Boundary. The therapist is Janus-faced on the group boundary. Once the group has begun, he focuses primarily inward on what is occurring inside the group, but he must also at times be ready to shift the focus outward toward the environment if the group is to remain viable.

Managing the group environmental boundary is particularly important for those psychotherapy groups embedded in psychiatric inpatient or day hospital systems (Astrachan, Flynn, Geller, and Harvey, 1970; R. H. Klein and Kugel, 1981; C. A. Rice and Rutan, 1981; R. Klein and Brown, 1987). Many psychiatric hospital systems have multiple tasks such as treatment of patients, training, research, and social control of patients, which often impact each other. In addition to group psychotherapy, other task subsystems such as activity therapy, individual psychotherapy, milieu therapy, pharmacotherapy, and art therapy also abound. The possibilities for unrecognized conflict between various tasks and task subsystems are legion. On a psychiatric hospital ward, Levine (1980) illustrated, through his use of a psychotherapy group as a "milieu biopsy," that the conflicts of the larger system around values, work, and unrealistic fantasied expectations were played out in the psychotherapy group.

Because of the permeability of the boundary of the psychotherapy group, what appears to be individual psychopathology of the patient often in fact may reflect pathology of the system. If the psychotherapy group is to maintain integrity and be a functioning part of the work system of the inpatient unit, the therapist must maintain rapport with other staff members, negotiate conflicts of schedule, clarify and resolve possible role conflicts if he has roles in other aspects of the system, and clarify criteria for information crossing into and out of the group. Delineating the boundaries of the psychotherapy group in relation to the larger system enables conflicts to be identified and negotiated as an alternative to unacknowledged covert struggles between subgroups or their representatives. Stanton and Schwartz's (1954) pioneering work on the hospital as a social system demonstrated that such covert struggles often lead to agitated patients winding up in seclusion rooms.

In more disturbed individuals, such as lower functioning borderline and psychotic patients who have poorly developed internal boundary management subsystems and are part of relatively undifferentiated family systems, the management of the group external environment boundary is crucial in treatment. I reported elsewhere (Skolnick,

1985) on a clinical situation in which the exercise of greater autonomy in a member of a psychopharmacology group provoked repercussions in the larger mental health system, the family, and the judicial system—all of which rebounded to the medication group to exert pressure on the therapist.

> A young man had entered the program from a forensic ward where he had been committed for making threatening remarks about the President of the United States. He came to the program overmedicated, subdued, and content to let his family, the family lawyer, and the Secret Service manage his personal and biochemical boundaries. The task of the medication group involved the pharmacotherapist and the patient with consultation from other group members determining medication and dose.
>
> In the course of the work, the patient realized that he had surrendered too much control of his personal boundaries to others and that his current dose of medication was causing painful side effects that were interfering with treatment. A decision was made to lower the dose of the antipsychotic medication. Within a few days, a halfway house counselor, the family lawyer, and a representative of the Secret Service were exerting pressure on the therapist to restore the previous dose of medication. The therapist held firm. Disturbances in other members of the family that had been bound by controlling the sickness in the designated patient began to emerge as the patient showed improvement.

As illustrated in this vignette, boundary decisions are not simply exercises of technical or intellectual understanding, but at times require the therapist to endure intense anxiety and fears of retaliation from the environment in order to preserve the integrity of the therapy.

The social systems conceptual framework, with its attention to careful delineation of task, role, and boundaries, enables therapists to work more effectively in different roles in different task groups with the same patients within a hospital ward or therapeutic community. For example, the clinical director of an intensive day treatment therapeutic community may also function as group psychotherapist, consultant to the patient government, family therapist, and member of the community. In such a situation, one must be clear about one's tasks, roles, and the boundaries between groups, in order to effectively utilize different facets of self and avoid serious confusion. For instance, this same person could make interpretations of unconscious group dynamics and transference in a small psychotherapy group, lead patients and staff in a community meeting in the task of distinguishing the problems of the real exercise of authority from problems arising from transference and countertransference, and follow instructions from a patient in a community food committee on how to make the salad.

Some roles and tasks within a treatment system are incompatible, however, as illustrated by the following example:

> In a long-term day treatment system, requests from outside agencies for records and assessment interviews of patients to determine eligibility for Social Security, Medicare, and disability entitlements presented serious role and task conflicts. Not surprisingly, it was discovered that many of the patients' fears of having Social Security payments cut off intensified as they began to make therapeutic progress, often culminating in defensive regressions and undoing of hard-won therapeutic gains.
>
> Based on the belief that staff transactions with these outside agencies compounded treatment resistance, treatment boundaries were made less permeable to third parties. A policy was developed not to report to third parties except to verify patient attendance at the program, and to refer all requests for assessment of patient capacity to professionals outside the treatment system.
>
> This policy met resistance from the patients, who now had to arrange these evaluations. However, the greatest resistance to this boundary decision came from the larger mental health institution of which the day treatment program was a part, which feared that if patients were not receiving disability payments, reimbursements to the mental health system would be reduced.

The experience of working with patients who have not developed adequate boundary subsystems of their own, or who have an investment in surrendering these functions to others, underscores the significance of careful monitoring of the boundaries and integrity of the treatment system. Changes in such patients and alterations in treatment boundaries often elicit swift and intense reactions from the environment. Since these patients, with their permeable boundaries, are susceptible to absorbing pathological projections from any source and tend also to projectively identify their health into others on whom they depend, they are very vulnerable to subtle external pressures to remain dependent part-objects on the bottom rung of the ladder in hospitals and treatment systems for the chronically ill—what Goffman (1961) described as "total institutions" (p. 4). If treatment is to be effective for these patients it is therefore essential that subsystems with regulated boundaries be established for them, in which they can safely exercise their own authority and have the opportunity to learn from experience.

The importance of the group/environment boundary in the outpatient group is often more subtle than in the inpatient group, but it must be considered. The outpatient group therapist must relate the outpatient group to a possible variety of individuals and other groups such as referral sources, individual therapists, credentialing bodies, third-party payers, mental health organizations that authorize or house the group, and family members of patients. The intergroup nature of the outpatient therapy group not infrequently confronts the therapist when therapeutic success in the group leads to a disruption of family equilibrium of a group member, or an individual therapist expresses disagreement about the treatment approach in the group.

Serving as Catalyst and Protector. In coming into contact with the emotional life of the therapy group, the individual is confronted with primitive impulses and feelings usually not in his awareness. He may also be thrown back to a murky world of part-objects and anxieties characteristic of the paranoid-schizoid position, in which an inner sense of goodness is preserved mainly by denial, splitting, and projection of rage, envy, and badness into others. Because these experiences are at variance with the ego ideal, feelings of vulnerability and shame (Eisold, 1985) may result. It is therefore important for the survival of the nascent group that the therapist convey an empathic understanding of the threats to the self that are inherent in the process of joining.

As inevitably happens in any effective therapy group, some patients, because of their "valences" and vulnerabilities, are placed at considerable risk. These patients, overloaded with feelings or impulses that may feel unbearable, are prime candidates to flee or to be exported from the group prematurely or to be thrust into roles in which they are pecked at, like Prometheus, by the group. It is an important part of the therapist's role to protect members from such overload by vigorously interpreting this dynamic or otherwise intervening to reduce the pressure on the member and enable other group members to reassume their share of the problem.

Performing this function, even when it entails confrontations with the group, is an important factor in establishing the group as "good-enough" to trust. Each member knows, at least unconsciously, that he could also be the group victim. Most psychotic patients have been scapegoated severely in their lives, and because of the primitive nature of their defenses tend to scapegoat others when threatened. Successful group treatment of these patients often hinges on the appreciation and response to scapegoating. It is often necessary in treating these patients for the therapist to be able to contain and process the experience of being hated and the experience of being hateful without reactively projecting this back into the group.

There are also circumstances—for instance, at times of group inertia—when the therapist may act to catalyze the projective process. The first step in gaining access to the shadowy sides of self often requires the projection of what is felt to be too threatening in one's self into the group or other members.

With groups of especially vulnerable or rigidly defended patients, the therapist may function at times as a titrator of interaction. For example, when the group is in a quiescent equilibrium for too long, a therapist may provoke interaction between himself and the group or between members by encouraging un–self-conscious expression of feeling and thoughts as they occur, asking questions, commenting on nonverbal behavior, or sharing his feelings. At other times it might be important to slow down the process through frequent interpretations or soothing comments in order to prevent an uncontrolled escalation. Reframing a frightening situation in a group to highlight its positive potential can be a useful technique to detoxify or bring anxiety into tolerable limits. For example, the expression of murderous feelings by one member toward another can be framed by the therapist as an opportunity for everyone to learn about how to manage rage toward others constructively.

On those occasions when interpretation, reframing, or empathic reflection do not serve to reduce anxiety or threatening behavior to bearable levels, particularly with more disturbed patients, the therapist may need to rely on the more managerial aspects of his role. For example, the therapist may utilize psychodrama techniques, such as role reversal, to manage a dangerously escalating fight between two patients while other group members are encouraged to participate as doubles. In extreme situations the therapist, again acting in a managerial capacity, may need to firmly invoke the provision in the treatment contract against physical intimidation by requesting that members threatening violence leave the group until they choose or are able to conduct themselves within the limits of acceptable group behavior. The therapist's titration in the systems framework can be conceptualized as catalyzing when boundaries between subsystems are too impermeable and as slowing down interaction when boundaries become too permeable.

Often groups will resort to exporting across the psychological boundary of the group into nonmembers (such as spouses, bosses, friends, children, or "them") particularly painful realities, feelings, or themes (Ganzarain, 1977). As a boundary regulator for the group, the therapist is faced with deciding whether to refrain from intervening (because of a judgment that what is being projected is beyond the group's containing capacity at the moment) or to bring back the issues and feelings more directly into the group through interpretation (because the group is strong enough to use this material in the conversion and differentiation process). While it is the therapist who makes most of these decisions in the early phases of the group, in later phases other group members can assume this function through growing awareness, greater interpretive capacities, and increased judgment.

Processing Information and Interpreting. Input and processing of information is essential in the survival and development of complex living systems. From a social systems perspective, the group therapist plays a vital role in the processing of information. In systems terms, he regulates, stimulates, decodes, and interprets in order to provide group members opportunities to assimilate new information that emerges from the group experience about feelings, behavior, and relationships between self and others, both past and present. Such new information plays a crucial role in the transformation of the self–other schemas in the minds of group patients from the anachronistic models of childhood into more integrated, realistic, contemporaneous, and flexible representations and in helping patients achieve more effective, satisfying interpersonal relationships.

Particularly in the early phases of the group, the therapist is called on to function as the primary communication expert. Other group members are usually focused on the manifest level of communication and oblivious to other levels of meaning. The effective therapist is capable of tuning in simultaneously to several different levels of communication. He processes intonations, body language, and emotional expressions embedded in the content, and he makes inferences about meaning.

Much of the un–self-conscious communication of group members is geared toward relational maneuvering rather than dialogue between persons. Each member unconsciously attempts to maneuver every other member into configurations that fit internal models of self–other constellations (Ezriel, 1952). The therapist can decode and interpret these covert communications into more explicit language. The manifest level of communication often refers to "there-and-then" phenomena that the therapist may choose to translate into "here-and-now" messages, in order to make the tensions and conflicts within the group system more explicit. The therapist is sometimes able, through these interpretations of group experience, to bring back within the boundaries of the group what the members are unconsciously trying to project out of the group or into a subgroup or individual. After a meaningful confrontation and examination of covert "here-and-now" issues, the therapist may choose to shift the time focus of the group back to "there-and-then" to assist members to better understand their own histories and their relationships with family and significant others.

As an information-processing expert, the therapist also decides on which level of the group to focus his interventions. Communication flow in the group simultaneously reveals aspects of the intrapsychic systems of individuals, interpersonal subsystems, and the group as a suprasystem. The therapist may choose to focus an intervention on the group as a whole, an individual, or a subgroup, depending on where he believes the intervention is most likely to be received and worked (Astrachan, 1970; Singer et al., 1975; Horwitz, 1977). For example, when a group encounters a conflict that provokes intense anxiety, members may defend against full awareness of this conflict by creating the illusion that the one member who happens to have the valence to manifest the issue overtly is the sole owner of the problem. If the individual used in this way is able to proceed with work on the problem without being disabled by the projections of other group members, the therapist may choose to make interpretations addressed to the intrapsychic system of the individual. If the interpretations are constructively used by the individual, this individual provides work leadership while the group profits vicariously. Later, the therapist can interpret more explicitly the shared group aspect of the conflict, and other members can experience their own parts more directly. If, on the other hand, the individual is sufficiently disabled by the group projections that he is at risk of becoming a casualty, the therapist should focus interventions on the group-as-a-whole defensive collusion in order to protect the individual from being further exploited, thus helping the group find a more enabling way to work the issue.

Consider the following vignette:

> A group with a male therapist had been struggling with neurotic conflicts about sexuality but had been unable to express these issues openly. During one session the group engaged in an animated discussion about the pros and cons of allowing explicit sexuality on television and the U.S. Attorney General's campaign to stamp out pornography, which suggested to the therapist that the issue and the related transference issues were coming closer to the surface.
>
> One of the women in the group began to behave seductively toward the men in the group, including the therapist. The group covertly encouraged this activity until it became more blatant, then confronted the woman, accusing her of using her sexuality in a manipulative way. The woman then began to cry.

The therapist here has several choices. One option is to initially focus on the crying patient by encouraging her to speak about what she is feeling or offer an individual interpretation because he believes that she has access to links between the group situation and previously repressed sexual attraction to her father and fear of retaliation from mother and siblings. If this patient is able to explore these issues, it is likely that it will bring comparable feelings to the surface in other members who have been projectively identifying their sexuality into the woman behaving seductively. Furthermore, it is likely that the therapist will eventually be able to work back to the common group tension and the transference to the male therapist.

Alternatively, if the therapist believes that the crying patient is overloaded with guilt and shame as a result of the forceful projection of sexuality and badness into her by the group, he may first focus on the group, emphasizing how it is using the member to avoid experiencing sexual conflicts, perhaps fearing retribution from the (Attorney General) therapist. In yet a third alternative, he could focus on the relationship issues between members from an interpersonal perspective.

No matter what level is addressed, the group as system and each member as subsystem are affected by the intervention. It is useful to keep the group as a system in mind even though one might be ostensibly addressing only a part of the system. The social systems perspective enables the therapist to assess and intervene at different levels and parts of the system, much like one might work with different objectives on a microscope with a microtome, the choice ultimately depending on a judgment involving task, circumstances, and therapist preference.

POTENTIAL PITFALLS

Group Relations Conferences sponsored by the Tavistock Institute in England and by A. K. Rice in the United States have provided a fruitful arena for studying and further developing Bion's penetrating insights about groups, incorporating understanding derived from social systems theory (Rioch, 1970). These conferences, utilizing an experiential learning format, provide participants with opportunities for intense encounters within this perspective. The deeper understanding of group process that can be gained has considerable relevance to group psychotherapy.

However, a misleading stereotype of the "Bion" small group consultant has become part of the folklore surrounding these conferences.

In this stereotype, the consultant is portrayed as an enigmatic, detached presence who "sits behind his face," making cryptic interpretations. This portrait of the consultant conjures up an omniscient, godlike figure who reveals profundities, rather than a human being in role who is interacting and struggling to learn through experience.

This stereotype in part grows out of the basic assumption dependency group, which often plays a dominant role in conference life. However, not infrequently consultants collude unconsciously with the group to support this illusion because of narcissistic countertransference in which they are enticed and intoxicated by exalted reflections of themselves, using this role as insulation from the pain, responsibility, and confusion inherent in group experience. Despite its fundamental contradiction with systems thinking, residues from early psychoanalytic tradition, in which the role of psychoanalyst is viewed as a noninteractive neutral projection screen interpreting the patients' transference from a detached position, may also have subtly reinforced this stereotype.

Another difficulty arises when the behavior of a study group consultant in group relations conferences is used too literally as a model for the role of the group psychotherapist, because of the distinctly different tasks involved. The study group has the educational task of providing an experiential opportunity for emotionally stable adults to learn about group dynamics, while the psychotherapy group has the task of promoting psychological change in emotionally disturbed patients. Although there is often considerable overlap in process in the two types of groups, the consultant and the group therapist will often need to make very different types of interventions to remain in concert with their respective tasks.

Therapists who overidentify with the "Bion" stereotype in psychotherapy groups run the substantial risk of promoting an iatrogenic vicious cycle in which their behavior produces undermining regressions in the group, which confirm interpretations of the group's primitive transference state (Gustafson and Cooper, 1978). On the other hand, group therapists who dismiss the "Bion" perspective in reaction to this stereotype miss opportunities to enrich their work and have only a partial understanding of what is going on.

The social systems perspective provides the therapist with a conceptual flexibility not as yet found in any other framework. As a metatheory it can enable therapists to bridge and utilize the richness of disparate psychological, biological, and sociological theories, different time frames, and varying levels of focus. The utilization of this perspective gives the therapist an array of ways to formulate a given moment in the group and also an array of choices about how to intervene. If the therapist relies too heavily on detached intellect to understand the group, the choices might well become so numerous and seemingly arbitrary that he could be overcome by a paralyzing directionlessness. However, if the therapist follows Bion's principle of staying attuned and informed by one's subjective experience, then the risk of information overload or sterile intellectualizing is reduced.

The responses of a therapist during a group session are analogous to the behavior of a seasoned tennis player in a match. The tennis player painstakingly practices hitting balls in numerous ways with numerous spins and theories of stroke production, developing a large repertoire of possible responses. Once in a match, if this knowledge is internalized, he can be attuned to the present moment and be able to respond to many levels of information, including such factors as speed, trajectory of the ball, and position of his opponent, choosing among many possibilities in his repertoire almost instantaneously as the ball heads his way.

However, there are risks. The conceptual flexibility of systems theory can also be misused by the therapist as an intellectualized defensive buffer against the uncertainties and anxieties of the group experience or as a rationalization for interventions driven by countertransference. The intellectual possibilities and the sense of being able to manipulate variables can become so intriguing and seductive that a detached grandiosity can overtake the therapist. This can seriously interfere with one's appreciating that one is a human being struggling with others in the human realm, in which ambiguities and paradoxes defy complete mastery.

Social systems language also does not provide a language that communicates to most people in the realm of feelings. The effective therapist must therefore often use system notions as a tool in his private thinking and translate such constructs as "boundary subsystems," "suprasystem," and "throughput" into everyday language that relates more directly to human experience.

CLINICAL EXAMPLE

Eight sessions of an outpatient psychotherapy group in which a patient's threat of suicide leads to a developmental crisis in the group will illustrate interventions by the therapist from a social systems perspective.

The group consisted of four women and three men, ranging in age from late twenties to late thirties, who suffered from neurotic and characterological disorders. Prior to the crisis, the group had been working for several months on themes of disillusionment with and loss of parents and the difficulties of establishing intimate, committed adult relationships. Despite a sense of cohesion, there was also considerable resistance to shifting from the emotional assumptions of disgruntled, dependent children to more adult perspectives.

Five members had been in the group for two to three years. Bob and Barbara had been group members for five years. Bob was planning termination. Martha was the only group member who met with the therapist individually on a regular basis. The group contract stipulated that all individual meetings held between therapist and members of the group part were considered grist for the group mill and would not be held in confidence.

In an individual meeting Martha revealed a plan to commit suicide. She indicated that she would spare everyone's feelings by making her death appear accidental. Martha had emphasized for years that her life felt like endless servitude. She experienced little about herself except that she was either empty or evil. Only by serving others did existence become bearable. Death afforded her the only hope for peace.

Martha's mother emerged in the material as a domineering, narcissistic woman who for over thirty years claimed to be dying, with an assortment of ailments including heart disease and cancer. Martha's memories of childhood were dim except for caring for her younger siblings, fear of disturbing her mother, and terror of her father's rages. She could recall no childhood friends or interests except reading and listening to music alone. At age seventeen she married an older man after two dates. Initially seeming paternal, he emerged after marriage to be an alcoholic. When she entered therapy at age thirty, Martha feared that her two sons were becoming addicted to drugs and failing in school. In the course of therapy, Martha finished a college degree and rose from clerk to executive as a result of technical brilliance and slavish devotion to her mentor, a narcissistic female boss.

In individual therapy the patient slowly allowed a strong attachment to the therapist to develop, despite her great discomfort with feelings. In the sessions the therapist often felt himself to be needy, ill, and exhausted, with the patient as a dedicated, oversolicitous nurse. When the therapist judged their relationship to be secure, Martha entered the group. Initially, she assumed the role of everyone's mother or nurse, but she became overwhelmed by the group experience, and for months sat silently. In her dreams the group appeared as monsters and vampires, but positive transference to the therapist kept her from fleeing. As she gradually recovered her equilibrium, she was able to resume her accustomed role as solicitous mother. She made insightful interpretations about others and nodded sympathetically when others spoke, but said little about herself. Martha's primary defense involved projectively locating her dependent, aggressive, and sexual feelings into her sons, alcoholic husband, therapist, boss, and group members, leaving her depleted, without a sense of self. She attended to these projected aspects of herself by solicitude toward the recipients of the projections. At times the group tentatively challenged her behavior, but usually preserved her as the embodiment of a nurturing, omniscient mother and leader of a basic assumption dependency group.

In the individual session in which Martha disclosed her suicide plan, the therapist struggled with feelings of fear and overwhelming responsibility that were probably similar to the feelings evoked in Martha by her mother. It became clear in this session that Martha's emerging feelings of jealousy and resentment seemed to her to threaten to destroy everyone. The urgency to kill herself seemed to be fueled by the need to kill off the developing awareness of self. Though tempted to hospitalize Martha, the therapist concluded that he was identifying with her fear of the omnipotent destructiveness of negative feelings. The actual risk of imminent suicide seemed low, particularly after Martha entered into an agreement not to act on her plan. While the risk to the comfortable group equilibrium was considerable, the growth opportunity both for Martha and the group also seemed high if the crisis could be handled within the group rather than by exporting Martha and the problem to a hospital.

In the next group meeting, Martha said nothing about her suicide plan, behaving in her usual fashion as the nurturing mother. The therapist felt filled with tension, while group members, including Martha, seemed nonchalant and relaxed. In an effort to redistribute some of the tension back to Martha and the group, the therapist encouraged Martha to reveal to the group the suicide plan that she had shared with him in the individual session. Martha refused. By the terms of the contract negotiated with the group, the confidentiality boundary surrounded the group as a whole, including individual meetings. The therapist therefore was authorized to reveal to the group what Martha had shared with him without violating confidentiality. The therapist sympathized with Martha's fear of exposure and felt pressure to hold her secrets. However, he reasoned that not sharing his knowledge of Martha's crisis would collude with Martha's encumbering defensive role and shield the group from facing its defensive exploitation of her pathology. On this basis he decided to recount his meeting with Martha.

The group appeared stunned and Martha was enraged. The therapist felt less isolated now that Martha and the group were involved. Initially, members attempted to understand Martha's despair. However, these efforts were soon supplanted by efforts to encourage, advise, and shame Martha out of her feelings. Martha revealed her weariness about being compelled to prop up so many people, perhaps doing more harm than good, particularly with her children. "Everyone would be better off without me," she said ominously. Martha was now opening the boundaries of her inner world as she became more like her mother, a mother who dominated others through threats of abandonment by dying.

Martha's persona as the good mother began to disintegrate. For the first time she expressed resentment about being exploited and angrily scolded the group for not giving her something—at least the right to kill herself. As Martha refused to comply with the group's pressure to renounce her despair, the group turned away from her and cast plaintive glances at the therapist. The therapist interpreted this process as a demand to fix Martha and return the group to its previous comfortable state in which the group felt protected from disillusionment with parental figures like Martha and himself. This interpretation was followed by a long silence. The therapist then continued, "I feel pressured to protect all of you from having to know about Martha as a struggling person." Long silences and a few strained perfunctory interchanges characterized the rest of the meeting. The therapist felt exhausted and that night dreamt that he was driving a bus that crashed because of his negligence, killing all the occupants.

The next session echoed the previous one as the group tried to maneuver Martha back into her caretaker role while avoiding any exploration of their own feelings. However, Martha resisted the group pressure and uncharacteristically continued to express anger and resentment. The therapist emphasized with the group's realistic apprehensions about Martha, but also suggested that group members were struggling to keep familiar illusions about Martha and parental figures alive even though the demise of these illusions might be essential for everyone's development. The group ended once again with members and therapist anxious and discouraged.

An hour later, Pat, another member, called the therapist to express alarm that she had seen Martha walking alone down a dark street, looking desperate. She expressed guilt that she had not stopped to check on Martha, but she had felt too afraid. Pat had earlier revealed in the group that her mother, while psychotically depressed, had tried to kill Pat and herself. Pat had been unable to connect this trauma from her eighth year to her terror of closeness with others now.

At the next meeting the therapist recounted Pat's phone call and wondered whether it might be connected to feelings about Pat's mother. The tense impasse continued. Silences were punctuated by attempts at small talk that filled the time. The therapist, frustrated and feeling responsible for the predicament, revealed that he felt punished by the group for involving them with Martha's suicidal crisis. Helen blurted out that her problems seemed insignificant compared to Martha's and that nothing she said to Martha seemed to help. The therapist felt that Helen was speaking on behalf of the group. Feeling beleaguered, he attempted to revive the work group by pointing out that the group was acting as if its only alternative was to restore Martha to her good mother role, when in fact there were opportunities to understand everyone's feelings and conflicts. Nevertheless, the group did not budge from its preoccupation with Martha, even though she had earlier implied that she no longer felt suicidal.

This struggle continued over the next two sessions. Bob, whose termination was scheduled for the following week, emerged as a work leader without followers. He attempted to explore his feelings about leaving and encouraged others to share more about what was happening within themselves. Although it seemed clear that Bob had achieved a great deal over five years and that his termination was appropriate, several members expressed concern that Bob was jumping ship and felt others might follow. Helen speculated that there might not be any members left when the new person, who was scheduled to join the group in three weeks, arrived. The new member was referred to by several as "urgently needed new blood," with the implication that the transfusion might be too late.

The therapist felt the life draining out of the group. While in previous sessions it had seemed that the crisis involved saving Martha, now it felt as if the dying patient was the group itself. Occasionally, a member made an attempt to express a feeling or share a problem, but others would not respond. The therapist pointed out the pattern and suggested that the group was at risk of starving itself to death by the members' refusal to feed each other. Helen commented that she had suffered too many losses in her life, including a boyfriend who had committed suicide, and that she didn't want to invest in people if they wouldn't always be there. When the therapist found himself entertaining fantasies of terminating the group and finding members who were willing to invest more, he realized he was being sucked into the prevailing group culture. He struggled with this feeling as he pointed out that if one waited for guarantees from others before getting involved, it was likely to be a long wait.

In the next meeting, Lori began by revealing a dream about a woman friend sleeping in the same bedroom with her. In the dream the woman moved toward her bed with a knife in her hand. Lori desperately ran to the group for help, but instead reached the therapist's kitchen, where she began messily stuffing herself with food. She then felt too ashamed to show her face in group. Despite what seemed to be an obvious metaphor for the group predicament, no one—including Lori—worked with the dream. After a few minutes of silence the therapist commented, "I feel that Lori's dream is a glimpse of how withholding is making us ravenously hungry. Shame about needy feelings seems to be keeping people from helping each other. The lack of response to Lori's dream is another example of the way we are starving ourselves."

As he made this comment, the therapist heard a scolding quality in his own voice, a sign to him of his growing exasperation. After a silence, Pat mentioned that next week she would be late for the group because she was meeting a man. "He is forty years old going on six," she complained. She described him as demanding and whiny, particularly when she didn't gratify his every wish. Helen and Lori joined in about the big-baby–men they had known and their infuriating ways. The therapist's irritation at the group's ignoring his interventions led him to consider that the "big baby" being talked about was him. He also reflected to himself that he was not the only big baby in the group and that the other members were projecting that part of themselves into him and men outside the group.

Trying to help members deal more directly with this split-off part of themselves, he acknowledged his own "big babiness" but also interpreted the denial and projection of their "babiness." Lori then reminded the group that she was going on an archeological dig in a couple of months and wanted to make sure that she wasn't charged for the missed sessions. (During the past troubled month of the group there had been a number of absences from the group.) Lori continued, "Well, doctor?" The therapist felt all eyes on him, waiting to see how he would respond to the challenge of an important boundary.

The therapist responded that he wished they could all go on a dig together to understand what was happening in the group, for everyone knew the policy that members were charged whether they attended the session or not. He sensed that with Lori's leadership, the group was testing to see if the therapist could solve the group's problems without their assistance. The therapist heard anger in his voice; he experienced himself fighting for the life of the group against the patients as adversaries. Martha spoke, after several weeks of silence, to say that no one wanted to hear her feelings. Larry responded by saying that he missed the times that she used to pick him up and bring him to the group or take him home. Phil asked why Larry didn't drive. "I guess I am afraid of the responsibility," he replied.

In the ensuing ten minutes it seemed as if the task of the group were to persuade and advise Larry about the procedures for acquiring a car and a driver's license. The problem of taking initiative and responsibility in the group was now being put into Larry. It was a relevant issue for Larry, and he was a willing recipient of the projection. The lively tension seemed to drain out of the group as Larry and the group fell into a "yes, but" pattern. The therapist suggested that people were handling their difficulties with "driving" by trying to "fix" Larry. "Let's all get into the back seat and let the damn therapist do the driving! After all, we are paying him," Helen exclaimed, with the apparent assent of all the members. The therapist remembered his dream about driving the bus that crashed.

Silence followed, but tension seemed to return to the group, indicating that more people were now struggling with feelings. Pat glanced repeatedly at her watch and rolled her eyes. The therapist recalled seeing that expression many times in the past month and realized that since Pat had called him to express her concern about Martha she had seemed sullen and antagonistic. When the therapist pointed out Pat's nonverbal communication, she exploded, "I am tired of you picking on me and you'd better quit it." The therapist reminded her that she had said very little in the group since Martha had spoken about suicide, and that in general she had been very cautious about revealing her feelings in the group. "This is not a trustworthy group," she responded, with an increasing edge to and tearfulness in her voice.

At this point the therapist became aware of an impotent rage, not unlike feelings that he had experienced in quarrels with his mother and wife, and he began to worry about countertransference. He felt that the group was continuing its struggle with him through Pat. Pat interjected, "You are turning the group against me, and if you speak to me again I am leaving." With that comment her tears flowed freely.

The therapist felt that this was a crisis in the development of the group. Intense hatred and deep suspicion had surfaced. The therapist, though intimidated, felt strongly the importance of not being silenced by Pat, for that would tell the group that he had no confidence that they could endure these feelings together. He struggled inwardly to contain rather than react and to understand his involvement in a complex transference–countertransference matrix.

The therapist then made a decision to address the group problem by initially interpreting Pat's complex transference. He suggested that Pat was living out with him and the group the frightening family interactions that surrounded her mother's psychosis and attempts to kill her. Furthermore, she had transferred fears of her mother to

Martha and rage toward father for not protecting her from her mother to the therapist. The family scenario had been reenacted when he had failed to understand the magnitude of Pat's terror the night she saw Martha walking alone. The therapist acknowledged that he may have acted callously toward her but also felt manuevered in part into this role by her provocative nonverbal communication.

Martha flushed and declared that she felt she should step in between Pat and the therapist to protect Pat from more abuse. Martha then remembered repressed scenes from her childhood in which she had thrown herself between her father and brother to prevent violence. Experiencing the therapist as well intentioned but frustrated enabled her now to imagine her father as a person whose volatility was a result of his having to live with a sick wife for so many years and also bear the burden of taking care of a number of children who were often unruly. Martha added that she could now experience her parents more as struggling persons than mysterious and frightening forces and could also see herself now as a sad and frightened little girl.

The session ended with a great deal of unexplored intense feeling. Pat was still crying, and the therapist felt uncertain whether any of them would meet again.

Everyone was present at the next meeting, and Pat began the meeting by indicating that she had decided to stay in the group and to work on her difficulty with closeness. Several members talked about what the struggle had been about for them. Larry revealed a rage related to the suicide of his father that had broken through his depression and numbness in the previous session. Helen admitted feeling jealous of Martha's "special" relationship with the therapist and compared this to her family, where she was expected to be a model for her acting-out sister, whom she felt was more valued by their father. Lori spoke of her terror of growing up and her smoldering rage at her father, who abandoned the family in her childhood. She linked this with her anger at Martha and the therapist for abandoning their roles as parents. A sense of camaraderie prevailed in this meeting, as if the group had lived through a painful crisis together and had survived. Martha shared a dream in which she felt shocked to discover that she was wearing a nursing bra in public while everyone looked at her exposed breasts. She began to work on her tendency to overfunction for everyone, seeing that this might stultify the growth of others.

In the next meeting the new member was taken in. The group presented itself as having vitality and receptivity. Lori described a romantic triangle that had developed at work and a dream transparently full of oedipal themes. The group worked spontaneously with

Lori's dream and began to examine the covert rivalries and attractions in the group. The therapist felt more like another member of the group than the embattled work leader struggling against a group collusion. Nor did he feel like the central figure, despite the oedipal material being presented. He made few interventions, more facilitating than interpretive. Despite important changes in the group—the export of one member and the introduction of another—the group maintained its essential structure and gave evidence of shifting into a new developmental phase. Though the therapist entertained the possibility that what appeared to be a significant developmental step for the group might in fact be a "flight into health" impelled by the loss of one member and the addition of another, subsequent meetings confirmed that genuine change had occurred.

DISCUSSION

In these sessions, group members experienced aspects of the complex subterranean connections and maneuvers between themselves, the therapist, and figures of their inner worlds, providing a glimpse of how archaic inner worlds can distort and shape experience of the here-and-now group. Martha and the group underwent transformation of the rigidified groups in their minds, permitting more receptivity to experience with new people. The recursiveness of change is illustrated: Martha's transformation forced the group to undergo transformation; the group's transformation forced Martha to undergo transformation. The therapist came to appreciate that the individual meetings with Martha did not constitute a separate concurrent therapy, but rather was a key subsystem in the larger group system. Most importantly, this example illustrates how the therapist's experiencing and imagining these interrelationships enabled him to move back and forth between Martha and her suicidal crisis and the group and its life-and-death developmental crisis without sacrificing either.

Most of the effective interventions made by the therapist can be understood as either management or delineation of a variety of boundaries. The decision to bring into the group material that had emerged in the therapist–Martha dyad, but had been excluded from the group, disrupted in dramatic fashion the restricted matrix of roles and steady state of the group.

The challenge to some key group boundaries established by the group's contract became pronounced during the crisis period. Lateness, increased absences, and amnesia for the task brought the therapist into continual confrontation with the group. The more the boundaries were broken, the more the integrity of the external group boundary and the life of the group were threatened. Holding to the boundary about payment for missed sessions in the face of the challenge led by Lori seemed to be a turning point that helped reestablish a task orientation and renewed appreciation by the members of their roles as empowered workers as well as dependent patients.

The members of the group, in their anxiety, managed their own psychological boundaries through an unconscious collusion involving mechanisms of denial, splitting, and projective and introjective identification, in ways that threatened to obstruct group work. For example, when Martha abdicated the maternal role, the group projectively located all strengths and resources in the therapist so as to preserve the fantasied childlike attachment to the omnipotent parent—but at the same time depleted themselves of the ability to understand what was happening to them. Other examples of rearrangement of psychological boundaries include the projection of entitlement into the "big-baby–men" outside the group, of passivity into Larry, and of rage toward the therapist into Pat. Through use of his own experience and subsequent interpretation of the ways the group defensively redistributed impulses, traits, and feelings, the therapist helped members re-own split-off parts of themselves. As a result, members were able to mediate the boundary between their inner worlds and the outer worlds of others more effectively and to convert defensive communication to more genuine dialogue.

The therapist also managed task boundaries by focusing the attention of the group on different levels and parts of the system. Prior to the crisis with Martha, the therapist had functioned primarily as a facilitator and interpreter of member-to-member interactions, utilizing an interpersonal frame. The crisis with Martha stirred up intense anxieties in group members, who retreated to regressive group defenses that oscillated between basic assumption dependency and fight–flight. This crisis threatened the cohesion and the holding and containing capacities of the group, without which the interpretive working through of dynamic object relations could not proceed. During this period, the therapist felt pressured to abandon his role as therapist in favor of becoming a dependency leader or face a mass evacuation of patients or destruction of the group, as reflected in his dream of the bus crash. By containing and then interpreting his experience in terms of the group-as-a-whole transference and firmly managing group boundaries under attack, the therapist was able to help the group weather its crisis and reclaim its capacity to hold, contain, and work.

That the group was then able to assist as the therapist and Pat first identified and then worked on intense transference and countertransference signaled that the threat to the group was abating. After clarifying the transference–countertransference matrix between Pat and himself, the therapist eventually returned the focus to the group as a whole and the part played by other members. With the crisis resolved, the group appeared to enter a new phase in which member-to-member focus predominated.

Psychotherapy groups evolve developmentally over time if conducted well, but oscillations inevitably occur in response to short-term changes in tension between predominantly basic assumption culture and work culture, calling for the therapist to focus on different levels of the system. The therapist who thinks in systems terms can choose the level of intervention based on his assessment of receptivity and opportunity and the need to maintain and develop the holding and containing capacities of the group.

The therapist relied heavily on his personal experience to inform him about what was transpiring at covert and unconscious levels of the group. This required a continuous monitoring of his own role/person boundary, in which he made discriminations between what in his behavior was an appropriate unfolding of his role, what was a reaction to transference or projection from the patients, and what was a derivative of his own unresolved conflicts and transferences.

For example, the therapist was aware of feeling sexual attraction to Pat, while at the same time he was also aware of feeling that she was to blame for the group impasse. These feelings were evidence that the therapist had counterprojectively identified with Pat's introject of her father (he had engaged in incestuous behavior with his daughters and had scapegoated Pat as the culprit of his family difficulties). The angry confrontation between the therapist and Pat was a modified reenactment of Pat's inner selfobject world. This enactment resonated with the inner selfobject world of other members. For example, Martha experienced a protective urge to stand between the therapist and Pat and was able to remember for the first time that her father had been violent toward her younger siblings.

The permeability of the therapist's personal boundary, his transparency, and his receptivity to the role of Pat's father had catalytic benefits in this instance. However, if the therapist had not also processed his feelings toward Pat and arrived at an understanding of the mosaic of projective and introjective exchanges across boundaries, he might well have escalated the conflict with Pat, thus contributing to the deterioration of the group situation.

In addition, the therapist recognized that his feelings toward Pat were intensified by the way they resonated with some similar feelings toward his wife and mother. This enabled him to make interpretations that did not imply that Pat's transference was solely responsible for the emotional turmoil in the group, but was also the result of complex unconscious contributions of all present. If this understanding had not been included in the interpretations, they might well have been experienced by Pat as a repetition of her father's scapegoating rather than as constructive and clarifying.

A clear notion in the mind of the therapist about his role, task, and person provides both a frame of reference to detect important intrusions into his person and a holding framework that enables him to dip into the group experience, function as a container for feelings and impulses that cannot yet be experienced by group members, and not lose his way. This capacity in the therapist is often the nidus that eventually enables group members to evolve empathic understanding of themselves and others.

The therapy group embarks on a psychological, social, and developmental odyssey. As in the clinical example, when the work proceeds, it leads inevitably into an immersion in the mysterious and frightening forces of unconscious fantasy and an interlocking web of projections and introjections of the inner worlds of the members and the therapist. The deep anxieties about Martha's threatened suicide almost paralyzed the group. Further, the disorganization, fragmentation, and loss of illusion that is an integral part of the developmental process in psychotherapy can be experienced as a threatened psychological death. Apprehensions about Martha's threatened suicide and anxieties provoked by the developmental process were inextricably intertwined.

In many respects the therapist follows the lead of the group. However, during crisis it is often necessary for the therapist to lead a reluctant group into confrontation with and exploration of an amorphous, frightening, and shadowy world. It is during these times that the therapist must also serve as a manager of the boundaries and group process and a container for intense anxiety, as well as a reservoir of optimism that psychological resurrection is a probable outcome of the journey. Clearly, an understanding of the group as a social system can be an invaluable companion on this journey.

REFERENCES

Astrachan, B. M. (1970), Towards a social systems model of therapeutic groups. *Soc. Psychiat.*, 5:110–119.

—— Flynn, H. R., Geller, J. D., & Harvey, H. (1970), Systems approach to day hospitalization. *Arch. Gen. Psychiat.*, 22:550–559.

Bacal, H. (1985), Object relations in the group from the perspective of self psychology. *Internat. J. Group Psychother.*, 35:483–501.

Baker, F. (1968), Review of general systems concepts and their relevance for medical care. In: *Systems and Medical Care*, ed. A. Sheldon, F. Baker, & C. McLaughlin. Cambridge, MA: MIT Press.

Bertalanffy, L. von (1968), *General Systems Theory*. New York: Braziller.

Bion, W. R. (1959), *Experiences in Groups*. New York: Basic Books, 1961.

—— (1970), *Attention and Interpretation*. London: Tavistock Publications.

Bridger, H. (1985), Northfield revisited. In: *Bion and Group Psychotherapy*, ed. M. Pines. Boston: Routledge & Kegan Paul, pp. 87–107.

Durkin, H. (1972), Group therapy and general systems theory. In: *Process in Group and Family Therapy*, ed. C. J. Sager & H. S. Kaplan. New York: Brunner/Mazel, pp. 9–17.

Eisold, K. (1985), Recovering Bion's contribution to group analysis. In: *Group Relations Reader 2*, ed. D. Colman & M. H. Geller. Washington, DC: A. K. Rice Institute, pp. 37–48.

Ezriel, H. (1952), Notes on psychoanalytic group therapy. *Psychiat.*, 15:119–126.

Foulkes, S. H. (1975), *Group-Analytic Psychotherapy: Method and Principles*. New York: Gordon & Breach.

Frank, J. (1957), Some determinants, manifestations, and effects of cohesiveness in therapy groups. *Internat. J. Group Psychother.*, 7:53–63.

Freud, S. (1921), Group psychology and the analysis of the ego. *Standard Edition*, 18:67–143. London: Hogarth Press, 1955.

Ganzarain, R. (1977), General systems and object-relations theories: Their usefulness in group psychotherapy. *Internat J. Group Psychother.*, 27:441–456.

Goffman, E. (1961), *Asylums*. New York: Anchor Books.

Gould, L. (1989), Exploring origins of personal authority. Paper presented at the 9th Scientific Meeting of the A. K. Rice Institute, New York City, May.

Grotstein, J. (1989), Chaos, meaninglessness and the black hole: A new psychoanalytic paradigm for psychosis. Paper presented at Sheppard Pratt 26th Annual Scientific Day, Baltimore, MD, April.

Gustafson, J. P., & Cooper, L. (1978), Collaboration in small groups: Theory and technique for the study of small-group process. *Human Relations*, 31:155–171.

Hirschhorn, L. (1988), *The Workplace Within*. Cambridge, MA: MIT Press.

Horwitz, L. (1977), A group-centered approach to group psychotherapy. *Internat. J. Group Psychother.*, 27:423–440.

—— (1983), Projective identification in dyads and groups. *Internat. J. Group Psychother.*, 33:259–279.

James, D. C. (1984), Bion's "containing" and Winnicott's "holding" in the context of the group matrix. *Internat. J. Group Psychother.*, 34:201–213.

Kellerman, H. (1979), *Group Psychotherapy and Personality*. New York: Grune & Stratton.

Kernberg, O. F. (1980), *Internal World and External Reality*. New York: Jason Aronson.

Kibel, L., & Stein, A. (1981), Group as a whole approach: An appraisal. *Internat. J. Group Psychother.*, 31:409–427.

Klein, E., & Gould, L. (1973), Boundary issues and organizational dynamics: A case study. *Soc. Psychiat.*, 8:204–211.

Klein, M. (1959), Our adult world and its roots in infancy. *Human Relations,* 12:291–303.

Klein, R. H. (1977), Inpatient group psychotherapy: Practical considerations and special problems. *Internat. J. Group Psychother.,* 27:201–214.

——— (1983), Some problems of patient referral for outpatient group psychotherapy. *Internat. J. Group Psychother.,* 33:229–241.

——— Brown, S. L. (1987), Large group processes and the patient staff community meeting. *Internat. J. Group Psychother.,* 37:219–238.

——— Kugel, B. (1981), Inpatient group psychotherapy: Reflections through a glass darkly. *Internat. J. Group Psychother.,* 31:311–328.

Langs, R. (1977), *The Therapeutic Interaction: A Synthesis.* New York: Jason Aronson.

Lawrence, W. G., & Robinson, P. (1975), An innovation and its implementation: Issues of evaluation (Document No. CASR 1069). London: Tavistock Institute.

Levine, H. B. (1980), Milieu biopsy: The place of the therapy group on the inpatient ward. *Internat. J. Group Psychother.,* 30:77–93.

Lewin, K. (1950), *Field Theory in Social Science.* New York: Harper Brothers.

Lofgren, L. (1976), A process-oriented group approach to schizophrenia. In: *Treatment of Schizophrenia,* ed. L. J. West & D. E. Finn. New York: Grune & Stratton.

Lyth, I. M. (1989), *The Dynamics of the Social: Selected Essays,* Vol. 2. London: Free Association Books.

Marshall, R. J., & Marshall, S. V. (1988), *The Transference-Countertransference Matrix.* New York: Columbia University Press.

Miller, E. J., & Gwynne, G. V. (1972), *Systems of Organization: Control of Task and Sentient Boundaries.* London: Tavistock Publications.

——— Rice, A. K. (1967), *Systems of Organization: Control of Task and Sentient Boundaries.* London: Tavistock Publications.

Neumann, E. (1955), *The Great Mother.* New York: Pantheon.

Newton, P. M., & Levinson, D. J. (1973), The work group within the organization: A sociopsychological approach. *Psychiat.,* 36:115–141.

Pines, M. (1978), The contribution of S. H. Foulkes to group analytic psychotherapy. In: *Group Therapy—An Overview,* ed. L. R. Wolberg, M. L. Aronson, & A. R. Wolberg. New York: Stratton Intercontinental.

Redl, F. (1942), Group emotion and leadership. *Psychiat.,* 5:573–576.

Rice, A. K. (1953), Productivity and social organization in an Indian weaving shed. *Human Relations,* 6:297–329.

——— (1969), Individual, group and intergroup processes. *Human Relations,* 22:565–584.

Rice, C. A., & Rutan, J. S. (1981), Boundary maintenance in inpatient therapy groups. *Internat. J. Group Psychother.,* 31:297–309.

Rioch, M. J. (1970), Group relations: Rationale and technique. *Internat. J. Group Psychother.,* 20:340–355.

Rutan, J. S., & Alonso, A. (1982), Group therapy, individual or both? *Internat. J. Group Psychother.,* 32:267–282.

Scheidlinger, S. (1982), On scapegoating in group psychotherapy. *Internat. J. Group Psychother.,* 32:131–143.

Singer, D. L., Astrachan, B. M., Gould, L. J., & Klein, E. B. (1975), Boundary management in psychological work with groups. *J. Appl. Behav. Sci.,* 11:137–176.

——— ——— ——— ——— (1979), Boundary management in psychological work with groups. In: *Exploring Individual and Organizational Boundaries,* ed. W. G. Lawrence. New York: Wiley.

—— Shapiro, E. R. (1988), Discovering links between early and family roles and current organizational roles: A loved and feared task. Paper presented at A. K. Rice Institute. Festschrift in honor of Dr. Margret Rioch's 80th birthday, Washington, DC, March 19.

Skolnick, M. R. (1985), A group approach to psychopharmacology with schizophrenics. *Yale J. Biol. Med.*, 58:317–326.

Slater, P. (1966), *Microcosm*. New York: Wiley.

Smith, K. K., & Berg, D. N. (1987), *Paradoxes of Group Life*. San Francisco: Jossey Bass.

Stanton, A., & Schwartz, M. (1954), *The Mental Hospital*. New York: Basic Books.

Sutherland, J. D. (1965), Recent advances in the understanding of small groups, their disorders and treatment. *Psychother. Psychosom.*, 13:100–125.

—— (1985), Bion revisited: Group dynamics and group psychotherapy. In: *Bion and Group Psychotherapy*, ed. M. Pines. Boston: Routledge & Kegan Paul, pp. 47–85.

Trist, E. L., & Bamforth, K. W. (1951), Some social and psychological consequences of the long-wall method of coal getting. *Human Relations*, 5:6–24.

Turquet, P. (1974), Leadership: The individual and the group. In: *Analysis of Groups*, ed. G. S. Gibbard. San Francisco: Jossey-Bass.

Whitaker, D. S., & Lieberman, M. A. (1964), *Psychotherapy Through the Group Process*. New York: Atherton Press.

Winnicott, D. W. (1965), *The Maturational Process and the Facilitating Environment*. New York: International Universities Press.

Yalom, I. (1970), *The Theory and Practice of Group Psychotherapy*. New York: Basic Books.

13

Summary: The Role of the Therapist

DAVID L. SINGER, Ph.D., HAROLD S. BERNARD, Ph.D., and
ROBERT H. KLEIN, Ph.D.

"Role"—"The part or character which one has to play, undertakes, or assumes. . . . Chiefly, with reference to the part played by a person in society or life . . ." (*The Compact Edition of the Oxford English Dictionary,* Vol. 2, 1971, p. 2567).

As applied to work efforts such as conducting a psychotherapy group, the term "role" connotes a constellation of activities or functions geared toward achieving a task. The authors in this section were asked to articulate, describe, and illustrate the ways in which one takes on the role of group therapist when working from their particular theoretical perspective. More specifically, they were asked how they framed the therapeutic task, the therapeutic contract, and the change process. They were also asked to write about their role definition of the group therapist—including strategy, techniques, and areas of responsibility; definition, understanding, and use of countertransference; and management or use of self-in-role. Essentially, we wanted to get a sense of how a group therapist working from the self psychology, the object relations, and the social systems perspectives attempts to coordinate the activities of all concerned to produce the desired results.

Interestingly, we believe what emerged were some very different viewpoints and emphases concerning what the desired results are, which activities and whose activities needed to be coordinated, and how to go about the task of coordinating them. Of critical importance for this chapter is that these authors appear to be pursuing overlapping, but somewhat different, tasks in the approach to group therapy they describe. In many ways these perspectives do not turn out to be competing or incompatible either/or approaches. Rather, they show up as different methods of pursuing different goals, which in some respects may be capable of productive integration and synthesis.

In what follows, we will attempt to highlight where we believe the areas of difference and convergence lie—especially as they pertain to the group therapist's role—and will suggest implications for the practitioner.

CONCEPTUAL OVERVIEW: THE THERAPEUTIC TASK

As we have noted in an earlier chapter, all three of the theories addressed in this volume are interpersonal in their fundamental thrust. One's personality is not seen as primarily derived from, and cannot be understood adequately in terms of, instincts, drives, defenses, and their vicissitudes. Rather, life is with people. The human being is viewed as an intrinsically social creature who must be understood both developmentally and in terms of current functioning from the perspective of self-in-relationship to others, in both "real" and fantasied relationships, conscious and otherwise. Although similar in the view that personality is rooted in the world of relationships—past and present—there are also critical differences amongst the therapeutic tasks that the three authors in this section describe themselves as pursuing in their approaches to group therapy. And, indeed, each of the three theories appears to highlight a somewhat different psychological level on which the psychotherapeutic enterprise is focused—different areas of dysfunction or psychopathology and different aspects of psychological life.

Ashbach and Schermer present self psychology as addressing ways in which group therapy may be used to enhance the self system. The goal is to effect increased cohesiveness, vitality, and strength of that sector of the personality termed the "self" and to work toward resolution of associated issues in the narcissistic domain. Members are selected on the basis of having disorders of the self marked by fluctuations in self-esteem that are preoedipal in origin and are characterized by an internal split between the "grandiose self" and the "depleted self." During group sessions, particular attention is paid to members' selfobject transferences as they manifest themselves—how members relate to others in the group based on their own narcissistic needs. Though concerned with relationships, because attention is centered on the selfobject aspects of these relationships, the therapeutic focus is essentially intrapsychic—facilitating the capacity to realistically value oneself, the capacity of the self to develop stable attachments to others, and the capacity to respond realistically rather than catastrophically to slights and deprivations experienced in the world.

Ashbach and Schermer clearly acknowledge that they are *not* presenting a total approach to group therapy based upon self psychology. Rather, they see themselves as describing how a group therapy grounded in self psychology can be particularly useful in working with one sector of the personality, and one set of problematic issues. For the more heterogeneous groups characteristic of day-to-day outpatient practice, they recommend a much broader approach than one focusing on the self system alone and, indeed, specifically recommend a model of group therapy that combines self psychology and object relations perspectives.

As he describes it, Tuttman's object-relations-based therapy is geared toward alleviating the contaminating effects of early identifications and unconscious fantasies, which tend to interfere with present-day reality interactions with others. His object relations approach to group therapy focuses on dyadic interpersonal transactions: relations between self and others around a variety of developmental issues, and conflictual domains, both preoedipal and of later origin. This could include, but would not be limited to, difficulties or deficits involving the self system, and narcissistic issues.

As articulated by Skolnick, social systems theory provides a set of metaconcepts through which to understand the organizational aspects of group psychotherapy and their implications for its successful conduct. The therapy group is seen as a social system with both a work task and an emotional life. Particular attention is paid to the group as a whole and its relations both with the individuals who comprise it and the environment(s) to which it is linked and of which it is a part. The therapeutic focus is on the individual-in-the-group qua system.

While partially rooted in open-systems and organizational theory, Skolnick's brand of social systems group therapy has its psychological grounding in the work of Klein, Bion, and the British object relations school. Group therapy is seen as affording opportunities to transform the relatively closed, archaic aspects of the inner self–other world into a more open system that can serve as the springboard for the development of the self. This occurs as the group attempts to deal with its emotional life in the here-and-now, and as each member, via projective identification as a primary mechanism, is induced to take on various social-emotional roles for which he has a particular proclivity or "valency," and which embodies unwanted aspects of the group's emotional life.

In practice, this brand of social systems–oriented group therapy could potentially encompass all of the levels and issues that serve as the focus of self psychology (the self system and narcissistic issues) and object relations (internal representations of self and others as they affect sense of self and interpersonal relations) approaches as described by the other two authors in this section. In a sense then, this social systems perspective completes a set of approaches characterized by increasingly inclusive levels of focus ranging from self through dyad to system. Skolnick also notes that a social systems–based organizational perspective might be combined with other psychological theories just as well, yielding a brand of group therapy that would be different in terms of the psychological *content* that would be addressed, yet similar in its attention to boundary issues and to multilevel perspectives on the relationship of individual members to different aspects of the group-qua-system.

How do the differences in focus and concern of the therapeutic tasks embraced by these three approaches to group psychotherapy spell themselves out in terms of the role and function of the group therapist? This is the issue to which we now turn.

THE CHANGE PROCESS AND THE ROLE DEFINITION OF THE GROUP THERAPIST

As one would expect, the differing perspectives on therapeutic task manifested in the three approaches to group therapy under consideration are reflected in their conceptualizations of the change process and of the group therapist's role definition. Ranging as they do in focus and therapeutic aim from self on the one hand to system on the other, it is not surprising that the view of both the change process and the therapist's role becomes broader and more complex as one examines the self psychology perspective, then object relations, and finally the social systems approach to group therapy, in turn.

Ashbach and Schermer are clear in their assertion that from a self psychology point of view, therapeutic change in the state of the self comes about through the process of "transmuting internalization." The therapist is seen psychologically as an integral part of the group, not a neutral outsider. The members introject the empathic, valuing, and soothing qualities of the therapist as he listens empathically to their concerns; emotions; states of fragmentation, depletion, and fragility; and their self-esteem fluctuations. These, in turn, are evoked in the ongoing group as part of the selfobject transferences (mirror, idealization, twinship, and merger) that emerge and that are revivals of the developmentally phase-appropriate and legitimate needs of the self during childhood. Over time, members no longer need to rely almost exclusively on external agents for regulation of self cohesion and self-esteem, having developed the capacity to provide these for themselves.

For this process to occur, a high degree of safety and group cohesiveness needs to be first cultivated, and during the process of group development the therapist must become an integral part of what are seen as members' incomplete and deficient self systems. Ashbach and Schermer assert that the primary role requirement of the self psychology group therapist is to continually provide in the here-and-now an experience-near and empathic understanding of the state of the members' selves. In particular, the therapist is responsive to expressions of narcissistic injury involved in entering and joining the group, including the difficulties of identifying oneself as a patient and loss of specialness in the group, as well as potential exposure, vulnerability, and diminution of the self. Although connections are made to memories and past experience, this appears to play a secondary role.

Other issues affecting the self system, particularly the emergence of selfobject transferences, arise during subsequent phases of the group. The role of the therapist here, too, is to interpret them in an empathic and experience-near fashion. While the therapist will certainly be alert to individual member "valencies" for taking up certain group roles, as well as the interpersonal and group-as-a-whole phenomena that emerge, these are not interpreted. Rather, they are managed in such a way as to maintain experienced safety and cohesiveness of the group. In particular, the therapist attempts to continually regulate the levels of stimulation and drive intensity in the group, keeping them within tolerable limits. To forestall potentially destructive processes such as scapegoating, which might either close down narcissistically vulnerable members or drive them out, the therapist acts to reframe behavior and make other unifying and deescalating interventions.

In summary then, in Ashbach and Schermer's view, the self psychology–oriented group therapist aims to promote transmuting internalization in self deficient and narcissistically wounded members by empathically responding to expressions of self system deficit or narcissistic injury and by being the facilitator of a group climate that promotes appropriate selfobject functions in the context of "optimal frustration," thus promoting the development of stronger and more adaptive psychic structures.

From Tuttman's object relations perspective, addressing as it does a wider and more inclusive range of patients and psychological issues, change comes about in members through three major interlinked processes: internalization of some of the therapists' qualities—especially the capacity for a nonjudgmental, calm optimism; the creation of a safe atmosphere in the group—a holding environment; and exploration in the group of the unconscious repertoire of object representations that influence the behavior of each member and that underlie acting out. In the ongoing group, members' regressive inclinations, the repetition compulsion, and the projection of unconscious wishes and fantasies onto one another and the therapist by members are evoked. Old unresolved issues and internalized representations of others are recapitulated and are lived out, for all to see. With the help of the therapist, this provides members a "second chance" to gain insight into these issues and work them through.

Whereas for Ashbach and Schermer's self psychology, empathy and introjection of therapist qualities (transmuting internalization) are both necessary *and* sufficient conditions for change, for Tuttman's object relations–based therapy, empathy, and introjection are necessary but *not* sufficient. It is the insight into and working through of distorted internalized representations that emerge that are crucial for the kind of change being sought in the object relations group. Given his view of the change process, Tuttman sees the role of the leader in an object relations group as having several dimensions. First, the therapist should model in the group an empathic but judgmentally neutral observing and learning stance. Second, the leader's role is to promote a group atmosphere in which it is safe for members to experience and share their fantasies, wishes, impulses, feelings, and fears—an atmosphere of "spontaneity and subjectivity." The notions of the "container," "mother group," and the "holding environment" are all relevant for Tuttman. Often, he claims, if a conducive group atmosphere is created and the therapist provides adequate "identificatory qualities," group members will be encouraged enough to do the necessary exploratory work themselves.

When group resistances are too strong, however, interpretations by the therapist of the ongoing dynamics are in order. Tuttman suggests that these should be made in an empathic way that acknowledges patients' experience and takes into account the developmental stage of the group. Interpretations should be informed by the therapist's awareness of manifestations of unconscious and archaic basic assumptions as well as of the projective identifications, introjections, and splitting mechanisms of group members. While Tuttman is keenly alert to the role of group-as-a-whole dynamics, his examples suggest that preferred interventions of the object relations therapist focus on the interactions between dyads of individual members and among the network of dyadic relationships, rather than on the emotional life of the group as a system or on tensions and issues common to the group as a whole.

Skolnick, too, acknowledges the role of empathy, introjection, and insight (both historical and contemporary) in the therapeutic change process. However, he asserts that from his social systems perspective, it is promoting change in how members behave in the group toward each other, the group, and the environment that is the most central aspect of the therapeutic process. This leads him to focus attention primarily on the here-and-now of the group. Skolnick describes how, in the ongoing group, members come to maneuver each other and the therapist into an unfolding series of group configurations that externalize their internal worlds and recapitulate issues from their families of origin.

To use these events creatively for therapeutic purposes, the social systems approach more than any other makes considerable use of group-as-a-whole and system-level interventions. These tend to focus on how individuals or subgroups (e.g., a therapist–member pair) have come to take on or express unwanted or intolerable aspects of the group's current collective emotional dilemmas on its behalf. An arena is thus created in which therapist and members may together explore these roles, issues, and processes, separating fantasy from reality and judiciously making linkages to members' histories. Ideally, through the therapeutic process described by Skolnick, members come to identify empathically with and reown aspects of the self heretofore hated/feared, disowned, and projected onto others and the group. This, in turn, leads to greater integration, self acceptance, and emotional freedom, thus enlarging and enriching members' possibilities for being-in-the-world. In many ways, this is quite similar to Tuttman's object relations perspective, but with the group-as-a-whole and systemic levels of analysis put center stage.

The role of the therapist as conceptualized within a social systems perspective is probably the latter's most unique contribution. Skolnick claims that while at any given moment the intervention of a social systems group therapist may not differ from that of a self psychologist, an object relations therapist, or many others, the social systems–oriented group therapist will be thinking about and making many decisions based on considerations outside the realm of more traditional theories. The social systems–oriented group therapist serves as what Skolnick terms, "a catalyst and protector of the group enterprise" as well as a "processor and interpreter of information." As with the self psychology and object relations group therapist, the social systems therapist attempts to create what is termed a "holding environment" or "group matrix." However, Skolnick is explicit that much of what will need to be contained and processed in this safe environment is rage and hatred; a point currently the subject of lively debate within the field.

What is most unique to a social systems–based approach, however, is the heightened attention to boundaries and boundary transactions, the idea that group therapists need to be vitally concerned with monitoring and/or managing a variety of boundaries as they work: task boundaries; time boundaries; membership boundaries; confidentiality boundaries; boundaries concerning therapist and member roles, group culture, and ground rules; the therapist's own role/person boundaries; and group/environment boundaries. If the external boundary (that is, the boundary between the group and its environment) is not managed well, the conditions necessary for the effective continuity of the group may be compromised. If key internal boundaries are neglected, according to Skolnick, the necessary emotional container or holding environment is compromised and members will consciously or unconsciously resonate to this threat by withdrawal, acting out, and so forth. Furthermore, if key boundaries are not spelled out clearly and kept in view by the therapist, opportunity is lost for using the subtle ways in which members relate to and treat each other, the therapist, and the group through adherence or nonadherence to these boundaries as material for therapeutic exploration.

THE THERAPEUTIC CONTRACT

The notion of the "therapeutic contract" refers to the shared understanding—formal or informal—between therapist(s) and members about the basic ground rules and assumptions governing the group and its work. The contract can be viewed as a frame within which participants authorize each other to work within the group; it defines the role of both therapist and member. In practice, the contract may be more or less explicit and more or less specific; it may be set forth clearly at the outset or allowed to evolve over time; it may be entered into by members more or less willingly and with more or less awareness and more or less power to control its content, and it may have very different content from group to group around such issues as outside contact between members or payment for missed sessions (Singer, Astrachan, Gould, and Klein, 1975).

Ashbach and Schermer do not address the notion of contract *per se*, but do allow us to infer how they manage the contracting process. Arrangements are handled explicitly, with therapists "instructing" members during pretherapy individual appointments about the necessary fee and commitment. During the initial session "other group rules are stated," which include a prohibition on physical contact, minimal contact outside of group, the importance of putting feelings into words, and members' responsibility to share their experiences and difficulties with others as freely as they can. Clearly these authors seem to believe that for the self psychology group, firm management of these issues by the therapist is conducive to creating the kind of safe atmosphere that will facilitate the work of the group.

Tuttman, on the other hand, believes that the purposes of an object relations group are best served by a less tightly structured and more ambiguous atmosphere in which arrangements in the group are allowed to evolve gradually over time. His rationale is that the more open-ended the group, the more members will feel that their spontaneity and subjectivity are valued. According to this view, when difficult issues arise (such as whether members should be charged for missed sessions) and the therapist is tested by the members, as he invariably will be, opportunities are provided for everyone to react and fantasize. With effective therapist leadership the situation can be worked through and an appropriate policy established. Different groups, he observes, develop different styles and norms. One major benefit of this approach, according to Tuttman, is that the therapist does not then get cast in the role of an autocratic controller, which he believes would constrict the group. While this approach to contracting may be useful and effective, in our experience it is more *laissez-faire* and less structured than that used by other object relations group therapists with whose work we are familiar.

From the social systems perspective, managing the establishment of the group contract is a critical part of the group therapist's role, since the contract is seen as defining the critical boundaries of "social reality" within which the therapeutic work of the group will take place. Skolnick emphasizes that this should be done in a collaborative way, with the therapist willing to offer clarifications and explanations. For Skolnick, key elements of the contract include acknowledgment that the experience of authority and responsibility is crucial to the patient role; highlighting that regular and punctual attendance is crucial to developing the necessary group cohesiveness (emphasized by charging at least something for missed sessions); confidentiality; the notion that whatever happens between members of the group (including individual sessions between members and the therapist[s]) is group business and should be brought back to the group; the agreement that patients will not leave the group without several weeks notice; and a prohibition on physical violence or intimidation. Skolnick also emphasizes that how the therapist relates to the boundaries established in the contract, as much as anything else, will contribute to the tone and culture of the group.

In summary, within the self psychology and social systems perspectives as represented here, early and explicit work around the therapeutic contract is a key piece of the therapist's role. This is in marked contrast to the object relations perspective presented by Tuttman, where issues are allowed to emerge within the group and are then worked with both therapeutically and "administratively." Interestingly, exponents of all three theories view their method as facilitating a culture that will encourage openness and sharing by members. And all three perspectives tend to share similar views of the appropriate ground rules and similar views of the member role as ideally carrying a great deal of responsibility for the work of the group.

THERAPEUTIC STRATEGIES: MANAGEMENT OF COUNTERTRANSFERENCE, THERAPIST SELF-DISCLOSURE, AND THE USE OF SELF-IN-ROLE

The authors represented in this section have all commented astutely on the wealth of material at varying psychological levels that emerges during the course of any session and over the life-span of the group. Therapeutic technique consists of making judgments and choices about what one will attend to, what one will respond to, and how one will respond. A key element for all three theories is evocation of, and work with, transference phenomena, although they understand and use these phenomena in somewhat differing ways.

Ashbach and Schermer describe the therapeutic strategy of the self psychology group therapist as centering around the reframing of members' goals, concerns, and experiences from a perspective that brings their narcissistic components to the fore. Using the technique of "vicarious introspection," from the very outset the therapist becomes immersed in the selves of the members, continuously and empathically interpreting these narcissistic issues back to the members as they emerge. This, in turn, evokes a group regression to points of narcissistic fixation in which members' various selfobject transferences, fluctuations of self cohesion and experiences of narcissistic injury emerge over time. Special attention is paid by the therapist to the mirror, idealizing, twinship, and merger selfobject transferences and their connection to vacillations of the selves of the members between the poles of grandiosity and depletion. These are then interpreted back to the members together with the implicit or explicit message that this is a "state" which will pass, not a "forever reality." Typically these interpretations focus on members' phenomenological intrapsychic experience, even though interpersonal and group dynamics may be taken into account in framing the intervention.

Each stage of group development has associated with it issues and dilemmas that have narcissistic components, and each member's transferential variations on these themes can be evoked and empathically articulated by the therapist and group. Table 1 in Ashbach and Schermer's chapter provides a very useful guide or road map to this technique. Along the way, the therapist encourages and models tolerance for affect and provides leadership in pointing out connections between affects and memories. The therapist also models the capacity to experience narcissistic needs and injury in a modulated manner and, through his behavior, demonstrates healthy expression of more mature narcissistic strivings and satisfactions.

The self psychology group therapist is presented by Ashbach and Schermer as behaving in a rather "real" or emotionally available way in the group, with a group leader who explains and teaches a fair amount at the outset and who, especially in the early stages of the group, meets members' needs for direct empathic response and is not at all a blank screen. However, this does not imply that their technique includes a great deal of therapist self-disclosure. Rather, they argue for great selectivity in this domain.

Ashbach and Schermer support the view that considerable "role strain" and a wide range of reactions will inevitably be stimulated in the therapist on many levels by a wide array of influences in the self psychology group, and they believe that these should all be subsumed under the rubric of countertransference. If therapists are skilled in sorting out their own issues from those stimulated in them by individual members and the group, Ashbach and Schermer claim, there is much to be learned about what is going on by examining these countertransference reactions. If not, unresolved issues surrounding shame, entitlement to pleasure, tolerance of strong affect, and needs for narcissistic gratification may lead to therapist acting out and a variety of errors. These might typically include a loss of empathy, working at a level of narcissistic development different from the patients' level, and difficulty in setting limits.

While Ashbach and Schermer do advocate discussion with the group of therapist errors (especially empathic failures and narcissistic slights) and see this as adding to the "user friendly" quality of the self psychology therapist, they do not believe that in the normal course of events a great deal of sharing of therapist countertransferential feelings and dilemmas is useful, as it might tend to overload patients, leave them feeling attacked or abandoned, or spoil the mirror and/ or idealizing transference. On the other hand, they do acknowledge that when used judiciously and selectively, and in ways that are in tune with the state of the self of members, sharing of here-and-now countertransferential reactions—especially at times of therapeutic impasse—can be a very powerful technique that touches patients at a deeper and more emotional level than usual. Overall, the authors stress that their approach stays well within the traditional psychoanalytic framework when it comes to therapist self-disclosure and use of self in the group.

Tuttman presents the object relations group therapist's technique as somewhat less active and directive. Having described the therapist as starting up the group with relatively low structure, he offers a therapeutic stance in which the therapist acts more as a catalyst than a leader as the group evolves. Interpretations are made only when the individuals or the group appears "stuck in resistance." A great deal of emphasis is put on the importance of the therapist's allowing members to experience fully their developmentally determined needs as they emerge in the group without unnecessary therapist intrusion in the form of interpretations. In his brand of object relations therapy, the work of deciphering and examining internal mental representations of others, disentangling projective identifications, and making connections between transferentially dominated current behavior and past experience is best done by the group and the therapist together. The therapist serves as teacher and guide rather than doing most of the interpretive work. In this way the group itself ultimately comes to be the therapeutic agent in the fullest sense— "Bion's work group," as Tuttman says.

While Tuttman does not advocate a great deal of self-disclosure of the therapist's experience in the group, at the same time he does not advocate therapist distance, aloofness, or disengagement. Rather, he suggests that the object relations therapist adopt a stance of providing what is neecessary at the time, given the state of the group and the individual members. At the outset this might well involve empathic reflections, but for the most part he advocates remaining "neutral," refraining from direct interaction with individual members unless the need is so great that a patient might, for example, experience this as duplicating an earlier abandonment. Interestingly, Tuttman describes his technique of using stories about other patients and their problems as ways of communicating his understanding and empathy of members' current experience and dilemmas. His goal is to respond "realistically and therapeutically" to what the patient needs.

If group processes evoke countertransferential behavior from the therapist, Tuttman believes that sharing and exploring this with the group can be productive modeling, which promotes member growth. However, he does not advocate a great deal of self-disclosure of internal experience—countertransferential or otherwise—by the therapist. While the object relations group therapist will experience the tugs and pulls of role suction as a result of the group's process, and experience impulses and feelings not characteristic of himself as a result of patient transference and projections, Tuttman believes it is usually better to monitor and process this experience internally, using it as a basis for later intervention rather than sharing it with the group, but he does not provide a rationale for this position.

A broader range of therapeutic techniques appears to be used by social systems group therapists such as Skolnick. He suggests that in the early stages of the group, soothing empathy can be offered to members who are confronting the real dangers and threats to the self inherent in group life, while at the same time interpersonal and group-level interpretations can be made about underlying collective neurotic and psychotic anxieties and defenses with which the group appears to be collectively grappling. Interpretations are also made about the meanings for the individual members and the group as a whole of the ways in which members are relating to various group boundaries and ground rules (e.g., time, confidentiality, contact outside the group, payment of fees).

A crucial difference between the social systems approach presented by Skolnick and the other approaches in this section concerns self-disclosure and the use of the therapist's experience in the group. Skolnick, like Ashbach and Schermer, observes that if the therapist really joins the group emotionally, his boundaries will become permeable to it. The therapist will inevitably be stirred up by the group, will feel the tugs and pulls of role suction, and will receive parts of the projective identification processes at work in the group. This is the "transference–countertransference matrix." A key therapeutic technique for the object relations–based social systems therapist is to become aware of and contain the experience stimulated by this complex interweaving of psychological influences, digest it, and then include it within an intervention that will be responsive to both the group situation and the individual patients' therapeutic needs. Thus, as contrasted with the self psychology and object relations group, during its middle and later phases Skolnick's social systems group will include a considerable number of interventions in which at critical times the therapist shares what experiences he is "carrying on behalf of the group" or what the therapist feels he is "being asked to do by the group" as part of a larger interpretation of the group as a whole's current psychological dilemma and an articulation of various members' roles or valencies within it. The trick here for the therapist is not to act out the aggressive or narcissistic needs in the process of sharing the experience that has been induced in him by the group process.

DISCUSSION

What has emerged in this section are considerable areas of commonality and several areas of difference among the self psychology, object relations, and social systems approaches. In all three, the therapist is concerned with creating a safe holding environment, providing empathic responsivity for the members during the early phases of the group (though to differing degrees, to be sure), and maintaining awareness of phenomena that are occurring at the intrapsychic, interpersonal, and group-as-a-whole level. And in all three, transference reactions of members within the group are used as a basis for therapeutic work—albeit differently in each. Also, all three points of view acknowledge the powerful role suction and countertransferential pulls that affect the therapist and highlight the importance of self-awareness for the therapist in managing these dilemmas and avoiding acting them out to the detriment of the group and the work.

Key differences were several. One area of difference concerns the nature of the phenomena highlighted and addressed by the therapist in interventions: the impact of the self by self psychologists; intrapsychic experience and interpersonal relations by object relations therapists; and the range of phenomena ranging from internal experience to group-level dynamics by the social systems therapist.

Another area of difference concerns types of interventions. The self psychologist tends to use empathically framed interpretations about the state of members' selves. Object relations therapists tend to interpret the ways in which members symbolize themselves and each other and project parts of themselves onto each other and the therapist. Social systems therapists do all of the above plus use their own internal experience to interpret group-level dynamics and the various projective processes at work in the group. The self psychology therapist thus appears most "experience-near" and "real," and least "distant" in stance; the object relations therapist most "neutral"; and the social systems therapist most varied—both in terms of the psychological level on which interventions are framed and aimed (intrapsychic;

interpersonal; group; and systemic) as well as in the stance of the therapist (ranging from empathically "experience near" for the patient to the more distant, yet revealingly provocative, participant-observer). Finally, the social systems therapist is particularly concerned with managing a variety of boundaries—especially between different subsystems of the group—which is not a matter of systematic concern to therapists of other persuasions.

Yet another aspect of the three chapters summarized and discussed here is worthy of special note. Psychodynamic psychotherapy was for years characterized by, and criticized for, its focus and reliance on clarification of feelings and interpretations of the history and dynamic underpinnings of behavior as its primary tools. Ashbach and Schermer, Tuttman, and Skolnick all demonstrate in their chapters how far the field has come since then. While not making reference to the empirical literature or theoretical conceptualizations surrounding the use of various therapeutic techniques, the methods they describe and their comments about the group leader's role exemplify the widened and increasingly flexible and sophisticated technical repertoire available to contemporary therapists. As would be indicated if one extrapolated the results of studies of the therapeutic relationship in individual therapy and the literature on cohesiveness in group therapy, all of the authors in this section highlighted their concern for the creation of a safe, supportive, and exploration-facilitating group environment (read "therapeutic relationship" in individual therapy language) as a primary technical concern. Furthermore, there was shared concern with defining appropriate and effective ways of productively sharing the therapist's experience for therapeutic ends.

Moreover, each theoretical perspective appears to have identified interventions and techniques other than clarification, confrontation, and interpretation through which to pursue therapeutic aims. Ashbach and Schermer describe the positive reframing of resistance as a way of forestalling flight and keeping clients' narcissistic injuries within tolerable limits in the self psychology group. They also describe the use of other techniques familiar to cognitive-behavioral therapists, such as cognitive restructuring of feelings and behavior and the teaching or coaching of clients in more adaptive ways of handling emotional upset. In a similar vein, Tuttman describes techniques focused on empowering the group and its members in relation to therapist authority, and on therapist story telling—a favorite technique of many child clinicians (e.g., Gardner, 1971) and others for delivering therapeutic messages, including interpretations, in a minimally threatening and maximally acceptable way. And Skolnick describes the judicious use of provocation for therapeutic ends.

In our view, these are developments and directions to be applauded. Understanding the origins of behavior, experience, or suffering does not necessarily dictate how one might go about facilitating change. Until now, psychodynamic psychotherapies have typically been long on insight and understanding of the genesis and dynamic underpinnings of maladaptive behavior, psychopathology and emotional distress, but short on innovative intervention techniques. A rich array of intervention techniques for use in both individual and group therapy has been developed in recent years by clinicians working within other theoretical frameworks. We believe that some of these techniques might be of immense value to the psychodynamically oriented group psychotherapist of any school, under appropriate circumstances and with appropriate clients, for addressing the kinds of issues outlined in the papers by the authors of the three chapters under consideration here. These might include the newer techniques already mentioned (e.g., positive reframing of resistance); the use of specific structured exercises and homework—possibly including use of the genogram and family-of-origin work; and the use of specific expressive techniques such as projective drawings in the group. There are also "uncovering" and "reparative" techniques—typically, but not necessarily, associated with hypnotherapy and hypnoanalysis—such as guided fantasy, visualization, and age regression which have been found highly effective as a means for recovering and reintegrating repressed or dissociated memories with appropriate clients—especially those suffering the sequelae of trauma. The point is that with the additional power available from theoretical advances in self psychology, object relations theory, and social systems theory comes the opportunity to design new and powerful interventions as well. While we recognize the potential dangers of becoming "technique oriented," and indiscriminately combining techniques based upon different theoretical rationales which may have incompatible implications, this remains a fertile field for creative exploration and innovation.

There is one further issue, raised by Skolnick, which we would like to highlight: the danger posed to clients if group therapists attempt to transpose whole cloth the leader role and intervention techniques developed for various *training* groups (e.g., T-groups and group relations/Tavistock groups in which members are provided with opportunities to learn about interpersonal relations, authority and unconscious dynamics in group life) to *therapy* groups, whose primary task is to assist members in overcoming emotional distress and dysfunction. Training group members, at least overtly, are enrolling to learn about group life; not enrolling as patients expecting *relief* from internal pain and distress, as are therapy group clients. And training group consultants are not functioning as therapists, whose primary concern is fostering the growth and welfare of the individual. Rather, in the training group, the leaders' primary task is, it is hoped, to provide *learning,* which is different from (though not mutually exclusive with) therapy or personal growth. These different tasks and roles require different decisions about the conduct of the group at key choice points if the group is to succeed and casualties are to be avoided. As Skolnick rightly points out, and as has been noted elsewhere (Singer et al., 1975), vague boundaries surrounding the task of a group can put members with weak or diffuse internal boundaries at psychological risk.

In closing, we wish to share with the reader some metaphoric images. Metaphor can reveal and it can conceal. For better or worse, the following role images were evoked in us by the authors in this section as they described their work and the role of the group therapist from their perspectives. That all three authors are men should be kept in mind; how women might have written these chapters and what images they might have evoked is yet another fascinating question.

We saw the self psychology therapist as protective mentor, who by gentle instruction, coaching, and modeling helps members attend to their inner life, identify their deficiencies and wounds, and heal over time.

We saw the object relations therapist as a warm and wise uncle who encourages group members to better understand how they see and relate to each other and who stimulates them to find ways of accepting and relating to each other more realistically and satisfactorily.

And finally, we saw the social systems therapist as a samurai leader who, like a composite of the many characters depicted on the screen by Toshiro Mifune, through the force and integrity of his own personality, bonds the group together, helping them to face the "ghosts" in the ancient castle, which, indeed, turn out to be the "ghosts" in themselves.

Needless to say, to some extent, these images reflect an amalgam of the personal styles, gender, idiosyncrasies, and stages of adult development of the authors of the three chapters, as well as the underlying assumptions and values of the theories they describe, and, indeed, something about ourselves. Nonetheless, for us these images do seem to capture something unique about each approach. We leave that for the reader to judge.

It is hoped that all three authors in this section have contributed to new ways of thinking about the therapist role which will enable group therapists to think more systematically about matching therapist stance and technique to the specific task at hand with the specific patients in a given group.

REFERENCES

Compact Edition of the Oxford English Dictionary, The, Vol. 2. (1971), New York: Oxford University Press, p. 2567.

Gardner, H. (1971), *Therapeutic Communication with Children.* New York: Science House.

Singer, D., Astrachan, B., Gould, L., & Klein, E. (1975), Boundary management in psychological work with groups. *J. Appl. Behav. Sci.,* 11:137–176.

14

Conclusion

ROBERT H. KLEIN, Ph.D., DAVID L. SINGER, Ph.D., and
HAROLD S. BERNARD, Ph.D.

In this final chapter we wish to address several broader, overarching concerns relevant to the object relations, self psychology, and social systems models for conducting group psychotherapy that have been described in this volume. More specifically, the following issues will be considered: (1) To what extent do each of these models provide a coherent, internally consistent body of theory and technique for the practice of group psychotherapy? (2) Can each of these approaches be differentiated both from a traditional/classical approach to group psychotherapy and from one another? (3) Does the social systems model, as presented in this volume, constitute an approach to group psychotherapy that is comparable to the object relations and self psychology approaches, or is it simply a different type of model? (4) Can these theories and techniques be reduced, combined, and/or integrated, and if so, to what extent, or do they remain mutually exclusive and incompatible?

COHERENCE AND INTERNAL CONSISTENCY

This volume, which has been organized into three sections (recent theoretical developments, applications to patient care, and considerations of therapist role), contains three chapters from different authors representing each of the three perspectives—object relations, self psychology, and social systems. We might begin this discussion, therefore,

389

by asking whether those authors writing from the same perspective seem to be talking the same language or at least sharing similar ideas about what they view as the key issues. More precisely, can we identify a coherent, internally consistent body of theory and technique that is clearly linked with each particular perspective?

In order to answer this question, of course, it is necessary to keep in mind that the authors contributing to each section were asked to focus on specific questions so as to preserve integration but limit redundancy across the volume. Furthermore, some differences between authors maintaining the same perspective are likely to exist solely as a function of person, style, and points of emphasis. Bearing these considerations in mind, we believe that our first question can be answered in the affirmative.

Thus, for example, while our object relations authors might all agree that there is no single object relations theory, all underscore the critical importance of certain key concepts. Foremost among these is the notion that people are object-seeking, not simply satisfaction-seeking. From this point of view, ego development, and the striving for object relationship, unfolds across a series of stages and initially occurs entirely in the context of the infant–mother dyad. How individuals develop in relation to the important significant others in their lives, especially the mother, is of paramount importance. Rather than focusing on the taming and discharge of impulses as does classical drive theory, the critical issues in development from an object relations standpoint involve internalizing and externalizing relationships, attachment and separation, and the unfolding of various forms of introjective, splitting, and projective processes that are the primary developmental and psychological mechanisms for ensuring continuity of relationships in the presence of contradictory loving and hating feelings (Hamilton, 1989).

From this perspective, the experiences of early childhood with primary objects become part of an internal drama that is carried within as memory and is subsequently reenacted. In the repetition of these internalized family dramas, propelled by efforts at attachment or mastery or both, the individual plays one or more of the roles. New experiences, rather than being fully experienced in their contemporary form, are assimilated into the templates created by the old dramas.

In the context of the group, these unconscious reenactments result in individuals playing out particular roles, selecting and inducing others to assume the necessary reciprocal roles to permit the externalizing of their internal dramas. The group setting provides the interpersonal stimulus field that evokes the unconscious paradigms that underlie each individual's internalized (part-object) relationships. The work of the psychotherapy group is to establish a safe holding environment that will enable its members to reenact and to examine their distorted internal dramatizations. This is accomplished largely via the interpretation of conflicts between various levels of unconscious partial self and object representations; the fantasies, relationships, defensive operations and affects involved in these schemata; and the effects these have upon past and present interactions with others. When the group serves as an effective container, the primitive, disowned, split-off, distorted aspects of the self can be recovered and the restrictive grip of archaic family dramatizations can be loosened, thereby resulting in modification of both internal and external object relations.

From the self psychology point of view, as presented here, there is also considerable agreement regarding the major theoretical premises, the focus of the work, and the role of the therapist in group psychotherapy. The central concept is the development of the self which organizes experience, serves as an existential agent that initiates action, and has a separate line of narcissistic development that continues throughout life. The individual is seen in terms of his ongoing subjective state, with issues of continuity, cohesion, differentiation, regulation, and esteem as the crucial dimensions (Pine, 1988). These functions are initially mediated by the parent who, through empathic attunement, integrates and modulates for the baby. Since the parent is an object who performs these self modulation functions on behalf of the infant, the parent is construed as a selfobject (Hamilton, 1989).

The cornerstone of human experience involves the relationship between the self and its selfobjects. The presence, availability, consistency, and responsivity of selfobjects profoundly affects development. In contrast to a more traditional/classical psychodynamic point of view, this is a deficit model, not a conflict model. The primary determinants of anxiety do not derive from pressure for instinctual gratification but from disturbances in self–selfobject relationships. Individuals unconsciously seek what they previously missed, in the form of mirroring, idealizing and alter-ego functions, to permit the development of a vital, cohesive self.

Patients experience current selfobject "failures" in the psychotherapy group as echoes of unresolved past disappointments suffered at the hands of faulty selfobjects. Successful group psychotherapy involves working through selfobject failures and disruptions, thereby restoring and/or creating what is needed for further development. It is not the interpretation of unconscious structural conflict that promotes change, but the provision of necessary, phase-specific, legitimate but previously unavailable selfobject functions by an experience-near, empathic therapist and group. Via the process of transmuting internalization, individuals gradually take over the necessary functions initially provided by others outside of the self.

With regard to the social systems model, all of our authors indicate that this is a metatheory concerned with the interplay of sentient, social-psychological, and technical factors in group life. Although this is not a motivational theory per se that focuses specifically on individual development, on a dynamic level its roots lie within the psychoanalytic tradition, especially the contributions of Melanie Klein, Wilfred Bion, and the British school of object relations. On a structural and organizational level, its roots may be traced to von Bertalanffy's notions about general systems and to the work of Miller and Rice, which emphasized a sociotechnical approach to task performance. From this perspective, psychotherapy can be thought of as a throughput process with input, conversion, and output phases. The psychotherapy group itself can be viewed as a social system, that is, a whole unto itself, with both a work task and an emotional life. The individual members, the group, and the environmental context in which it is operating can all be thought of as hierarchically linked interactive open systems that share common laws of operation and reciprocally influence one another.

Within one and the same group, there are two groups present: the work group, with its consciously agreed-upon work task, its logical and scientific ways of proceeding, and its allegiance to external reality, and the basic assumption group (dependency, fight–flight, pairing), with its unconscious tasks, its illogical and irrational ways of proceeding, and its allegiance inward to the world of fantasy and drive gratification. A central concern from this perspective is how to effectively harness the emotional energy and vitality of the basic assumption group in the service of accomplishing the given work tasks of the psychotherapy group.

Crucial to understanding this perspective is the idea that interaction in the group takes place across various boundaries (Singer, Astrachan, Gould, and Klein, 1975). The group psychotherapist must remain concerned with monitoring or managing transactions across both internal boundaries (e.g., those surrounding task, time, confidentiality, therapist and member roles, group culture, etc.) and external boundaries (e.g., those determining the relationship between the group and its environment). This model also highlights how group members relate to designated authority and how they exercise their own authority to work at the agreed-upon primary task. The social roles members assume in the group by virtue of their unconscious predispositions, or "valences," and the functions they fulfill on behalf of themselves and others are systematically examined.

From this point of view, interpretations are made primarily at the interpersonal and group-as-a-whole levels. This level of focus, coupled with the maintenance of abstinence and technical neutrality on the part of the therapist, tends to promote regression in the group. By establishing a clear contract that enables the group to serve as a holding environment or container, opportunities can be created for interpretation and recovery of members' projectively disowned feelings, impulses, and fantasies.

In our opinion, then, each of the authors representing each of these three perspectives does seem to be talking the same language, that is, focusing on a core set of concepts that serves to provide an internal consistency and coherence for each model. But perhaps a word of caution needs to be inserted here. It should be noted that we are comparing and contrasting how our authors think about group psychotherapy and what they say they do during sessions. What they actually do across sessions was not observed; rather, it was reported. Although our authors did provide detailed clinical examples, these were, of course, selected by them to illustrate core clinical precepts. Were we to observe the actual behavior of these senior clinicians during ongoing group psychotherapy sessions, we might be more impressed with their similarities than with their differences. Put another way, we might discover that their conceptual differences can be more easily distinguished than can their techniques and actual clinical practices. With increasing levels of clinical experience and expertise, group psychotherapists, like their individual therapist counterparts, may learn to apply a core set of concepts and techniques that have proven to be clinically effective, regardless of theoretical persuasion.

SIMILARITIES AND DIFFERENCES

Let us now turn to our second question: Can each of these approaches be differentiated from a traditional/classical approach to group psychotherapy and from one another?

By a "traditional/classical" approach we mean one that is based upon drive theory. From the point of view of drive psychology, the individual in the group can be thought of in terms of "the vicissitudes of, and struggles with, lasting urges, forged in the crucible of early bodily and family experience, and taking shape as wishes that are embodied in actions and in conscious and unconscious fantasies" (Pine, 1988, p. 572). As a result of the internalization of parental and societal constraints, these wishes are eventually experienced as dangerous and unacceptable. Hence, psychic life pivots around the notion of wish and urge, defenses against them, conflict, and its resolution. This process, based upon instinctual drive and epigenetically unfolding psychosexual stages, is marked by the emergence of anxiety, guilt, aspects of shame, inhibition, symptom formation, and pathological character traits (Pine, 1988).

To begin with, it is important to note that both the object relations and self psychology models constitute developments that evolved from within the field of psychoanalytically informed psychodynamic psychotherapy. In addition, the dynamic component of social systems theory is itself rooted in the contributions of the British school of object relations. Hence, it is not surprising to find that all of these approaches share certain fundamental precepts with more traditional drive theory. For example, all (including drive theory) endorse the importance of psychic determinism, unconscious mental functioning, and primary process, that aspect of thinking based upon symbol, metaphor, and irrational connection among ideas, which is impervious to reality (Pine, 1988). Furthermore, all subscribe to a developmental model, although the content (specific stages, their sources, and their sequence) differs across approaches. All emphasize the importance of repetition and reenactment, and all make clinical use of transference and countertransference phenomena. It also could be argued that the practice of traditional psychoanalysis, with its reliance upon concepts such as transference, countertransference, resistance, and the Oedipus complex, is based upon a psychology that emphasizes problems of relatedness, that is, a type of object relations theory (Bacal, 1985). In general, when conducting the psychotherapy group, all three perspectives underscore the importance of establishing a safe holding environment, providing sufficient empathic responsivity, attending to transference and countertransference responses, and remaining alert to phenomena that are occurring at the intrapsychic, interpersonal, and group-as-a-whole levels.

Nevertheless, object relations, self psychology, and social systems approaches reveal some important departures from drive theory. Thus, while drive theory is based upon the drive-defense paradigm that focuses on how the individual organism discharges its impulses, these approaches emphasize that the individual is also object-seeking from birth, not simply satisfaction-seeking. These are multiperson approaches that emphasize interpersonal relationships, especially the importance of early (preoedipal) relationships. Personality cannot be understood solely in terms of an isolated entity with drives forcing relentlessly outward, the defenses mobilized to deal with them and the process of conflict resolution; yet this is the reductionistic, linear model of causation offered by drive theory. Even with the development of ego psychology, with its emphasis on the individual's capacities for adaptation, reality testing, and defense and the availability of these capacities for dealing with the inner world of drives and the outer world of reality demands, relationships with people were still viewed as being maintained primarily to gratify drives or to defend against their unwanted expression (Pine, 1988; Hamilton, 1989).

In contrast to both drive theory and ego psychology, these models (which rely upon concepts such as splitting and projective identification, the notion of container/contained, the development of selfobjects, and the idea of transmuting internalization) are concerned with interactions between individuals who together form a more complicated system. These are nonlinear, circular models of causation that focus on the dyad—the infant and the parent and their interaction—to understand personality development. These approaches hold that the individual must be understood from the perspective of self-in-relation-to-others; they describe interactions across boundaries, stressing the importance of complex patterns and relationships, not linear causality (Hamilton, 1989).

In addition, each of these approaches differs from traditional drive theory and from one another in a number of more specific ways. Object relations theory, for example, holds that the ego does not develop as a result of conflict between libidinal instincts and societal prohibitions, but is instead present from birth and develops in the context of the object relationship that forms between the infant and the mother. Consistent with this notion is the idea that primary anxiety is separation anxiety, not that which is aroused by the threat of forbidden impulse discharge. In its most extreme form, this is experienced as a state of total aloneness, with the prospect of panic, annihilation, and disintegration of the ego (Alonso and Rutan, 1984).

Thus, from this perspective, the primary problem for the individual is how to preserve the continuity of relationships, not how to modulate impulse discharge so as to conform to societal demands. The concept of inner and outer reality provides the model for understanding infantile ego development: The infant moves from an autistic cocoon containing primitive affects to seeking people into whom he or she can projectively deposit these primitive feelings and who become his or her outer reality. As described by Alonso and Rutan (1984), it is the attachment process that serves as the bridge between inner and outer reality. The boundaries between self and others, that is, between inner and outer reality, become more fully differentiated with increasing maturity.

Over the course of time, the other members of a psychotherapy group can come to represent one aspect of outer reality that resonates with one aspect of the individual's inner reality. The individual's transference distortions can then be subjected to the group's reality testing, thereby setting the stage for interpretation of the distortions. Thus, the reenactment on an interpersonal level of various object relationships with associated affects, wishes, defenses, and fantasies links the intrapsychic level of individual member functioning with the social system level of the group. The therapeutic focus in the group tends to remain the dyadic interpersonal transactions, with the group examining internal representations of self and others as they affect the sense of self and interpersonal relations.

The primary feature that distinguishes self psychology from the other approaches is its focus upon the development of the self. In fact, it might be argued that self psychology constitutes a particular form of object relations theory in which interactions within the group are considered in terms of their effects on one's sense of the self (Bacal, 1985). From this perspective, narcissism is not regarded simply (some would say "pejoratively") as a less mature form of object love that serves as a defense against involvement with an external object. Instead, self psychology posits a separate line of narcissistic development that continues throughout the life cycle. Selfobject transferences, and the ways in which they may come into conflict with each other, express developmentally phase-legitimate selfobject needs.

The therapist who adopts this framework is not trying to work through defenses against anxieties related to the expression of unacceptable forms of object relations in the group, which from a more traditional point of view may be derived from unconsciously warded-off instinctual drives and their vicissitudes (Bacal, 1985). Instead, based upon the notion of a deficit as opposed to a conflict model, the self psychology therapist is concerned with working through defenses against anxieties associated with the expression of legitimate but previously thwarted selfobject needs. Unavailable selfobject responsiveness accounts for the patient's understandable and not necessarily distorted and/or maladaptive reactions, which are repeated in the here-and-now interactions in the group. Aggression is not regarded as an inborn drive but as a by-product arising from the frustration of legitimate narcissistic needs. In contrast to object relations theories, splitting is not a congenitally determined developmental step; it is a fragmentation that arises as a consequence of inadequate empathic attunement (Hamilton, 1989).

Hence, what the patients are conveying is of more importance than what they are concealing. It is through the provision of experience-near empathic attunement during the group that individual members gradually acquire the capacity to overcome the inevitable slights and injuries arising from interactions with unresponsive selfobjects and to maintain self-regulatory functions that permit the development of cohesiveness, differentiation, self-esteem, and a sense of inner vitality. From this point of view, the level of therapeutic focus in the group is primarily intrapsychic, examining the self system and narcissistic issues.

What most distinguishes the social systems model from the other perspectives is not its dynamic component, which is rooted in, and extends to, the group contributions emanating from the British school of object relations, but its emphasis on the structural, organizational aspects of the psychotherapy group as a system. The therapist who adopts a social systems perspective is making assessments, formulating therapeutic strategy, implementing clinical decisions, and initiating interventions based upon considerations outside the realm of the other theories. From this perspective, the therapist is concerned with identifying and regulating transactions across both internal and external boundaries, and with the relationships between hierarchically organized interacting open systems that share common laws of operation and reciprocally influence one another. Particular attention is devoted to the group as a whole, the environmental context in which it is embedded, and to the individual-in-the-group-qua-system. With regard to the task of psychotherapy, efforts are made to transform the relatively closed, archaic aspects of group members' inner self–other worlds (and, as a result, the group as a whole) into more open systems that permit new learning, integration, and change. In contrast to the object relations and self psychology approaches, therapeutic interventions, directed largely to the here-and-now in the form of interpretations, are focused primarily upon the interpersonal and group levels.

To summarize, all of these models endorse certain fundamental precepts of psychoanalytic thinking (e.g., psychic determinism, unconscious mental functioning, primary process), subscribe to a developmental approach, and emphasize the importance of repetition and reenactment. All underscore the importance of establishing a safe holding environment, providing sufficient empathic responsivity, attending to transference and countertransference responses, and working clinically with phenomena occurring at various levels (intrapsychic, interpersonal, and group). In contrast to traditional drive theory, however, these are not linear causality models, focusing on drive, defense, and conflict resolution. Rather, they are multiperson approaches that emphasize that individuals are object-seeking from birth, not simply satisfaction-seeking. They focus on interpersonal relationships and systems transactions to understand individual psychological development.

Hence, differences can be identified between each of these models and traditional drive theory at both conceptual and technical levels. There are clear differences (some major, some minor) with regard to how normal development and psychopathology are understood; the nature of the change process and the task of psychotherapy; how the group can be used to promote growth; the role definition of the group psychotherapist; the range of techniques and types of interventions to be employed by the therapist; and the primary level of focus (intrapsychic, interpersonal, group) at which to conduct psychotherapeutic work in the group. Furthermore, additional differences between these approaches have been highlighted in previous chapters, where the nature of the therapeutic contract, the role of therapist self-disclosure, and the use of therapist experience during the group were discussed in detail.

IS SOCIAL SYSTEMS THEORY A DIFFERENT TYPE OF MODEL?

At this point, it may be useful to consider our third general question: Does the social systems model, as presented in this volume, constitute an approach to group psychotherapy that is comparable to the object relations and self psychology approaches, or is it simply a different type of model? As one of our colleagues recently put it, are we trying to compare "apples and a pear"?

To begin with, social systems theory as presented here is not a theory about individual motivation or development, nor is it a theory about psychotherapy per se. In fact, with the exception of family systems theory, we are unaware of any particular version of social systems that purports to be a conceptual and epistemological clinical theory. More specifically, while object relations and self psychology represent two theoretical positions about the content, process, and dynamics of mental life, the unique contribution of social systems theory is its focus upon structure.

Looked at in this way, social systems may be thought of as independent of any particular dynamic content, but also as a theory that can be combined with virtually any psychodynamic clinical theory. With its unique emphasis on boundaries and boundary maintenance/regulation, hierarchical organization and interaction between systems, and the common laws of operation that characterize social systems at various levels of complexity, it is a metatheory that is at a different level of abstraction. As such, it is neither a conflict nor a deficit model of human development, but a growth/change model that is relevant for understanding all open living systems.

Furthermore, it then follows that one could be, for example, an object relations theorist without embracing open-systems theory, and that, conversely, one could hold almost any psychodynamic clinical position and embrace an open-systems perspective. As a case in point, those of us in the group relations field have always worked with the integration of two conceptually distinct paradigms: a paradigm of psychic life based on the object relations position elaborated by Bion into his basic assumption theory, and a paradigm of structure based upon the open-systems theory of Miller and Rice (Gould, 1987, personal communication).

TOWARD AN INTEGRATIVE APPROACH

Let us now turn to our last question: Can these theories and techniques be reduced, combined, and/or integrated, and if so, to what extent, or do they remain mutually exclusive and incompatible?

In general, we would argue that these models, together with traditional drive theory, provide complementary rather than contradictory perspectives from which to understand group psychotherapy. The idea that these approaches complement one another is based more upon clinical experience than upon detailed theoretical or epistemological considerations. Furthermore, this idea implies that these approaches can be combined to augment and enrich our understanding of the group psychotherapy enterprise beyond that which can be achieved through the exclusive application of a single perspective.

To be sure, we are not unique in advocating this position. In recent years much effort has been devoted to integrating individual and group-dynamic models, especially with the development of the group-as-a-whole approaches, and to linking more traditional with newer models of psychoanalytic thinking. Thus, for example, Horwitz (1977), Kernberg (1983), Kibel (1987), Scheidlinger (1974), and others have maintained an interest in applying object relations theory and ego psychology to group dynamics in order to promote the understanding and resolution of emotional/relational difficulties in group psychotherapy. Alonso and Rutan (1984) suggest that, in the practice of psychodynamic group therapy, object relations theory can be viewed as a conceptual framework that adds to the classical Freudian structural theory. Durkin (1982) has maintained that a traditional psychoanalytic approach can be meaningfully combined with a systems perspective to significantly enhance the power and scope of group treatment. Ganzarain (1989) has advocated employing general systems theory together with object relations theory. In one of the most scholarly and impressive contributions to this area of concern, Ashbach and Schermer (1987) presented a framework for integrating group psychology with psychoanalytic theories of object relations, the ego, and the self.

At this point in its development, group psychotherapy has achieved the status of a distinct therapeutic modality. Yet it remains an amalgam of many different theories with no single prevalent comprehensive theory (Roth, Stone, and Kibel, 1990). We believe this is the case, in large part, because each of the available theories offers a view of the broad range of clinical realities one encounters in the course of conducting group psychotherapy. Each theory speaks to an aspect of those clinical realities that is vitally important, but none holds an exclusive view of the "truth," a situation that is consistent with the state of knowledge in the field of group psychotherapy.

Our view of how to combine or integrate these different perspectives is most similar to that articulated by Pine (1988, 1990). In his discussions of individual psychotherapy, Pine has eloquently described how different theories lead therapists to approach the material produced during the clinical session with different questions in mind, that is, with different potential ways of thinking about the associative content and the accompanying affect. These typically serve as silent, nonverbalized ways of guiding and grounding our listening, providing the means by which therapists begin to organize and to make sense out of the clinical material. We believe that these theoretical frameworks and the questions they enable therapists to generate are equally suitable for use in the group as well as the individual therapy situation.

Thus, from the perspective of drive psychology, which calls attention to the taming, socialization, and gratification of drives, we would be alert in the group to the following questions: What wishes are being expressed and how do they relate to consciousness; what are the underlying fantasies and how do they emerge as a compromise between wish, defense, and reality; what are the defenses employed against the wishes and how effective are they; to what extent is guilt present as a result of the operation of conscience; are symptoms and inhibitions present that signal faulty compromise formations between wish, defense, conscience, and the patient's historical realities; are characteristic, ego-syntonic modes of functioning apparent; and have early under- or overgratifications of particular drives resulted in early fixations and tendencies toward regression under certain conditions (Pine, 1988)?

From an object relations point of view, which focuses on how we carry within us the history of our significant relationships yet try to free ourselves from their constraints to permit the assimilation of new experiences in contemporary terms, therapists might ask the following questions: What old object relationships are being reenacted and who is occupying which roles; are patients behaving as they or as their parents did; is a particular patient's behavior designed to meet his or her parents' wishes or expectations; to what extent are group members relying upon primitive defenses, including denial, splitting, and projective identification; is group interaction characterized by the externalization of part-object dramas; what early passive experiences are being actively repeated in order to master trauma, to repeat pleasure, or to hold onto those relationships to preserve continuity; and "to what degree are these relations, as carried in memory, enacted in identification, or repeated in action . . . veridical renditions of what happened in childhood" (Pine, 1988)?

With regard to the self psychology perspective, which emphasizes the forming of a differentiated, coherent, and whole sense of self that effectively regulates self-esteem and serves as a center of initiative, another series of equally important and relevant questions might be generated. For example, do patients manifest stable, differentiated self-boundaries; to what extent are mirroring, idealizing, or twinship needs being expressed; what self–selfobject relationships are being established, and how do patients deal with the inevitable slights, disruptions, and injuries that occur in these relationships; are fantasies or enactments of merger associated with panic over loss of boundaries; is discontinuity of the self, including derealization and depersonalization, apparent; are patients able to establish and to maintain a stable sense of self value; do patients experience themselves as the center of actions in their own lives; and "what pathological efforts to right imbalances in [each patient's] state of self are present—grandiosity, denial, flights into activity, disdain of others" (Pine, 1988)?

Similarly, the social systems perspective, with its unique emphasis on the structural and organizational aspects of the psychotherapy group as a system, leads the group psychotherapist to yet another important set of considerations. For example, how clearly are internal and external boundaries located, established, and maintained; how are members and leaders recruited into and discharged from the group; are internal structural boundaries (e.g., time, task, and role) consistent with the functions the group is designed to fulfill; are transactions across boundaries being adequately monitored and regulated to ensure the presence of stable, interacting open systems that are conducive to growth and change; how are individual patients, subgroups, the group as a whole, its leaders, and the larger system (e.g., the hospital or clinic) in which it operates relating to and mutually influencing one another; to what extent is the group functioning in a work as contrasted to a basic assumption mode; how is authority being assumed and expressed within the group; what roles are patients occupying, on whose behalf, and how are they being deployed by the group; and to what extent is the group enabling patients to recover and to reintegrate their primitive, disowned part-objects that have been projectively deposited into others?

In certain respects, the proposed integration of these different perspectives in a supplementary or complementary manner is readily apparent and does not appear to pose any particular problems for the clinical practitioner who is not overly concerned with resolving epistemological issues. In other respects, however, the proposed integration does pose some significant dilemmas for the working clinician.

More specifically, it seems reasonably clear and straightforward that the social systems framework can be effectively combined with either a traditional, object relations, or self psychological point of view. This stems primarily from the fact that social systems theory provides a metatheoretical framework focused on structural and organizational issues, not just the specific content and meaning of mental life. Thus, only by maintaining a social systems perspective can one recognize the role and place of the therapy group within the larger system of the hospital or clinic and begin to understand the reciprocal, multilevel functions and relationships that evolve. Furthermore, as noted by Durkin (1982), for example, the therapist who relies exclusively upon traditional psychoanalytic theory has no way to change the structure of the group, since that theory deals only with individual personality structure. By contrast, the social systems therapist, who views the three levels of the group (intrapsychic, interpersonal, and group) as isomorphic, understands that structural and behavioral change at any one level will generate change at the other two levels. Monitoring transactions at the boundaries can serve to "catalyze the dormant potentials of those systems whose boundarying is dysfunctional" and generate new modes of interacting (Durkin, 1982).

Similarly, most psychodynamically trained group psychotherapists have always been concerned with the merging of intrapsychic, individualistic structural theory and interpersonal object relations theory. In the context of the group, where a dialectic is readily observed, object relations has supplemented traditional drive theory. This is familiar territory for group therapists since the highly individualistic, conflict-based structural theory has never fit entirely comfortably into the interpersonal matrix of the therapy group (Alonso and Rutan, 1984). Of course, one must accept the notion that human beings are object-seeking and not simply satisfaction-seeking; if one does, then object relations can be thought of as complementing the topographic, genetic, economic, and structural models. If one views attachment as primary, then ego functions can be thought of as designed primarily to ensure and to preserve relatedness and only secondarily to modulate drives; impulses can be understood in the context of relationships that provide the backdrop against which impulses are played out (Hamilton, 1989). In either case, one can maintain the position that individual character is shaped by interconnected early, bodily-based and object-related experiences (Pine, 1988).

The prospect of combining self psychological with traditional psychodynamic approaches to group psychotherapy seems equally possible. One can hold the view that drive theory is most relevant for treating "structural neuroses," while self psychology is most useful in working with early, preoedipal disturbances. Or one can maintain the view that drive theory and a psychology of the self constitute different, complementary perspectives about the same set of clinical phenomena. Furthermore, with regard to object relations, one can view self psychology as a special version of object relations theory that focuses on self–selfobject relationships. These two perspectives, then, can also easily be viewed as supplementing or complementing one another.

Thus, it would appear that the three different perspectives presented in this volume can be utilized together to attend to critical structural characteristics of the group as a system and to organize the content of group psychotherapy sessions in diverse and complementary ways. As suggested by Pine (1988), such an integrated framework permits the therapist to maintain evenly hovering attention without prematurely forcing the clinical data into unnecessarily restrictive categories.

However, we believe that the more challenging aspects of integrating these different approaches are encountered once one moves beyond data gathering and hypothesis formulation in clinical work to the level of making what one hopes will be mutative interventions. There are important differences between these approaches with regard to their respective theories of therapeusis: that is, their respective views of how change takes place, what needs to change in order to promote health, and what the therapist needs to do to facilitate matters.

In particular, whether one believes in a conflict versus a deficit model has a different set of implications for the role and technique of the therapist, especially with regard to the relative emphasis one places on interpretation as compared with empathy. To what extent is it the more neutral, experience-distant interpretation of unconscious wishes, malfunctional or ineffective defenses, or repetitively reenacted distorted old object relations that leads to change? Is such interpretation of more importance when dealing with certain types of patients, such as those with structural neuroses? When offered to more seriously disturbed patients, are such interpretations experienced as damaging, mortifying, or humiliating? Conversely, should greater attention be devoted to establishing a safe holding environment with increased emphasis given to providing experience-near, empathically attuned responses to enable such patients to feel understood, validated, and not alone? To what extent is it important not to interpret too early the patients' experiences of feeling mirrored or being able to join with an understanding and/or idealized therapist?

Not only must the type and level of patient disturbance be considered in decisions about therapist technique, but in dealing with groups we must also remain sensitive to the developmental level and the developmental tasks facing the group as a whole. Particular theoretical issues and techniques may be more or less relevant as a function of the stage of group development at a particular point in time. In the early phases of development, for example, one may need to be alert to establishing a safe holding environment and to the impact of the joining process upon individual group members. Under such circumstances, the use of a more empathic stance may prove to be timely and effective. This may be particularly so when one is dealing with more seriously disturbed patients, where such a large proportion of the therapeutic work involves the establishment of a therapeutic alliance, that is, the development of a trusting and cohesive group.

Similarly, interventions addressed to the group as a system may be particularly germane as a group moves in and out of various phases of group life, when there are disruptions in the therapeutic frame of the group, and/or when shared emotional dilemmas arise that affect all the members. In contrast, the use of clarification, confrontation, and interpretation may be more in order during later phases of group life, when the group is already well established as a safe holding environment that can provide its members with suitable supports as needed, and/or when dealing with healthier patients who can tolerate the anxiety that is aroused by such technique and still remain able to carry on productive work.

It would appear that self psychology, in contrast to the other approaches described here, ascribes considerably more importance to the relational, empathic and noninterpretive aspects of the therapeutic encounter. However, while this approach may be particularly useful in working with those patients who suffer from more profound disturbances in their sense of self, the exclusive maintenance of an empathic stance may be conducive to making certain kinds of countertransference errors that may interfere with effective treatment (Cooper and Perry, 1988). For example, does the deficit model lead the therapist to rely upon inexact interpretations and/or to equate "empathy" with "nourishment"? In the course of empathically responding to legitimate, phase-appropriate but previously unfulfilled selfobject needs, to what extent is the therapist gratifying these needs as opposed to interpreting them, as one would from an object relations position? Under what conditions is gratification of patients' selfobject needs therapeutic or antitherapeutic? In addition, does the therapist sustain and reinforce the patient's belief that he or she is an unwitting victim whose difficulties are the direct result of past traumatic experiences suffered at the hands of faulty others who are unloving and unresponsive? Furthermore, does the maintenance of a reciprocal empathic attunement inhibit or delay the expression of rage within the transference and the recognition and exploration of the patient's own aggression and projective defenses?

Thus, although we believe that the perspectives of object relations, self psychology, and social systems theory can be meaningfully combined to augment and enhance one another, the preceding questions and other equally important ones remain to be further explored. We can only hope that the discussion in this volume will encourage practicing clinicians to attempt to incorporate some of the recent contributions from object relations, self psychology, and social systems thinking into their work with psychotherapy groups.

REFERENCES

Alonso, A., & Rutan, J. S. (1984), The impact of object relations theory on psychodynamic group therapy. *Amer. J. Psychiat.*, 141(11):1376–1380.

Ashbach, C., & Schermer, V. L. (1987), *Object Relations, the Self, and the Group.* New York: Routledge & Kegan Paul.

Bacal, H. A. (1985), Object relations in the group from the perspective of self psychology. *Internat. J. Group Psychother.*, 35(4):483–501.

Cooper, A. M., & Perry, S. W. (1988), The relationship of models of the mind to clinical work: Self psychology. *J. Amer. Psychoanal. Assn.*, 36(3):741–748.

Durkin, H. E. (1982), Change in group psychotherapy: Therapy and practice: A systems perspective. *Internat. J. Group Psychother.*, 32(4):431–439.

Ganzarain, R. (1989), *Object Relations Group Psychotherapy: The Group as an Object, a Tool, and a Training Base*. Madison, CT: International Universities Press.

Hamilton, N. G. (1989), A critical review of object relations theory. *Amer. J. Psychiat.*, 146(12):1552–1560.

Horwitz, L. (1977), A group-centered approach to group psychotherapy. *Internat. J. Group Psychother.*, 27:423–440.

Kernberg, O. (1983), *The Internal World and External Reality*. New York: Jason Aronson.

Kibel, H. D. (1987), Inpatient group psychotherapy—where treatment philosophies converge. In: *Yearbook of Psychoanalysis and Psychotherapy*, Vol. 2, ed. R. Langs. New York: Gardner Press, pp. 94–116.

Pine, F. (1988), The four psychologies of psychoanalysis and their place in clinical work. *J. Amer. Psychoanal. Assn.*, 36(3):571–596.

—— (1990), *Drive, Ego, Object, and Self*. New York: Basic Books.

Roth, B. E., Stone, W. N., & Kibel, H. D. (1990), *The Difficult Patient in Group: Group Psychotherapy with Borderline and Narcissistic Disorders*. Madison, CT: International Universities Press.

Scheidlinger, S. (1974), On the concept of the "mother group." *Internat. J. Group Psychother.*, 24:417–428.

Singer, D. L., Astrachan, B. M., Gould, L. J., & Klein, E. B. (1975), Boundary management in psychological work with groups. *J. Appl. Behav. Sci.*, 11:137–176.

Name Index

407

Subject Index